D0686002

THE KABUKI THEATRE

1. One of the greatest contemporary Kabuki actors, Nakamura Kichiemon (1886–1954), as Kumagai in *The Battle of Ichinotani*.

rnst, Earle.
he Kabuki theatre /

1974.
33305212719789
u   11/05/07

The Kabuki Theatre

Earle Ernst

University of Hawaii Press
HONOLULU

First published in 1956 by Oxford University Press

Copyright © 1974 by The University Press of Hawaii
All rights reserved
Library of Congress Catalog Card Number 73–91460
ISBN 0–8248–0319–1
Printed in the United States of America

93 94 95 96 97 98   6 5 4 3 2

University of Hawaii Press books are printed on acid-free
paper and meet the guidelines for permanence and durability
of the Council on Library Resources

For
ALEXANDER M. DRUMMOND

εἰσὶν γὰρ δή, ὥς φασιν οἱ περὶ τὰς τελετάς,
"ναρθηκοφόροι μὲν πολλοί, βάκχοι δέ τε παῦροι·"
οὗτοι δ' εἰσὶν κατὰ τὴν ἐμὴν δόξαν οὐκ ἄλλοι ἢ
οἱ πεφιλοσοφηκότες ὀρθῶς.

ΦΑΙΔΩΝ

Contents

List of Illustrations

7. The Nakamura-za in Edo at the beginning of the Genroku period (c. 1688).

In order to show both the interior and the exterior of the theatre, the artist considerably reduced its proportions. The Nakamura-za at this time accommodated an audience of about 1500.

The facade of the theatre was enlivened with posters. The two on the right, drawn in the same style as the Kabuki posters of today, depict scenes from the play being performed. Above the entrance are billboards on which are written the names of the five principal actors. Above these is the *yagura*, on front of it the crest of the theatre, on the side the inscription *kyōgen-zukushi* (plays of more than one act) and the name of the theatre owner, Nakamura. The poster to the left of the entrance bears the title of the play, *The Nagoya Lottery*, while those to the left of it give the titles of its four acts. It is the second of these which is being played on the stage according to the placard attached to the *metsukebashira* on stage-right. At this time the Nakamura-za had a second story of *sajiki* (boxes) above those shown. The area just in front of the stage was covered with the long, narrow roof permitted on 23 November 1677. The *hashigakari* (bridge) was at this time almost as wide as the stage proper. [*Waseda.*]

8. *Kaomise* ('face-showing') performance at the Ichimura-za, Edo, November 1764.

The theatre at this time was completely roofed. The stage shows a typical interior-exterior Kabuki setting. The interior is placed beneath the Nō roof and consists of a platform with a painted perspective behind it. The forestage is a garden, separated from the stage-right area by a gate. Placards with the name of the play and of the scene are attached to the pillars of the Nō roof. The balcony-like area above the stage is purely decorative and serves no theatrical purpose. In the up-right corner of the stage are spectators in the *rakandai*. At the down-right corner of the stage is the draw curtain, which opened from stage-left to stage-right, as it does in the present doll theatre, so that the narrator-musicians seated at stage-left are first revealed. In the Kabuki today, the curtain opens in the opposite direction.

The 'aisles' of the theatre were raised wooden passageways.

This period was the culmination of inventiveness in devising varieties of theatrical posters, including posters announcing the cast of characters, the plays being performed, the actors' names, scenes from the plays, and the *jōruri* performers. The front of the theatre was also adorned with flags and pennants. There were two front entrances to the *sajiki*. Platforms at the entrance (*yobikomidai*) were provided for barkers. The *yagura* continued to be decorated with the crest of the troupe. [*Waseda.*]

9. An Edo theatre about 1802.

The play being performed is the 'congratulatory' piece, *The Soga Confrontation*; the actors playing the Soga brothers are on the *hanamichi* at the *shichi-san*. Shortly before the time of this print the Nō roof had been removed from the Kabuki stage. Poorer spectators are crammed into the *yoshino* and the *rakandai*; the use of these areas declined after 1817. The forestage shows considerable expansion, for it was now the principal acting area. The *ayumi-ita*, the raised passageway on the right of the print, was used, after 1772, as the 'temporary' *hanamichi*. An inclined plane can be seen at the point it joins the stage. The entire pit is divided into *masu*, each accommodating seven people, and the *masu* next to the *sajiki* are raised above the level of the pit so that they become *takadoma*. Seats in the odd-shaped *masu* next to the *hanamichi* were cheaper than

18. For the dance *The Wisteria Girl*, instrumentalists are seated on stage-right, singers on stage-left. [*Shochiku.*]

19. A scene from Chikamatsu's *Yūgiri and Izaemon*, a doll theatre play performed in the Kabuki, with the narrators and musicians seated on the platform at stage-left. [*Shochiku.*]

20. The *michiyuki* scene of *The Loyal Forty-seven Rōnin*.
   The musicians' platform on stage-left is painted to tie in with the setting. Hanging above the stage is a *tsurieda* of cherry blossoms. At the rear of the stage, barely visible, is the stage assistant. [*Shochiku.*]

21. The setting for 'Moritsuna's Camp.'
   The 'inner proscenium,' including the *geza* on stage-right, is painted a flat black. Although this is not a dance piece, the *shosabutai* (dance-stage) is laid on the permanent stage floor, for the act involves considerable dance movement. The presence of the two standing lamps (*andon*) on the upstage platform indicates that the scene is taking place at night. The backdrop of sea and mountains is used to create a sense of space around the actors seated on the platform. The 'secondary' room on stage-left is enclosed with *shoji*. [*Shochiku.*]

   Illustrations 22–56 appear as a group following page 152.

22. Setting for *Kasane*, typical of the exterior setting using a raised upstage area.
   On stage-left a river is indicated by blue cloth laid on the stage floor. The principal acting area is the undisguised floor of the stage. [*Shochiku.*]

23. A scene from *The Loyal Forty-seven Rōnin*, with the usual arrangement for showing two separate interiors, the downstage area being exterior. [*Shochiku.*]

24. A scene from *Hiragana Seisuiki*.
   Upstage is the *nami-ita* ('wave-board'), which is the conventional indication of ocean. Seated in front of it are *hana-shiten*, the brilliantly costumed 'flower-warriors.' The stage-floor is covered with a gray floor cloth. The line of the revolving stage can be seen at the lower edge of the photograph. [*Shochiku.*]

25. *The Soga Confrontation.*
   The upstage wall is brilliant gold and blue. Above the stage is a *tsurieda* of plum blossoms. [*Shochiku.*]

26. *The Subscription List*, which is played with the Kabuki version of the Nō setting.
   Togashi, played by the late Uzaemon, stands at stage-left, Benkei, played by the late Matsumoto Kōshirō VII, at stage-right. [*Haar: Tuttle.*]

27. The Hamamatsu-ya scene of *Benten the Thief*.
   Benten Kozō, played by the late Kikugorō VI, has been disguised as a woman but now reveals himself. The pseudo-official, played by the late Matsumoto Kōshirō VII, is seated on the upstage platform. [*Shochiku.*]

DIAGRAMS

Preface, 1973

BUT haven't things changed, I'm asked, in the some twenty years since you wrote this book?

Yes.

Last summer the Farmers' Association of Fujinomiya, a town at the foot of Fujiyama, chartered a plane, and the farmers flew to Paris for a vacation. Another result of affluence is the National Theatre, opened 1 November 1966, just across the street from the Imperial Palace grounds in Tokyo. A handsome, superbly equipped building, it is dedicated to preserving, promoting, and developing Japanese traditional theatre arts. Within it are two theatres. The larger, seating 1,746, used principally for Kabuki, provides all the scenes and machines a Kabuki connoisseur could want—both the permanent and the temporary *hanamichi* of the late eighteenth-century theatre, for example, and the world's largest revolving stage, sixty-five feet in diameter, containing sixteen trap-lifts. The smaller theatre, seating 630, used to stage a variety of native music and dance, has the special machinery required for doll theatre performances.

Evidence is abundant, however, that new theatre buildings, no matter how elegant and well equipped, do not guarantee compelling performances nor theatrical innovation. The National Theatre engages the foremost Kabuki troupes, presents Kabuki plays in their entirety rather than doing collections of the choicest scenes from them, revives plays that have been neglected, and conducts research on the correct historical methods of production. While preserving the past, the theatre also encourages contemporary playwrights to write pieces based upon the Kabuki form; the most spectacular production of a new play was of that written by Mishima Yukio, which exploited contemporary sado-masochistic violence as well as all the scenic and mechanic resources of the National Theatre. The theatre has broken with the past by instituting formal classes in actor training as opposed to the traditional, slow and laborious, teacher-disciple system, with the result that teaching is done rapidly and systematically.

Although Kabuki tickets are increasingly expensive, the houses are full at the National Theatre and elsewhere. Probably a larger percentage of the population now sees Kabuki than ever before. Not live, of course, but on television. The National Theatre either plugs into a relay car outside the building or transmits by microwave from the top of it. And so the television audience could see the entire eleven acts of *The Loyal Forty-seven Rōnin*, running time about twelve hours. A lot more foreigners have seen Kabuki. It's obligatory for the stylish tourist in Japan, and then the Kabuki's been abroad— a tour of the United States, two tours of Europe—and on the whole critics and audiences were impressed. More has been written about the Kabuki by foreigners in the past twenty years than was before, and one can see, fairly regularly, Kabuki plays produced in English in American university theatres. Kabuki performances don't seem to be dwindling. A Kabuki actor has remarked that if it should disappear in Japan, it will not be lost, for production will go on in the United States.

I solemnly inveighed, I notice, against forcing American notions on the Japanese. True, there was propagandizing in 1945 and later, but the Japanese didn't have their present consumer society forced upon them. They like all the appliances, enjoy built-in obsolescence. Television commercials run even longer than ours. McDonald's flourishes. There seem to be as many knives and forks as chopsticks. The 'Western Room' may survive in a few old houses, but the new ones consist almost entirely of Western rooms. A plastic imitation of traditional straw matting for the floor is available. The *tokonoma* is not to be found in the high-rise apartments. Factories smoke where rice grew.

But perhaps in historical perspective there is less to this than meets the eye. The Japanese have always loved novelty, whether native or foreign, and have set great store by foreign technology, particularly since 1868. A Japanese film company employee told me in 1946 that he became convinced Japan would lose the war when he saw Disney's *Fantasia*, a print of which the army had found in Singapore; Mine-san, the cook, couldn't figure out why Japan had lost the war until she saw a jeep and henceforth ascribed defeat to that automotive wonder. But the Japanese seem to have the ability to live without schizophrenia both in a traditional Japanese world and in a 'modern' one, a psychological adjustment that doubtless had to be made following 1868. Their modern world, seen in all its hideousness as you leave Haneda airport, is readily discernible. Their traditional world is less obvious, more tenaciously held, a world of habit, of taste. It is the world in which Nō plays are presented, every weekend in Tokyo, in very much the same way they were costumed, acted, danced, and sung five centuries ago. And the Japanese who goes to the Nō on Sunday may very well have been to an all-Beethoven concert on Saturday.

And so it seems that bad modern taste need not drive out good traditional taste or that Kabuki will vanish because a poor musical-comedy version of *Gone With the Wind* played to packed houses.

Japanese theatre has really changed little in the past twenty years. Straight plays, old or new, native or foreign, still run only a month, but the modern actor now adds to his income by working in television, as do some of the young Kabuki actors, who are capable of playing equally well in the realistic mode. Some young actors experiment in off-off-Broadway fashion, but their work attracts even smaller audiences than the conventional play. Although the government pays the staff at the National Theatre, the Kabuki must make its way commercially there as elsewhere. As film eroded the theatre audience, television now erodes the film audience. Foreign theatre-workers urge the Japanese to preserve the Nō, preserve the Kabuki, and some Japanese wonder how or why.

But Nō and Kabuki go on, like the tea ceremony, the doll theatre, court music and dance, and the pinball machine, which is no longer a fad but an institution. A sizable number of Japanese find deep satisfaction in them.

In October 1972 one could step out of the din and pollution of Tokyo into the Kabuki-za to see Kichiemon's grandson play Togashi in *The Subscription List*, a role in which his grandfather excelled. He's not yet as good as his grandfather was, but he will be. The set was precisely the same as it's always been and so was the music. The audience was perhaps a little more restrained than the one grandfather played to, but they came and went at will, they ate, and some seemed to have little notion of what was going on theatrically, though whatever it was, it was estimable. And there were those, perhaps a majority, who shed tears when Yoshitsune forgives Benkei for having struck him. As long as audiences weep at that moment of the play, a moment so purely Japanese that it is emotionally inaccessible to most foreigners, traditional Japanese sensibility will be alive and the Kabuki will nourish it.

EARLE ERNST

Honolulu, Hawaii
15 October 1973

Preface

THE purpose of this book is to outline the form of the Kabuki theatre, considering it throughout as an expression of Japanese life and culture. The work is intended for the reader with little or no knowledge of this form of theatre; therefore, I have frequently mentioned the Western theatre in order to establish points of reference for understanding the Kabuki. Since a theatre with three centuries of history cannot be described adequately in a single volume, the book does not pretend to be an exhaustive treatment of the subject, but I hope it will serve to arouse interest in a theatre which until about 1900 received relatively little attention either from foreign or Japanese scholars. No major form of world theatre has had as little written about it in Western languages as the Kabuki.

The chief reason for the indifference of the Japanese scholar to the Kabuki was that it was a popular theatre which he thought unworthy of serious consideration. This attitude was adopted by most foreigners in Japan, with the notable exception of such writers as Alexandre Benezet, Maria Piper, Zoë Kincaid, Serge Elisséeff, and, more recently, Faubion Bowers. (A list of the important books on Kabuki in Western languages is given in an appendix.) Japanese acceptance of the Kabuki as a 'respectable' form of theatre underwent some acceleration in the 1930's, when, along with increasing chauvinism, Japan found renewed interest in its native forms of artistic expression. The revival of Japanese interest in the Kabuki today has risen in part out of the nostalgia of a defeated nation for its colorful and romantic past.

The present American interest is partially the result of a sizeable number of Americans having seen, and having been intrigued by,

Kabuki performances during the Occupation. This fact alone, how-ever, does not account for the powerful attraction the Kabuki has exerted on Americans. At the beginning of the century many percep-tive Americans saw Kabuki and dismissed it as either incomprehen-sible or naïve. That the playwright Paul Green has described the Kabuki as 'in the main, the finest theatre art in the world' suggests that our conceptions of the theatre have undergone profound changes in the last forty or fifty years.

It is significant that on the only occasion that Kabuki has been played outside Japan,[1] at Leningrad and Moscow in 1928, Russian audiences found nothing new or startling in the performances. There was nothing in it, they felt, which had not been seen in the productions of Vsevolod Meyerhold. Meyerhold, at that time a leading *régisseur*, had begun his career in the Moscow Art Theatre, which, under Stanislavsky, was devoted to the realistic school of acting. However, Meyerhold broke with the realistic theatre and formulated a highly stylized, nonrepresentational manner of production. Although Russian audiences viewed the 'feudal' subject matter of the Kabuki with dismay, their familiarity with Meyerhold's productions had pre-pared them to accept the nonrealistic and frankly theatrical idiom of the Kabuki.

The contemporary movement toward a theatre freed from late nineteenth-century naturalism seems to have gained more ground in Europe than in America. But in recent years, despite the general unwillingness of producers to forgo the commercially reliable realistic production, our more adventurous directors and playwrights have made commercial successes of plays not patterned after the con-ventional realistic theatre. Forty years ago the mode of production of such plays as *Death of a Salesman* and *Cat on a Hot Tin Roof* would have been incomprehensible to American audiences. Today such pro-ductions are widely acceptable; but if *The Girl of the Golden West* could be re-created now in the same form in which Belasco staged it, audiences would probably find its straining for 'realistic' effects

[1] Of late, dance performances by the Azuma Tokuho troupe in the United States were widely billed as Kabuki. The facts are these: Although the Azuma dancers are undeniably a highly proficient group, their expression differs from that of the Kabuki theatre; a Kabuki troupe containing women is a contradiction in terms; none of the Azuma dancers is a professional Kabuki actor. The use of the word 'Kabuki' was understandably resented in Japan, but few Americans who saw this troupe were aware that they did not see the genuine article.

more amusing than impressive. Our notions of what constitutes good theatre have changed.

In total effect, the Kabuki is profoundly different from any of the forms the historical Western theatre has taken, but its techniques of expression, examined singly, are not as alien as one might suppose. During a recent sojurn in the United States, a young Kabuki actor, Onoe Kuroemon, saw what he felt were Kabuki-like effects in some American productions. In becoming familiar with the Kabuki, I was repeatedly astonished to find close similarities between Kabuki techniques of expression and the theories of production set forth by such contemporary theatre workers as Adolph Appia, Gordon Craig, Georg Fuchs, Leopold Jessner, and Bertolt Brecht. Gordon Craig, for example, felt the affinity between the Oriental theatre and what the Western theatre should be when he wrote, in 1905, 'The East still boasts a theatre. Ours here in the West is on its last legs. But I look for a Renaissance.' Under the influence of men such as Craig our theatre has begun to free itself from the domination of realism. And I believe it is for this reason that we are now capable of appreciating the nonillusionistic, uncompromisingly theatrical form of the Kabuki.

Even so, first acquaintance with the Kabuki performance is likely to be bewildering. But with continued acquaintance one finds, beneath the unfamiliar surface, comprehensible, and, after a time, profoundly moving theatre experience. If Americans can attain to this understanding of the Kabuki, perhaps Japanese culture is not the obscure, unintelligible matter that many Westerners have assumed it to be.

At this point in history our future, for good or ill, is bound up with that of Japan: For good, I believe, if we meet on a level of cultural equality; for ill, if we continue in the folly of creating the impression abroad that American ideas and American ways of doing things are the only ultimately correct ones. Fortunately, the vigorously advertised myth that the Occupation of Japan had uprooted native culture and had converted the country to 'democracy' has now been generally recognized as the fiction which it was, even though some Americans continue to deceive themselves with surface appearances. Japan admires our humanitarianism, our technical skill, and our neon lights, but it has little patience with our efforts to make it abandon its cultural patterns and to substitute those of the United States. A disturbing phenomenon of our time, unsettling to many Americans, is that although we have provided foreign countries with vast quantities of money and materials, many foreigners feel, at best, indifference, at worst, downright hatred toward us. There are many reasons for their feelings, but a basic one is that although we have accepted world leadership, we have not yet accepted the responsibility of respecting the validity of cultures other than our own. Until we do, we will not find the mutual understanding upon which solid friendship must be based. In the past, the West has made little effort to understand the East; the seeds of this ignorance have borne bitter fruit and may do so again. Only by understanding and respecting the culture of Japan can we hope to penetrate beneath deceptive surface appearances and to find common ground in the essential humanity that underlies cultural differences.

EARLE ERNST

Honolulu, Hawaii

Acknowledgments

IN gathering the material for this book, I consulted the standard Japanese authorities whose books are familiar to anyone who is interested in the Kabuki and who reads Japanese. For readers with such an interest and ability, I feel that a bibliography of these familiar works would be gratuitous, and I have not supplied one. However, I should not like to create the impression that my study represents exhaustive research in Japanese sources. On the contrary, I deliberately avoided using Japanese materials until late in my work. My primary object was to look at the contemporary Kabuki as a living theatre, and this, I felt, could not be done if I allowed myself at the beginning to be influenced by the points of view of Japanese writers. The greater part of the material, by far, I obtained in the time-consuming, rather haphazard way of attending Kabuki performances and talking with Kabuki actors and members of the Kabuki audience.

Of the large number of Japanese who helped me, I will mention only a few. At Waseda University, Dr. Kawatake Shigetoshi, head of the Department of Theatre, provided me with historical materials, as did Kurahashi Takeshi, of the Department of English. Members of the Shochiku Company (the organization which is the sole producer of Kabuki today) were invariably helpful, both in occupied and sovereign Japan, particularly the president, Otani Takejirō, and my friend Yoshida Matsuji of the Production Department. The actors from whose performances I learned most about Kabuki are Ichikawa Ebizō, Onoe Shōroku, Onoe Baikō, Matsumoto Kōshirō, Nakamura Tokizō, the late Onoe Kikugorō, and, especially, Nakamura Kichiemon, whose recent death has created a vacancy in the Kabuki theatre that will not soon be filled.

Among American friends, Stanley Yamamoto performed innumerable indispensable services. Laura Korn undertook the disagreeable task of painstakingly reading the first draft of the manuscript and offered helpful criticism. Colleagues at the University of Hawaii—Shunzo Sakamaki, Yukuo Uyehara, Florence Maney, and Dorothy George—gave me valuable advice. To my former teacher, the late Henry Alonzo Myers of Cornell University, I owe many of my ideas concerning the nature of tragedy. I am particularly indebted to Serge Elisséeff, chairman of the Department of Far Eastern Languages at Harvard University, for suggestions and corrections which, out of his comprehensive knowledge of Japan, only he could have made.

In acknowledging the help I have received, I must also acknowledge the errors and infelicities as my own; without the generous assistance given me they would have been more numerous.

Photographs were obtained from the Waseda Theatre Museum, the Charles E. Tuttle Company, the Iwanami Publishing Company, the Shochiku Company, and Namino Chiyo.

The writing of the manuscript was made possible by aid from the Rockefeller Foundation, to which I owe special thanks, particularly to Charles B. Fahs, Director of the Division of Humanities.

E. E.

Le théâtre est toujours la secrétion d'une civilisation ; la société, dans sa forme actuelle, a le théâtre qu'elle mérite.

LOUIS JOUVET, *Refléxions du Comédien*

Note: In Japanese, the five vowels are pro-nounced as they are in Italian, always using, however, the close *e* and *o*. All syllables end in vowels or diphthongs, with the exception of those ending in *n* (which sometimes in trans-literation becomes *m*), or followed by a double consonant. There is no accent, except that occasioned by the long vowel sound.

Contrary to the usual Western practice, in Japanese the surname precedes the given name.

CHAPTER I

Introduction

BEFORE 1868 and the opening of Japan to Western influence, the Japanese evolved three distinct types of native theatre, one of which was the Kabuki. These three survive today.

First to develop was the Nō, synthesized principally out of indigenous materials into a precise form toward the end of the fourteenth century. The Nō was an aristocratic form of amusement, formal, restrained, and soon static. Although it greatly influenced the other forms of native theatre, it remained primarily the theatre of the intellectual and the well-to-do. Only after the end of World War II did Nō theatres become public playhouses. Foreigners, however, influenced by attitudes of late nineteenth-century Japanese, have shown great interest in the Nō, with the result that many Nō plays have been translated and that an impressive body of information concerning the Nō is available in Western languages. The foreigners' preoccupation with the Nō cannot be ascribed to snobbishness. In the Nō they found plays of greater literary value than in the more popular forms of theatre and discovered in the Nō performance an austere art form in which certain aspects of Japanese culture are idealized. The precise form of this theatre also appealed to some deep instinct in the Westerner. But there was in addition the satisfaction for him that the serious Nō plays are underlaid with a comprehensible and compact body of belief, derived largely from the Amidist strain of Buddhism, which gives the plays a constant ideological core lacking in the other forms of Japanese theatre.

The doll theatre and the Kabuki, the other principal forms of native theatre, appeared almost simultaneously at the end of the

1

sixteenth century. Both were distinctly popular theatres, deriving their raw materials from the contemporary scene and from popular history. The doll theatre achieved its greatest popularity and created its best plays during the first half of the eighteenth century; thereafter the number and the popularity of the doll theatre troupes declined. Today this form of theatre survives only in the performances of one troupe, Bunraku, whose name to most Japanese is now synonymous with doll theatre.

Unlike the Nō with its aristocratic acceptance, the Kabuki had to make its way commercially, depending for its existence upon the approval of nonaristocratic audiences. Mere survival made it necessary for the Kabuki to use men in the roles of women, to adapt to its uses both the style of acting and the plays of the doll theatre, to take dramatic material both from the Nō and from contemporary event. All this has given the Kabuki its vitality—the vitality of a healthy organism capable of adjusting itself to a constantly changing environment. But this requisite pattern for survival also made the Kabuki a theatre lacking precise dramatic form, embodying various styles of acting, irregular, racy, violent, and, at times, sensational and cheap. The Kabuki does not represent the purest form of Japanese cultural expression. But it provides a comprehensive insight into average Japanese tastes and reveals much of Japanese culture not expressed in the Nō or in the doll theatre.

According to tradition, the first Kabuki performance was given in Kyōto in 1596, but it was during the Tokugawa, or Edo, period (1603—1868) that Kabuki developed its distinctive form. Since the evolution of Kabuki is unintelligible out of its historical context, a brief description of the configuration of these centuries is necessary.

Throughout the period from 1338 to 1590, Japan was variously involved in civil wars between rival fiefs. Toward the end of the sixteenth century, the successive military and political coups of Nobunaga, Hideyoshi, and Ieyasu at last brought about a general peace. In 1603 Tokugawa Ieyasu (1542–1616) received from the Emperor the title of *sei-i tai-shōgun* ('barbarian-subduing-great-general') and became the ruler of Japan in Edo, the present Tōkyō. With the establishment of the Tokugawa Shōgunate, or as it was also called, the Bakufu ('tent-government'), the Tokugawa line became the undisputed political power. Ieyasu did not thoroughly consolidate his position until he had vanquished the heirs of Hide-yoshi by taking the castle of Ōsaka in 1615, but thereafter Japan was free from domestic and foreign wars under a firmly established system of feudal government. Throughout the Tokugawa period the Emperors of Japan, although they remained the spiritual figureheads of the country, were politically impotent, as they had been, generally, since the thirteenth century. However, on 4 January 1868 the Imperial House was restored as the nominal ruling power of Japan, and Tokugawa supremacy ended.

An historical fact of extreme importance to the development of the unique form of the Kabuki was that during most of the Edo period Japan was isolated from the rest of the world. The isolation of the country, like the majority of the policies of the Shōgunate, was a measure of political expediency. To understand why this policy seemed desirable, we must briefly recapitulate the events which led to it.

In 1542 three Portuguese were shipwrecked on a small Japanese island, and within a few years of this inadvertent discovery of the country Portuguese traders had begun to call at Japanese ports. On 15 August 1549 Francis Xavier and two other Jesuit missionaries landed in Kagoshima and began to preach the Christian religion. The Jesuits were generally successful in their enterprise, particularly since the feudal lords came quickly to believe that the missionaries could exert influence upon the Portuguese traders from whom they wished to obtain trade articles and firearms. In fact, in the hope of attracting traders, the lords of some fiefs ordered their subjects to embrace Christianity. In 1568 the Jesuits were received by Nobunaga (1534–1582), then the most powerful feudal lord in Japan, and he thereafter treated them with considerable friendliness. Nobunaga's successor, Hideyoshi (1536–1598), who unified Japan in 1590, also showed kindly feelings toward them. But seeing a number of southern feudal lords converted to Roman Catholicism, Hideyoshi apparently feared that their new faith might serve as a bond between them and against him. Hideyoshi, in 1587, issued an edict that all missionaries were to leave, although traders might continue to call at Japanese ports. This edict was not seriously enforced, however, until 1597, when Hideyoshi became convinced that the missionaries were agents for foreign political designs. He had nine of them executed. In the few remaining years of his life, Hideyoshi did not enforce the edict, perhaps fearing that traders would no longer visit the country. On coming to power in 1603, Ieyasu was equally tolerant for similar considerations. But beginning in 1612, on what he considered

3

irrefutable evidence of Spanish and Portuguese plans for aggression, Ieyasu pursued a consistent policy of ridding the country of the missionaries, and that policy was continued by his son Hidetada (1579–1632). Christianity was now firmly believed, and with good reason, to be a manifestation of foreign aggression. In 1624 Hidetada decreed that all Spaniards, whether missionaries or not, should leave. Hidetada's son, Iemitsu (1603–1651), continuing his persecution of Christians both native and foreign, closed Japan to the rest of the world. All Japanese were forbidden to leave the country in 1637, and in the following year native Christianity was almost completely wiped out with the massacre, at Shimabara, of approximately 37,000 converts. After 1641 Japan was almost completely cut off from the contemporary culture of the rest of the world. Chinese merchants could trade at Nagasaki, and a small group of Dutch traders was allowed to remain on the small island of Deshima in Nagasaki harbor. When the Shōgun Yoshimune was in power (1716–1745), he permitted the limited circulation of certain Dutch books obtained from the traders; 'Dutch learning,' as it was called, was one of the few sources of foreign influence during the Tokugawa period.

Tokugawa faith in the principle of isolation was manifested not only in shutting the nation off from the rest of the world, but also in carefully maintaining differentiated areas within the country. Segregation became a matter of practical politics. Not all the fiefs were kindly disposed toward the Tokugawa line, and the lords of these provinces were known as the *tozama-daimyō* (outside lords) in contrast to the *fudai-daimyō* who were hereditary vassals to Ieyasu. So that the outside lords could be prevented from conspiracy against the Bakufu, an efficient 'censor' system was set up in 1617; and at strictly guarded barriers established throughout the country every traveler was carefully examined. Roads and bridges were deliberately kept in poor repair so that travel would be discouraged. The outside lords were also prevented access to the Emperor in Kyōto, a potential source of political unrest, by the presence of the *shoshidai*, a Tokugawa official placed in Kyōto ostensibly to be of service to the Emperor and his court, but in actuality serving to prevent intercourse between the Emperor and the outside lords. A further device for preventing conspiracy was that of *sankin-kōtai* ('alternate attendance') by which lords were required to spend their time alternately on their fiefs and in Edo, while during their absence from Edo their wives and children were obliged to remain in the city as hostages.

4

Japan was broken up into a succession of isolated areas, from the isolation of the country at large, down to sections of city streets which were closed at the end of every day. The policy of segregated areas contributed to the development of regional dialects as well as certain regional cultural differences. The Kabuki of Kamigata (the Ōsaka-Kyōto region), for example, showed the influence of the good breeding and quiet ways of the Imperial Court, while the Kabuki of Edo reflected the rawness and hardness of a young, brash city. These differences were of degree rather than of kind (the Japanese have always been great travelers) and did not lead to the development of unique forms of expression. However, the contemporary Japanese concern for defined areas, both in art and in life, although it seems to have its origin in pre-Tokugawa Japan, was no doubt strengthened during the Edo period.

The Shōgunate also, logically enough, placed great faith in the isolation of groups of artisans and merchants. Trade guilds, called *za*, had come into economic importance in the fourteenth century. *Za* (the word means 'seat') developed out of groups, including musicians and dancers, privileged to practise their trades within the precincts of a shrine or temple; in addition to meaning *guild*, *za* also came to be, and remains today, a word for theatre. In the Edo period the guilds reinforced the Tokugawa ideas of social stability. Trades tended to become hereditary, and this pleased the Bakufu. Guilds, even those of street peddlers, were licenced. The concentration of the production of a certain commodity in a single guild meant that free business competition could be inhibited and that the Shōgunate could deal easily with the entire group of artisans or merchants. It further gratified the government to see the members of a guild concentrated and segregated in a certain area. Some such areas in Japanese cities continue to bear the names of the artisans who occupied them during the Edo period, and there is still an observable tendency of similar trades to congregate in the same locality.

The policy of the Shōgunate toward the guilds was very much the same as that toward the theatres. Troupes of actors, like the guilds, became hereditary units called *gekidan*, a system of organization which obtains today. In the larger cities theatres were permitted to be built only in specified areas. In Edo after 1657 theatres were restricted to the areas of Sakae-chō, Fukiya-chō, and Kobiki-chō; in Kyōto to the region of Shijōgawara; in Ōsaka to Dōtombori. These areas continue to be theatre sections in their respective cities today. In 1841 the Three Edo Theatres were required to move to Saruwaka-chō, the present Asakusa, which remains the gaudiest of Japanese theatrical centers.

The official policy of segregation of actors and theatrical troupes was summed up by Ogyū Sorai (1666–1728), scholar and adviser to the eighth Shōgun, Yoshimune:

> People are easily influenced by the behavior of actors and prostitutes. Recently there has been a tendency for even high ranking people to use the argot of actors and prostitutes. This habit has become a kind of fashion, and people think that those who do not use such words and phrases are rustics. I am ashamed that this is so. Such a tendency will result in the collapse of the social order. It is therefore necessary to segregate actors and prostitutes from ordinary society.

The attempt to prevent association between actors and other citizens had been made before Sorai's birth and continued after his death. There were constant regulations against *wakiaruki* (the actors' walking outside their areas). That actors frequently disobeyed this injunction is implicit in the fact that it was frequently repeated. In January 1661 actors were forbidden to leave their assigned areas, and a year later they were again specifically told not to go abroad 'either on foot, in a palanquin, or on horse.' A regulation of April 1671 stated, 'Recently people have been seeing actors at tea-houses, and actors have been coming into the pit of the theatre. This is contrary to previous regulations and hereafter actors and spectators will observe this rule.' In March 1678 it was announced that 'Actors have been visiting the houses of samurai and merchants, remaining there for a long time, and sometimes even staying the night. This is incompatible with regulations issued previously. . . . It is illegal for actors to board anywhere but at an actor's house. An actor may not rent or loan a room to men employed in other work.' In May 1689 some Edo actors were discovered performing a play outside the theatre area; as punishment all Edo performers were required to present themselves at police boxes to show that their hair was no longer than half an inch. In August 1695 actors were specifically forbidden to go aboard ships, and in January 1699 and April 1703 these prohibitions were repeated, together with the strongly worded suggestion that actors would do well to shave their foreheads. This list could be greatly prolonged, but these examples serve to illustrate the constant vigilance on the part of lesser officials against the actors' mingling with other citizens even when, during the period of 1680 to 1709, the Shōgun was Tsunayoshi, a notorious friend of actors.

The attempt of the Bakufu to prevent intercourse between Kabuki actors and other citizens continued to the end of the Tokugawa period, but it is perhaps typified in the incident known as the Ejima Affair, which has served as source material for songs, stories, and plays. The incident sums up much of the attitude of the government toward the theatre, and the punishment meted out by the Bakufu had a permanent effect upon the Kabuki.

Ejima, head of the women of honor at Edo Castle, harbored a passion for Kabuki actors. On 19 May 1713, accompanied by several ladies in waiting, Ejima went to the Yamamura-za, one of the four Edo Kabuki theatres, where, during the performance, she amused herself by having some thirty-five of the actors invited to her box, there to exchange pleasantries and drink sake. But since the principal actors of the theatre, Ichikawa Danjūrō II and Ikushima Shingorō, being engaged in the play declined her invitation, Ejima returned to the castle somewhat displeased. Subsequently, two men attached to the Court, wishing to curry favor with Ejima, decided to approach the recalcitrant actors. Ichikawa gave a polite, though contrived, refusal, but Ikushima was easily persuaded. The theatre manager was induced to place his home, accessible from the theatre through a secret door, at the disposal of the couple, and the assignation was quickly arranged. The actor apparently heard no more of Ejima until 26 February 1714. On that day the widow of the Shōgun Ietsugu intended to visit his tomb at the Zōjō Temple, but being ill, she sent Ejima in her stead. Ejima set out with a company of some one hundred attendants and performed the necessary duties at the temple. On the way back to the castle, the entire party detoured slightly out of its way and went to the Yamamura-za. There they drank a good deal of rice-wine and almost disrupted the performance with their noisy merriment. The Shōgun could not have been greatly distressed by this disgraceful behavior, being only five years old at the time. But when news of it reached the Shōgun's councillors, in the form of a report from the secret police, they took quick and drastic action. Ejima and a younger brother were exiled to a small island, and her older brother was executed. Ikushima, one of his fellow actors, and the theatre manager were also exiled, but to a different island than that to which Ejima was sent. Sixty-seven court maids were put under

7

house arrest at the homes of relatives.[1] The four Edo theatres were closed immediately and the Yamamura-za was torn down and closed forever. When the three other theatres in Edo were permitted to reopen, they were subject to severe restrictions upon their architectural arrangement and their hours of performance.

The attempt to segregate actors from the rest of society was not based upon moral considerations such as those which prompted the Puritan attack on the English Renaissance stage. It grew, like the policy of nation isolation, from the central political philosophy of the Tokugawa line: to preserve for all time the feudal structure established by Ieyasu. In time, adherence to Tokugawa principles came to be regarded by the Shōgunate as 'moral,' but this was a political, not a religious, view. The official attitude was stated by Ogyū Sorai when he wrote, 'Morality is nothing but the necessary means of controlling the subjects of the Empire. . . . Morality may be regarded as a device for governing the people.' Repressive or hortatory edicts, the substance of Shōgunate government, were designed to preserve the social stratification, the economic structure, and the moral climate which had prevailed in the time of Ieyasu; consequently, all change, whether in manners, thought, or wealth, was looked upon by the Bakufu as subversive. Tokugawa social philosophy was summed up in a statement attributed to Ieyasu: 'If one is ambitious, there will be no limit to his ambition. It is therefore necessary to avoid ambition and to be content with one's present lot.' A constant concern of the Shōgunate was to prevent social change; it was for this reason that Kabuki actors were forbidden social prominence or influence.

The hierarchy of Tokugawa society consisted of four groups: the court nobility (*kuge*), the warrior class (*bushi* or *samurai*), the farmer, and the townsman (*chōnin*). The court nobility languished, politically ineffectual, in the ancient capital of Kyōto until the end of the Tokugawa period. At the beginning of the period, the warrior class was strongest both politically and economically. The farmer was next in social importance, at least theoretically, since the economy was agrarian. The townsmen, who included all workers who were not farmers, were the lowest recognized social group.

To the Shōgunate the most disturbing economic development of the Edo period was the rise of the townsman to greater financial importance than the warrior class. This phenomenon was primarily the result

1 Japanese accounts of the Ejima affair differ considerably in details. The present account is a composite of various Japanese sources.

of the gradual change from rice to money as a means of exchange and the consequent transition from an agricultural to a monetary economy. In the process the townsman became increasingly wealthy, while both the warrior and the farmer became increasingly poorer. With this economic verity the Shōgunate was unable to cope. It exhorted all citizens to be frugal, it debased currency, it cancelled the debts of the warrior class, it insisted that every man conduct himself appropriately according to his class. Occasionally in a moment of indignation it might confiscate the estate of a townsman, as it did that of the Kabuki actor Ichikawa Danjūrō VII (1790–1855), but such acts were relatively infrequent and were scarcely part of a consistent economic philosophy. Although the Bakufu was genuinely concerned about the economic distress of the warrior and the farmer, it was incapable of adopting any economic measures other than negative, repressive ones which it thought would maintain the status quo.

The rise of the Kabuki theatre, as well as that of the coeval doll theatre, was linked with the rise of the townsman, for it was the *chōnin* who principally attended the Kabuki, and the Kabuki became the expression of the townsman's artistic tastes and ethical beliefs. The Nō theatre was familiar to the commoner, but the Kabuki was lustier stuff, more suited to the tastes of a newly important economic class than the esoteric Nō. In the creation of their culture the townsmen did not ignore the Nō; on the contrary, the wealthier members of the class took up this aristocratic form of amusement with all the snobbish fervor of the *nouveau riche*, and the Nō was made to supply material for the Kabuki. (For this reason the Nō seems to have been somewhat sullied as an amusement for the warrior class; in its desire to preserve a decent aesthetic differentiation between warriors and commoners, the Shōgunate at a banquet in 1711 substituted ancient music for the customary Nō performances.) Constantly borrowing its materials from dance, legend, and history, the Kabuki was established by the end of the eighteenth century as a definite cultural form of the *chōnin*, and its flowering coincided with the emergence of the townsmen as a strong economic class. It was during this period, called Genroku,[2] that Tokugawa society reached what may be called its

[2] Throughout the Tokugawa era, periods of years were designated by name, as they had been, generally, since 645. A new era name was announced when any presumably significant event took place—the abdication or enthronement of an emperor, a great catastrophe, or a felicitious occasion. Since 1868 the names of periods have been changed only upon the enthronement of an emperor.

period of social and economic equilibrium. (Officially, the Genroku period was from 1688 to 1703, but historically its influence remained well into the 1740's.) Although at this time the *chōnin* had got their hands on most of the money, the warrior class was not yet reduced to penury nor was the farmer yet in the dire straits which later brought him to rioting and in some instances to cannibalism. The synthetic culture of the townsman existed comfortably alongside that of the samurai.

The Kabuki was suspect from its beginnings because it was not a traditional form of theatre like the Nō, and therefore like all new things it could only grudgingly be given a place in a governmental scheme of things dedicated to eternal sameness. The word from which *kabuki* derived, *kabuku*, a now obsolete verb of the Momoyama period (1573–1603), originally meant 'to incline,' but by the beginning of the seventeenth century it had come to mean 'to be unusual or out of the ordinary' and carried the connotation of sexual debauchery.[3] Furthermore, the Kabuki was a manifestation of the culture of that perplexing social class, the *chōnin*, which was coming to have an economic strength out of all proportion to the social position assigned it. The Bakufu seemed willing enough to allow the townsmen the Kabuki as a controlled and carefully supervised amusement. But when the composition of the Kabuki audience reflected a leveling of the precise social hierarchy that the government felt necessary to its continued existence, the Shōgunate invariably resorted to oppressive measures. Despite the fact that he had Kabuki actors appear in Edo Castle, or perhaps because of it, Iemitsu, the third Shōgun, was the first to take strongly repressive action against the Kabuki. (It was this same Iemitsu who closed Japan to the outside world and who directed the massacre at Shimabara.) On 23 October 1629 the first form of Kabuki, Women's Kabuki (*onna-kabuki*), which had its inception in the dances of Okuni in Kyōto in 1596, was prohibited. The Kabuki actresses immediately resorted to the subterfuge of staging performances in which, reversing their previous practice, men played male roles and women female roles, but this evasion was ended in 1630. In prohibiting Women's Kabuki the Shōgunate pointed to its

[3] There is evidence that the word *kabuki* was used as early as the ninth century to describe actors. However, this use was not continued, and the meaning of the word had changed completely by the sixteenth century.

Kabuki is now written with three Chinese characters which mean *song*, *dance*, and *skill*. The choice of these characters is somewhat arbitrary, for in the past several phonetically suitable characters have been used.

immorality, and it is true that many of the performers were prostitutes, but the morality about which the government was concerned was less sexual than political. With the disappearance of women from the theatre their roles were taken over by long-haired handsome boys, and women never again appeared on the public stage in Japan until after 1868.[4] Young Men's Kabuki (*wakashū-kabuki*) enjoyed as great a popularity as that in which women played. The boys took pains to make themselves attractive to their audiences, and this was their undoing. Certain of the samurai who gathered in the theatre found themselves unduly attracted to the boys, and such attachments led, in 1652, to two samurai brawling publicly over the favors of an actor. The incident came to the attention of the Shōgunate, and on 27 July 1652 Young Men's Kabuki was forbidden. According to legend, it was only through the efforts of Murayama Matabei, a theatrical manager, that the Kabuki theatres were permitted to reopen. Murayama is reputed to have gone to the offices of the city authorities responsible for enforcing the edict and there to have staged a hunger strike. The theatres were permitted to reopen, but without the handsome boys. Commanded to cut off their forelocks, they suffered a vast loss of allure. Now they were no longer cute boys but grown men. The resultant form of Kabuki was called 'Male' Kabuki (*yarō-kabuki*),[5] but theatre managers, afraid the government would take offence at the very word *kabuki*, for many years did not use it publicly at all. Instead, the performance was described as *mono-mane-kyōgen-zukushi*—'a display of performances imitating things'—and the theatres were not referred to as Kabuki theatres but as playhouses.

Eventually, the Shōgunate could no more control the mingling of warrior and townsman in the theatre than it could control the hopeless confusion of these groups outside the theatre. Samurai whose lords had dismissed them or those whose lords had been deprived of their fiefs became the cast adrift *rōnin* ('wave-men'). The *rōnin* lived among the townsmen, influenced their ethical notions, and married their daughters. Wealthy commoners bought their way into the nobility. Against the wishes of the Shōgunate, farmers left their

---

[4] There is an isolated instance of two women dancers, Kasaya Sankatsu and Kasaya Shinkatsu, being permitted to perform in Kyōto in 1665.

[5] It was the shaved forehead (*yarō-atama*), the usual male hairdress, which gave rise to the term *yarō-kabuki*. Men playing women's roles at first covered their heads with an arrangement of cloth, but about the middle of the eighteenth century the use of wigs began.

farms and took employment in cities. At last there came about a certain economic and social fusion, completely at variance with the Tokugawa scheme for a social hierarchy. It was principally these socially displaced people who made up the Kabuki audience and thus established the Kabuki theatre, in the mind of the Shōgunate, as a source of constant suspicion. For reasons which we shall see, the government had little reason to fear the Kabuki theatre as a breeding ground of subversive ideas; even so, the Bakufu clearly discerned that the theatre should not be allowed to deal with politics or history of the Tokugawa period, and the Kabuki was forced to use either remote or disguised history or contemporary triviality as material for its plays.

In view of this official attitude and the resultant restrictions against the Kabuki, it seems surprising that the theatre could exist at all. The doll theatre was less harshly dealt with. Even the Shōgun Ietsuna (1639–1680), who among other repressive actions forbade the translation of European books and any writing concerning the government, on three occasions had doll theatre performers appear at his palace. But any drama involving living actors, amateur or professional, was suspect. In January 1697 amateur performances were forbidden. However, an examination of the influence of the Shōgunate's other restrictions on the life of the Japanese reveals that policies concerning minor matters were seldom enforced with any consistency. Official vacillation in enforcing edicts against the Kabuki resulted, eventually, in the actors and the theatre managers developing a consummate ability to deceive the officials, and it was this ability which, to an appreciable degree, enabled the Kabuki to exist. Subterfuge became a stock-in-trade of the Kabuki not only during the Tokugawa period but in modern times as well. In 1945 when the leader of a theatrical troupe was told that performances would thereafter be subject to American censorship, he remarked, wryly, 'How do the Americans think they will go about censoring us? During the War, we deceived even the Japanese police.'

The Shōgunate apparently did not believe in the outright extermination of Kabuki. The majority of the Shōguns were indifferent to Kabuki and one was even favorably inclined to it. A Kabuki performance was given within Edo Castle on 20 February 1607 before Ieyasu's son, Hidetada; but there is evidence that in the following year Ieyasu himself had Kabuki players driven from his castle in Sumpu, the present Shizuoka, to which he had retired when he left the office of Shōgun. According to the *Tokugawa Jikki*, a history of the Tokugawa family, Kabuki actors performed, as we have seen, in Edo Castle for the third Shōgun, Iemitsu. However, the Kabuki actors enjoyed their heyday of governmental approval during the incumbency of the Shōgun Tsunayoshi (1680–1709). Because of his great love of the Nō theatre, Tsunayoshi installed two troupes of performers in Edo Castle, one of which was selected from among the sons of the nobility. In 1690 he not only engaged the services of some ten or a dozen Kabuki actors to train his noble charges but also raised the Kabuki actors temporarily to the rank of lesser nobility. Never afterwards, until the twentieth century, was the Kabuki actor held in so high official esteem. Although there seem to have been periodic restrictions against the theatre whenever catastrophes, either natural or social, occurred, the actors were never reduced to the position of the social outcasts, *hinin*, on whom a member of the warrior class was free to test the sharpness of his sword. In 1708 the chief of the *hinin* petitioned Tsunayoshi to include the Kabuki actors among the social outcasts and his petition was refused. On the other hand, the actor was never permitted to buy his way or marry into the warrior class. The policy of the government toward the Kabuki seems to have been about the same as that toward the farmer: Both were permitted to survive, but at a level of bare subsistence.

Although the Shōgunate failed in its efforts to prevent a shift in economic power from the warrior class to the townsman, it succeeded brilliantly in spreading its system of ethical propaganda, the popular acceptance of which was in part responsible for the continuance of the regime. Basic Tokugawa political philosophy was contained in the *BukeHatto*, the *Laws of the Military Houses*, a document promulgated in Ieyasu's name in 1615. This was, in essence, a sumptuary code to which successive Shōguns added further exhortative edicts. Aware that the civil wars preceding his coming to power had been made possible by double-dealing and shifting loyalties among the feudatories, Ieyasu had established the idea of feudal loyalty at the center of Tokugawa political theory; and the *Buke Hatto* was designed to promote and strengthen this concept. The principles of the *Buke Hatto* were further reinforced by the encouragement given to the study of Confucian ethics as they appeared in the writings of Chu Hsi. Chu Hsi's work had been known in Japan from the early fifteenth century, but it was not until the end of the sixteenth century that it became widely circulated. In its emphasis upon a precisely defined

13

hierarchy of social relationships and its insistence upon loyalty and orthodoxy the work was admirably suited to Tokugawa needs. During the Edo period this brand of Confucian philosophy became established as official thought, if not almost as state religion. Its principles were accepted not only by the warrior class but at last permeated the thinking of all social groups, when, toward the end of the seventeenth century, pursuit of Confucian learning became something of a nation-wide craze.

As a result, a curious manifestation of the rise of the townsmen is that although the *chōnin* created new forms of artistic expression in the Kabuki, in the doll theatre, in the graphic arts (the wood-block print of the *ukiyoe*, for example), they did not create similarly distinctive political and ethical patterns of thought. About the middle of the eighteenth century began the dissemination of *shingaku* ('heart-learning'), a school of thought directed at the ethical and cultural improvement of the townsman. *Shingaku* was an easily comprehensible philosophy which borrowed its elements rather indiscriminately from ancient native religious beliefs, from Buddhism, and, particularly, from official Confucianism. The movement had the tacit approval of the Shōgunate, for it was entirely traditional in subject matter and was, in large part, a translation of Chu Hsi Confucianism, which in the hands of official scholars became increasingly abstruse, into concrete, nonspeculative precepts applicable to the lives of the commoners. As such, it provided a suitably orthodox moral code for the increasingly wealthy merchants. Since the teachers of *shingaku* were themselves commoners, the movement can be described as a cultural expression of the townsman. However, there was nothing in the ethical teaching of *shingaku* which was not completely conformist and orthodox, while, on the contrary, in the arts the townsman created such distinctive expression as the poems of Bashō (1644–1694) and the short stories of Ibara Saikaku (1642–1693). In effect, the townsmen accepted the Confucian code of ethics and patterned their lives, their morality, and their theatre on it. The overwhelming public sympathy for the forty-seven *rōnin* who avenged their lord in strict accord with Confucian ideals of loyalty is evidence of the degree to which these ideals pervaded popular thought; and there is an instance of rioting farmers bearing banners proclaiming that even a farmer cannot serve two lords. The citizenry dedicated itself to the idea of loyalty and to a whole-hearted acceptance of Tokugawa ethics. The merchant, like the farmer, suffered the restraints put upon him with no incitement to social change or revolt. Even the overthrow of the Tokugawa line in 1867 was not led by the *chōnin* or the farmers, who might have much to gain from its success, but by disaffected members of the warrior class. The ethical and moral climate of the Kabuki, therefore, and of the doll theatre as well, is almost purely orthodox Chu Hsi philosophy, and one looks in vain in the Kabuki repertoire for an original idea, much less for overt social criticism.

The only non-Confucian intellectual movement which appeared during the Tokugawa period was a potentially dangerous one which the Shōgunate itself, ironically, unwittingly encouraged. It was an anti-Confucian system of thought which eventually led to the re-establishment of Shintō, a native pre-Buddhist religion. The movement had its beginnings in the work of Yamazaki Ansai (1618–1682) and others and was carried on by Kamo-no-Mabuchi (1697–1769) and Motoori Norinaga (1730–1801). One result of the revival of interest in native religious belief (and with it a renewed interest in native literature) was a growing sense of nationalism which previously had been little developed in Japanese thought. This aspect of the movement was no doubt pleasing enough to the Bakufu, but it was accompanied by a hidden corollary. At the center of Shintō belief is the notion that the Emperors are descended in an unbroken line from the sun-goddess Amaterasu and that the Emperor is both the spiritual and political head of the State. Toward the end of the eighteenth century, as these concepts were mingled with the Confucian notions of hierarchical loyalty, it became increasingly obvious that the Tokugawa line had usurped the divinely given power of the Emperors. In the politically confused days after Commodore Perry's disturbing appearance at the harbor of Uraga in 1853, the cry of Japanese patriots was *sonnō jōi*—'honor the Emperor and expel the barbarians'—a concept which could not have been held had not the Shōgunate permitted the revival of Shintō. The Shōgunate's error of judgment helped lead the way to the destruction of the Tokugawa line, the restoration of the Imperial House, and the beginning of a new and decidedly different period in Japanese history.

Japan had begun foreign trade under treaties signed between 1854 and 1859, but with the Restoration of 1868, under Emperor Meiji, Japan abandoned its policy of isolation from the rest of the world. It almost seemed that native culture would disappear under the flood of foreign ideas and inventions which swept across the country and that the Kabuki would be shattered by the impact of a foreign form of theatre. The Kabuki was temporarily shaken, but it recovered from the blow; and it does not seem likely that in the second great influx of Western influence following World War II the Kabuki is about to be swept away. In modern times the Kabuki has shown an inability to absorb and express new ideas in terms of its own idiom, and it may well be that it will never be able to do so. Nevertheless, the hold of the Kabuki on the Japanese people is strong today, and there is every evidence that its strength will continue. The fact remains, however, that the Kabuki is a form of theatre so intimately related to the economic, political, and social atmosphere of the Tokugawa period that it has not been capable of significant development since 1868.

Some Japanese scholars have attempted to show parallels between the development of the Elizabethan theatre and that of the Kabuki. The Kabuki had its beginnings in the city of Kyōto at the time Shakespeare was writing his first plays. Within a short time boys began to play the roles of women in Kabuki as they did on the Elizabethan stage, and the physical Kabuki theatre showed certain spatial similarities with the Shakespearean. Chikamatsu Monzaemon (1653–1724), probably the greatest playwright of Japan, is almost invariably referred to by the Japanese as the 'Shakespeare of Japan.' The rise of both Kabuki and of the Elizabethan drama was concurrent with the rise of an increasingly wealthy and powerful class of commoners. In both countries a new age had begun: in England, the Renaissance; in Japan, a period of peace following centuries of war.

These parallels are interesting. But the spirit of the age in the two countries was almost antithetical. The Elizabethan theatre was born out of a time in which the mind explored new frontiers of time and space and in which the individual assumed a new dignity. During the whole of the Tokugawa period the Kabuki existed and developed within the narrow geographical and intellectual confines imposed on the country by the Shōgunate. The theatre of Shakespeare was unfettered, acquisitive, ranging freely through the whole of European culture. The Kabuki was restricted, both politically and intellectually, to an unquestioning and placid acceptance of the status quo, its spiritual frontiers no wider than its geographical ones. A certain spiritual freedom was apparent toward the end of the seventeenth century, when there was high living and an unusual lack of restraint. But this was a purely social phenomenon growing out of sexual licence, the elevation of courtesans to public figures, the pursuit of fashion, and a craze for all that was novel in decoration and amusement. A characteristic quality of the period is that of an inquisitive, fun-loving people attempting to provide themselves amusement despite the exhortation of the Shōgunate to austere behavior. The tension arising because of the government's repression of.the natural inclinations of the people was relieved in an inordinate concern with the trivial, a concern said to be typical of imprisoned people. A certain kind of hairdress would do and no other. The Edo fireman was prepared to sell his wife and children into prostitution to buy the first bonito of the season. The public paid admission fees to gaze upon a dinner table properly set by a master of this intricate art. After the middle of the period a preoccupation with decorating food and making trivial variations on the themes of a few simple dishes reached proportions which probably can be explained only in psychiatric terms. In none of this was there anything of the powerful forces that set man at the center of the universe during the Renaissance. A comparison of the plays of Shakespeare with those of Chikamatsu supplies striking evidence of the wide dissimilarities between their ages. The only Japanese renascence lay in the revival of the ancient religion, Shintō, and in renewed interest in native literature.

Although thought control and isolation from the outside world resulted in a politically and intellectually almost static society, during the two and a half centuries of the Tokugawa period the Kabuki, and Japanese art in general, had the opportunity to develop techniques of expression undisturbed by forces from the world outside or by political change within. The deeply rooted Japanese respect for tradition, and with it the reverence for etiquette and formalism, preceded the Tokugawa period, and it was this quality of the national character which in large part permitted the long continuation of the Tokugawa regime. To this was added the national acceptance of Confucian ethics and the growing lack of differentiation in artistic tastes according to social classes. The result was the formulation of an aesthetic vocabulary which was understood and appreciated throughout the country. The innovations and developments in the graphic arts and in the Kabuki were gradual, never showing a violent break with traditional forms, and thus the Japanese artist never faced the situation of being 'too advanced' or being 'ahead of his time.' So profound a difference of expression as that between Bach and Berlioz or between Molière and Strindberg did not occur during the Tokugawa period. While Western drama was undergoing the changes of concepts and of productional methods that characterized its movement from

17

Shakespeare to Ibsen, the Kabuki, feeding on no original materials other than innocuous contemporary events, continued to sharpen and refine its means of expression. Since artistic innovations were those of technique rather than of intellectual concept, the spectator was 'accustomed' to what he saw and moved generally in the same world of perception as the artist. A certain type of hairdress, make-up, or costume stated immediately to the Kabuki audience the complete nature of the character who wore it. The way in which an actor held a pipe communicated at once the whole of his social background. A phrase of music played on the samisen, a single gesture could economically evoke a time, a place, a mood. Japanese art had traditionally expressed itself in nonrealistic idiom, but to this basic impulse was added the clarity made possible, in the Tokugawa period, by a generally uniform view of actuality. The Kabuki had little to say politically, but what it had to say artistically could be expressed immediately, trenchantly, and with no possibility of misinterpretation. Its expression perhaps became somewhat overrefined, inbred, and precious. But within the narrow world of Japan, the Kabuki was enabled to create a vocabulary of expression which was concise, shorn of the nonessential, and, in a word, nonrepresentational.

The terms presentational theatre and representational theatre have been used to describe antithetical forms which the theatre may take. The Kabuki, because of the nature of its means of expression and the quality of its rapport with the audience, can be called presentational. This is an abstract term, not referring to a specific historical theatre, but useful in outlining a general form, such as that which the theatre took in Greek civilization of the fifth century, in the Elizabethan public playhouse, in the contemporary theatre of Meyerhold, or in vaudeville. In the presentational theatre the actor does not lose his identity as an actor. The audience does not regard him as a 'real' person but as an actor acting. His make-up, costume, movement, and speech emphasize the difference between the actor and the concept of a 'real' person that exists in the mind of the audience. The stage is a platform for acting, not a disguised area. The stage is distinguished from the rest of the theatre building, but it is not conceived to be spatially discontinuous from it. The actor, the audience, and the performance exist within the same psychologically undifferentiated world. The actor is therefore permitted to communicate with his audience directly, for both occupy the same world of aesthetic actuality.

At the opposite pole from the presentational theatre is the representational. This generalized form appeared in the Greek theatre of the fourth and third centuries, in the European medieval mystery plays, but it probably reached its ultimate statement in the theatres of Antoine and Belasco at the turn of the century. In the representational theatre every effort is made to convince the audience that the stage is not a stage and that the actor is not an actor. To this end the stage is disguised by the use of settings, properties, and lighting so that it will appear to be a specific and 'real' place. Various technical means are employed to create in the audience a sense of spatial discontinuity between the auditorium in which they sit and the stage on which the play is being performed. In essence, the stage becomes an area of illusion, while the auditorium remains a part of actuality. The actor, although he may have to resort to highly 'unreal' methods to do so, seeks to convince the audience by his make-up, costume, movement, and speech that he is a 'real' person, not an actor acting. Since he must give the appearance of behaving as though the audience did not exist, he can communicate with the audience only by indirect means.

Although the Kabuki is presentational theatre, if one were to read Japanese comments on the theatre without seeing the performances of plays, he would be inclined to think that the theatre was concerned with the literal reproduction of reality on the stage. Even Zeami Motokiyo (1364–1443), who was the leading force in the creation of the Nō theatre, wrote in his earliest treatise that the purpose of the Nō actor was 'imitating things' (mono-mane). The first Kabuki performers, actresses dressed in contemporary costumes, dancing simple pieces, appeared even more 'realistic' to their audiences than the Nō performers. The first Kabuki performances which resembled plays rather than dances were called 'plays imitating things' (mono-mane-kyōgen), and, as we have seen, this nomenclature was used for some years instead of the word kabuki. The Genroku actor Sakata Tōjurō (1647–1709) expressed the opinion that 'a Kabuki actor should present reality on the stage,' while Ichikawa Danjūrō I (1711–1783) introduced the argot of contemporary Edo samurai into the Kabuki. Sadoshima Chōgorō (1701–1757) in his Diary wrote what sounds like a description of fairly realistic acting:

Movement and attitude should be accompanied by a proper expression of the eyes. In acting, movement and attitude are the body, but the expression of the eyes is the soul. When the soul is lacking, nothing is left; there is only dead movement and dead attitude. Only by vital accord between

19

movement, attitude, and expression of the eyes can living acting be created.

In his book *A Primer of the Kabuki* (1762), Tamenaga Ichō defined 'imitating things' as 'imitating truly and realistically the behavior of young and old, male and female, aristocrat and poor, priests and laymen.'

The truth of the matter is that when Japanese actors and theatre critics spoke of 'realism' and 'imitating things,' they were not referring to the realism of the representational theatre but to the quality that can be called theatre reality. It is difficult for a Westerner to imagine a less 'realistic' form of theatre than the Nō or the Kabuki. Judged relatively, the Nō is the less 'realistic' of the two,[6] but the Kabuki, which is based upon dance, and moves always in precisely designed rhythm and gesture toward the static, nonrealistic attitude called the *mie* (rhymes with *we say*) is no less stylized and presentational. We must distinguish between 'realism' as it appears in the representational theatre and is an attempt to make the performance appear to resemble 'real life' to the greatest degree possible, and theatre reality, which arises when the vocabulary of expression of a given theatre form, whether representational, presentational, or combining elements of both, is accepted by the audience as theatrically believable and aesthetically valid.

Although the structure of the theatre building and the trappings of the stage have a certain relation to the creation of a sense of theatre reality, this condition arises primarily out of the quality of the rapport which exists between the spectator and the performance. The theatre does not create its vocabulary of expression in a vacuum, but builds it up laboriously out of the vocabulary of aesthetic communication which its society has evolved. Therefore, the theatre embodies, for good or bad, the complex of attitudes, beliefs, customs, and aspirations of that society, as well as the economy or lack of economy by which these qualities can be communicated. The degree to which the theatre of a given society is capable of summing up that society and expressing it in a communicable vocabulary is the degree to which the spectator will be convinced of the theatre reality of the performance. The theatre reality of any given performance is consequently dependent upon its speaking in the same social and aesthetic vocabulary as

[6] In the early fifteenth century, the Nō performance was apparently much less stylized than it is today, permitting greater freedom of movement and using a faster tempo.

that shared by the audience. In a static society, the vocabulary of expression tends to endure unchanging; in a changing society the vocabulary of expression differs from one generation to the next.

It is therefore generally true that in the past the closely integrated, stable society has evolved a theatre expression which is presentational, while the society swept by doubt and confusion, and lacking a commonly shared social faith, has created a representational theatre. In the late nineteenth century, for example, such men as Richard Wagner, Friedrich Nietzsche, and Adolph Appia regarded the rise of naturalism as evidence of cultural disintegration. They, along with others, saw the evolution of the naturalistic theatre as the result of an increasing lack of communication and hoped there could be created a new vocabulary of expression which would eschew the literal for the suggestive, the poetic, and the nonnaturalistic. The movement in the contemporary Western theatre away from a strictly naturalistic mode of expression is undoubtedly in part due to the efforts of modern *régisseurs* affected by such ideas, but the results of this movement have appeared more obviously in the realm of stagecraft than in acting or playwriting. It is easier to fashion new methods of staging than it is to formulate a new vocabulary of expression for the actor and the playwright. Despite the important influence that these innovations have had upon the contemporary Western theatre, it remains, by and large, both on the stage and in the film, representational expression. It may well be that the quality of our age is such that it is capable of expression only in the representational theatre, which, according to Nietzschean thought, by its very existence reveals the absence of aesthetic communication among men.

Although the Kabuki was prevented from dealing to any significant degree with the actual stuff of human existence, it nevertheless reflected in the nineteenth century the theatrical symptoms of a society in ferment. There appeared in the Kabuki a concern with delirium, suffering, and pain, with the vulgar, vicious, and murderous, with blood, shock, and horror. The lofty and grandiose heroes of the historical play (*jidaimono*) were succeeded by the thieves, ghosts, and suffering wives of 'living' domestic plays (*kizewamono*). *Aragoto* ('rough-business') acting, completely stylized and nonrealistic, was followed by a manner of acting somewhat more appropriate to the depiction of characters drawn from the contemporary commoner's life. Viewed from within Kabuki history, this was undoubtedly a movement toward realism in the theatre. But so strong

21

was the Japanese love of the traditional means of Kabuki expression that these innovations did not destroy it but were absorbed into it. Consequently, the 'realism' of the nineteenth-century Kabuki bears little resemblance to the realism of the late nineteenth-century Western theatre or to that of the fourth-century Greek theatre in which the actor Polos was able to move his audience to grateful tears by using, when he played Electra, not a property urn supposedly containing the ashes of Orestes, but an urn containing the ashes of his own recently dead son.

The Kabuki occasionally employs touches which viewed through a Westerner's eyes appear to be thoroughly realistic in intent. In the performance of *Summer Festival*,[7] a play first presented in 1762, the hero after committing a murder removes his clothes and douses himself with several buckets of water. But the purpose of this act is not to convince the audience of the authenticity of the performance by the use of actual materials. The use of water is dictated by the fact that the play is one that is always performed in the summer and the splashing about of water is thought to create a pleasurably cooling effect upon the audience. (Ghost plays, also because of their chilling effect, are invariably performed in the summer.) This is a typical instance of the way in which 'realism' is used in the Kabuki: to surprise, shock, or delight. Kabuki 'realism' differs basically from that of the representational theatre in that it is momentarily imposed upon a highly stylized, nonrealistic performance, while the realism of the representational theatre is consistent and organic, pervading every part of the illusory world erected behind the proscenium. The hero of the play mentioned above is not naked when he removes his clothes preparatory to splashing the water over himself; he is dressed in a skintight costume on which tattooing is painted. Similarly, when 'realism' appears in the traditional Japanese graphic arts, it is concentrated within a given area, such as the feathers of a bird, the skin of a tiger, the single flower, and does not invest the entire area of the picture which other-

---

7 Most Kabuki titles are fanciful in the extreme, being only with difficulty read and understood by the Japanese, because the playwrights adopted the convention of using highly poetical titles which could be written with either five or seven Chinese characters. For this reason, the Japanese have given most plays brief, popular titles. In choosing appropriate English titles for the plays I have been somewhat arbitrary mostly for the sake of brevity. Some are taken from the long Japanese titles, others from the shorter ones, and a few are free improvisation. The reader who wishes to identify the plays by Japanese titles will find a list of these in an appendix.

wise is suggestive rather than literal. In the same way, the 'realism' of the Kabuki is concentrated in the isolated gesture and attitude or in the specific theatrical property.

Thus the Japanese use of the phrase 'imitating things' no more implies representationalism than Aristotle's 'imitation of an action' means the literal reproduction of actuality in the theatre. The attitude of the Kabuki toward realism in general was summed up by the late Kabuki actor, Nakamura Kichiemon, who, when asked why women were not used on the Kabuki stage, looked at the questioner incredulously and replied, 'But that would be too real!'

Of all the arts, the theatre is probably the least transmissable from one culture to another unless the cultures have many common characteristics. A poem, a picture, a vase may be studied at leisure in the attempt to understand the artistic idiom in which it speaks. But the theatre is a shifting quantity, ephemeral even within the culture that creates it. It does not exist either in the script of the play performed, or in a description of the performance, but only in the performance itself. And theatre reality can exist only when audience and performance meet in the same world of aesthetic communication. Many Westerners accept as the only theatre reality that of the representational theatre. A Balinese dance play with its masked figures creates theatre reality for its Balinese audience, but a performance of *John Loves Mary* with the original New York cast would not. To understand the Kabuki, we must be prepared to look at it from the point of view of the culture which created it rather than impose upon it our acquired notions of the form in which the theatre should express itself.

The introduction of the Western representational theatre into Japan has had an effect upon contemporary Kabuki playwrights, but their plays constitute a negligible part of the Kabuki repertoire. Today the Kabuki continues to preserve its traditional means of expression based upon rhythmical movement, dance, and music, and to present, in its monthly changes of program, a living museum of Kabuki by the performance of pieces chosen from all periods of its history.

CHAPTER II

The Development of the Physical Theatre

THE present Kabuki theatre building represents a compromise
between the form it had developed before 1868 and the form of
the Western theatre. The new Kabuki-za in Tōkyō, which opened for
performances on 21 November 1889, imitated the Western theatre
only in its exterior; the interior remained purely Japanese. But the
Yūraku-za, which was built in Tōkyō in 1908 principally for the
purpose of presenting Western vaudeville, was Western inside and
out, while the Imperial Theatre, constructed in 1911, was modelled
on the conventional European opera house. Following the earthquake
of 1923, which resulted in the destruction of most of the theatres in
Tōkyō, the Kabuki theatres were rebuilt, generally, in the style of
Western theatres, with chair seats, aisles, floors raked toward the
stage, prosceniums, and front drop curtains.

However, the Kabuki theatre auditorium today has certain features
which distinguish it from the conventional Western arrangement.
Most prominent is the relation of the width of the proscenium opening to the depth of the auditorium, which spatially, and therefore
aesthetically, differs from the relation of these two areas in the usual
Western theatre. The proscenium opening of the present Tōkyō
Kabuki-za is approximately ninety feet wide. The depth of the auditorium is about sixty feet. Thus despite the size of the theatre which
seats 2600, no spectator, unless he is seated at the rear of the second
balcony, is much more than sixty feet from the stage. This physical
arrangement of the theatre has important aesthetic implications which
will be discussed later. A second distinguishing characteristic of the

auditorium is the *hanamichi*,[1] a passageway approximately five feet wide running from the rear of the auditorium to the stage. It joins the stage at a right angle on the stage-right side,[2] which in Japan is called the 'western' side of the auditorium, while the opposite side of the house is called the 'east.' (These are merely theatre terms and have nothing to do with the geographical orientation of the building.) The *hanamichi* is as important an acting area as the stage (*butai*) itself. Although it is used primarily for important entrances and exits, it exerts an aesthetic force on the whole of the Kabuki performance.

A third distinguishing characteristic is the presence of *sajiki* on both sides of the orchestra. These correspond to boxes in the Western theatre both in their position relative to the stage and in their social implications. But in some theatres the *sajiki* differ from the Western boxes in that they are without chairs. Instead they are floored with *tatami*, the thick mats of rice straw which cover the floors of all Japanese houses, and the spectator sits on a cushion on the *tatami*. The *sajiki* are the only remaining evidence in the present theatre of the seating arrangement which prevailed in the Kabuki theatres until the early twentieth century. Today the rest of the Kabuki theatre is provided with Western style theatre chairs, just as uncomfortable as those in the New York theatres.

The shape of the auditorium is rectangular, and the first and second balconies are built around three sides of the auditorium as they are in the European opera house. The spectator in the side sections of the balconies is seated not facing the stage, but facing the opposite side of

---

[1] The word *hanamichi* is written in Japanese with two characters meaning *flower* and *way, path,* or *street.* One explanation of the origin of the word, apparently unverifiable, is that at one time it was customary for actors' admirers to place flowers on this playing area. Before the appearance of the *hanamichi*, an Edo theatre, the Nakamura-za, in 1687 installed a platform on which to display flowers sent to actors, but where it was placed in the theatre is not known. It is possible that the *hanamichi* derived its name from this earlier platform.

Foreigners have got into the habit of translating *hanamichi* as *flower way* or *flowery way*, and this no doubt gives the word a quaint, Oriental flavor. But to the Japanese, *hanamichi* no more means *flowery way* than *cupboard* literally means *cup board* to the English-speaking.

[2] Throughout, the term *stage-right* refers to the area on the actor's right as he stands on the stage facing the audience; *stage-left* is the area to his left. (British terminology is often the opposite.) *Upstage* is used to mean the area of the stage farthest from the audience, *downstage* the area of the stage closest to it.

the house. This arrangement affords him a good view of the *hanamichi* and derives not from European models but from earlier forms of the Kabuki theatre building. The fact that this orientation prevails, rather than that toward the stage, is some evidence of the continuing force of the *hanamichi* as an acting area.[3]

The proscenium differs in no way from the usual Western one. The present Tōkyō Kabuki-za is provided with four conventional front curtains of silk which drop from the flies, each handsomely designed and embroidered. These curtains are more attractive to the foreigner who cannot read Japanese; for when he can, he realizes that each is in part an advertisement of the business company which donated the curtain to the theatre. This practice is not, however, the result of imported Western commercialism. From the time of the earliest permanent Kabuki theatres, the merchants, tea-houses, and geisha houses in the vicinity of the theatres were accustomed to providing materials to the theatres as a means of advertisement.

The drop-curtain (*donchō*) as such was introduced into the theatres after 1868, and at this time inexpert Kabuki actors, as well as those who took to playing in foreign style plays, were called, derogatively, *donchō-yakusha* ('drop-curtain actors'). Curiously, during the Tokugawa period small temporary theatres such as were set up in shrine and temple grounds were strictly forbidden to use any kind of curtain other than a drop curtain, while only the government-authorized theatres were permitted to use the *hikimaku*, the draw curtain that was associated with Kabuki performances. In addition to its drop curtains, the Kabuki theatre today still uses the *hikimaku* when the play being performed is 'pure' Kabuki. This curtain is drawn off and on from the stage-left wing by a stage assistant who pulls the onstage edge of the curtain, concealing himself behind it. The opening and closing of the curtain is accompanied by a gradually accelerated beating together of wooden clappers (*hyōshigi*) and the movement of the curtain across the stage is correspondingly accelerated.

This kind of draw curtain appeared in the Kabuki theatre with the performance of the first two-act play (*tsuzuki-kyōgen*), *Secret Visit to*

[3] The introduction of seats into the Kabuki theatre, though undeniably modern and modish, is at variance with the necessary bodily movement of the spectator. He must look in two directions: at the stage and at the *hanamichi*. The former chairless Kabuki theatre allowed for his free movement, while the conventional Western theatre seat does not. This is a minor instance of the innumerable ways in which the adoption of foreign customs by Japan has resulted in stylish discomfort.

Imagawa, in 1664 in Edo.[4] On this occasion, a black curtain was used, and a black curtain remained generally in use for almost a century. The present Kabuki curtain of alternating vertical bands of black, rust, and green was not generally adopted by Kabuki theatres until after the Meiji period. According to tradition, the curtain of this pattern is believed to have been introduced into the theatre when the manager of the Nakamura-za in Edo performed a service for the Shōgun Iemitsu (1603–1651) by supervising the unloading of cargo destined for the Shōgun. Among other rewards, Iemitsu gave the Nakamura-za the sail of the boat, which was made in the pattern and colors of the present Kabuki curtain. Toward the end of the eighteenth century, curtains of similar pattern but of different colors were generally in use. Another variety of draw curtain is that given to an actor by an admirer or group of admirers, bearing the actor's *mon*[5] as well as the name of the donor. This kind of curtain is seen less frequently today than the traditional Kabuki curtain.

Directly behind the proscenium is a structure which can be called an 'inner-proscenium' for want of a better term. There is no Japanese word for it. This structure is purely native in origin and has no counterpart in the Western playhouse. On stage-right and stage-left it is approximately six feet wide, sharply angled in toward the center of the stage, and extending upward to the height of the outer proscenium, which in most theatres is about twenty feet high. These two vertical sections are joined at the upstage edge at the top by a horizontal piece about three feet wide, parallel to the front of the stage. The whole is of wood and is painted a flat black. The vertical sections on either side of the stage consist of two stories each. On the

[4] Dates concerning theatrical history are based principally upon Suda Atsuo, *Nihon Gekijō Dokushi Hyō*, Tōkyō, 1935.

[5] There is no very satisfactory word in English for *mon*, although the word *crest* is sometimes used. *Mon* were originally used only as decoration of the curtains around a general's battle headquarters, a use which is preserved in the stage decoration of battle plays such as 'Kumagai's Camp' and 'Moritsuna's Camp.' But with the compilation of the *Genealogy of the Nobility* (1641–1644) the *mon* came to be used on almost every conceivable household article and on the clothing of even the meanest members of a samurai household. The custom spread to townspeople and even to actors, and since that time has been preserved in the theatre both as decoration and as a dramatic device of recognition within the play.

From 1670 the Nakamura-za in Edo had used a crane as its *mon*, but in 1687 the government forbade the further use of this *mon* because the daughter of the Shōgun was named *Tsuruhime* ('crane-princess').

stage-right side, the lower story is the *geza*, or, as it is sometimes called, *hayashibeya* (orchestra room). It is occupied by musicians and sound-effects men, who are able to see the stage through a long rectangular opening which is screened with bamboo blinds painted black. The story above is a room with a smaller opening, similarly screened, which is now used principally as a point from which workers in the fly gallery may observe the stage. The upstage edge of this structure is called the *metsukebashira* ('facing pillar,' or 'pillar on which the actor fixes his eye'), although in the present theatre there is no pillar there. The reason for this will appear later. The stage-left structure is similarly arranged architecturally, but in the performance of certain plays a platform six feet wide, three feet high, and three feet deep is placed against this structure on the stage level. On this platform are seated a samisen player and a narrator-singer. In the upper surface of the platform is a small revolving stage, the use of which permits a new pair of performers to appear, during the course of a long play, without undue delay. When the play is not one using this technique, or when the narrative and descriptive element of the play is not of great importance, this platform is not used, and the two musicians are placed within the first-story room behind a screened opening which is very much like the musician's room on the opposite side of the stage. On other occasions, the front of this first-story room is removed and the opening used for the entrances and exits of actors. Under this circumstance, the samisen player and the narrator-singer, if required, are placed in the second-story behind a screened opening. Whether the bamboo blind is raised or lowered depends upon the historical and traditional precedent surrounding the play being performed. When the play is one that has been adopted into the Kabuki from the repertoire of the doll theatre of the first half of the eighteenth century, the musical-narrative element is called *chobo* and therefore the second-story area is called *choboyuka* (*chobo* floor). The upstage edge of this stage-left structure is called *daijinbashira* ('prime-minister's pillar'), a term derived from the Nō theatre.

The whole 'inner proscenium' preserves the essential features of the architectural arrangements for accommodating musicians and singers which had been arrived at before 1868 and projects this arrangement into the proscenium stage of the West. Spatially, and as we shall see later, aesthetically, it sets off the downstage area of the stage which on the Kabuki stage proper (as opposed to the *hanamichi*) is the playing area of greatest strength.

The stage itself, in wing space, position of lighting instruments, facilities for flying scenery,[6] and so forth, follows the Western model. However, the stage retains the use of machines which were developed by the Japanese independently of their development in other countries. These are the *seridashi*, the *seriage*, and the *mawari-butai*. The *seridashi* is a trap-lift[7] which brings scenery from below to the level of the stage floor and vice versa. This invention of Namiki Shōzō seems to have first appeared in November 1727. In the present Tōkyō Kabuki-za there are three such lifts, the largest measuring forty-eight feet by twelve and a half feet, the next measuring twenty-seven feet by ten feet, and the other somewhat smaller. After its appearance in the Kabuki theatre, this new means of changing settings was soon appropriated by the actors as an effective device for making entrances and exits. The first use of the *seriage* (the trap-lift for the actor) appeared in 1736. Today the same trap-lifts are utilized both for raising and lowering actors and scenery, but the linguistic differentiation between them remains. The invention of the revolving stage (*mawari-butai*) is also credited to Namiki Shōzō; it was first used in an Ōsaka theatre, the Kado-za, on 22 December 1758. In 1827 Hasegawa Kambei elaborated the design of the revolving stage by the introduction of a second revolving stage (*janome-mawashi*) within the circumference of the first, this inner stage capable of being moved in the opposite direction from the outer stage; most of the contemporary Kabuki theatres retain the *janome-mawashi*. The revolving stage of the Tōkyō Kabuki-za is fifty-nine feet in diameter in a proscenium of about ninety feet.

In total effect, the present Kabuki theatre building does not show immediately any striking differences from the conventional Western playhouse. But the conventions of acting, the concepts of theatre space, the relation between actor and audience—all the elements that distinguish between the physical arrangement of the theatre and the uses to which it is put—still show the effect of the theatre

[6] In Japanese theatre vocabulary, the area of the flies outside the 'inner proscenium' is distinguished from that upstage of the 'inner proscenium.' The former is called *hioi* (*sunshade* or *awning*), a term surviving from the earliest Kabuki theatres, which used the roof of the Nō stage; the latter is called *sunoko*, and in this area all 'flied pieces' (*harimono*), backdrops, and the like, are hung.

[7] Because of its brevity, the term *trap-lift* is used throughout to describe the general type of theatre machine which is more precisely designated by such terms as *opera trap*, *appearance trap*, *disappearance trap*, and *stage elevator*.

from which the Kabuki had developed before it was subject to foreign influences. To understand this development, we must turn to a brief consideration of the historical development of the physical theatre.

The earliest Kabuki stage was, according to tradition, a spot in the dry river bed of the Kamogawa in Kyōto, where in 1596 a Shintō priestess named Okuni of Izumo performed Buddhist dances.[8] Therefore, later, when government censure of actors became a part of political philosophy, actors were frequently referred to as *kawara-kojiki* (river bank beggars). At Okuni's first performance the spectators sat on the grass, and it is probably for this reason that a Japanese word for play, *shibai*, is written with two Chinese characters meaning *turf* and *to sit*. Okuni's success grew; in 1603 she went for a tour throughout Japan and on May sixth of that year was invited to perform at the Imperial Palace in Kyōto. During her tour, Okuni and her troupe performed on one of two kinds of permanent stages: the *kagura* stage or the Nō stage. The *kagura* stage was, and still is, a stage for the performance of sacred dances, permanently erected within the precincts of Shintō shrine grounds. It is simply a rectangular platform, roofed or unroofed, and inconvenient for the presentation of plays requiring entrances, exits, and the change of costumes. However, the Nō stage, also to be found in Shintō shrine areas as well as in Buddhist temple grounds and on the estates of the nobility, provided a dressing-room, an effective entrance for actors, and another entrance which could be used by musicians and singers. It was, in brief, a stage which offered greater technical facilities than the *kagura* stage. Therefore, when Okuni built a semi-permanent theatre in Kyōto in the summer of 1604, it was only natural that her theatre should be modelled on the contemporary Nō stage.

This stage was, moreover, a kind of stage which was familiar to her audience. It is erroneous to regard the Nō performances of this time as a purely aristocratic amusement. Although the aristocracy supported the Nō troupes, in general, there were frequent occasions when the most ordinary individuals could see Nō performances, and there is every evidence that these were popular with the commoners. These performances were called *kanjin*-Nō ('subscription' Nō)

---

[8] Whether Okuni actually existed or is merely a composite legendary character is a perplexed question, but in either event her name is a rallying point in early Kabuki history. If she did not exist, it would have been necessary to invent her.

because, since they were given for the purpose of raising money for a temple or shrine, admission was charged. *Kanjin*-Nō was also sometimes performed on the estate of a lord as a benefit for the lord's Nō actors. Several features of the physical arrangement of *kanjin*-Nō, purely utilitarian in origin, were taken over by Women's Kabuki. The public performances of Nō required that those who did not pay be kept from seeing the performances, that a place for collecting money be set up, and that order be maintained, particularly since nobility was likely to be present. The area surrounding the Nō stage was marked off with posts driven into the ground, and between these were hung straw mats. A single entrance between two posts was provided, and in order that admission could be readily collected, only enough space was provided for one person to squeeze through at a time. The entrance was called *nezumi-kido* ('mouse-door'), presumably because the spectators had to creep in like mice, and this name for the entrance to a theatre was retained for at least a century and a half.

When *kanjin*-Nō was performed at the estate of a lord, guards were provided to keep order, and there was erected over the single entrance a *yagura* ('watch-tower' or 'turret'), which contained a large drum used to call reinforcements, and three weapons—a pole, a lance, and a double-pronged lance—which the guards could use at appropriate times to protect the aristocracy. The *yagura*, although it soon came to serve no practical purpose in the public theatres, was an architectural feature of every Kabuki theatre built between 1604 and 1878, when for the first time a Tōkyō theatre, the Shintomi-za, dared to break with tradition. At first the drum in the *yagura* was used to signal the beginning and end of a performance, but in 1679 the government forbade its use on the grounds that it sounded too much like a battle drum. This prohibition, like others the government made concerning the theatre, was apparently not much honored, and in 1684 the regulation was reissued. Thereafter the *yagura* came increasingly to have superstitious significance. When the theatre was not prospering, the *yagura* was cleaned out and tidied up in the hope of placating evil forces, and toward the end of the eighteenth century a placard was placed on the *yagura* for the purpose of protecting the theatre against fire. In general, the *yagura* became a symbol of the spirit of the theatre, although some Japanese writers hold that it was the symbol of the subservience of the theatre owners to the government. After 6 May 1726, when the government prohibited the

31

opening of unlicenced theatres, the word *yagura* came to have the meaning of 'permission to operate a theatre.'

At the time Okuni constructed the first temporary Kabuki stage, the Nō theatre which she used as a model did not differ in any essential way from the modern Nō stage. It consisted of two principal architectural areas: the stage proper (*butai*), and the 'bridge' (*hashigakari*). Both were roofed in the style of Shintō shrine architecture. The pillars supporting the roof over the stage had come to have conventional spatial values for the actor and were named. The pillar at the point where the *hashigakari* joins the stage is the *shitebashira* ('the pillar of the principal character'). Having reached this point after his entrance on the *hashigakari*, the principal character pauses there to announce who he is and where he has come from. The pillar directly downstage of this is the *metsukebashira* (the pillar he faces, or on which he fixes his eye). On the downstage-left corner of the stage is the *wakibashira* ('pillar of the subordinate character') or, as it is also called, the *daijinbashira* ('prime minister's pillar'), because in many of the early Nō plays the subordinate character was a prime minister. The stage floor is divided into three principal areas, although these are not indicated architecturally. The upstage area is the *atoza* (rear stage, or literally, 'rear seat') and is occupied by the *hayashikata* (orchestra) which consists of two or three drummers and a flute player. The flute player is at stage-left, and therefore the pillar nearest him is known as the *fuebashira* (flute pillar). A narrow platform (on the same level as the stage, however), stage-right of the *wakibashira*, is the *waki-za* ('subordinate character stage') so named because of its proximity to the *wakibashira*, and here sit the eight or ten members of the chorus (*ji-utai*). The rear wall of the stage and of the *hashigakari* as well as the narrow wall upstage-left are wooden. The *atoza* wall (called *kagami-ita*, 'mirror-board,' because of its acoustical properties) is painted with a stylized pine tree (*matsubame*), while the upstage-left wall is painted with bamboo. This painting is a conventional reminder of the Nō stage when it had no rear wall and natural scenery provided the background. In one of the earliest forms of the Nō stage, the length of the *hashigakari* was at a right angle to the front of the stage. About the 1570's it was placed at an obtuse angle of about 130 degrees to the stage, joining the stage on the upright side. This angle was gradually decreased and by about 1615 it had assumed its present form of being at about a 120 degree angle to the stage. Along the down-stage edge of the *hashigakari* is a railing,

EVOLUTION OF THE NŌ STAGE

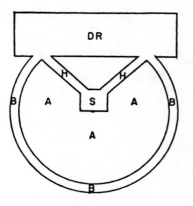

I DENGAKU-Nō 1348

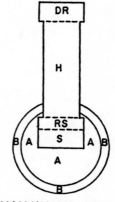

II. KANJIN-Nō 1464

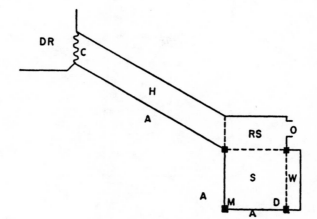

III NŌ STAGE c. 1615

A	Audience	O	'Hurry'-door (*okubyō-guchi*)
B	Boxes (*sajiki*)	H	'Bridge' (*hashigakari*)
C	Curtained entrance (*agemaku*)	RS	Rear stage (*atoza*)
D	*Daijinbashira*	S	Stage proper (*honbutai*)
DR	Dressing-room (*gakuya*)	W	*Waki-za*
M	*Metsukebashira*		

EVOLUTION OF THE KABUKI STAGE (I)

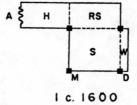

I c. 1600

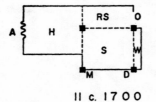

II c. 1700

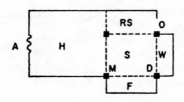

III c. 1710

A	Curtained entrance (*agemaku*)	O	'Hurry'-door (*okubyō-guchi*)
D	*Daijinbashira*	RS	Rear stage (*atoza*)
F	Forestage (*tsukebutai*)	S	Stage proper (*honbutai*)
H	'Bridge' (*hashigakari*)	W	*Waki-za*
M	*Metsukebashira*		

EVOLUTION OF THE KABUKI STAGE (II)

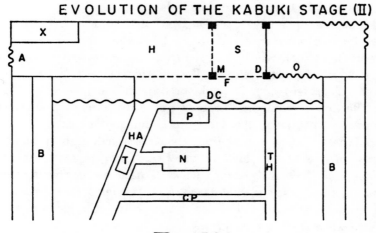

IV c. 1780

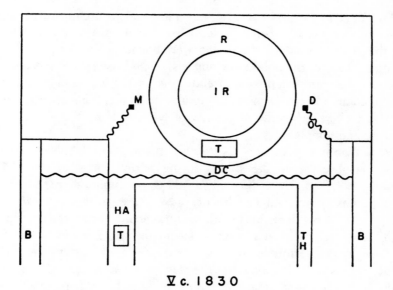

V c. 1830

A	Curtained entrance (*agemaku*)	M	*Metsukebashira*
B	Boxes (*sajiki*)	N	*Nanoridai*
D	*Daijinbashira*	O	'Hurry'-door (*okubyō-guchi*)
DC	Draw curtain (*hikimaku*)	P	Pre-forestage (*harigashi*)
F	Forestage (*tsukebutai*)	R	Revolving stage (*mawari-butai*)
H	'Bridge' (*hashigakari*)	S	Stage proper (*honbutai*)
HA	*Hanamichi*	T	Trap-lift
I	Inner revolving stage (*janome-*	TH	Temporary *hanamichi*
	mawashi)	X	*Rakandai*

35

in front of which at regular intervals are planted three pine trees which have the poetic values of heaven, earth, and man. The offstage end of the *hashigakari* is separated from the dressing room by a curtain (*agemaku*), which is raised from the bottom by two bamboo poles when the actor enters. Behind this curtain is the 'mirror room' (*kagami-no-ma*). Here, before an entrance, the actor studies his reflection in a mirror in order to get into character. The principal actors' entrance is on the *hashigakari*, but another entrance to the stage is provided by a small door about three feet high in the up-left corner of the stage. This is the *kirido-guchi* ('hurry' door) or *okubyō-guchi* ('coward's'-door) which is used by musicians, chorus, subordinate actors, and stage assistants. It is also sometimes called the 'stomach-ache door' because of the posture the performer must assume when passing through it.

Although today the Nō stage is ordinarily enclosed in a larger building, the original roof over the *hashigakari* and the stage is retained. The early Nō stages were independent architectural units set, however, near another building so that when the sliding doors on the side of the adjacent building were opened, this area provided a seating place for the nobility or officials, while less favored spectators, such as the commoners who attended *kanjin*-Nō, stood or sat in the unroofed area between the building and the stage. This arrangement is still to be seen in the placement of Nō stages on the grounds of shrines and temples.

A similar arrangement of spectators, implying social differentiation, is to be observed in the annual spring performances at the Mibu temple in Kyōto. Here didactic religious pantomimes, instituted in 1300, are performed on a rudimentary Nō stage which apparently has preserved its original fourteenth-century form. Spectators who pay admission are seated in a building facing the stage, while those who do not pay are permitted to stand in the open area, about fifteen feet wide, between the building and the stage. The same spatial arrangement prevailed in a temporary theatre built for a performance of *dengaku-nō* (a pre-Nō form) in 1348. Favored spectators sat on a circular platform which was divided into 'boxes' called *sajiki*, while the less important members of the audience sat on the ground close to the stage. The floor plan of this theatre immediately suggests similarity with the spatial arrangement of the Elizabethan public theatre.

Okuni-kabuki, or *onna-kabuki* (Women's Kabuki) as it soon came to be called when other troupes appeared, adopted, in general, the form that the Nō theatre had assumed for performances of *kanjin*-Nō.[9] The theatre area was marked off with a fence of straw matting about seven feet high supported by vertical poles. There was a single entrance for spectators with the *yagura* above it, on the front of which a billboard was hung. This earliest form of Kabuki theatre showed the social differentiation which was characteristic of the seating for *kanjin*-Nō. Since the entrance to the theatre was opposite the stage, the placing of a platform for *sajiki* along this side of the theatre, facing the stage, was impractical. Therefore the *sajiki* were constructed along the stage-right and stage-left sides of the theatre at right angles to the stage. The rest of the auditorium was bare earth on which the spectators sat on crude straw mats. This area was known as the *doma* ('earth floor') and the word serves today as the designation of the orchestra or pit in modern theatres. During the first quarter of the seventeenth century there were five to seven *sajiki*, about six feet square, along either side of the theatre, and these were raised some three feet above the ground. The *sajiki* were separated from each other by wooden partitions; there were railings at the front of them, and curtains or bamboo blinds were hung, not only for decorative elegance but also to protect the occupants from the gaze of the vulgar. In the event of a sudden shower, the occupants of the *doma* sat under the *sajiki* for shelter. The only portions of the theatre that were roofed were the *sajiki*, the stage, and the *hashigakari*, the last two retaining the typical roof of the Nō theatre.

Although on the whole the stage was a copy of the Nō theatre stage, it showed some departures from it. The normal arrangement of the Nō theatre placed the dressing-room at the end of the *hashigakari*; in the *onna-kabuki* theatre (c. 1604–1629) the dressing-room (*gakuya*) was placed directly behind the stage. It was originally an unroofed platform hung about with curtains, but was later walled with wood or plaster. The *hashigakari* was shortened so that it was about ten to twelve feet in length, although its width—about six feet—remained the same. There was a railing on the downstage side and the three pine trees of the Nō theatre were planted in front of it. The entrance to the *hashigakari* was curtained. Unlike the Nō *hashigakari* which was placed at an obtuse angle to the stage, the Kabuki *hashigakari* was

9 It is interesting historically that when Okuni opened her semi-permanent theatre in Kyōto, she began, on 23 October 1604, with a five-day performance of *kanjin-kabuki* to raise funds for her shrine in Izumo. *Kanjin*-Nō gradually disappeared with the development of Kabuki.

built at a right angle to the stage, although perhaps in the very earliest Kabuki stages it retained the angle of the Nō *hashigakari*. The musicians, who at this time were the drummers and the flute player of the Nō, were seated on the *atoza*. Since the Kabuki did not use a chorus, the *waki-za* (the area for the chorus at stage-left) was not technically necessary, but it seems nevertheless to have existed in some theatres. Unlike the Nō, the rear of the stage and of the *hashigakari* was not a wooden wall, but consisted of a curtain, probably of vertical alternating bands of red and white. This curtain separated the stage from the dressing room and continued across, on stage-left, to the fence surrounding the theatre area. No entrances were made through this curtain to the stage, nor was there an entrance in the area of the 'hurry'-door of the Nō stage. The stage floor about 1604 was raised some two and a half feet above the ground, and the sides of the structure below the stage floor level were unenclosed. Within twenty years the height of the stage increased to 2·9 feet in order to improve the sight lines for the increasing number of spectators. The stage proper was never larger than 17·9 feet square or smaller than 11·9 feet square. The entire theatre area measured 53·6 feet by 59·6 feet.[10]

This, in general, was the form that the Kabuki theatre had achieved by the first quarter of the seventeenth century.

Subsequently the development of the physical theatre was in the main shaped by three forces: the prevalence of fires, governmental restriction, and the gradual movement away from the form of the Nō stage. Most of the innovations in theatre architecture were first introduced in Edo, rather than in the more conservative Kabuki theatres of Kyōto and Ōsaka.

Fires flourish everywhere in Japan, but judging by the number of times the Edo theatres were destroyed as compared with the destruction by fire of the theatres of Ōsaka and Kyōto, the fires in Edo were not only more numerous but were also more widespread. As a case in point, the first permanent theatre in Edo, built in 1624 by Saruwaka Kanzaburō, was destroyed by fire forty-six times during the one hundred and seventy years of its existence. The euphemism for these fires was 'the flowers of Edo,' and until 1728, at which time the

---

[10] Japan has its native system of linear measurement. A basic unit is the *shaku* which today is 0·994 feet. Since the translation of Japanese measurements into feet and inches results in unwieldy figures, I have used tenths of a foot rather than inches.

population of Edo was about 750,000, there were no fire brigades organized among the citizens. 'Probably,' James Murdoch suggests, 'the Bakufu dreaded a possible menace in any such popular organizations as this measure would involve.' But even after the formation of the fire-brigades of Edo (which were colorful groups that soon found their romantic way into the Kabuki plays), fires continued to ravage the city. Some of these fires began in the theatres and thus provided a convenient excuse for the government authorities to enforce regulations having to do with theatre construction and the locations of theatres. Since frequent rebuilding of theatres after fires provided ample opportunity for architectural innovations, the Japanese were never encumbered with permanent theatre structures which could influence the form of the play and the method of acting. On the contrary, the form of the theatre building was eventually determined by the nature of the performance. Although for reasons of conservatism, economy, and governmental restrictions the theatres were usually rebuilt in much the same form they had previously, the rebuilding of theatres every three or four years, on the average, permitted the series of minor changes in the theatre building which over almost three centuries resulted in quite a different architectural form from that with which the Kabuki stage began.

Although the Kabuki had been subject to government regulation before, the first strong stand against it was taken on 23 October 1629, when the presence of women on the stage was forbidden. Shortly afterwards, the appearance of more than three actors on the stage at any given time was prohibited, and this resulted in the stage, which was now generally 17·9 feet square, being reduced to 11·9 feet square. A spate of government regulations affecting the Kabuki continued to be issued subsequently, but none of these were particularly concerned with the physical theatre until the regulations following the Ejima Affair in 1714.

By this time the theatres had greatly increased in number and in size. When the first permanent theatre in Edo was built in 1624 (the Saruwaka-za, which later became the Nakamura-za) the population of Edo was 150,000. By the end of the seventeenth century the population had increased to 500,000, and the increase was reflected in the number of theatres. In 1628 in addition to the Saruwaka-za, there were six smaller theatres. The Miyako Dennai-za, a Kabuki theatre, was built in 1633, and in the following year Maruyama Matasaburō constructed the 'large' theatre that was later to become the Ichimura-za. In 1642 the Yamamura-za, which was to come to grief in 1714, was opened. By 1652 Edo had four large Kabuki theatres, three doll theatres, eight small theatres and an indeterminate number of temporary ones, both legal and illegal. At the time of the great fire which began on 18 January 1657 and supposedly started in a theatre, there were thirty theatres in Edo, all of which were burnt. Of these only nineteen were permitted to rebuild: four large theatres, eight small theatres, five doll theatres, and two theatres in which children danced. Permission was given in 1660, however, for the building of the Morita-za, which opened in April of that year; this theatre and the Nakamura-za, the Ichimura-za, and the Yamamura-za were known as the Four Edo Theatres. Some of the smaller theatres were also performing Kabuki, as were the *miyaji-shibai* (troupes performing on temporary stages in the precincts of temples and shrines).[11] In 1661 five such companies were authorized to perform for one hundred 'fair days' in the temples and shrines of Edo, but judging by the number of regulations issued against other *miyaji-shibai*, a considerable number of troupes must have been performing without government permission. Toward the end of the century the number of doll and puppet theatres, and theatres for dancing, music, and singing also increased. At this time a doll theatre accommodated 400 to 500 spectators, while a large Kabuki theatre accommodated 1500 to 1600.

In Kyōto and Ōsaka, where the population was more stable, the growth of the number of theatres was much less spectacular. In 1656 a Kabuki actor in Kyōto quarrelled with a spectator in the theatre, drew his sword, and injured him. The government officials seem to have felt no great concern for the injured man, but they objected strongly to a man who wasn't a samurai, and particularly a Kabuki actor, drawing a sword. As a result, all Kyōto theatres were closed for thirteen years, and in 1669 only four theatres were permitted to reopen.

The theatres were also increasing in size. When the Saruwaka-za was rebuilt after a fire and reopened in November 1651, it was 47·7 feet wide and 89·5 feet deep (or according to another source, 48 feet wide and 77·5 feet deep). About 1690, after six more fires, the size of this theatre had increased to 65·6 feet by 89·4 feet. There is

---

11 Temples and shrines on the whole encouraged these performances. Not only did they attract potential worshippers but they also provided a source of income from the theatrical troupes themselves.

some evidence, although it is open to question, that in 1689 the two largest theatres in the city of Kyōto (the Ryōgaiya Denyemon-za and the Izutsuya Sukenojō-za) measured 96·4 feet by 180·9 feet, and 87·4 feet by 180·9 feet respectively.

The straw mat fence around the theatre area had been replaced by a bamboo fence, and this in turn was gradually replaced by a wooden one, so that by 1655 the wooden fence was standard construction in all Kabuki theatres. This wooden fence was generally used in the doll theatres earlier than in the Kabuki theatres. The wooden fence (*itagakoi*) eventually became the outer wall of the building, thus facilitating the development of a roof over the pit. During the first half of the seventeenth century a sunshade made of straw-matting was on some occasions stretched over the pit, but nothing resembling a permanent roof appeared until 1677. On January 23 of that year, two Edo theatres, the Ichimura-za and the Nakamura-za, were permitted by the government to install a wooden roof which partially covered that part of the pit next to the stage. Although the roof stretched across the *doma* a length of thirty feet, it was only ten feet wide. Even so it offered shelter to a sufficient number of spectators, other than those who could afford the *sajiki*, to permit the theatres to operate for the first time during rainy weather. About 1673–1675 the earthen floor of the *doma* was covered with rudely made *tatami* (thick rice-straw mats) which replaced the earlier used *mushiro* (thin mats of straw).

The height of the *sajiki* had gradually increased so that by the 1670's they were in most theatres about four feet above the ground. About 1685 the height of the *sajiki* had increased so that, in effect, the original *sajiki* were raised until they became a second story and a first story of *sajiki* was installed beneath them. About 1690 the two-story *sajiki* of the Nakamura-za in Edo were both six feet high. (In 1651 the floor area of each *sajiki* in this theatre was four feet square).

The increase in the number of *sajiki* and the decrease of their floor space is evidence of the growing popularity of the theatre at this time among the samurai and the wealthier townspeople, for it was they who occupied these seats. The government policy toward the theatre was a vacillating one; although it exhorted the warriors and townspeople to avoid the baleful influence of the theatre, it made no direct laws against their being there. However, the government believed that, once in the theatre, such spectators should not be hidden from the rest of the audience or from any government official who might drop in on a tour of inspection, apparently on the grounds that their being exposed to all eyes would arouse their native shame and act as a deterrent to further theatre-going. To this end, a government war was waged against the trappings with which the *sajiki* were outfitted.

In addition to the curtains and bamboo blinds which were installed in the early *sajiki*, during the first half of the seventeenth century red cloth hangings over the front railing and a folding screen at the rear of the box were added. In 1649 the government issued an order prohibiting the use of these screens, curtains, and bamboo blinds. Immediately the theatres began to use *kōshi*, frames of close wooden lattice work, placed at the front of the boxes. These had not been forbidden because they had never been used before. The *kōshi* had the advantage of being immediately portable, so that should intelligence come of the imminent arrival of a government official in the theatre, the *kōshi* could be quickly removed and hidden from his sight. This deception did not long continue, for after a few years the theatres gradually restored to use the curtains, bamboo blinds, and folding screens, and in 1668 they were again prohibited. By this time the luxuriousness of the *sajiki* had been increased by the installation of thick straw mats of good quality on the floor.

The dressing-room (*gakuya*), placed behind the stage, was now covered with a permanent roof, but the roof was architecturally independent of that over the stage. By the middle of the seventeenth century, the interior of the *gakuya*, which was essentially a single large room, showed a division into two levels, the second level resembling a loft along one side rather than a second story. In the early 1680's in the Morita-za in Edo, a second loft was added, and this arrangement formed the basis of a later division of the *gakuya* into three stories. At this time some parts of the dressing room had thick straw mats on the wooden floor. At about the same time two passageways were built behind the *sajiki* and these permitted access both to the *sajiki* and to the dressing room. Some theatres built covered passageways leading from the theatre to adjacent 'play-tea-houses.'

After 1644 the stage became more architecturally defined by the enclosure with wood of the bottom of the stage proper and of the *hashigakari*. The rear of the stage proper in the early theatres was curtained, but during 1624–1644, it became customary, in a number of theatres, to place a folding screen in front of this curtain. After 1655 the increasing tendency was to adopt the rear wooden wall of the Nō stage for both the stage proper and the *hashigakari*. In some theatres the rear wall was painted with the stylized pine tree (*matsubame*) of the Nō theatre. A further borrowing from the Nō theatre was the up-left 'hurry'-door which was introduced into the Kabuki theatres during the 1670's and was hung with a curtain like that which covered the entrance to the *hashigakari* on the opposite side of the stage. The roof over the stage and *hashigakari* became more elaborate in design during the 1670's. The only feature of the Nō stage abandoned during this time was the three pine trees planted in front of the *hashigakari*; these disappeared toward 1650. In general, the stage increased in size. The *hashigakari* was gradually extended toward the pit, while the stage proper increased its width on stage-left by the addition of the *waki-za* of the Nō stage, on which the Nō chorus sat. This area was not used by musicians and singers in the Kabuki theatre until about 1730. In 1684 the stage proper in the Ichimura-za in Edo was 29·8 feet wide.

The *hashigakari* began to expand about 1650. Previously it had been approximately six feet deep, the same depth as the *atoza* (rear stage); but by about 1700 it had been so extended toward the pit that it lacked only three or four feet of being as deep as the stage proper. The expansion of the *hashigakari* toward the audience did not provide the actor additional space in which to play, for the *hashigakari* continued to be used only for entrances, while the stage proper remained the area for extended acting. However, a desire to increase the size of the principal acting area appeared in the occasional, though apparently rare, use during the 1660's and following of a forestage (*tsukebutai*) which was attached to the front of the stage proper. The forestage does not seem to have been used extensively, but it was later to become a very important area of the stage.

The significant developments in the physical theatre up to 1714 were, then, the movement in the architecture toward the combination of the separate units of which the theatre was composed into an integrated building, and the increasing size of the stage, which was reflected in the increase in the width of the theatre area. The theatre area was now surrounded with permanent walls which would eventually support a roof, but at this point the dressing room, the *sajiki*, and the stage still retained their separate roofs. The expansion of the *hashigakari* toward the audience and the occasional use of a forestage is the first evidence, in the physical theatre, of a pattern of stage movement toward the audience which is one of the strongest forces in the Kabuki performance.

After the unfortunate visit of the court lady Ejima to the Yamamura-za in 1714, the assets of the Yamamura-za were confiscated by the enraged Bakufu, and this theatre, as well as *miyaji-shibai* in nine different places, was never permitted to reopen. On 6 February 1714 the government issued a series of regulations which, at least temporarily, affected theatre construction. The intent of these regulations seems to have been to restrict the size and the convenience of the theatres, thus discouraging spectators from attending them, and also to prevent nonprofessional contact between audience and actors in the theatre buildings and in the adjacent tea-houses.

The 1714 regulation forbade the construction of any theatre more than one story high and the construction of *sajiki* on two levels. This meant that the seating area of the *sajiki* was reduced by one-half. The wooden roof authorized in 1677, which had partially covered the *doma*, was now prohibited, and only the loosely woven straw matting (*mushiro*) previously used over the *doma* was permitted. The passageways behind the *sajiki*, running parallel to them and connecting them with the dressing-room, were prohibited, as well as the passageways which in some theatres led to the adjacent tea-houses. *Zashiki*, reception rooms, were forbidden in the tea-houses, for it was here that actors sometimes met members of the audience after a play, and it was in such rooms that women of Ejima's stripe stooped to folly. On 9 March 1714 another regulation was issued which prohibited the use of any lamps or fires within the theatre building and ordered all theatres to conclude their performances by six p.m.

With the disappearance of the Yamamura-za, only three large Kabuki theatres remained in Edo: the Nakamura-za, the Ichimura-za, and the Morita-za; and these, called popularly the Three Edo Theatres (*Edo Sanza*), remained the leading theatres until the Restoration in 1868. On only one point affecting the architecture of the Kabuki theatres did the government abandon its firm stand. On 6 October 1718 it permitted the theatres to cover the *doma* with a temporary roof of *tomabuki*, a thick rush matting which kept out most of the rain, and the theatres began to perform on days on which the rain was not too heavy.[12] Within a few years the theatres had

---

[12] An amusing anecdote involving a pun is told of this occasion. The word for love scene in the Kabuki is *nuregoto*, which means, literally, 'moist business.' In a curtain speech at the Ichimura-za in Edo just after permission to erect a roof had been received, the leading actor said, 'Hereafter we will not do any more love scenes (*nuregoto*), for we have received permission to put up a roof.'

44

begun, without government permission, to install wooden roofs. The Kabuki theatre owners seem to have been a brave lot in their defiance of the government, or perhaps through long experience they could accurately estimate the lengths to which they could go before the government would again close the theatres. In any event, their disregard of the 1714 regulations is shown by the following regulation which was issued in 1723:

> Article I: There has recently been a tendency to build theatres with two or three stories. This must stop, and theatres must be one-story buildings as before.
> Article II: Passageways from *sajiki* to the dressing room and to tea-houses will be removed. A spectator may not call upon an actor or see the actor in a tea-house. It is also illegal to see an actor at his residence.
> Article III: Hanging bamboo blinds in the *sajiki* is prohibited. Curtains and folding screens in the *sajiki* must also be removed.
> Article IV: Theatres have been building permanent roofs on theatres so that performances can be given on rainy days. This must stop. Only temporary roofs may be used.
> Article V: Recently the clothing and costume of actors has been more and more gorgeous. Hereafter costumes will be made of cotton only.
> Article VI: The use of lights in the theatre is strictly prohibited. The performance must end by four p.m.
> Article VII: The installation of reception rooms in tea-houses is prohibited.

Having forbidden, in Article IV, a permanent roof, the government abruptly changed its mind, and in the same year ordered the Three Edo Theatres to install complete wooden roofs, to cover them with tiles (tiles had been used on Edo houses since 1603), and to plaster the walls of the theatre. The change in policy was brought about by a sudden concern for fire prevention. By 18 April 1724 the Three Edo Theatres were tiled and plastered and for the first time had complete roofs. On 27 November 1726 they all burnt down and continued to do so in the following years as they had done before. Tiles were expensive and once having been subject to fire they were no longer usable; therefore the theatre owners hit upon a plan which both was economical and also, since the officials knew nothing of it, kept the officials satisfied. The theatre owners tiled only the front of the theatre roof, the portion which could be easily seen, and omitted to tile the rest of it. This deception was apparently successful for sixty-eight years, for it was not until November 1794 that the government again ordered complete tile roofs; but the habit had become fixed, and in January 1807 the government had to repeat its demands.

The newly tiled and plastered theatres of April 1724 also had restored the two-story *sajiki* of 1714, and these continued to be used in the theatres thereafter. The only one of the 1714 and 1723 regulations that remained constantly in effect was that which forbade the use of fire and lamps in the theatre. In the 1780's the officials permitted the use of *kantera*, small metal hand lamps, but they were insufficient for general stage illumination at night. These lamps were on occasion attached to the end of a long pole, the opposite end of which was held by a stage assistant, and used to illuminate the face of the actor. This lighting device was called *tsura-akari* ('face-light'), and its use survives today in the performance of certain plays. A Kabuki performance at night was not given until 1878 at the Shintomi-za in Tōkyō where gas lamps had been installed. Before this, the only stage lighting was the daylight which entered through *shōji* (the paper-covered wooden frameworks which serve as windows in Japanese buildings) placed behind the *sajiki* closest to the stage on the second story level. There is evidence that some theatres had curtained openings in the roof to provide general illumination for the auditorium.

The Kabuki theatre building continued to divorce itself from the physical theatre of the Nō. By 1830 it had arrived at the general form which it was to maintain until subject to the influence of Western theatre buildings.

On 6 May 1726 the government forbade the opening of any theatre which did not have a licence, and although the functioning of this provision was slightly different in Kyōto than in Edo and Ōsaka, it was enforced throughout the nation. Thus no new theatres were built, other than authorized ones that had burnt down, until after the Restoration in 1868.

The population of Edo increased from approximately 750,000 in 1725 to 1,367,840 by 1787. It is doubtful whether the increased population would have supported a greater number of theatres had they been authorized. The second half of the eighteenth century was marked by famines in 1749 and 1757, and by the great famine of 1783–1787 which culminated in rice riots and the looting of shops and houses in 1787. From about 1750, as a result of the famines, peasant uprisings were frequent; the practice of infanticide among farmers unable to support their children grew to such proportions that it had to be prohibited by edict in 1767. The first cracks had appeared in the walls of the Tokugawa edifice, and the troubled conditions of the times were reflected in the economics of the theatre. The large audiences of the first twenty-five years of the eighteenth century diminished considerably.

At this time the staff and actors of a Kabuki theatre numbered, on the average, one hundred and fifty, which is only a little smaller than the usual contemporary group. According to Tokugawa ethics, the managers were responsible for the continued employment of the theatre staff and the actors, yet government regulations did not permit them to increase the income of the theatres by increasing seating capacities. On 24 December 1734 the Morita-za went bankrupt. The manager and the managers of the other two theatres feared that if the theatre were allowed to close there might be occasion for the government to keep it closed permanently and that such a fate might eventually befall all theatres. They therefore devised a scheme whereby their theatres could be kept open though bankrupt. This was the system of *hikae-yagura*. The *yagura* was the tower-like structure at the front of all Kabuki theatres, and the word had come to mean 'permission to operate a theatre,' but the *hikae-yagura* ('duplicate'-*yagura*) was an individual who was prepared to take over the management of a bankrupt theatre until such time as the manager was able to find sufficient funds to pay his bills. The *hikae-yagura* of the three theatres were called into service eleven times between 1784 and 1823. On 3 October 1794 the managers conferred about the possibility of a change in the regulations affecting their theatres, thinking undoubtedly, as did the Shōgunate, that changes in regulations might remedy economic conditions. Their meeting produced no observable results.

About the middle of the eighteenth century, the doll theatres, performing the plays of such gifted writers as Chikamatsu Monzaemon and Takeda Izumo, surpassed the Kabuki in popularity. But toward the end of the century, particularly in Edo, these theatres had greater financial difficulties than the Kabuki and the number of doll theatres decreased.

In order to increase seating capacity and income, theatre managers quietly ignored governmental restrictions and increased the size of Kabuki theatres.[13] By 1807, the Kabuki theatre buildings on the

13 In 1782 the Ichimura-za in Edo was 59·6 feet wide by 79·5 feet deep. By 1797 this theatre had increased to 78·6 feet wide by 119·2 feet deep, and in the same year the Morita-za was 65·5 feet wide by 119·2 feet deep. The Nakamura-za in 1806 was 65·6 feet by 129·2 feet and when it was rebuilt after a fire in the same year it was increased to 74·6 feet by 129·2 feet.

average were 27·8 feet in height and were higher than the other buildings on the street. The government held that this height made fire-fighting difficult and ordered, in 1807, that the maximum height of theatres hereafter be 23·8 feet. Heretofore the roof over the pit had been the common gable roof, but this new regulation brought about an architectural problem. The common gable roof could not be supported, because of the width of the building, without a considerable decrease in the height of the outer walls of the theatre, which would, in turn, necessitate internal changes in the established theatre architecture. The problem was solved by the substitution of three parallel gable roofs over the pit.

During the late 1730's the early 'mouse-door' disappeared, and two front entrances to the pit were substituted; in addition there were two front entrances that led to the corridors directly behind the *sajiki* on both the first- and second-story levels. About 1736 began the process of dividing the pit into three different areas according to the price of admission. The tickets for the space closest the stage were the most expensive, those for the rear of the *doma* the cheapest. The sections were at first separated by bamboo railings, but later the railings were changed to raised narrow wooden passageways on which spectators walked to their seats. There were, however, no reserved seats until in 1766 the Nakamura-za in Edo instituted a system of marking off a few areas on the stage-left side (the 'east' side) of the pit for reserved seats. The system proved popular, and in August 1772 the rebuilt Nakamura-za and Ichimura-za installed similar 'boxes' on both sides of the theatre in front of the *sajiki*. They were called *shikiri-masu*, which means, literally, partitioned boxes, but the name was soon shortened to *masu*. By 1773 the number of *masu* in both these theatres had been increased to thirty-six and they covered half the pit area; by 1797 seventy percent of the pit of the Nakamura-za was converted to *masu*. The Miyako-za, a smaller theatre, had already completely converted its pit into *masu* in 1793. During this period each *masu* accommodated seven people. In 1772 the *masu* measured approximately five feet four inches square, in 1797 about five feet by four feet eight inches, in 1807 about four feet six inches by four feet eight inches. In general they remained this last size until 1841.

Shortly after 1800, the *masu* directly in front of the *sajiki* were raised above the level of the pit, and in the Ōsaka theatres another row of raised *masu* in front of the previously elevated *masu* was added. This practice was followed in some of the Edo theatres, and this raised area of the pit (*doma*) was called the *takadomo* (high *doma*). The stage-right and stage-left sides of the *doma* were thus built up in step-like levels, so that eventually in conjunction with the *sajiki* above them, the *takadoma* constituted a three-level structure.

The number of *sajiki* increased proportionately with the size of the theatre, and a new area for *sajiki* was added at the rear of the pit on the second story level. Nine of these *mukōsajiki* ('*sajiki* on the opposite side') were installed in the Nakamura-za in 1724, and the innovation spread to other theatres. At this time the total number of *sajiki* in this theatre was forty; by 1784 the number in both the Nakamura-za and the Ichimura-za had increased to sixty-nine, but generally in the late eighteenth-century theatres the number was about sixty. Although the theatre building was now completely roofed, vestigial portions of the original roof over the *sajiki* remained. Injunctions against the use of screens, blinds, and curtains in the *sajiki* continued to issue from the government and to be ignored.

The *hashigakari* continued to expand. In 1724 the railing at the front of it and the Nō roof above it were removed. A kind of *sajiki* was installed on the second-story level at the rear of the *hashigakari*, but this was purely decorative and was not used for spectators. At this time the *hashigakari* lost all evidence of its original relation with the Nō stage, although the area continued for some time to be called *hashigakari*. Shortly after the beginning of the eighteenth century, the *hashigakari* had become as wide as the stage proper; but in spite of its increased width, it was still used primarily as an area in which to make entrances rather than as an area for extended acting. The original extension of the width of the *hashigakari* was brought about by the desire to keep the entrances and exits upon it as close to the audience as possible and also to provide a better view of the *hashigakari* for the spectators in the second-story *sajiki*. But when it became the same width as the stage proper the *hashigakari* lost its architectural differentiation, even though the sight lines had been improved. At the same time, the increasing depth of the theatres reduced the effect of the procession-like entrance of the actor, achieved, in the earlier theatres, on the *hashigakari*. This was unsatisfactory to both actor and audience. Entrances and exits on a long, relatively narrow platform had become necessary to the form of the play and had also created a significant part of the actor's technique.

For these reasons, the *hanamichi*, which was in reality a new *hashigakari*, appeared in the theatres between 1724 and 1735. The construction of the *hanamichi* was probably suggested by the presence of the raised wooden passageways which served as the aisles of the theatre, and possibly by the existence of somewhat similar passageways in the contemporary wrestling arenas. The *hanamichi* ran from the rear stage-right side of the *doma*, where the entrance to it was hung with a curtain, and joined the front edge of the stage at an obtuse angle of about 110 degrees. Thus its angular relation to the stage was about the same as that of the Nō *hashigakari*. The *hanamichi* was, and is, theoretically divided lengthwise into ten equal parts, and its area of greatest strength is at the point which is three-tenths of its distance from the stage, or, from the other direction, seven-tenths of the distance from the curtain through which the actor enters at the rear of the auditorium. This important area is therefore called the *shichi-san* ('seven-three'). In the late 1730's the strength of this area was reinforced by the addition of a small platform extending from the stage-left side of the *hanamichi* called the *nanori-dai* ('name-announcing-platform'). This platform was first used in the November performances, *kaomise* ('face-showing'), which opened the new theatrical season and in which the actors who would appear during the year were introduced to the audience. On these occasions the actor stood on the *nanori-dai* for his introduction, and in plays such as *Just a Moment* the area was used for extended acting by the chief character. The *nanori-za* ('name-announcing-seat') of the Nō theatre, which is the area on the stage proper occupied by the actor just after he leaves the *hashigakari*, serves a similar spatial function. The strength of the *shichi-san* was further reinforced subsequently by the installation of a trap-lift in the *hanamichi* at this point, upon which characters, particularly supernatural ones, could make entrances and exits. This trap-lift, called the *suppon*,[14] is retained in the present Kabuki theatre.

From about 1772 on, another passageway through the pit to the stage was used by the actor. This was the *ayumi-ita* ('stepping-board'), a raised wood passageway at right angles to the front of the stage, by means of which spectators entered the *masu*. The successful use of the *hanamichi* probably suggested the use of this passageway as a secondary *hanamichi*. The *ayumi-ita* was a little lower than the

---

14 The word *suppon* means *snapping turtle* and was probably applied to this machine because of the analogy with the appearance and disappearance of the actor's head as he was raised and lowered.

level of the stage floor; therefore when it was first used by the actor, a length of board was laid at the point where it joined the stage, forming an inclined plane. As the use of this passageway to the stage increased, it came to be called the *higashi-hanamichi* (east-*hanamichi*) or, more frequently, the *kari-hanamichi* (temporary or 'improvised' *hanamichi*). Following the establishment of its use, toward 1780 still another passageway for the actor through the audience was employed. This was the *naka-no-ayumi* (center passageway), which was, in reality, the wooden partition which separated the second class seats from the third class seats. It was constructed across the width of the theatre and connected the *hanamichi* with the *kari-hanamichi*. The passageway, less used than the other two, was employed in this fashion: The actor entered the *hanamichi* at the rear of the theatre, moved to the stage and across it to stage-left, entered the *kari-hanamichi*, moved toward the rear of the pit, went across the *naka-no-ayumi*, and made his exit through the curtain at the end of the *hanamichi*. The movement was always clockwise. Today the *naka-no-ayumi* is never used, and the *kari-hanamichi* only rarely, but the stage business of watching a nonexistent character exit on the *kari-hanamichi* and the *naka-no-ayumi* is preserved in a number of plays with stage business dating from the time of these passageways.

The stage proper showed some expansion in width, but a greater expansion in depth because of the general adoption of the forestage. The forestage (*tsukebutai*) had previously been used in a temporary, tentative fashion, but from about 1736 it was a permanent part of the theatre architecture. Shortly after 1745 it became the principal acting area. At first the forestage was attached only to the front of the stage proper, but after the *hashigakari* had become the same width as the stage, the forestage was gradually widened in the direction of stage-right. In the 1770's a second smaller forestage, placed in front of the original forestage, was added. The stage-left area, that of the *waki-za* of the Nō theatre, was also widened between 1716 and 1763, and about 1730 the musicians and singers began generally to use this area rather than the *atoza*.

The 'hurry'-door of the Nō theatre, which had previously been in the up-left corner of the stage proper, had by this time been moved downstage. In 1717 at an amateur performance in the city of Nagoya, the musicians and singers were moved from their position on the *atoza* to a second-story level platform above the 'hurry'-door on stage-left. This practice was imitated in other Nagoya theatres. In

1728 the Takemoto-za, the famous doll theatre of Ōsaka, apparently influenced by the Nagoya theatres, moved the musicians and singers to the stage-left area on the stage level, a position they have since occupied in the doll theatres and also in the Kabuki theatres when a play of doll theatre origin is being performed. The practice of placing musicians and singers on stage-left subsequently spread to Edo, and the two-story stage-left structure remained the area for musicians and singers until after 1868. The second-story level, with an opening in the front which was screened with a bamboo blind painted black, came to be known as the *chobo-yuka* (the floor for the musical-narrative accompaniment). When the architecture of this stage-left area assumed a permanent form, a room was placed just within the 'hurry'-door for the use of musicians and sound effects men, who are to be distinguished from the performers of the musical-narrative accompaniment. This room at stage level was called the *hayashibeya* (orchestra room) or more frequently the *geza*. This word is most frequently written with two Chinese characters meaning *to sit* and *below* and had its origin in the fact that the musicians were placed below the musical-narrative performers.[15]

The removal of the musicians from the *atoza* and the use of the forestage as the principal acting area permitted the unhampered use of the rear of the stage by the scene designer. The Kabuki stage in its beginnings used only simple properties and the stylized pieces of scenery (*tsukurimono*, 'fictional things') which were common in the Nō theatre. However, in the last quarter of the seventeenth century, the stylized set pieces of the Nō had in some instances been converted to more representational miniature models of temples and palaces. As early as the beginning of the eighteenth century, small wagon stages (*hikidōgu*) were used to carry small set pieces onto the stage, but it

[15] Since the written word *geza* can be read literally as 'lower-seat,' there has developed a popular, though untrue, explanation of the etymology of *geza*. In the Japanese theatre, *shimote* ('lower-hand') is the term for stage-right, while *kamite* ('upper-hand') is the term for stage-left. At present the *geza* is at stage-right, and the assumption is therefore made that the first character of *geza*, 'lower,' is derived from the word *shimote* ('lower-hand'). But since the *geza* did not assume its present position on stage-right until the end of the nineteenth century, this explanation cannot be true.

The words *kamite* and *shimote* undoubtedly derive from the position of the actor on the stage. The chief character in most plays wore swords, and as the actor stood center stage facing the audience his left hand was placed on the hilt of his long sword and was therefore higher than his right hand. Thus his left hand was the 'upper-hand' (*kamite*) and his right hand the lower one.

was not until some twenty-five years later that any remarkable scenic innovations were made. In general, extensive scenery was used earlier in the doll theatres than it was in the Kabuki, in part because the doll stage was smaller and therefore required less expensive scenic equipment. But the great popularity of the doll theatres and the resultant loss of popularity of the Kabuki toward the middle of the eighteenth century undoubtedly encouraged the Kabuki to make scenic innovations. The popularity of the dolls similarly caused the Kabuki actors to take over their repertoire and their acting techniques.

During the eighteenth century there was a great development of Kabuki theatre machines, all of which first appeared in the doll theatres of Ōsaka. The first trap-lift for small pieces of scenery appeared there in 1727 and was first used by the Kabuki at the Nakamura-za in Edo in 1736. In 1744 a trap-lift for actors was also installed in this theatre. A larger trap-lift (*yatai-seriage*) capable of thrusting up large pieces of scenery, such as temple gates and the walls of rooms, appeared in the Chikugo-shibai, a theatre in Ōsaka, in 1748. The Toyotake-za, one of the two leading doll theatres in Ōsaka, in 1757 used a trap-lift consisting of three sections which could be raised to various levels independently. The revolving stage, invented by the doll theatre playwright Namiki Shōzō, was used first in the Kado-za in Ōsaka in 1758. This stage revolved above the level of the stage floor and was not, in this form, immediately adopted by other theatres. In 1793 the Nakamura-za in Edo, in the play *History of Azuma*, first used the revolving stage in the form in which it exists today.[16] A trap-lift of complicated design which came through the stage floor at an angle first appeared in the Onishi-shibai in Ōsaka in 1759. The *gandogaeshi* was used in the Ōsaka Naka-no-shibai in 1761. This was a device for spectacular scene-changing by which a large piece of scenery, such as a roof, was turned on its side to reveal a new painted surface.

[16] A 'revolving stage' was used in the West as early as 1602 (in a triumphal arch erected in honor of the entrance of Albert and Isabella of Austria into Antwerp), and Inigo Jones designed two revolving stages, one suspended above the other, for the *Masque of Beauty* in 1608. These and subsequent uses of a revolving stage, however, were of a temporary nature. It was not until the end of the nineteenth century, with the rise of spectacles of realism, that revolving stages, employed in much the same fashion as in the Kabuki, were permanently installed in the theatres of the West. The first modern installation was that of Lautenschläger, credited with being the inventor of the revolving stage, in the Residenz Theatre, Munich, in 1896.

With the development of this machinery, the dark area beneath the stage and the *hanamichi* occupied by the stage hands was called *naraku*, the Buddhist word for hell. (The corresponding area in the Elizabethan public theatre was also known as hell.)

It will be noticed that all these inventions involved the stage floor and that none of them utilized the area above the stage. Although the principal reason for this practice is an aesthetic one, the presence of the Nō stage roof was a practical deterrent to the use of the space above the stage for stage machinery.

The Nō stage roof had served only one functional purpose in the Kabuki theatre. Both the title of the play and the titles of the individual scenes were written on long pieces of paper or board and these were attached to the *metsukebashira* and the *daijinbashira*, the two downstage pillars supporting the roof. After the middle of the eighteenth century, with the development of stage machinery and an increasing concern with stage decoration, the presence of these two pillars became more and more inconvenient, and there is considerable evidence that an effort was made to decorate them, in exterior settings, with scenic bushes and trees. In such settings, the edge of the Nō roof was hung with paper cherry blossoms, or, on occasion, with blossoming plum branches or pine branches. This decoration, *tsurieda* ('hanging branches'), remains a conventional decoration hung, in certain exterior settings, just within the top of the proscenium in the contemporary Kabuki theatre. The pillars were not disguised when an interior was represented, for they then much resembled the exposed roof supports of domestic Japanese architecture.

As the forestage increased in size and importance as an acting area, the stage proper beneath the Nō roof became increasingly the area for stage decoration. In the 1730's *shōji* and *fusuma*, sliding doors consisting of a wooden framework covered with paper, were placed against the rear wall of the *atoza*, and these indicated an interior to the spectator. About the 1760's a low platform (*jumbidai*, 'preparing'-platform) was built behind the sliding doors, and on it were placed painted flats which showed an exterior perspective scene (*tōmi*, 'distant view').

The use of Western perspective in Japan, appearing first in the wood block prints, seems to have followed upon the government's permission, after 1720, to allow foreign books to be brought into the country; among these were Dutch books illustrated with engraved plates in perspective. One of the experimenters with perspective was

Maruyama Ōkyo (1733–1795), who, during the Meiwa period (1764–1772), made perspective wood block prints to be viewed in a peep-hole box (*megane-e*), the same sort of toy as that which appeared during the Italian Renaissance. The influence of this popular toy (which is depicted in one of Harunobu's prints) is undoubtedly related to the use of perspective painting in the theatre. By 1760 typical Japanese sliding doors were placed on the stage-right and -left sides of the stage proper, so that this area bore a greater resemblance to the usual Japanese room. At this time, with the addition of the forestage, the stage proper was so far upstage that the presence of the sliding doors at its sides did not obstruct the view of this area. Also, during the 1760's, a raised platform was placed in this area in interior settings. Actors playing in this space were, most of the time, seated on the floor; the raised platform enabled spectators in the front of the pit to get a better view of the actors. Another of Namiki's inventions which appeared about this time was the *dengakugaeshi*, a scene-changing device by which each of the upstage *shōji* or *fusuma* was turned at the same time in its vertical axis, thus turning the upstage side toward the audience and presenting a new decorated surface.

The Nō roof and its supporting pillars remained in the Kabuki theatre until 8 April 1796. At that time, the Miyako-za, one of the 'small' Edo theatres, removed the Nō roof so that in the performance of the play *The Golden Pavilion* a representation of the Golden Pavilion of Kyōto could be built on the stage. In the following spring another Edo theatre, the Kiri-za, also removed its Nō roof. Hereafter the Nō roof was gradually abolished in all Kabuki theatres. But the areas in which the *metsukebashira* and the *daijinbashira* had stood retained these names, as do the corresponding areas in the present Kabuki theatre. Although the custom of hanging a paper or placard bearing the title of the play in these areas disappeared almost at once with the abolition of the Nō roof in the Edo theatres, the Ōsaka theatres continued for some time afterward to hang this sign on stage-left. The practice can still be seen in the performance of plays in the rural districts or at the annual performances of medieval pantomimes at Mibu temple in Kyōto.

With the introduction of the *hanamichi*, the stage-right area of the *hashigakari* declined in importance. The curtained entrance at this side of the stage was retained and used by actors, but the strongest entrance was that made on the *hanamichi* and, second to that, the entrance from the 'hurry'-door which had been moved to downstage left. After the appearance of the *hanamichi*, a portion of the *hashigakari* was put to another use. The upstage area of it was fenced off and was made a standing room area called *rakandai*[17] for which the lowest admission price was paid.

Toward the end of the eighteenth century a second story was added above the *rakandai*, to which admission was even cheaper. The second story was soon given the fanciful name of *yoshino*, a region south of the ancient capital of Nara noted for its cherry blossoms. The reason for this name was that when the Nō roof was hung about the eaves with decorative cherry blossoms, the spectator in the *yoshino*, who was on the same level, was able to see little but the cherry blossoms. Both the *rakandai* and the *yoshino* continued to be used during the first quarter of the nineteenth century. The use of these two areas, which were occupied by the poorest spectators, was the result of the pit having been divided up into boxes for which higher admission prices were charged. Today these areas no longer exist, and the cheaper seats of the Kabuki theatre, as in the Western theatre, are in the second balcony.

The dressing-room in 1716 was a large room with two lofts along one side of it. The 1714 regulation concerning the theatres expressly forbade theatres of two-story construction. Nevertheless, when the Nakamura-za opened, after rebuilding, on 27 January 1720, the dressing room was built in three stories. The manager of the theatre, fearing that the government might object to this architecture, and showing the Japanese faith in linguistic differentiation, called the three stories the first floor, the mezzanine (*chūnikai*), and the second floor. This semantic deception continued in use until the end of the eighteenth century. The three-story arrangement was adopted by the Ichimura-za and the Morita-za in 1724 (they no doubt waited to see if the Nakamura-za would be called to account) and remains at present the standard dressing-room construction. In the 1720's the custom arose of rehearsing on the third floor in the *ōbeya* (a large room for subordinate actors) and is retained today. At the end of the century the backstage area contained rooms for costumes, properties, and wigs, as well as rooms for the actors and the manager.

By 1830 the Kabuki theatre had moved entirely away from the influence of the Nō stage and had arrived at a form which was

17 '*Rakan*'-platform. *Rakan* are the disciples of Buddha, usually represented in Japanese painting as crowded closely together about the Buddha. The press of spectators in this corner of the stage was an obvious parallel.

2. Auditorium of the present Kabuki-za, Tōkyō.

The *hanamichi* (in the foreground) is usually uncovered, but in this instance it is covered with straw matting and thus converted, theatrically, to an interior area. Sunken footlights can be seen along the edge of the *hanamichi*. The capacity of the theatre is 2600. [*Iwanami.*]

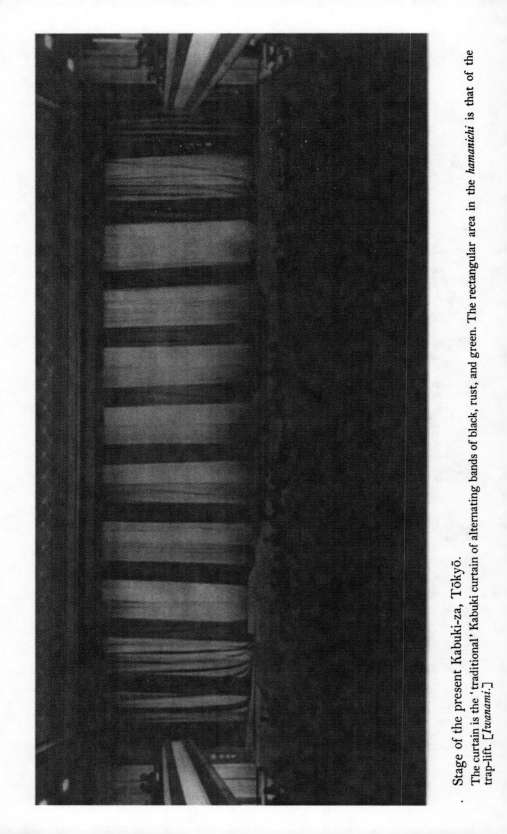

. Stage of the present Kabuki-za, Tōkyō.
The curtain is the 'traditional' Kabuki curtain of alternating bands of black, rust, and green. The rectangular area in the *hamanichi* is that of the trap-lift. [*Iwanami.*]

A *kanjin*-Nō performance on the estate of a feudal lord.

5. The contemporary Nō stage, which has shown no significant change
    since 1615.

The earliest Kabuki theatres were based upon this form of stage. Its
principal areas are the *hashigakari* (bridge), leading from the curtained
entrance of the dressing room to the stage, the *atoza* (rear stage) in which
the orchestra sits, and the *butai* (stage proper), which is the principal
acting area. The stage and the *hashigakari* are elaborately roofed, and
the pillars supporting the roof have conventional values in the movement
of the actor. The rear wall is painted with a stylized pine tree (*matsubame*).
The platforms and peony blossoms at the front of the stage are *tsukurimono* ('fictional things'), more flamboyant than is usual in Nō stage
decoration. [*Haar: Tuttle.*]

6. The Nō stage.

In the up-left corner of the stage is the low 'hurry'-door, used principally by musicians and chorus. The chorus is seated at the right of the photograph in the area called the *waki-za* (the stage of the subordinate character). The play is *Dōjō Temple.* [*Haar: Tuttle.*]

7. The Nakamura-za in Edo at the beginning of the Genroku period (c. 1688).

In order to show both the interior and the exterior of the theatre, the artist considerably reduced its proportions. The Nakamura-za at this time accommodated an audience of about 1500.

The façade of the theatre was enlivened with posters. The two on the right, drawn in the same style as the Kabuki posters of today, depict scenes from the play being performed. Above the entrance are billboards on which are written the names of the five principal actors. Above these is the *yagura*, on front of it the crest of the theatre, on the side the inscription *kyōgen-zukushi* (plays of more than one act) and the name of the theatre owner, Nakamura. The poster to the left of the entrance bears the title of the play, *The Nagoya Lottery*, while those to the left of it give the titles of its four acts. It is the second of these which is being played on the stage according to the placard attached to the *metsukebashira* on stage-right. At this time the Nakamura-za had a second story of *sajiki* (boxes) above those shown. The area just in front of the stage was covered with the long, narrow roof permitted on 23 November 1677. The *hashigakari* (bridge) was at this time almost as wide as the stage proper. [*Waseda Theatre Museum.*]

8. *Kaomise* ('face-showing') performance at the Ichimura-za, Edo, November 1764.

The theatre at this time was completely roofed. The stage shows a typical interior-exterior Kabuki setting. The interior is placed beneath the Nō roof and consists of a platform with a painted perspective behind it. The forestage is a garden, separated from the stage-right area by a gate. Placards with the name of the play and of the scene are attached to the pillars of the Nō roof. The balcony-like area above the stage is purely decorative and serves no theatrical purpose. In the up-right corner of the stage are spectators in the *rakandai*. At the down-right corner of the stage is the draw curtain, which opened from stage-left to stage-right, as it does in the present doll theatre, so that the narrator-musicians seated at stage-left are first revealed. In the Kabuki today, the curtain opens in the opposite direction.

The 'aisles' of the theatre were raised wooden passageways.

This period was the culmination of inventiveness in devising varieties of theatrical posters, including posters announcing the cast of characters, the plays being performed, the actors' names, scenes from the plays, and the *jōruri* performers. The front of the theatre was also adorned with flags and pennants. There were two front entrances to the *sajiki*. Platforms at the entrance (*yobikomidai*) were provided for barkers. The *yagura* continued to be decorated with the crest of the troupe. [*Waseda.*]

The play being performed is the congratulatory piece, *The Soga Confrontation*; the actors playing the Soga brothers are on the *hanamichi* at the *shichi-san*. The forestage shows considerable expansion, for it was now the principal acting area. The *ayumi-ita*, the raised passageway on the right of the print, was used, after 1772, as the 'temporary' *hanamichi*. The entire pit is divided into *masu*, each accommodating seven people, and the *masu* next to the *sajiki* are raised above the level of the pit so that they become *takadoma*. [*Waseda.*]

10. (*below*) The Shintomi-za, Tōkyō, about 1888.

This was the largest of the Tōkyō theatres at that time; the print shows a little over half of the auditorium. The *geza*, the music and sound effects room, was placed at stage-right, and the *choboyuka* for narrator-musicians was on stage-left at the level of the second-story *sajiki*. Both *geza* and *choboyuka* occupy these positions in the present Kabuki theatres. [*Waseda.*]

11. The contemporary use of both *hanamichi* and 'temporary' *hanamichi* in *Chivalrous Gorozō*.

Followers of rival samurai confront each other from opposite sides of the auditorium. [*Haar: Tuttle.*]

12. The exit of Nango Rikimaru and Benten Kozō in *Benten the Thief*, played by the late Nakamura Kichiemon and the late Kikugorō VI.

The exit is a humorous one, involving the blind man, on the left, whom the characters meet on the street. While this scene is played, the characters on the stage are immobile, but continue the act after the extended exit on the *hanamichi* has been completed. [*Shochiku.*]

13. *The Subscription List.*

The beginning of Benkei's triumphal exit on the *hanamichi* after the curtain has been closed. [*Haar: Tuttle.*]

14. (*above*) A *mie* in *Just a Moment*.
The square sleeves of the chief character are held up from behind by stage assistants.
[*Shochiku.*]

15. (*below*) The position of narrators and musicians on the stage of the doll theatre.
[*Haar: Tuttle.*]

16. Narrator and samisen player of the doll theatre, dressed in *kamishimo*.
[*Haar: Tuttle.*]

distinctly its own. An essential characteristic of the Kabuki performance is the intimacy between actor and audience, which is, of course, to some degree dependent upon the physical proximity of the actor to the audience. As the theatres increased in size during the eighteenth century, this intimacy was endangered, and the gradual expansion of the *hashigakari* toward the audience represents an attempt to restore it. The former relation between actor and audience was restored with the introduction of the *hanamichi* and the subsequent use of the temporary *hanamichi* and the *naka-no-ayumi* connecting the two *hanamichi*. With these passageways, the performance moved among the spectators in a form which is not exactly paralleled elsewhere in theatre history. The introduction of the forestage was also occasioned by the impulse to bring the performance close to the spectator, as was the use of a pre-forestage in the early 1770's. With the appearance of these new acting areas, the stage proper derived from the Nō theatre degenerated in importance and it was also, by the expansion of the other acting areas, reduced in size. The stage proper was largely delivered over to the stage mechanic and scene designer.

Between 1830 and 1868 the theatres showed no significant changes in size, and the number of theatres was, as before, limited by law. A fire starting in the backstage of the Nakamura-za on 7 October 1841 resulted in the destruction of all the Edo theatres. On 20 October the government forbade the reconstruction of the theatres on their former sites. On 19 December the Three Edo Theatres were ordered to move to the section of the city which later became known as Saruwaka-chō (the present Asakusa) where each was allotted a plot of ground measuring 65·6 feet by 108·3 feet. The government regulation fixing the height of theatre buildings at 23·8 feet does not seem to have been strictly enforced at this time, but the architect who had previously designed the buildings now rebuilt them, and they showed no significant change. The employment of the same architect, however, is a minor reason for their remaining the same size.

Toward the end of the 1830's worsening economic conditions and evidences of social unrest, such as the abortive rebellion staged by Ōshio Heihachirō in 1837, clearly foretold the eventual collapse of the Tokugawa Shōgunate. The government meanwhile attempted to cope with the situation in its established methods. It reissued currency in 1835 and issued regulations against spending money idly in 1838. In the interests of moral stability it forbade performances by temporary theatres in Edo in August 1836, in Ōsaka in May 1842, and repeated its prohibition in Edo at the end of 1842. In 1841 the chief minister of the Shōgun, Mizuno Tadakuni, instituted a series of reforms directed at almost all aspects of Japanese social and economic life; women were prohibited from employing hairdressers and from learning the *samisen* and *jōruri,* and the design of decorations on cakes was strictly regulated.

Financial depression of the country at large was reflected in the theatres. Audiences were smaller and the cost of materials greater. Little investment in scenery could be made and stock sets were commonly used. When the Three Edo Theatres were destroyed by fire following the earthquake of 2 October 1855, the managers had great difficulty in rebuilding because of the high price of construction materials.

But with the Restoration in 1868 came the removal of almost all the restrictions against the theatres, and they increased both in size and in number as economic conditions improved. On 21 September 1871 the municipal government of Tōkyō ('the Eastern capital'), as Edo was now called, issued a regulation which permitted the building of theatres other than the Three Edo Theatres, and in the spring of 1873 the number of theatres to be permitted in Tōkyō was fixed at ten. In August 1890 the regulation was amended so that ten 'large' theatres and twelve 'small' ones were permitted. The *donchō-shibai* (drop-curtain theatres), now performing a new kind of play influenced by Western models, were regarded as 'small' theatres. On 1 December 1900 the strict differentiation between large and small theatres was abolished, although theatres occupying an area larger than 7110 square feet were limited to ten within the center of Tōkyō. Five theatres were permitted in the suburbs. An amendment to the 1890 regulation provided that the theatres should be roofed with tiles, that the walls should be made of stone or brick, that there should be at least two staircases of stone or brick, that there should be more than two entrances, the main one being more than twelve feet wide. No restrictions were put on the height of the theatre buildings or on the ground area of the large theatres, and theatres were now permitted to be built in any section of the city.

In the spring of 1873 five new Kabuki theatres opened in various parts of Tōkyō. By 1900 there were seven larger theatres and four smaller ones.[18] The increase was less in Ōsaka, where only four new

[18] Now there are only four large legitimate theatres in Tōkyō, one performing Kabuki constantly, two others presenting Kabuki programs most of the time, the last devoted almost entirely to the revue.

theatres had opened by the end of the century, and in Kyōto, where only one new theatre had been built by 1899. Although the number of Tōkyō theatres increased and audiences were apparently large, the theatre owners frequently went bankrupt or were forced to sell their theatres. When this happened the name of the theatre was changed, and one Tōkyō theatre of this time bore five different names in rapid succession. Since no one, other than those in the three authorized theatres and their *hikae-yagura*, had had any experience in theatre management for several centuries, bankruptcies were to be expected.

The largest Tōkyō theatre in 1872 was the Morita-za, which was 107·3 feet by 196·8 feet, and it was not surpassed in size for twenty years. However, there was a gradual increase in the size of the theatres which were built toward the end of the century.[19] The Kabuki-za, which opened in 1889 and was the first Kabuki theatre to show the influence of Western theatre architecture, was 89·5 feet by 107·3 feet; in 1891 the Haruki-za, also influenced by the West, was 125·2 feet by 196·8 feet.

The arrangement of the auditorium was to some degree affected by government regulations. On 20 October 1886 a regulation fixed the number of persons permitted to occupy one *sajiki* or one *masu* (the boxes into which the orchestra level was divided) at four; while the August 1890 regulation stipulated that a passageway at least one foot wide be installed between every two *masu* and that a minimum ground area of eighteen inches square be provided for every spectator in the auditorium. When the Three Edo Theatres were moved to Saruwaka-chō in 1841, the size of the *masu* was reduced to four feet three inches by four feet five inches and the number of persons admitted to each *masu* was five. The total number of spectators that could be seated in the *masu* and *sajiki* was 1055 and probably five or six hundred more could be accommodated in the standing room both at the rear of the theatre and in the *rakandai* and *yoshino*. Exact figures on the capacities of the theatres are difficult to estimate, and no Japanese scholar has made a study of this aspect of theatre history. There is general evidence, however, that between the middle of the eighteenth century and the middle of the nineteenth, the capacity of the theatres almost doubled. When the Nakamura-za was rebuilt in 1856, both the *masu* and the *sajiki* were reduced in size to four feet

[19] In 1873 the Nakajima-za was 65·6 feet by 107·3 feet. In 1878 the Ichimura-za was 71·5 feet by 116·2 feet. In 1884 the Saruwaka-za was 77·5 feet by 149·1 feet. In 1885 the Chitose-za was 107·3 feet by 154 feet.

by four feet two inches, and five people were squeezed into this smaller area. The decrease in the size of the *masu* and *sajiki* indicates an attempt to increase the capacity of the theatre, since the theatre could not be expanded in floor area. The capacity of the Morita-za in 1872 was probably over 2000.

This theatre introduced certain changes in the architecture of the pit. Sliding doors were installed at the rear of the *sajiki*, and chairs were placed in a few of the *sajiki* at the rear of the theatre for the benefit of the foreigners who were beginning to come to the Kabuki. The rear of the pit was still given over to standing room (*oikomiba*). The number of levels of raised *masu* along the stage-right and stage-left sides of the pit was increased to three, which, with the *sajiki* above them, constituted four levels. The upper *sajiki* were thus assuming the characteristics of a balcony. With the Shintomi-za, rebuilt in 1878, the architectural detachment of this area was made; and the former second story *sajiki* became a balcony. The auditorium was gradually assuming an architectural form which, with the exception of its being rectangular, resembled the arrangement of the auditorium of the European opera house. This change in the construction, however, does not seem to have been in any way influenced by Western theatre architecture, but was an outgrowth of the characteristic architecture of the Kabuki theatre.

The new Shintomi-za[20] (the former Morita-za) made a few minor changes in the pit. Previously the standard practice was not to build the *sajiki* and the raised *masu* on the stage-left side of the auditorium as far forward as the front of the stage, for if this were done the spectators in this area closest to the stage would have little or no view of entrances made through the 'hurry'-door on stage-left. But in the 1878 Shintomi-za the *sajiki* and the raised *masu* were extended directly to a line parallel with the front of the stage. The change indicates the decreasing importance of the 'hurry'-door as an entrance to the stage in the Tōkyō theatres. In the Ōsaka theatres, however, this entrance continued to be an important one until after 1900. Today, important entrances are never made from this curtained opening on stage-left, and it is used much more frequently for exits than for entrances.

The Shintomi-za of 1878 also installed for the first time a flat wooden ceiling over the auditorium, which was said to have improved

20 The best known foreign patron of this theatre was ex-President Ulysses S. Grant, who attended a performance in 1879.

the acoustics considerably. Heretofore the theatre ceiling had been merely the unfinished underside of the roof. The rudimentary remainder of the early roof over the *sajiki* was discontinued, as were the *rakandai* and the *yoshino*. Subsequent theatre buildings followed this innovation.

The *hanamichi* was originally placed at an obtuse angle to the stage proper, but with the change of the pit floor into *masu* this angle was architecturally, as well as economically, inconvenient, for it meant that either the *masu* placed next to the *hanamichi* could not be made rectangular or that a certain amount of the pit area would have to be sacrificed. The problem was solved by building the *hanamichi* at a right angle to the stage proper, parallel to the temporary *hanamichi* on the opposite side of the auditorium. By 1872 all *hanamichi* were built in this fashion, as they are now. The earliest *hanamichi* were probably no more than a foot or so wide, but there had been a gradual increase in their width so that by 1889 the *hanamichi* of the Kabuki-za was about five feet wide and the temporary *hanamichi* was about two and a half feet wide. The length of the *hanamichi* depended, of course, upon the size of the theatre. In the Kabuki-za it was 59·6 feet long. Previously, in order to make an entrance on the *hanamichi*, actors had made their way to the rear of the theatre by passing through the corridor behind the *sajiki* (*ura-sajiki*) on the stage-right side of the building. In the 1872 Morita-za and the 1889 Kabuki-za this practice came to an end. A passageway was built beneath the floor of the auditorium so that actors could go from the dressing rooms behind the stage to the entrance to the *hanamichi* without being seen by the audience. The temporary *hanamichi* continued to be a standard part of the theatre building until about 1923; but when the theatres were rebuilt after the earthquake of that year, the temporary *hanamichi* were generally not rebuilt. Today the theatre chairs in the area of the temporary *hanamichi* are constructed so that they can be removed and a temporary *hanamichi* installed. But since use of the temporary *hanamichi* would decrease the capacity of the theatre and consequently reduce its income, this economic sacrifice is seldom made.

After 1868, the stage, following its previous pattern, continued to expand in width, and at the same time the depth of the auditorium was gradually decreased. Finally the auditorium assumed the form it has today, that of a rectangle with the stage on one of its long sides. The pre-forestage was generally in use in the Tōkyō theatres until the 1870's, although it was less used in Ōsaka and Kyōto. When the Morita-za was built in 1872, the pre-forestage was abandoned, and the entire stage now became an architecturally undifferentiated unit 65·6 feet wide. Other theatres followed this practice. Thus the actor could now be seen 'in the round' only when he was on the *hanamichi*. In the 1889 Kabuki-za, the largest theatre at that time, the stage was 78·6 feet wide and 71·5 feet deep, with a revolving stage 53·6 feet in diameter and an inner revolving stage 41·7 feet in diameter. This theatre, after subsequent rebuildings and remodellings, remains the largest theatre in Tōkyō today. However, the other new Tōkyō theatres showed a continued expansion of the width of the stage. In 1893 the stage of the Meiji-za was 49·7 feet wide; in 1894 the Ichi-mura-za stage was 68·5 feet wide; in 1899 the Hongō-za stage was 77·5 feet wide.

None of these theatres had the proscenium arch of the Western theatre. The proscenium arch made its appearance in Japan with the opening of the Yūraku-za in Tōkyō on 1 November 1908. This theatre was painstakingly modelled on the Western theatre, complete with chair seats, with number plates on them and hat racks beneath them, as well as a proscenium arch and a drop curtain. Smoking rooms and lounges were provided in the hope that the audience would confine its smoking and eating to these areas. The Yūraku-za stage was 23·8 feet deep, with a proscenium opening 35·7 feet wide and 17·9 feet high. The Imperial Theatre, a replica of the standard European opera house, seating 1700, opened in 1911. Its proscenium opening was 58·6 feet wide, and it was the first Japanese theatre to have an orchestra pit. The influence of the proscenium arch of this theatre was immediate, for in November 1911 the Kabuki-za began remodelling, and a proscenium arch was installed as well as a drop curtain. After the 1923 earthquake all Kabuki theatres were rebuilt with proscenium arches and chair seats. Only occasionally a small suburban or rural theatre is seen today without chair seats, its floor covered with straw mats.

With the introduction of the proscenium, the Kabuki theatre attained the form which it has today, with the 'inner-proscenium' of music and sound effects rooms placed just upstage of it. However, the 'inner-proscenium' structure had been established in the Kabuki theatres before the proscenium was incorporated into the theatre design. Shortly after 1868, the *geza*, the sound effects and orchestra room, was moved in most theatres from its position on stage-left to stage-right. Before 1868 on at least one occasion, the *geza* had been placed on stage-right because it was more convenient to the staging of a particular play. Placing the *geza* in this position permanently was probably due to the better view it afforded of the *hanamichi*; the musicians and sound-effects men could achieve better synchronization with the movement of the actor on the *hanamichi*.

Following the style of the two Western theatres, the Kabuki-za began to use the drop-curtain, which, historically, had been associated with the *miyaji-shibai*, the small, temporary, and frequently unlicenced theatres. The draw curtain had always been the prerogative and distinguishing mark of the government authorized theatres. Now, however, the previously despised drop-curtain appeared in a new light, for since it was used in foreign countries it was therefore of necessity, in this day of passion for things foreign, stylish, modern, and high class. The draw curtain, however, was not abandoned. In the remodelled Kabuki-za of 1906 a draw curtain of silk was used for the first time in two centuries. In a strangely generous mood, the government in March 1668 had permitted the authorized theatres to use draw curtains of silk crepe (*chirimen*), but in February 1683 this privilege was withdrawn and thereafter only cotton curtains were permitted.

As the theatres increased in size, the problem of lighting the stage became more acute, for even after 1868 lights within the theatres were still prohibited. The problem was partially solved by increasing the number of windows above the second story *sajiki*, and in the late nineteenth-century theatres these windows extended from the stage to the rear of the auditorium. The modern era in Japanese theatre lighting was ushered in with the installation of two gas chandeliers suspended over the auditorium in the Tōkyō Shintomi-za, which opened on 7 June 1878. The chandeliers illuminated both the stage and the auditorium. In August of the same year, this theatre began the first night performances in Kabuki history, beginning the plays at five p.m. and closing about eleven p.m. In February 1879 gas was installed in the Ichimura-za and in August of the same year in the Hisamatsu-za. The first use of electricity in the Japanese theatre was in August 1887 at the Chitose-za in Tōkyō, and thereafter its use spread quickly to other theatres.

Stage lighting equipment in the present Kabuki theatres is in no way different from that in the larger Western theatres. Border lights and spot lights are placed in their conventional positions behind the proscenium; footlights are generally used; batteries of spotlights are fixed at the front and at the rear of the second balcony to provide front lighting for the stage. In most theatres a small room at the rear of the orchestra level is used for 'special effects' lighting equipment. Generally, two rooms are installed on both sides of the stage at the level of the first balcony and these provide positions for cross-lighting the stage. The presence of the 'inner-proscenium' construction prevents the use of positions for lighting equipment directly behind the proscenium on either side of the stage. The *hanamichi* is lit from two positions: from the lighting room on the stage-left side of the theatre on the first balcony level, and from a row of sunken footlights installed along the edge of the entire length of the *hanamichi* on the stage-left side. A spotlight from the lighting room usually follows the actor as he moves on the *hanamichi*, while the footlights along the *hanamichi* provide general illumination. The *hanamichi* footlights are wired in three circuits, providing for the use of three colors.

In actuality it was the auditorium of the Kabuki theatre that was influenced by Western theatre architecture; the stage itself remained unchanged. Before 1868 the stage had become a unified spatial area with its inner proscenium; the relation between the two *hanamichi*, the stage, and the auditorium was firmly established. The adoption of the proscenium and the drop curtain, as well as the chair seats, had no roots in the essential quality of the Kabuki performance. These innovations were made solely in the fanatical craze for things Western and the desire to avoid being ridiculed for not knowing Western ways that absorbed most of Japanese urban thought during the first twenty years or so of the Meiji period. That there were not changes in theatre architecture earlier in the period is probably due to the fact that it is a little more difficult to import proscenium arches than it is to import watches.

The proscenium arch, which had originally appeared in the Western theatre as a decorative device, had gradually become a means of architecturally defining the division between stage and auditorium and separating the world of illusion from the world of actuality. By the time the proscenium arch reached the Japanese theatre, this aesthetic function of the proscenium was clearly and, it almost seemed, permanently established in the Western theatre. The elevation of the proscenium to this aesthetic prominence was accompanied by a visual and psychological penetration of space behind it.

The scene designer did away with the painted perspective backdrop and substituted carefully lighted sky domes or sky drops so that the illusion of depth could be maintained. 'Sky' continued upward and into the wings of the stage until the vision of the audience was cut off by the line of the proscenium or by carefully placed scenic units. In interior settings, windows and doors gave onto gardens, streets, hallways, or adjoining rooms. At the same time, the playwright and the actor were engaged in investing these new worlds with theatrical validity. A playwright such as Chekhov used an orchestra of sound effects to create the sense of a world of unseen offstage activity, while the actor oriented himself psychologically to these regions and in doing so moved farther and farther away from the audience. The proscenium performed the function of a rectangle through which could be observed a segment of an expanding universe whose nucleus was the stage.

There was no such penetration into the unseen areas of the stage in the Kabuki theatre, either psychologically or visually. On the contrary, only the observable limits of the stage had theatrical significance, and the pattern of movement of the actor toward the audience and away from the upstage areas was stated architecturally. The introduction of the proscenium arch into the Kabuki theatre was therefore not the result of artistic need but of snobbery.

Japanese students of the Kabuki seem agreed in the opinion that the form the Kabuki stage had achieved by the 1830's represents its highest development and that the innovations after 1868 are a movement away from the true nature of the Kabuki theatre. They feel that the presence of the proscenium arch, the disappearance of the temporary *hanamichi*, and the increase in the size of the auditorium and stage have brought about a lack of intimacy between actor and audience which is the antithesis of the basic nature of the Kabuki performance. Certainly, the primary impulse of Kabuki theatre architecture was to move the actor toward the audience. This movement is implicit in the widening of the *hashigakari*, in the development of the forestage and the pre-forestage, in the appearance of the *hanamichi*, the temporary *hanamichi*, and the passageway connecting them, and even, to a lesser degree, in the use of the *rakandai* and *yoshino* as seating areas on the stage. The drop curtain behind the proscenium sets off the stage as an area separate from the auditorium in a way that the Kabuki draw curtain does not. The Kabuki curtain is of thin material. Drawn by a stage assistant across the stage, it has about it an informal air quite the opposite of the drop curtain; it hangs loosely over the front edge of the stage; when closed, one side or the other may be lifted to permit seeing musicians and singers on the stage. In the main, the function of the Kabuki curtain historically was not to separate the auditorium spatially from the stage but simply to avoid the awkwardness of exits after a striking tableau at the end of a scene. It was not used to hide the stage during scene shifts, for with the development of stage machinery the scene shift became, and continues to be, one of the most exciting moments of the performance. However, in spite of the architectural changes in the theatre after 1868, a greater intimacy between actor and audience exists in the Kabuki theatre than in the contemporary Western theatre, not excluding such recent 'intimate' theatre as that called variously theatre in the round, arena theatre, and so forth. A large part of the intimacy in the Kabuki results from centuries of theatre custom which continues to triumph over the architectural form of the theatre building. The *hanamichi* remains, and, except in recent plays, serves all its original functions. The proscenium opening, because of the great width of the stage in relation to the auditorium, does not suggest a 'peep-hole' stage; the stage dominates the auditorium. During most contemporary performances the auditorium is only a little less brightly lighted than the stage, so that the two areas are not differentiated psychologically by light. The principal acting area continues to be the downstage one as it was on the forestage of the earlier theatres. Mere physical proximity in the theatre is no guarantee of the quality known as intimacy. The use of the *hanamichi* in the contemporary Western theatre would probably produce mild discomfort among most of the audience (as did the wedding procession in *Our Town*) and very little intimacy. But the Kabuki arose out of impulses, attitudes, and conceptions of beauty quite different from those which shaped the contemporary Western theatre. The Kabuki stage and *hanamichi* continue today to be architectural areas which both through historical association and present use assist in that elusive yet vital rapport between actor and spectator which produces the phenomenon known as theatre.

CHAPTER III

The Audience and its Attitudes

ALTHOUGH the Shōgunate thought to preserve its power by maintaining carefully drawn class distinctions, and although the end of the Tokugawa period was a time of social ferment, the long isolation of the country created a uniformity of habits, beliefs, and tastes among all classes. The farmer, the townsman, and the samurai moved in different hierarchical spheres but they shared a mundane world in which their differences were not of kind but of degree. The diet of all, except in times of famine, was essentially the same, consisting principally of rice with a few vegetables and a little fish, prepared according to a very few standard recipes. In fact for some twenty-five years under the orders of the Shōgun Tsunayoshi, the entire population of Japan was forbidden to kill any living thing, but the killing of fish was overlooked and the population lived, consequently, on a Lenten diet. The house of a townsman was more elegant than that of the peasant, but the architectural arrangement, the household articles, the system of heating, the furniture—all these had the same basic form, size, shape, and function. The wealthy townsman could warm his hands in winter over a charcoal brazier made of bronze while the peasant had to be content with one of clay and with somewhat less charcoal. The frames of the sliding paper doors of the townsman's house were made of cypress while those of the peasant were of pine. But there was no difference in the basic forms of the braziers or the sliding doors nor in their functions. Wealth could provide greater abundance of food and better quality of materials; it could purchase nothing essentially different in form or function. The code of morality and social behavior, based largely upon the

Japanese interpretations of the commentaries of Chu Hsi on the works
of the Chinese sages, at last permeated into all social groups, so that
finally the Edo fireman shared an ethical climate not immediately
distinguishable from that of the samurai.

Similarly, tastes in art were built up out of commonly shared
artistic experiences. The Nō was at first a purely aristocratic amusement, but as early as 1413 a *kanjin*-Nō was performed. Subsequently,
until the rise of the Kabuki, public performances continued, attended
by young and old of all classes, until Nō techniques and modes of
artistic expression were understood and appreciated throughout the
social hierarchy. In the early eighteenth century a group of reapers
from the province of Shinano offered a leading Nō performer suggestions which he accepted concerning the playing of a role. Identical
tastes in music and in the graphic arts were so widespread that, until
modern times, the body of artistic canon did not differ significantly
according to social stratification. A maid serving tea moved in a style
similar to that used at court ceremonies; shop clerks were taught to
sit, move, and stand in patterns used in the Nō and were intensively
drilled to speak in a manner closely resembling that of the Kabuki
actor. The identity of artistic taste, which meant a certain loss of
class distinction, was one aspect of the social scene which worried
the Shōgunate. It disliked the presence of the samurai in the Kabuki
theatre as well as the Emperor's singing, in 1718, a licentious song
of the commoners.

In the realm of the arts and in the Kabuki theatre, the general
similarity of tastes, attitudes, and feelings throughout the whole of
society permitted the development of a vocabulary of expression
which was, in the Western sense of the word, nonrealistic. During
the nineteenth century, when the society of Japan was undergoing
great internal stress, there was, judged solely from a Japanese point
of view, a movement toward realism in the Kabuki, but it was only
after 1868, in the ferment of social change and under the impact of
Western influence that realism, in the Western sense of the word,
appeared in the Japanese theatre.

Today the vocabulary of expression of the Kabuki remains
essentially nonrealistic, but it would not be fair to imply that the
audience today shows the same acceptance of its expression as did the
audience of the Edo period. The flood of Western influence that has
swept over Japan in modern times has not destroyed the traditional
forms of expression, but it has introduced new theatrical forms that

have attracted certain spectators away from the Kabuki and acquainted them with representational expression. Continued acquaintance with the representational film, for example, has unfitted many Japanese for understanding the presentational idiom of the Kabuki. After Japan was opened to the Western world, *shimpa*, a new theatrical form which appeared about 1888 and was more realistic than the Kabuki, attracted audiences who formerly might have attended the Kabuki. The *shimpa* audience consisted largely of country people who had found employment in the cities during the wars with China in 1894 and with Russia in 1904. However, with the showing of the first foreign film in December 1896 and the first Japanese film in April 1898 much of the audience that had patronized the *shimpa* turned to this new form of amusement and *shimpa* soon became unpopular. The Kabuki was, at that time, no longer the 'popular' theatre it had been during the early Tokugawa period. Although its audiences were not drawn from a particular social class, they consisted of those who through taste and education in its idiom were devotees of the Kabuki. At the end of World War II, this audience largely disappeared and was succeeded on the whole by the only people in Japan who could afford theatre tickets at that time, the black marketers. Japanese economic conditions have improved considerably since then, and at present the audience is a more representative one. However, a first-class Kabuki ticket at present costs the average white collar worker about one-twelfth of his monthly salary and few are in the position to pay this price. The great majority of the audience consists of the employees of a commercial company which has bought out the whole house or part of it for the performance and has distributed tickets among the employees and their families. The practice is not entirely altruistic, for the companies are permitted to deduct such expenses from their income taxes as entertainment costs. The custom of distributing free tickets, which was established during the Meiji period, provides a larger and more representative audience than the Kabuki could gain otherwise.

Many of these spectators are not educated in the idiom of the Kabuki. Some read their program notes assiduously in the hope of understanding what the play is about, and by the time they have finished reading, the play is over and they have not seen it. Others laugh, at the wrong places, at Kabuki techniques they do not understand. A few simply pay no attention to the play at all. Japanese theatre critics seem agreed that post-war audiences, though larger than pre-war ones, have considerably less understanding of the Kabuki. It is probably to the end of educating the audience that a number of books popularizing the Kabuki have appeared and that the Kabuki actors have instituted a program of performances for children so that they will grow up acquainted with this form of theatre expression.

But a curious fact strikes the foreigner. Even the people who know little or nothing of the Kabuki, other than that it is spoken well of by the intelligentsia, are eager to go to the theatre, not once but again and again, whether they buy their own tickets or are given them. Part of this attitude is undoubtedly due to the same snobbishness with which the Edo townsmen imitated the manners of the aristocracy, but there is also in it that deep strain of genuine admiration for traditional forms which lies at the root of Japanese thought.

In addition, going to the Kabuki is for many a novelty. The Japanese are a violently mercurial people, and, possessed of a strong natural curiosity, they are quick to seize upon anything new. Fads and crazes occur in other countries, but they seldom reach the virulent and epidemic proportions which they do in Japan. Opposed to this impulse throughout the Tokugawa period was the government policy of maintaining the status quo in every aspect of Japanese life, even the most trivial. Government policy had deprived the Japanese of innovations from abroad, and the impact of governmental authority upon the native love of novelty set up a tension which was relieved in the heedless and country-wide pursuit of a fad. In the first quarter of the eighteenth century the double suicide of lovers became so popular and widespread that the government deemed it necessary to forbid such frivolous behavior by edict. Later in the century the Japanese took up going to temples and hearing sermons with violent energy, not because of religious belief but only as a fad. With the end of the Edo period, the craze for things Western occupied the energies of most of the nation. Currently the consuming passion of the Japanese is playing pinball machines; at latest count there is one machine for every forty people in the country, and there is scarcely a spot in village, town, or city where one is out of earshot of their whirr and click.

Though the Japanese is a willing prey to almost any novelty, whether of foreign or local origin, he is also deeply reverent of tradition. The new never absorbs him to the point that he is unmindful of the past. As a result, he is capable of maintaining simultaneously what seem to be such great extremes of artistic attitudes that, at any given moment in history, it is difficult to fix the median line of his tastes. All the varied forms of artistic expression of Japan's past are accepted by a majority of the population (not necessarily by the scholar or artist) as having about equal merit. This attitude may be in part the result of racial and nationalistic pride which finds in every Japanese artistic expression an equal virtue. In any event, in architecture the Japanese admires both the chaste restraint of the room in which the tea ceremony is performed and the excessively gaudy, pretentious decoration of the temples at Nikkō. In painting, he is equally attracted by the austere understatement in black and white of the Muromachi period (1392–1573) and the lavish, colorful, crowded, profuse expression of the Momoyama period (1573–1603). In flower arrangement, he loves forms which are rigorously controlled and also those which are a welter of color and confusion. In ceramics, he approves both the simplicity of the tea ceremony bowl and the overdecorated surface of Satsuma pottery. It is not that similar wide variations in taste do not occur in other countries, but in Japan they exist simultaneously and are maintained throughout a majority of the population.

In the matter of taste as elsewhere, the Japanese have exhibited a recurrent pattern of behavior. They undergo a craze which is of intense but short duration. Thereafter, in the majority of cases, the virulent fever having abated, the new acquisition, whether it be a certain kind of tea cup, a style of hair arrangement, or double suicide, is absorbed into the main stream of Japanese culture and becomes part of a stable tradition. The Kabuki, existing in the forefront of popular taste, was particularly susceptible to the waves of novelty which swept its audience. But like Japanese culture in general, it gradually created a solid tradition which underlay all the agitation of novelty on its surface. And so there is in the Kabuki not only unrestraint, lavish detail, an almost uncontrolled line, but simultaneously, restraint, economy of statement, and exquisite control. That these characteristics should exist side by side in the same theatrical form complicates any explanation of the aesthetic of the Kabuki. Japanese scholars insist that the Kabuki is not the place to look for logic. Although no logical consistency may underlie a given Kabuki performance, it nevertheless has certain characteristics in common with, and derived from, other forms of Japanese art and expression, and these other forms are known and appreciated by the audience.

71

The people in a Kabuki audience have a deep love of nature. This love had its origins in the pre-Buddhist nature worship of the native Japanese animistic religion, and even today rocks, trees, and rivers are worshipped not in a spirit of awed propitiation but in thankfulness and appreciation. There is nothing in native Japanese thought which corresponds to a fear of natural objects such as appeared in Medieval Europe. Buddhist thought gave added impetus to this native characteristic, for Buddhism makes no distinction between man and nature and allows no sense of opposition between them. Man and nature are both part of a whole, and in merging himself with nature man can find 'self-submergence' and 'self-forgetfulness.' The Japanese express their love of nature in flower arrangements, in the cultivation of dwarf trees, in the indefatigable building of gardens. Japanese domestic architecture does not make a sharp division between exterior and interior. There are few walls in a Japanese house, and usually one or more sides of a room consist of sliding doors which can be opened to the outside, and in most instances the rooms give onto a garden. The architectural arrangement does not set man off from nature; and at all times of the year, in every Japanese home, even the poorest, there is a visible suggestion, either in the form of painting or natural objects, of the world of nature outside.

The objects chosen are appropriate to the season of the year, either factually or traditionally, so that they do not suggest spring during the fall or summer during the winter. The art object therefore shows an aesthetic continuity with the world of nature outside: The scroll painting depicting a snowy scene is hung during the winter, that of a summer landscape during the summer. In the same fashion the plays selected for the Kabuki program are appropriate to the season of the year. The plays performed during the winter abound in wintry scenes, while those selected for summer performance are concerned largely with events occurring in the summer.

The Japanese love of nature is of a particular kind. There is little admiration for flowers blooming in their natural state or placed casually in a vase; the flowers must be arranged in a formal design before they can exist on an aesthetic plane. Similarly, a free growing tree in its natural surroundings has less aesthetic force than one which is pruned and trained to a precise design in a garden. The design is not the topiary variety sometimes used in Western gardens in which bushes are pruned into the form of animals or geometrical figures; it is a design based upon and emphasizing the asymmetricality of nature. The most artistic of all Japanese trees is the *bonsai*, the potted tree which by pruning, training, and careful regulation of the soil is dwarfed so that it grows to no more than several feet in height. The *bonsai* is, in effect, a miniature tree, but it has two principal qualities which make it, for the Japanese, a work of art: In it, nature has been forced to submit to a design; and, although the design is based upon the asymmetrical forms occurring in nature, the *bonsai* resembles a real tree only indirectly. The design triumphs over the literal material of a tree and emerges on the surface, and it is the process of design which is aesthetically important, not the 'real' materials of which the *bonsai* is composed. In the graphic arts as well, the raw materials of nature have not been artistically acceptable until modern times under foreign influence, nor was any attempt made to use them directly and reproduce them in literal fashion. The painter Ogata Kōrin (1657–1716), like the artists of the Kanō school during the seventeenth and eighteenth centuries, kept sketch books in which he drew 'life-like' pictures; but these were merely studies for his work, the raw material from which he derived his paintings. He was not concerned with the reproduction of a 'life-like' surface but with reducing to a design the elements observed in actuality. The appeal of Fujiyama for the Japanese lies in its chaste form rather than its 'natural' giganticness.

The audience finds in the Kabuki a similar concept at work. The actor's gesture does not reproduce reality. Instead it is a rhythmic and designed ordering of the gesture observed in actuality. The design emerges on the surface of the gesture and therein lies its artistic validity. The setting is not conceived as an illusionistic representation of reality, but in terms of a designed, decorative background for the actor. The audience does not go to the theatre to be moved by images made to resemble those occurring in actuality, but by images clearly distinguished from reality by the precision of their design.

The visual perception of the Japanese people being acute, their artists have expressed themselves most frequently in visual images. It is significant that Japanese were made to deny Christianity not by oath but by treading upon a religious image. All of the Kabuki audience, with the possible exception of the child in arms, is familiar with the poetical form of the *haiku* (or variantly, *hokku* or *haikai*) whose images are generally visual. They all know, for example, the *haiku* of Bashō (1644–1694):

Furuike ya
Kawazu tobikomu
Mizu no oto

Literally translated,

An old pool
A frog jumps in
The sound of water

The *haiku*, like the Kabuki gesture, is rigidly designed. The first line contains five syllables, the second seven, the last five. Like most *haiku*, this one is unsatisfactory in English, for its effect lies in the juxtaposition of three concrete images, which outside the context of Japanese thought carry little meaning. A crude expansion of the immediate images of this *haiku* is that the old pool signifies permanence or perhaps the continuity of time, while the frog jumping into the pool implies the brief duration of life. The surface of the water is broken, the concentric ripples agitate it, but soon the motion dies. The brief movement of life has disappeared into the eternal unchanging. Even this general description of the 'meaning' of the poem is a falsification, for its poetic effect lies not in a precise intellectual concept but in a terse statement of sensuous images, producing a sense of the fragmentary and the isolated. This is one of the poem's chief qualities and one which is manifested both in other poetical forms and in the graphic arts.

This quality seems clearly to have its origin in Buddhist thought. Buddhism has ceased to be the vital, immediate force in Japanese life which it was formerly, but its centuries of influence continue to color the Japanese intellect and emotions. Although the Japanese schools of Buddhism show wide variations in theory, all are in general agreement about the nature of existence. Existence consists in the interplay of a plurality of elements whose true nature is indescribable and whose source is unknown. Combinations of these elements instantaneously flash into existence and instantaneously disappear, to be succeeded by new combinations of elements appearing in a strict causality. The momentary appearance of combinations of elements is conceived to be the only reality. Mind, matter, and time are unreal ideas. Mind is only a transitory state of consciousness arising out of the momentary meeting of observer and observed, both of which in the succeeding moment will have changed. There is no permanent matter, for substance has no continuity nor duration, being merely a manifestation of sense perception. Time is an empty concept invented

74

by the mind; the past has no existence because it has ceased to be, the future is unreal because it does not yet exist. The only concrete reality is the moment, which like the image from a single frame of motion picture film is instantaneously followed by a new and different frame and image. The visible world is therefore flamelike, shifting, and evanescent, possessed of no durable validity.

The world of the Japanese artist under the influence of this doctrine differs considerably from that of his Western counterpart. The Western artist generally inhabits a world in which mind, matter, and time are relatively tangible things, in which actuality tends to be a continuum. Although Western religious leaders have from time to time inveighed against the vanity and mutability of earthly existence and the things of the world, the artist has on the whole accepted the visible world as a reliable, continuous field for investigation. He has at times sought to capture the fleeting moment, but more often he has distrusted the brief appearance in his attempt to penetrate beneath the surface of a plurality of moments and to discover essential forms. Out of his myriad images of actuality he builds a synthetic world, an ordering of existence, a world of architectural solidarity which by its very construction implies his trust in the enduring aesthetic as well as philosophic validity of the world of perception. In doing so, he is intimately involved with the world in which he moves, but at the same time he feels a sense of opposition to it, for he must select and judge in order to erect his synthesis and to arrive at a view of life.

But for the traditional Japanese artist the world of perception has no such extension or permanence. It does not constitute a continuum of mind, matter, and time from which laws may be deduced or out of which an aesthetic or philosophic cosmos may be constructed. Existence is manifested in disparate, discrete moments in which neither the artist nor the object he observes has durability. He cannot 'order' such an existence; he can only seize upon actuality in the moment, since the moment is the only actuality. Actuality cannot, then, serve to sustain monumental patterns such as the Western artist has wrought out of space and time. Instead, the discontinuous glimpse of actuality, the brief juxtaposition of incidents, are the materials with which the Japanese artist works. These he assiduously observes and records, but he does not build with them nor impose 'interpretation' upon them; on the contrary, he tends always to the reduction of volume. Since the world of perception is in fluxion, the incident is isolated, incapable of synthesis with other incidents; an extended view of life cannot be erected. Traditional Japanese art does not see life steadily and see it whole, nor does it arrive at philosophical generalizations such as 'Beauty is Truth; Truth, Beauty.'

Japanese art tends always, as it does in the *haiku*, toward the isolation of the single, significant, visual moment. In the Nō performance, the point of greatest dramatic communication is reached in terse, strictly designed, visual, rather than vocal, images. In the Kabuki the highest points of interest are those in which the actor's movement resolves into a static attitude in a *mie* or in a tableau. The images of the Kabuki are not bound together by an inner coherence, nor do they build, one upon the other, to a cumulative effect. They follow one another in a simple progression in time, and the surface of the performance consists of an uninvolved succession of significant visual moments. The line of the Kabuki performance is not classic; it rather resembles the Gothic line of Western medieval art, without strong or regular accent, both convoluted and casual, nervous and grotesque. The monumental artistic structure, represented in Western art by the fugue or the tragedy, in which an inner complexity of forces binds together the outer surface, is unknown to Japanese art and to the Kabuki theatre.

The audience comes to the Kabuki not for a sustained comment on life, either tragic or comic, nor to witness the erection of a complex dramatic structure in time. It comes to the theatre to see a succession of striking images. The Kabuki had attained to the basic form it has today in the Genroku period, a time when the life and art of the townspeople revolved about the 'modern' world of pleasure, sensation, and shifting images recorded in the wood block prints of the *ukiyoe*. Although the Kabuki performance later underwent various modifications, the spectator views it today with the same attitude as that of the Genroku audience, and the colorful images of the Kabuki remain chiefly those of the world of sensation and pleasure. The audience does not appreciate the performance of a play; it appreciates the moment.

This attitude is made explicit in the audience's immediate reaction to moments of the performance. Virtuoso samisen playing is often used as a musical interlude in the Kabuki. The audience very seldom applauds at the end of the composition, but at exactly the points at which it is most pleased; and these are, in general, passages which show brilliant technique and execution. Translated into Western idiom, the audience would applaud during the performance of a piano concerto at exactly the point, not after it, at which the pianist was skilfully performing a particularly difficult passage; there would be very little or no applause at the conclusion of the composition. The actor too is applauded or shouted at as he achieves his best effects, not at the end of the play. The basic pattern of the Kabuki performance is a succession of high points rising like waves on the surface of a lake; there is no incoming tide flowing beneath them and sustaining them.

This general pattern of the Kabuki performance is also apparent in its visual effect. The visual centers of interest of the Kabuki stage are widely dispersed, as, for instance, when the attention of the audience is shifted from the actor on the *hanamichi* to the actor on the stage. Even when the *hanamichi* is not being used, the concern with keeping actors isolated in space requires that a relatively extended acting area be used. As a result, the audience does not see the performance as a concentrated whole, for the attention of a member of the audience may shift alternately from an actor five feet away to one fifty feet away. This visual readjustment contributes much to the audience's sense of the liveliness of the performance, but it also creates a lack of visual continuity; the performance is realized in a succession of bits of the play isolated in space. The representational theatre has tended to concentrate the performance within a carefully defined acting area whose dimensions (except in the upstage area of exterior settings) in general correspond to those of actuality, and although parts of this area may be used to the momentary neglect of others, nevertheless the *mise en scène* tends to exist as a visual total for the audience and to constitute, relatively speaking, a concentrated spatial area. The lack of such visual totality in the Kabuki perhaps bears some correspondence to the spatially dispersed *mansions* or *houses* of the European medieval drama or to the multiple stages of the Elizabethan public theatre, although the distances involved in the Kabuki are greater than those of the Shakespearean stage. Perhaps the argument could be sustained that the play written for the theatre in which disparate acting areas are widely separated in space results in casual construction and a multiplicity of scenes, while that written for the stage with a single spatial locale, such as that of French classical tragedy, results in a more concentrated, tightly-knit dramatic form (or, on the contrary, it may well be that the form of the play or that of the acting creates the form of the theatre). In any event, there seems to be a correlation between the relatively extended distances of the Kabuki acting areas, the impossibility of viewing the performance as a concentrated visual whole, and the concern of the audience not with the totality of the performance but with its vivid, spatially isolated moments.

For the audience the designed images of the Kabuki are at the same time nonrepresentational and yet specific in meaning. The gesture and attitude of the actor is always as precisely explicit as the stylized statement of the *haiku*. In a certain sense, the method of communication in the Kabuki is one of suggestion rather than of actual statement, but the quality of the suggestion is somewhat different from that frequently employed in Western poetry. There suggestion is usually created by a deliberate blurring of line or the omission of specific concrete images so that a stronger and clearer poetic concept will rise behind the surface of the poem. The method of suggestion in the *haiku* is the opposite, for the surface of the poem consists of precise, concrete images while beneath the surface lies the undefined and the unliteral. Whereas Western suggestion is most frequently achieved by the creation of a relatively broad, unspecific, diffuse surface, behind which a more or less precise and specifically defined image is brought into focus, the *haiku*, on the contrary, creates precise surface images behind which is an expanding field of weaker and weaker images. In this respect the *haiku* corresponds to the placing of large rocks in certain Japanese gardens. Only one-tenth of the rock is left exposed above the surface of the ground, while the remaining nine-tenths is buried. To the Japanese mind, the visible portion of the rock forcibly suggests the depth and size of the entire rock, the greater part of which is to be imagined. Both the *haiku* and the rock present literal images as a point of departure, which lead the way to less precise, more suggestive meanings below the surface images.

This method of suggestion is not, of course, unknown in the West. We do not see Helen of Troy in Homer, but the specific image of the effect of her beauty upon the old men. In the film, montage can set up a series of precise images which give rise to an expression not implicit in any one of them singly.

However, the suggestion of the Kabuki differs essentially from that which has been employed in modern times in the Western theatre. In the French Symbolist theatre, for example, a hieratic style of acting, intoning of lines, the utilization of nonrepresentational settings, together with the frequent use of scrim drops behind which the actors appeared, were designed to create an impression of misty vagueness and blurred outline. The artistic tenet that art is always suggestion, never literal statement, resulted in a theatrical surface deliberately made unspecific as a protest against the images of actuality in the naturalistic theatre. To a critic like Francisque Sarcey, this surface could suggest everything and nothing. But for the Kabuki audience no such vagueness exists. The gesture, the movement, the setting have immediate, specific significance because they occur at a point aesthetically midway between the reproduction of an image observed in actuality and the abstract image which is so far removed from actuality that it ceases to have specific meaning.

The Japanese artist may reduce a waterfall to two exquisitely controlled black lines, but these lines express the specific image of a waterfall; the artist does not depart from the basic form of the object. The writing of Chinese characters becomes art in Japan when, in the cursive style of writing, the complex lines of the character are reduced to a few flowing abbreviated strokes of the brush. The designed Kabuki gesture similarly omits all nonessentials but preserves the identity of movement observable in actuality. Nowhere does Japanese art break up or disintegrate the essential lines of a natural form. There is, consequently, no movement toward abstract or nonrepresentational forms such as exists in Western art.

The Japanese show simultaneously both a greater closeness to art and a greater sense of detachment from it than the Westerner. There is scarcely a Japanese home without a garden, however small, in which a larger world of nature is suggested by a few carefully selected trees, bushes, and rocks, arranged according to an asymmetrical yet rigid design. In every home there is a *tokonoma*, an area distinguished from the rest of the room, in which art objects are placed. These objects usually include a hanging scroll painting, an arrangement of flowers, leaves, or branches, or perhaps a dwarf tree. Sometimes a stone of interesting texture, form, and color is also included, set on a small wooden stand carved to accommodate its shape. The objects in the *tokonoma* are constantly being changed, for certain types of paintings and flower arrangements are traditionally appropriate to the seasons. A Japanese may have a hundred scroll paintings, but at most he hangs three in his *tokonoma* if they are painted as a series; the usual practice is to hang only one. As a result, the art objects in the *tokonoma* always have a certain freshness, a certain novelty, and one is thus constantly aware of their impact in the daily business of living. Art objects in Japan do not become staled by being constantly on view, nor are they conceived as being set apart from mundane existence. Every Japanese home has, in the *tokonoma*, its intimate, constantly renewed art gallery.

Although the Japanese are generally more familiar with art objects than the average Westerner, their attitude toward them is never confused by the lack of a clearly drawn line between art and reality. The typical Japanese art object, whether it be a painting, a dwarf tree, or a flower arrangement, has about it a nonrealistic aura created by the precise yet suggestive design of its surface and by the traditional processes by which the raw materials of actuality are converted, in the Japanese aesthetic, into objects of art. Western art, on the contrary, has moved at certain periods so close to the depiction of actuality that the problem of fixing a line of division between art and reality and of determining the quality of aesthetic distance and how it can be maintained have become matters of profound philosophical inquiry. But the Japanese, because of the inherent nature of their art, have never been concerned with these problems. The Japanese word for aesthetics, *bigaku*, did not appear in the language until about 1880 when Japanese artists came under the influence of Western artistic theories. The Japanese art object contains within itself to a large degree the quality known as aesthetic distance, and the average Japanese accepts this line of contact and division between art and reality without question or discussion.

The Kabuki audience is at all times completely, consciously aware that it is in a theatre seeing a play. Not only do all the visual elements of the performance—the costumes, make-up, settings, and patterns of movement—contribute to this awareness, but frequently the actors themselves draw attention to their being actors. In many plays there are passages of dialogue in which the actors make use of their own professional acting names. When, in *Just a Moment*, the leading character demands in a loud voice to know the identity of the person who approaches him, if Kichiemon was playing the role he replied, 'I am Kichiemon.' The leading actor in *Benten the Thief*, when disguised as a woman, proclaims that his favorite actor is himself. There are also frequent passages of acting in which the theatricality of the performance is pointed up. At the end of the 'female' version of *Just a Moment* after the curtain is closed, the actor Nakamura Tokizō is left alone on the *hanamichi*. Although he remains in the character of a woman, he is now a frightened embarrassed girl, quite the opposite of the militant woman who appeared in the play. He calls to a stage assistant to relieve him of the spear he carries and is distraught at the dreadful experience he has had. Then the stage assistant asks him to perform a Genroku *mie*, but he covers his face in shame and says he couldn't do it in front of all these people. After considerable urging, he agrees to do it, but he begs the audience not to laugh at his ineptness. He performs the intensely masculine *mie* to the great satisfaction of the audience. Then, reverting to being an embarrassed young woman, he runs from the *hanamichi* in confusion. In *Thunder God* two servants, sent down the mountain after dark, are very much frightened at having to make the trip. On the *hanamichi* they stop in horror, seeing something red in the distance. Their fear is dissipated, however, when they identify the object as the carpet in the balcony. In late 1945 under the pressure of contemporary events, the line was changed, and the frightening object was identified as a jeep.

Such passages as these are used for comic effect, but they also indicate a characteristic attitude of the Kabuki audience toward the performance. The actor Nakamura Kichiemon described the Kabuki performance as *hontō-rashii uso*, 'a plausible lie'; the audience, also recognizing the basic fiction of the theatre, is not required to suspend its disbelief, willingly or unwillingly, for it accepts art on the premise of its being nonrealistic.

The daily intimacy with art and at the same time the clear-cut recognition of the line between art and reality also make possible for the Kabuki audience the acceptance of the performance on an intimate, informal level and simultaneously on a level which maintains aesthetic distance.

The intimacy of the performance is manifested principally in the relation between the actor and the audience. Some Kabuki scholars feel intimacy to be one of the distinguishing characteristics of the theatre, and they complain that the size of the contemporary theatre militates against the intimacy which in the past existed in smaller theatres. The intimacy of actor and audience, however, having solid historical precedent, is part of the Kabuki tradition.

It was the feeling of intimacy with the actor which particularly distressed the government during the Edo period. The actor was sought after, admired, imitated in dress, and in all of this was raised to a higher social position, in the popular mind, than that to which he had been assigned by the government. The audience met actors at 'play-tea-houses' and groups of admirers organized themselves into clubs for the purpose both of advertising the actor's ability and of providing him with gifts. Intimacy with the actor outside the theatre was the basis of the attitude toward the actor during the performance. The Kabuki actor has always existed for his audience on a pre-established level of informality which, in essence, is not unlike the attitude of the audience of friends and admirers toward Western amateur actors, or of the fans of contemporary stage and screen performers, in which the performance is regarded more nearly as an extension of their ordinary good will toward the actor than as an art which is to be judged on a somewhat different basis. But the difference, in the Kabuki, was that the audience was capable of maintaining simultaneously a feeling of personal intimacy toward the actor and also high standards of judging artistic skill.

The adulation of the actor was most frequently expressed in the form of gifts, and both the 'play-tea-houses' and the theatres displayed them. The custom of displaying the actors' gifts in front of the theatres began in Ōsaka in the early eighteenth century and was shortly thereafter imported to Edo. Rice was still at that time the standard monetary unit, and bales of rice were a common gift. Today outside the front of the theatre there is usually a large wooden framework on which are placed some fifty or sixty large paper lanterns or imitation bales of rice, each bearing the name of an actor in the troupe which is currently performing. Gifts to actors have by no means disappeared today; a front curtain for the stage is given an actor who, having advanced in skill, is rewarded by receiving a new acting name rich in historical associations; or in keeping with the times an actor may be given an automobile.

During the performance the audience shows its approval or disapproval immediately and spontaneously by applauding or shouting. The curtain call is unknown in the Kabuki, as well as the stepping out of character to acknowledge applause which is sometimes practiced by the Western actor. The Kabuki actor remains completely in character however wild or amusing the acclamation from the audience. The enthusiasm of the audience generally occurs as the actor approaches the point of performing a *mie*. Then the male members of the audience are more likely to shout than to applaud, and these shouts, like almost every other aspect of the Kabuki performance, have their technical names. They are called *homegotoba* ('words of praise') or *kakegoe* ('shouts') and take a variety of forms. As the play approaches a *mie*, members of the audience frequently shout, '*Matte imashita!*' ('We've been waiting for this!'), while after the

mie the audience will shout the actor's name,[1] as well as such complimentary remarks as 'You're as good as your father was.' Actors are
sometimes given nicknames and these are also called out. The
late Ichikawa Sadanji, for example, because of his grave and dignified
manner was always called 'President.' Frequently members of the
audience will vie in praising the actor. In late 1945, one member of an
audience shouted at the actor Kichiemon, 'You're the best in Japan';
another, not to be outdone, cried, 'You're the best in the world'; a
third achieved the ultimate praise with 'You're MacArthur!'

Casual comments on the action of the play are also made, chiefly,
however, by the whiskey and sake drinking men in the audience. On
one occasion, when during a performance of *The Subscription List* the
character Benkei drinks a large quantity of sake, a convivial fellow
shouted, 'If you don't have enough I've got some more here.' Inexpert actors also receive their share of remarks from the audience,
the most distressing of which, to the actor, is being called a *daikon*.
The Japanese radish, *daikon*, is a large, white, cheap, common, rather
tasteless vegetable.

Although the actor does not acknowledge any of these shouts, he
too on certain occasions shows his intimate relation with the audience
by addressing it directly. Recently a certain actor had been ill and had
not appeared during the preceding month. When he recovered and
returned to the theatre, during the scene in which he first appeared,
the actor playing with him suddenly interrupted the scene, turned to
the audience, told them of Fukusuke's illness, assured them of his
complete recovery and his promise to try to please them in the future,
and concluded with 'Now let's get back to the play.' A rather more
formal nontheatrical contact is made between actor and audience in
the ceremonies known as *kōjō*, which are held when a actor receives
a new name or when a ceremony in commemoration of a dead actor
is performed. On these occasions, the entire troupe appears on the
stage and remains in a seated bowing position facing the audience;

---

[1] Scarcely any aspect of the Kabuki is uncolored by traditional practices.
Names, as well. After Ichikawa Danjūrō I (1660–1704) decided upon the
use of four names, all Kabuki actors followed his example. An actor therefore
has a *yagō* (a 'clan' name), a *gō* (a theatrical 'family' name), a *geimei* (a
theatrical 'first' name), and a *haigō* (a *nom de plume* for writing and painting). Besides these, the actor of course has his legal name as a private
citizen. The 'clan' name is the one properly called out in the theatre, but
many in the contemporary audience are ignorant of this nicety of theatrical
etiquette.

the chief actors make speeches, and the tone of the ceremony is one of intimate relation between audience and actor. The November *kaomise* ('face-showing') performance, dating from the early years of the eighteenth century, was originally an introduction of all the actors who would appear in the theatre during the ensuing theatrical season in a ceremony similar to the *kōjō*. Today, however, the *kaomise* generally consists of the performance of certain plays deemed suitable to the occasion rather than the introduction of the actors to the audience. During most of the Edo period, the theatre owner always appeared at the end of a performance to thank the audience and to request its continued patronage. Today this practice is lost; the modern equivalent is a strident loud-speaker voice thanking the audience for coming as well as appealing to them not to forget the articles with which they came. Meanwhile ushers stand at the exits bowing and expressing their thanks. This custom has also been transferred to movie houses.

At the same time that the audience is possessed of a feeling of close and intimate contact with the actor and the performance, it also recognizes that the images that the theatre sets up before its eyes, as stylized and yet as precise in meaning as the images of the scroll painting, are similarly not images reproducing actuality, but set off from actuality by their carefully designed surfaces. It is for this reason that the Kabuki does not need the proscenium arch as a 'frame' to set its figures off from the world of actuality, that it does not find it necessary to keep the stage lighted and to plunge the auditorium into darkness in order to maintain a line of division between stage and auditorium. The stage is not an illusory locale but a decorated platform for acting, spatially and psychologically differentiated from the auditorium in the way that the *tokonoma* is differentiated from the rest of a Japanese room.

The Japanese sense of spatial differentiation is very strong. Throughout the country, areas are set off one from another and the defined area has particular attributes. Today the West can in most instances surround a given area with a religious aura only by the erection of a relatively large building; the Japanese can make this conversion by a *torii*, consisting of two supporting pillars with a beam across their top, erected over a pathway. Or a small shrine can be set up on the top of a modern office building or at the side of a theatre and this area becomes possessed of sacred force. The outlines of the areas are not always so sketchily indicated. The Japanese home is almost invariably surrounded by walls or fences, and this impulse toward enclosure of an area shows a marked similarity to that which existed in Greek civilization. The defined areas exert a strong force on Japanese patterns of behavior. The cleanliness of the Japanese home is proverbial, yet in a Western style building, a different spatial and psychological area, the Japanese feels no compulsion whatever toward tidiness. Within a home, his or another's, the Japanese is one of the politest persons in the world, but outside it in a crowd he is among the world's rudest. This characteristic can scarcely be claimed as the exclusive property of the Japanese; Westerners have shown a similar propensity. But in Japan the extremes of this behavior are much greater, and although there are other contributing factors, the behavior is based principally on the conception of the defined area having an inherent force of its own.

The area of the *tokonoma* is marked off in a Japanese room by a single pillar, the trunk of a small tree, the bark frequently left on it, placed at one corner, and, usually, by the area being raised a few inches above the level of the floor of the room; the area is not otherwise visually differentiated. This area demands respect; one does not lie down with his head or feet in it nor place in it nonaesthetic materials. It is dedicated to the purpose of containing art objects. It does not correspond to the frame surrounding a picture, for the frame, when empty, has normally no aesthetic force of its own. The *tokonoma*, even when empty and awaiting the placement there of an art object, is in itself heavy with aesthetic significance. At the same time that the *tokonoma* is a spatially defined area, it is not a disparate area such as that enclosed by a picture frame. The art objects placed in the *tokonoma*, appropriate to the season, are intimately related to the actuality of the here and now and create an intensification of it. Therefore, although the *tokonoma* defines an area of aesthetic force, it does not set up a disparate, noncontinuous world.

The Japanese feeling for significant area is also marked in the conception of the playing area of the Nō stage. The 'bridge' between dressing room and stage differs in spatial quality from the stage proper, and the stage proper itself is divided, without the aid of visual indications, into disparate areas each having its peculiar quality. The Kabuki stage showed in its development a similar concern for the aesthetic qualities of its acting areas and distinguished carefully between the spatial function of the *hanamichi*, the forestage, and the stage proper. This conception of the inherent nature of the acting areas continues today, and the audience accepts it as it accepts the aesthetic force of the empty *tokonoma*. The areas of the *hanamichi* and of the stage do not, therefore, require scenic disguise in order to establish their force. They possess in and of themselves the force of theatre reality, and the scenic elements serve only as decoration, not as illusionistic disguise. There are obvious parallels with this conception of the acting areas in other forms of the theatre in other countries. The *orchestra* of the Greek theatre, the forestage of the Elizabethan theatre, and the early stage of Molière were similarly platforms for acting which did not derive their theatrical force from scenic indication. But in each of these instances the essential spatial quality of the areas came to be influenced by scenic elements which imposed their force upon the acting areas and which gradually translated them into representational locales. In the Kabuki, this phenomenon has not yet occurred; the Japanese concept of the inherent strength of defined areas, despite the influence of Western illusionistic theatre models, militates against this happening. The audience continues to accept the *hanamichi* and the stage as basic presentational platforms for acting.

The Kabuki runs the gamut of Japanese taste. On one hand there is restraint, austerity, economy of statement, strict design; on the other, lavishness, sumptuousness, luxuriance. Both these extremes are equally admired by the audience. Kabuki gestures and movements, though broader and less hieratic than those of the Nō, are, by the nature of their precise design and technical polish, restrained and austere. Although they have the power of immediate communication of emotion to the audience, they avoid representing the full, detailed reproduction of actual movement and gesture. Weeping, for example, is resolved into a rhythmical movement of the head and precise gestures of the hand; the audience would abhor the literal reproduction of this act on the stage. Similarly, the most impassioned movement in scenes of murder (*koroshiba*) is expressed in designed images which are as terse and nonrepresentational as those of the black and white scroll painting. But at the same time, the audience requires that the Kabuki be an eye-filling spectacle. Stage decoration, costuming, make-up are colorful, bold, rich, and luxuriant. Visual opulence provides at least half the pleasure of the theatre-goer.

The most frequently heard expression in the Kabuki theatre, other than 'It's pretty,' is 'It's pitiful,' and this last statement is evoked by the gratification that the spectator derives from the situation in the play. The emotions aroused in the audience do not have a very wide range. At the base of Japanese artistic thought lies the Buddhist concept that all things pass, that glory is evanescent, that all bright quick things come to confusion, and this notion constitutes almost the whole intellectual content of Japanese art.

For the Japanese the loveliest of trees is the cherry. The poem runs,

> Among flowers,
> It is the cherry;
> Among men,
> The samurai.

When the cherry trees are in bloom, the Japanese assemble beneath them, in time-honored custom, drink rice-wine, sometimes write poetry, and forget the bleakness of the Japanese winter. The trees are beautiful to see; but their beauty does not exist principally in their present loveliness: It lies in the concept that this beauty stands poised upon the brink of destruction, that within a few days the blossoms will have fallen. During World War II, the Special Attack Corps (the so-called suicide pilots) sang of their being like the cherry blossoms, shining for a moment against the sky, then plunged into darkness. The poignancy of the situation, the compassion of the observer toward it, create the essentially melancholy yet pleasurable quality in Japanese thought and art which Daisetz Suzuki describes as "'feeling' the sentiments moving in things about oneself." This attitude pervades traditional poetic expression and is the constant theme of the *haiku*, as, for example, in the now almost trite one by Chiyo (1701–1775):

> *Asagao ni*
> *Tsurube torarete*
> *Morai mizu*

Literally translated,

> The morning glory
> Has taken hold of the well bucket
> [I will] borrow water

The picture created is this: During the night, the morning glory vine has wound its tendrils around the well bucket. In the morning when the woman goes to draw water, she sees the flowers blooming. Rather than destroy this fragile beauty which only too soon will wither and be gone forever, she goes to borrow water from a neighbor. Ki no Tsurayuki (d. 946) wrote that poetry 'was invented by man, and poets have used it in numerous forms, in the greeting of flowers, in expressing envy of the birds, in giving their impression of the mists and the sadness they are made to feel by the dews.' This statement provides some indication of the essential quality of Japanese poetry and of the emotions most often expressed in Japanese art. The Japanese are not, contrary to Western legend, an unimpassioned people; their emotions are strong, frequently violent, and their outbursts of violence are mirrored in the Kabuki. But Kabuki violence is manifested only in moments. The basic and continuous ground of the performance is that of unresolved sadness. The constant dwelling on the poignant and the pathetic and the lack of concern for any strong intellectual element are manifested in the Kabuki by the audience's appreciation of prolonged, static scenes whose only dramatic content is long drawn out melancholy. The essential emotional quality of the Kabuki is the romantic, and a concern with the romantic is manifested throughout Japanese culture. The most popular Western composer is Chopin. The Japanese have a lively comic sense but this is only rarely manifested in the theatre; there are extremely few Kabuki pieces which are pure comedy or which provoke robust laughter. The spectator goes to the theatre not to laugh, but to weep.

But this attitude does not color the behavior of the audience when it is not absorbed in the play. Kabuki-going has always been an informal social affair, having nothing about it of the formality, if not solemnity, which is characteristic of contemporary Western theatre-going. The behavior of the Kabuki audience suggests parallels with that of the Greek theatre of the fifth century and that of the Shakespearean theatre, in both of which a holiday mood, abetted by eating and drinking, seems to have been the prevailing attitude. The 'play-tea-houses,' which were, however, not run by the theatre managements, appeared with the first permanent theatres and continued until after 1868. On the average, there were some ten or so large tea-houses and many more smaller ones in the districts to which the theatres were assigned. These served a variety of practical functions, all of which contributed to the cheer of the theatre-goer. Then, as now, spectators went to the theatre in groups rather than as individuals; this practice is attested to by the divisions of the theatre auditorium into *sajiki* and *masu* which accommodated at first seven people, later five, and then four. It is not unheard of today for as small a group as two or three people to go to the theatre, but a much larger group is the rule. Going to the theatre, like sight-seeing and

7. The comic dance, *Tied to a Pole*, adapted from a *kyōgen* of the Nō theatre. The setting is the Kabuki version of the Nō stage. The musicians and singers are seated in two tiers in the upstage area, singers and samisen players on the upper level, drummers below them. The man in black, facing upstage behind the actors, is a stage assistant. [*Shochiku.*]

8. For the dance *The Wisteria Girl*, instrumentalists are seated on stage-right, singers on stage-left.
[*Shochiku.*]

19. A scene from Chikamatsu's *Yugiri and Izaemon*, a doll theatre play performed in the Kabuki, with the narrators and musicians seated on the platform at stage-left.

[*Shochiku.*]

20. The *michiyuki* scene of *The Loyal Forty-seven Rōnin*.

The musicians' platform on stage-left is painted to tie in with the setting. Hanging above the stage is a *tsurieda* of cherry blossoms. At the rear of the stage, barely visible, is the stage assistant. [*Shochiku.*]

21. The setting for 'Moritsuna's Camp.'

The 'inner proscenium,' including the *geza* on stage-right, is painted a flat black. Although this is not a dance piece, the *shosabutai* (dance-stage) is laid on the permanent stage floor, for the act involves considerable dance movement. The presence of the two standing lamps (*andon*) on the upstage platform indicates that the scene is taking place at night. The backdrop of sea and mountains is used to create a sense of space around the actors seated on the platform. The 'secondary' room on stage-left is enclosed with *shoji*. [*Shochiku.*]

many other Japanese social activities, is seldom an individual undertaking. The Japanese seem happiest, whatever the occasion, when in a crowd. Formerly the 'play-tea-houses' made reservations for seats, and it was therefore to the tea-house that the theatre party first went, arriving there, during most of the Edo period, about six in the morning. Then, as now, the audience felt no great compulsion to get to the theatre at the beginning of a performance. The members of the theatre party took breakfast at the tea-house, and later were escorted to the theatre by a tea-house attendant who waited upon them during the rest of the day. Kabuki-going is inseparable in the Japanese mind with eating and drinking, and the tea-house attendant brought tea, rice-wine, and a variety of edibles which the audience continued to nibble on throughout the performance, as they do today. He also provided his patrons with programs bearing the crest of the chief actor (*mombanzuke*), programs illustrated with scenes from the plays (*ehon*), and broadsheets on which were printed the purple passages from the plays (*onseki*). Perhaps by commercial connivance between the theatre owners and the tea-house owners, the theatres were not provided with toilets while the tea-houses were. The running back and forth between tea-house and theatre brought about the building of passageways between the two about 1673–1680. These were forbidden in 1714, in 1723, and periodically afterwards, but in the same manner they used in dealing with other restrictions the theatre owners removed the passageways only for a token period and then installed them again. The theatre-goers returned to the tea-house for lunch, went back to the theatre afterwards, and during the long afternoon continued to divert themselves with further eating and drinking. Although the government ordered the performance to end by six, this rule too was not much observed, and the play frequently continued until it was completely dark. The theatre party then returned to the tea-house, where not infrequently a banquet was laid out in a *zashiki*, a reception room, to which actors were invited. After dinner, the actors entertained their patrons by dancing or by performing requested passages from plays. The tea-house owner performed an important social function in arranging assignations between theatre-goers and actors.

Only the well-to-do could afford the luxury of the tea-houses, but even the poorest spectator availed himself of the services of the *degata*, an individual who would reserve seats and have food and drink brought in from neighboring restaurants. The *degata* ('a person who goes out') continued to perform these functions until he was forbidden to appear in the Yūraku-za of 1908, and thereafter as Japanese theatres began to adopt Western ways, the *degata* gradually disappeared.

The 'play-tea-houses' have also vanished; the post-Restoration theatres provided both toilets and restaurants within the theatres. Toward the end of the eighteenth century small shops selling tea and food began to appear in the Ōsaka theatres, but this practice was not introduced to Tōkyō until the end of the nineteenth century. At present the basements and lobbies of Kabuki theatres are a warren of some twenty or thirty shops, bars, restaurants, and tea-rooms, which sell not only a great variety of both Japanese and Western food and drink, but also books and magazines concerning the theatre, photographs of actors, cotton towels bearing actors' crests, and an innumerable variety of souvenirs which are bought and given to friends who were unable to attend the theatre. Despite the general patronage of the eating places within the theatre, few members of the audience come to the theatre without boxes of rice which have been prepared at home, and the men are likely to appear carrying bottles of rice-wine or whiskey. And the Kabuki performance goes forward, as it did from the beginning, to a constant accompaniment of eating and drinking.

Kabuki performances, or for that matter all Japanese theatrical performances, have always been lengthy affairs; even the performances of modern plays of foreign origin are made to extend over a period of four hours. In 1868 a government regulation fixed the time of daily performances at a maximum of eight hours a day. Just before World War II performances were limited to six hours a day and usually began at four in the afternoon and continued until ten at night. At present the restrictions on the length of performances have been removed. Seven days a week, the matinee performance begins about eleven in the morning and continues until about four in the afternoon, and the evening performance begins at about four-thirty and continues until nine-thirty or later. Although intermissions are frequent and lengthy, occasionally running to twenty-five minutes, the person probably does not exist in Japan who is capable of giving sheer, rapt attention to what is happening on the stage for a period of four hours or more. No act of a Kabuki performance begins with a majority of the audience seated in the auditorium. This phenomenon also occurs in the Western theatre and has influenced its playwriting, but in the Kabuki theatre as much as fifteen or twenty minutes may pass before the audience, already in the theatre, reaches its seats. After that, there is constant activity and constant coming and going. Weeping children (the child is ubiquitous in Japan) are trotted up and down the aisles; babes are suckled; whiskey and sake bottles are passed about; conversations are held; tangerines are peeled and eaten and the peelings casually scattered beneath the seats. No act lasts longer than an hour and a half, and at its conclusion almost every member of the audience leaves the auditorium. The lobbies are then made hideous by a succession of announcements over a public address system, consisting mostly of requests that so-and-so go to the main entrance where someone is waiting to see him. An electric bell rings, at length and furiously, announcing the imminent beginning of the next act, but this warning is not widely accepted as the literal statement of an actuality. The act begins, and the audience returns to the auditorium as it pleases. Having been trained to it, the Japanese are capable of silence and concentrated attention when attending concerts of Western symphonic music, but the Kabuki is a different world, a purely Japanese world, in which only sporadic attention to the performance is possible. However casual the attention of the audience may be at the beginning of an act, the audience comes gradually, though never quite to the same degree as the Western audience, to concentrate on the play. The actors accept the widespread confusion in the auditorium as a natural occurrence and not as rudeness; they make no attempt to wait for quiet or to induce it by the technical means at their disposal. The appearance of an actor on the *hanamichi* can be a pacifying influence, but such entrances are ordinarily delayed until well after the act is under way. The actors in the opening scenes continue stoically though not a line can be heard. When the audience wishes, it will pay attention.

This is the Kabuki audience today. Japanese observers insist that its behavior is quite unlike that of the audiences before World War II, who were silent, who concentrated on the play, who did not come with children in arms, who did not eat and drink during the performance. Perhaps. But a study of the audiences depicted in prints of the Kabuki theatre from its beginnings convinces one that the present behavior of the audience is based firmly on historical precedent and that the Kabuki has always been attended much more nearly in a spirit of picnicking than in one of solemn observance.

CHAPTER IV

The Hanamichi

IN the architectural development of the Kabuki theatre, the growth of the playing areas was determined by the movement of the actor toward the audience, and the *hanamichi* was introduced to satisfy this basic impulse. The stage proper is the more formal of the two acting areas, while it is on the *hanamichi* that more intimate acting is performed. The *hanamichi* does not bring about intimacy by any significant change in the actor's technique of expression but by its unique function as an acting area.

The *hanamichi* is transmutable into three psychological areas: It is used as an area spatially and psychologically continuous with the stage; it can be related to the stage but defined as a spatially differentiated area; or it is used as a completely independent stage.

The *hanamichi* is ordinarily undecorated, but when it is used as a psychological extension of the stage, it is sometimes covered with a floor cloth of the same color as that used on the stage. A white floor cloth is used on the *hanamichi* to signify snow, a blue one to signify water, and more rarely, a gray one to signify bare earth. When the *hanamichi* is used as a corridor in the house which is represented on the stage, it is covered with the straw matting which is the ordinary covering of Japanese floors. In these circumstances, the character on the stage may be aware of the character on the *hanamichi* and extended conversations may ensue between them. In the short play *Just a Moment*, during the greater part of the action the chief character remains on the *hanamichi* and engages in conversation with his adversaries on the stage. In a scene of *Through the Iga Pass*, the central character while engaged in furious duelling on the stage carries on a dialogue with a character on the *hanamichi*. In the second scene of the fourth act of *The Loyal Forty-seven Rōnin*, two groups of retainers meet and mingle on the *hanamichi*, the one group coming from the stage, the other entering from the *hanamichi*. The scene is designed to show conflict and confusion, and the *hanamichi* is a projection of the locale of the stage into the auditorium.

But even when the *hanamichi* is covered with the same kind of floor cloth as that on the stage, it may still represent an area which, though related to the stage, is differentiated from it. It may be, for example, a pathway to a house on the stage. Under this condition, the characters on the stage and those on the *hanamichi* are not aware of each other. In *The Subscription List* when the chief characters enter the *hanamichi* they know that they are approaching a guarded barrier which is indicated not scenically but by the characters present on the stage. Theatrically, however, they cannot see the characters on the stage, nor can those on the stage see those on the *hanamichi*. An extended passage of acting ensues on the *hanamichi* at this point, and although the *hanamichi* is a mountain pathway which leads to the barrier, and is thus spatially related to it, it becomes, theatrically, a disparate area. In this and other plays, the *hanamichi* and the stage proper become two different psychological areas with two distinct fields of activity, so that together they constitute a kind of simultaneous setting. In *The Subscription List* and in other plays in which dancing is done on the *hanamichi*, no floor cloth is used to indicate the locale of the *hanamichi*; its identity is established by the lines of the play. This practice is followed perhaps half the time when the *hanamichi* is used. Its identity as a locale is also conveyed to the audience by the movement of the actor, a more effective means, generally, than the use of the floor cloth, since the surface of the *hanamichi* cannot be seen by the greater part of the audience seated on the orchestra level. The actor's movement indicates that he is walking through snow, that he has stumbled over a stone, that he is stepping delicately over mud-puddles, and so forth. In *The Exile of Shunkan* the *hanamichi* becomes shore and ocean; the beating of the waves on the shore is not indicated by scenic devices but by the movement of the actor.

The use of the *hanamichi* as a completely independent stage occurs at the end of a play or act. The curtain is drawn on the stage and the actor (in most cases only one, and the principal one) who before the closing of the curtain was related to the characters on the stage, is alone on the *hanamichi*. His period of acting is relatively short and does not at most extend much beyond five minutes. In this usage, the *hanamichi* has scarcely any feeling of a specific locality, but is rather a platform for the actor's display of virtuosity.

The *hanamichi* is always lit when it is used, and the lighting matches that on the stage; if the stage lighting is atmospheric, that of the *hanamichi* will also be. In the large majority of cases, however, the lighting of the *hanamichi* is purely arbitrary and its only purpose is to illuminate the actor. When the *hanamichi* is not used, it ceases to exist theatrically, and the stage becomes the only acting area.

The theatrical function of the *hanamichi* is, then, to extend the psychological area of the performance through the audience. The degree of extension was greater when the temporary *hanamichi* was also used; characters could enter on opposite sides of the theatre and from their position on these two passageways could make the entire auditorium an acting area. Today, since all important entrances and exits are made on the *hanamichi*, it exerts a strong force upon the actor who is on the stage when the *hanamichi* is being used. In doing so, it reinforces the basic pattern of Kabuki movement toward the front of the stage and directly toward the audience. When characters on stage engage in conversation with characters on the *hanamichi*, those on the stage usually take a position at stage-left. Thus the line of theatrical force is extended out over the heads of a considerable part of the audience. On some occasions the psychological force of the *hanamichi* is utilized even though no actor appears on it. In *The Drum of Matsuura*, the sound of the battle drum, which marks the climax of the play, comes from behind the curtained entrance to the *hanamichi*, and the acting of the chief character at this point is oriented toward the rear of the theatre. He moves to the very edge of the stage, showing his joy that the forty-seven *rōnin* have completed their revenge. Similar sound effects from the rear of the theatre are used in 'Moritsuna's Camp'[1] with a similar extension of the performance over the audience to the rear of the theatre. In *Just a Moment*, the chief character calls out several times from behind the curtain at the end of the *hanamichi* before he makes his entrance. But even without sound effects and actors, the *hanamichi* can still exert theatrical force. A notable example is the use made of it in the first scene of the fourth

[1] Throughout, the titles of acts of plays are enclosed in quotation marks. The titles of complete plays are in italics.

act of *The Loyal Forty-seven Rōnin*. Hangan has received orders to commit suicide, and the elaborate preparations for his death have gone forward; but before his death he must speak with his chief retainer, Yuranosuke, and Yuranosuke has not yet come. All of Hangan's intensity on the stage is directed toward the *hanamichi*, on which Yuranosuke will make his entrance; the *hanamichi* is lighted and becomes a vital force through the auditorium without the presence of the actor.

As previously mentioned, the *hanamichi* is conceived of as being divided into ten equal parts with the most important acting area occurring at the *shichi-san* ('seven-three'), a point seven-tenths of the distance from the curtained entrance to the *hanamichi* (the *agemaku*,[2]) and three-tenths of the distance from the stage. The *hanamichi* is weakest as an acting area at the rear of the theatre, but it grows progressively stronger toward the *shichi-san*. This concept of its varying strength is apparent in the technique of the actor as he moves forward upon the *hanamichi*. The delineation of the character and his state of mind is shown as the actor steps through the *agemaku*, but thereafter as he moves toward the *shichi-san* he continues to build up the initial impression, so that it reaches its strongest expression when he arrives at the *shichi-san*. Here he pauses, and the direction of his acting takes a different turn. The original attitude of the character was a purely subjective one, an exploitation of the mood with which he entered the *hanamichi*, but now at the *shichi-san*, the character makes the adjustment to the situation into which he will move when he enters the stage. When this adjustment has been shown and has been established in the mind of the audience, the character moves onto the stage into a new dramatic field, that of relationship with the characters on the stage. This pattern is not always followed, for some entrances consist merely of the actor running the length of the *hanamichi* and onto the stage. However, all important entrances are constructed on this basis.

The character Kumagai, in an act of *The Battle of Ichinotani*, has beheaded his son so that he can substitute his son's head for that of a young warrior, Atsumori, and so save his life. As Kumagai enters the *hanamichi* and moves slowly toward the *shichi-san*, his anguish grows more and more apparent. At the *shichi-san* he stops. On the stage his

---

[2] *Agemaku* means 'rising curtain,' although actually the curtain is drawn to one side when the actor enters or exits. The name is inherited from the Nō theatre curtain which is lifted from the bottom.

wife, who knows nothing of the sacrifice he has made, is kneeling within the gate to the house, awaiting his return. He controls his anguish, thinks of what his wife must yet endure, and shows his determination to carry through his deception so that Atsumori can be saved. As he turns to move toward the stage, he tucks into his sleeve the Buddhist rosary he has been carrying. This movement subtly suggests what will become clear at the end of the act: that Kumagai has already determined to give up the life of a warrior and to become a Buddhist monk.

All this acting is done in pantomime, as is most of the acting on the *hanamichi*, although soliloquies may be given occasionally at the *shichi-san*. The elaborate and extended entrance of the character Sukeroku on the *hanamichi* consists of a series of stylized postures and dance movements demonstrating his bravery and valor, his pride, cleverness, and energy, his championing of the rights of the people, and (although the significance of the movement is lost on most of the contemporary audience) his thanks to the merchants who, at the beginning of the eighteenth century, furnished the various articles of the costume he wears. By the time Sukeroku reaches the stage to confront his rival Ikkyū, there is no doubt in the mind of the audience that in any conflict Sukeroku will be the victor.

The entrance of Genzō in 'The Village School' is another well known passage of acting on the *hanamichi*. Genzō has been ordered to behead the son of his lord, a child that he has pretended is his own. Being found out, he is aware that he cannot escape with the child and that he will have to submit. His state of mind is apparent as he enters the *hanamichi* and his despair grows stronger as he moves toward the *shichi-san*. There he pauses, and an idea crosses his mind: Perhaps he will be able to substitute the head of one of the pupils in his school. With this change in the direction of his thoughts, he moves onto the stage where the school children are seated at their desks.

Important characters do not always enter the *hanamichi* alone; they are frequently accompanied by a retinue. In such cases the pattern of acting of the central character remains the same, and he pauses at the *shichi-san* to display his attitude toward the situation which he is about to enter on the stage. Two people frequently enter together— friends, lovers, brothers, a mother and child—and follow the same pattern, although the expression is now in duet form. However, in *Benten the Thief*, in which the five heroes of the play enter on the *hanamichi* one after another, the *hanamichi* is used in a somewhat atypical manner. In this scene each of the heroes performs a *mie* just after he comes through the *agemaku* and then moves forward.

In the Western theatre great care is taken to 'build up' the entrance of an important character both by the playwright and by the director. The important character must, in standard practice, be talked about by lesser characters, the audience's interest in the character must be whetted, and when he finally appears he must make as significant an entrance as possible. At his entrance the actor must establish, almost simultaneously, the essential quality of the character, his present state of mind, his relation to the other characters on the stage, as well as his rapport with the audience. The Kabuki actor is concerned with identical problems, but he is provided with different technical means of coping with them.

The Western director must first of all, in most cases, direct attention to the entrance through which the important character will appear. This he does by certain groupings of the other characters on the stage, sometimes by light or sound effects, or by combinations of these techniques. In the Kabuki light is brought up on the *hanamichi*, and, shortly thereafter as the *agemaku* is opened, the sharp sound of the iron curtain rings scraping against the curtain rod directs the attention of the audience to the *hanamichi*. The audience turns physically toward the *hanamichi* as one turns to see an important person enter a room. The required physical adjustment to a new area of interest gives the spectator a lively sense of 'things happening' together with a sense of physical participation in the performance itself. As the actor moves forward on the *hanamichi* he is first concerned, as we have noticed, with the expression of the essential nature of the character (if this is his first entrance in the play) as well as with the present mood of the character. He moves forward a distance of some forty feet to the *shichi-san*, and during the whole of this distance (which is as great as the width of the stage in the average Western theatre) he is concerned with only two things: establishing the nature and present state of the character and establishing rapport with the audience. His proximity to the audience and the audience's reorientation from the stage to the *hanamichi* separate the character from involvement with the field of theatrical interest on the stage, and thus the actor is enabled to bring the character into sharp focus, over a considerable acting area. Pausing at the *shichi-san*, his new mood, attitude, or direction of thought or emotion is clearly indicated by his pattern of movement or, more rarely, by his words. He is not bound at any point on the *hanamichi* (or in the play at large) by realistic considerations of time and may prolong his actions throughout the length of the *hanamichi* as long as is necessary to strengthen the impact of the character upon the audience. As he leaves the *shichi-san*, he enters into the psychological area of the play, his progressive delineation of the character and its relation to the play firmly established in the mind of the audience. The Kabuki actor, then, 'takes one thing at a time' when making his entrance, unlike the Western actor who must, generally speaking, deal with all these expressions simultaneously in very much more limited space and in an area usually shared by other actors.

Lesser characters, in one's or two's, also use the *hanamichi* for entrances, but these are usually rapid and do not show the pattern described above. The entrances of messengers, servants, and the like are a simple progression from the rear of the *hanamichi* to the stage. They are usually accompanied by a rapid beating of wooden clappers, directing the attention of the audience to the *hanamichi*, and they are chiefly used to create a sense of excitement in battle scenes or other scenes of violence.

For exits, the areas of the *hanamichi* are used in reverse fashion. The actor moves out of the area of the stage and of the play to the *shichi-san*. Here he indicates by a *mie* or by a pattern of movement the shift in attitude of the character from his participation in the events of the play to the more subjective, personal emotions of the character apart from the situations of the play. Having done this, he moves toward the rear of the *hanamichi*, the force of his acting weakening, though he remains completely in character, as he approaches the *agemaku*. Not infrequently, the tempo of the movement, after the actor leaves the *shichi-san*, is gradually speeded up, particularly if the character is moving toward an offstage confrontation. In this circumstance, his movement may be accompanied by an accelerating beating of wooden clappers or of a drum. But the manner of exit is not conventionalized to the point of inflexibility, and varies considerably according to the character.

The hero of *Izayoi and Seishin*, a priest, overcome by temptation, has stolen money from a passerby, Motome. During a struggle Motome dies of a heart attack. The hero is filled with remorse at his act and feels that he must commit suicide to atone for it. But after several attempts to stab himself, he realizes that he lacks the courage.

He seizes the money he has stolen and runs to the *hanamichi*. At the *shichi-san*, he pauses, and in pantomime shows his transformation from a sensitive, conscientious priest into a furtive, professional thief. He moves toward the *agemaku* in his new character, his whole manner and movement that of a sneak thief.

The most impressive exits on the *hanamichi* are those called *maku soto hikkomi*: 'exit outside the curtain.' The curtain is drawn across the main stage, and the actor is left alone on the *hanamichi*. Usually the stage-right end of the curtain is lifted and pulled upstage so that a samisen player can stand in this corner of the stage and provide a musical accompaniment for the exit, or so that incidental music from the *geza* can be clearly heard. One of the best known exits of this kind is that of Benkei at the end of *The Subscription List*. Benkei has succeeded through cleverness, not brawn, in getting his master Yoshitsune through the guarded barrier which has been set up to apprehend him. In order to do so, Benkei has had to commit what in feudal ideology is an almost unforgivable sin. To convince the keeper of the barrier that Yoshitsune is merely an unimportant servant he has had to strike his master. However, Yoshitsune has forgiven Benkei. As the play draws to its close, Benkei drinks, pretends to be drunk, and dances before the barrier guards. Still dancing, he herds his followers and Yoshitsune before him and they make a rapid exit on the *hanamichi*. The curtain is closed. Benkei, standing just outside the curtain, remains motionless for a time. Then he shows his continued grief at having had to strike Yoshitsune and his private relief that the barrier has been passed. He moves to the *shichi-san*, and there, in a powerful *mie*, displays his strength, his deep devotion to Yoshitsune, and his indomitability. Then, holding his traveller's staff in his left hand, his right hand extended before him, alternating three steps on the right foot with three on the left, he dances to the rear of the *hanamichi* in the kind of exit known as *roppō*.[3] The dance is an ecstatic expression of his triumph.

The character Kumagai also makes his exit outside the curtain. Kumagai's plan has succeeded and the head of his son has been accepted

---

[3] The word is said to have been derived from *roppōgumi* or *roppōshū*, which were organizations of proud-spirited commoners ready to assert themselves against the retainers of the Shōgunate. They wore a distinctive costume, set styles in manners and dress, and even evolved a special manner of speech, known as *roppō kotoba*, distinguished by its harsh and nasal delivery.

by Yoshitsune[4] as the head of Atsumori. Toward the end of the play, Kumagai removes his armor, revealing himself dressed in the clothes of a mendicant Buddhist priest, his head shaved. Putting on straw sandals and the circular straw hat of the traveller, he moves to the *hanamichi* leaning on a staff. As he reaches the *shichi-san*, Yoshitsune calls to him. He turns, and Yoshitsune lifts the head of Kumagai's son so that he can look at the face of his child for the last time. Kumagai stares at it for a moment, and then in a broken voice cries, 'The sixteen years of his life! Only a dream . . . a dream.' He weeps, his legs give way beneath him, he sinks to the floor. The curtain closes. Kumagai's grief subsides, he slowly rises, and pathetically brushes the dust from his clothes. From the rear of the *hanamichi* comes the sound of battle drums and the clash of arms, grating on his raw nerves. There passes through his mind thoughts of the days of his generalship and of the evanescence of his glory. Then his thoughts return to the present, and he prepares to go. Again the battle drum sounds. But Kumagai has already withdrawn from the things of the world, and the battle drum no longer exists in his past or in his present. He moves toward the *agemaku* a broken old man, his only purpose in life to pray for the soul of his son.

A somewhat curious exit outside the curtain is that of the evil magician Nikko Danjō in *The Famous Tree at Sendai*. The warrior Arajishi has seized a large rat which carries in its mouth a scroll containing the names of a group of conspirators among which is Nikki Danjō. After a struggle, the rat escapes from Arajishi, runs to the *hanamichi*, and disappears into the trap-door at the *shichi-san* (the trap called the *suppon*) in a cloud of smoke. Immediately after, Nikki Danjō, transformed from a rat into a human being, dressed in mouse-colored clothes, and holding the scroll in his mouth, slowly ascends on a trap-lift. Arajishi defies him from the stage in a *mie*, and the curtain closes. Nikki Danjō makes a series of mystical passes with his hands and then turns toward the *agemaku*. He has given himself the mystic power to walk on smoke, and his extremely slow, quiet exit conveys the impression of this rare form of locomotion.

The actor usually walks from the *hanamichi*, but sometimes other means of exit are used. A rather unusual one is the exit of the hero in a scene of Chikamatsu Monzaemon's *The Girl of Hakata*. Here the stage and the *hanamichi* are covered with a blue floor cloth, painted

[4] Minamoto Yoshitsune (1159–1189), one of the most colorful men in Japanese history, figures throughout Japanese plays, poetry, and novels.

with stylized waves, representing the ocean. In the center of the stage is a large pirate ship, from which the pirates, suspecting the intentions of the hero, have thrown him into the sea to drown. After the curtain has closed, a small boat is pulled from the stage, by means of ropes from behind the *agemaku*, toward the rear of the *hanamichi*. Just after the boat has passed over the *shichi-san*, the hero appears through the trap-door and pulls himself up into the boat. The boat with the hero aboard is then pulled to the rear of the *hanamichi*.

The *hanamichi* is sometimes used for what might be called a 'continuous' exit and entrance, in which the character exits from the *hanamichi*, the set is changed on the stage, and the character re-enters almost immediately on the *hanamichi* in a mood continuous with that of his exit. This occurs in *Mirror Mountain* when the heroine, having been grievously used by the villainess of the piece, shows in her actions at the *shichi-san* that the only escape from her difficulties is death. She makes a very restrained, infinitely sad exit. The scene shifts to her home, and almost at once she re-enters the *hanamichi*, her expression and attitude exactly the same.

There are no sharp, incisive beginnings and endings in the Kabuki such as those produced in the Western theatre. Even when the curtain is drawn across the stage on a static tableau the effect is rather that of the 'slow dissolve' of the film than that of the decisive finality of the Western drop curtain; and even when the drop curtain is used in the Kabuki it is not employed, as in the West, at varying speeds so that it becomes, theatrically, a means of heightening the dramatic intent of the performance. The Kabuki drop curtain never rises on a scene of great dramatic intensity, nor does it fall just at a climax, but always considerably after the climax has been reached. The Kabuki curtain, whether the native draw curtain or the Western drop curtain, is not used as a theatrical device closely integrated with the form of the play, but merely as a means of concealing the stage from the eyes of the audience.

Exits and entrances on the *hanamichi* have a similar feeling of filmic 'fading in' and 'fading out.' As the actor moves along the *hanamichi* to the *shichi-san* the form of the character becomes progressively stronger, while when he moves away from the *shichi-san* to the rear of the *hanamichi* the reverse is true. After the actor disappears through the *agemaku*, he leaves behind him, in the opinion of Japanese critics, a quality called *yoin*—a continued, fading reverberation, the effect of the shadow of the emotion of the character left upon

101

the audience. The character does not exist, aesthetically, after he goes through the *agemaku* (in the way a character may exist in the Western theatre even though he has left the stage) but rather the fading outlines of his form, the withdrawal of his passion, hang for a moment in the air of the theatre after the character has vanished. Considered in its complete function, the *hanamichi* 'fades' the actor into the sharply focussed action of the play on the stage and 'dissolves' him out of it, to a certain degree in a literal, visual sense, but more strongly in the sense of the character's impact upon the audience.

Most of the time the *hanamichi* is used as a kind of private, personal stage for the character, as opposed to the stage proper where he mingles with other characters and becomes part of a theatrical complex. For on the *hanamichi* the character not only puts forward the world of his individual being but also projects his attitude toward the world of the play existing on the stage. The action of the character on the *hanamichi*, although sometimes accompanied by words, is a soliloquy in movement, and like the soliloquy is a point of more intimate contact with the audience than when the character is engaged with the other persons of the play. On the *hanamichi* the character is also free from psychological involvement with settings and, except to a very limited degree, with properties. Nothing interposes between the actor and the audience, and therefore the actor, in this intimate relation with the spectator, uses the *hanamichi* as an area for improvisation, suiting his acting to the mood of the specific audience. Although the acting on the stage, subject to the influence of other actors, the setting, and the music, does not vary from performance to performance in any significant detail, the performance of the lone actor on the *hanamichi* may show considerable variation arising out of his feelings toward the audience and theirs toward him. Improvisation occurs particularly when the curtain is drawn across the stage and the *hanamichi* becomes an independent area, and in this circumstance, the actor, when he has a 'good' audience, will considerably prolong and intensify his acting.

The *hanamichi* is constantly used as an entrance for large groups of characters: a lord in a palanquin with his retinue of servants, a band of soldiers, warriors on horseback, and the like. When the temporary *hanamichi* was used, opposed groups lined up on the two *hanamichi* and confronted each other from opposite sides of the theatre, the leader of each group taking his position at the *shichi-san*. This technique was used, for example, in *Chivalrous Gorozō* when the

102

rival samurai and their followers meet. Today one group lines up along the length of the *hanamichi*, the other on the left side of the stage. Despite the loss of the temporary *hanamichi*, one of the characteristics of the Kabuki performance is its processional quality arising out of the frequent passage of large groups of people through the auditorium. In this circumstance, unless the group has a leader who stops at the *shichi-san*, the *hanamichi* is undifferentiated in the strength of its areas, the whole of it exerting a similar force over the auditorium.

The position of the *hanamichi* at stage-right increases the strength of this side of the stage. Why both the *hanamichi* of the Kabuki and the *hashigakari* of the Nō stage should have been joined to the stage at the right rather than at the left is a matter for pure speculation. In the plan of a stage for *dengaku-nō* in 1348 (the floor plan is shown on page 33) two *hashigakari* were used which joined the stage at an angle on both the right and left sides. But the Nō stage abandoned the passageway on the left and retained only that on the right; and when, in the Kabuki theatre, the *hashigakari* lost its original force, the *hanamichi* appeared joining the stage proper on the right side. Thus the stage-right area of the Kabuki stage became a psychologically stronger area than stage-left. On the Western stage the stage-right area is, similarly, a comparatively stronger area than stage-left. This phenomenon has been explained as resulting from the Westerner's reading from left to right so that in watching a play, his eyes move habitually to his left, which is, in theatre terms, the stage-right area. However, in Japan, where this area is similarly strong, the spectator reads not from left to right but in the opposite direction. He also reads down the page, not across it. The explanation of the strength of the stage-right area seems, therefore, to lie in some other sphere of activity than reading the printed page.

The movement of the actor on the *hanamichi* through the auditorium, the interplay between the actor on the *hanamichi* and the actor on the stage, the width of the front of the stage and the length of the *hanamichi*—all these necessitate physical movement on the part of the audience, both when watching the progression of the actor on the *hanamichi* or his movement across the stage. The spectator thus makes a series of visual and bodily adjustments to an acting area measuring a total of some one hundred and fifty feet, looking at one moment, perhaps, at an actor ten feet away from him and at the next moment at an actor fifty feet distant. The spectator is not hypnotically fixed in a single visual direction as he is, generally speaking, when viewing a film, or, to a lesser degree, when watching a representational Western play. And so the spectator participates physically in the performance to a greater degree than does the spectator in any Western form of entertainment except possibly the three-ring circus. In the Kabuki there is the same sense of multiple areas of interest and the corresponding physical movement which creates in him the feeling of immediate involvement with the performance. This sense of physical participation, in conjunction with the pre-established atmosphere of intimacy between actor and audience, creates a world of immediate theatre reality over the whole of the auditorium. In the representational theatre the genesis of the force of the performance begins behind the proscenium and the audience must be drawn into this field of theatre activity. In the Kabuki the entire force of the performance is directed outward, both from the *hanamichi* and from the stage, so that the focal center of the performance is created in the midst of the audience.

CHAPTER V

Elements of the Performance

THE basic quality of the Kabuki performance grows principally out of two concepts: The actor is the principal means of expression; the stage and the *hanamichi* are platforms for acting rather than representational areas. These two ideas are, of course, closely related since the stage is essentially the province of the actor rather than that of the scene designer. Kabuki stage settings are elaborate, large, and spectacular, but only rarely do they and the stage machinery dominate the actor. On the contrary, the most spectacular stage effects are those which are created to show the actor to best advantage. Furthermore, since the Kabuki is not concerned with creating a world of illusion and since the performance derives from the actor, persons who are not actors (in the sense that they are not characters in the play) can appear on the stage during the performance to facilitate the expressiveness of the actor.

The stagehands, dressed in black work clothes, are usually seen on the stage at the end of a scene when the setting is being changed, as it usually is, before the eyes of the audience. On these occasions, which are most frequently those on which the revolving stage is used, the stagehands bring on and set up flats or gather up the floor cloth and deposit it on the revolving portion of the stage. The stagehands may also appear during the course of the play. Platforms bearing one or more actors are sometimes pushed up- or downstage by stagehands, particularly in dance pieces. But the stagehand appears most frequently on stage during the performance in order to remove some piece of scenery which is no longer needed and which will impede the movement of the actor. Gates, indicating the entrance to

a house or garden, are often brought on or removed during the course
of an act. In 'Anniversary Celebration,' for example, a garden gate
figures prominently in the early part of the act, which is marked by a
series of significant exits and entrances through the gate. But
toward the end of the act the gate is no longer required, and the area
it occupies must be used by the chief character in the final tableau. A
stagehand therefore comes on stage and removes the gate. Toward
the middle of 'Moritsuna's Camp,' it is necessary to show that a
mother is not permitted to see her young son, who is held prisoner
in the house. Up to this point the entrance to the house has not been
indicated scenically, but now a stagehand brings on a gate which will
show clearly the division between interior and exterior so that the
separation of mother and son can be visually indicated. After this
scene has been played, there is no further dramatic use for the gate
and a stagehand removes it. When the stagehand appears during the
course of the play he does his work as quickly, quietly, and self-
effacingly as possible. When he is working backstage setting up the
next scene while another is being played, however, he is a changed
character, and a good deal of the beginning of an act is accompanied
by thumping and pounding behind the scenes as a new setting is
being put up on the unseen part of the revolving stage. The stage
screw is a refinement unknown to the Japanese stage; a Japanese
stage brace ends in a metal point which must be pounded into the
stage floor. The only people in the audience disturbed in any way by
this racket are the foreigners.

The personal servant, as it were, of the actor on the stage is the
kurombo or the *kōken*. The two are distinguished by their costumes, not
their functions, for they are in actuality the same persons. The
kurombo ('black fellow'), sometimes also called *kurogo*, is dressed
entirely in black, a black hood covering his head and face. The *kōken*
(assistant) is dressed in *kamishimo*, the Edo period formal dress, and
his face is not covered. Whether the *kōken* or the *kurombo* will appear
in a particular piece depends upon the costuming of the actors in the
play. Usually in the plays in which the actors appear in *kamishimo* the
kurombo is used, for in this circumstance the necessary visual differentiation between the actor and the *kōken* would be destroyed. However,
in such elaborately costumed pieces as *The Subscription List, Lion
Dance,* and *The Arrow Maker,* there is no possibility of the *kōken* being
confused with the actor. Therefore the use of the *kōken* is determined
by his visual suitability to the stage picture. The same is true of the

kurombo, for although he is usually dressed in black (which in Oriental artistic convention makes him invisible), in winter scenes when the stage is covered with a white floor cloth indicating snow, the *kurombo* appears dressed entirely in white.

There is no appropriate name in English for these men because a function corresponding to theirs does not exist in similar form in the Western theatre. They have been called both property men and prompters, but these words describe only a part of their work. *Stage assistant* is probably a more appropriate term in view of the variety of their activities.

The number of these men on the stage at any given time varies; there may be a stage assistant for every actor in the scene, or there may be none at all. Their presence on the stage is purely utilitarian, and they come onstage when needed. Unless the action of the play requires that the actor enter the stage carrying a certain property, the property is given to the actor at the appropriate moment by the stage assistant and removed when it is no longer needed. In general, no property is allowed to remain before the eyes of the audience, or, from another point of view, to detract from the presence of the actor, after it has served its dramatic purpose. When the actor has finished with a particular property—a letter, a pipe, a Buddhist rosary—he places it behind him and the stage assistant, who usually takes a position behind the actor, removes it. Properties can be invested with as great dramatic power in the Kabuki as they are in the Western theatre, and perhaps their dramatic power is even greater, for they appear only when needed and are removed immediately when they are not required. Their force is not dulled by familiarity. The same effect can, of course, be achieved in the representational theatre, but only after considerable labor on the part of the playwright, the director, and the actor. The property must either be carried on the stage by an actor or some logical reason must be provided for its being on the stage, and, once there, it must remain until the end of the act or scene unless some motivation can be supplied for its removal. It is interesting to speculate upon the number of butlers and maids who have found their way into the Western theatre solely because no other character in the play could perform the function of bringing in or removing the dishes.

The Kabuki costume is a rather complicated affair, sometimes weighing as much as fifty or sixty pounds, consisting of several layers of kimono which must be carefully arranged when the actor sits on the floor, moves to a new position, or performs a *mie*, for at no moment in the performance is an ungraceful costume line permitted. The stage assistant is constant in his attention to the actor's costume, arranging its folds or adjusting its line. The actor frequently removes his right arm from his kimono, preparatory to fighting or other strenuous activity, and at the conclusion of the action replaces it; in this he is helped by the stage assistant. A fairly common occurrence is what may be described as a partial change of costume (*hada wo nugu*); the kimono is held in place by a wide band, the *obi*, around the waist, and the upper part of the kimono is removed to reveal another kimono of different pattern and color beneath. In this case, the stage assistant helps the actor out of the upper part of the kimono and arranges it around the actor's waist. Sometimes the outer kimono is entirely removed, with the help of the stage assistant, to show a different costume beneath it. A more rapid costume change is that known as *hikinuki* ('pulling-out') which is used for the most part in pure dance pieces. For this, the parts of the outer kimono are loosely sewn together; at the appropriate moment, the stage assistant deftly pulls out the threads with which the costume is basted together, the parts of the kimono fall from the actor's body, and a new costume is revealed. This almost instantaneous costume change requires considerable dexterity on the part of the stage assistant, for it is effected with no pause in the dance movement. All costumes removed during the course of the play, unless they are to be reworn, are unobtrusively taken from the stage by the stage assistant at the earliest convenient moment. Probably the most striking costume in the entire Kabuki is that worn by the chief character in *Just a Moment*, a costume which traditionally requires nine times as much material as the ordinary Kabuki costume. In this play two stage assistants are required to manipulate the costume, which is distinguished by enormous square sleeves kept in shape by steel ribbing. Toward the end of the play, the stage assistants remove the steel ribs so that the actor is able to move freely in a scene of fighting. Having conquered his enemies, the character performs a *mie*, and at this point the stage assistants hold up the exaggerated sleeves, restoring them to their original squareness so that the *mie* is made more striking.

The stage assistant assiduously sees to the comfort of the actor. He brings the actor water or tea during a long scene, he supplies him with the Japanese equivalent of a handkerchief, he wipes the perspiration from the actor's face after a strenuous scene. These acts are usually performed with the actor facing upstage. The actor is often required to sit in a kneeling position, his legs under him, for a considerable time. Even though the Japanese are trained to this position from childhood, when unduly prolonged it results in impaired circulation and the actor has difficulty in rising. In long scenes, the stage assistant places a low wooden seat under the actor so that his circulation will not be cut off. The only other kind of 'seat' seen on the Kabuki stage, other than the cushions (*zabuton*) on which the Japanese ordinarily sit and an occasional folding chair for dignitaries, is a stool approximately two and a half feet high which is used by important characters in long scenes. This is placed behind the actor by a stage assistant and the actor sits on it, as Queen Victoria is reputed to have done, without having first to ascertain its presence. Conventionally, the actor sitting on this stool is conceived to be standing, and it is provided merely for his comfort.

The stage assistant helps in the management of large or cumbersome properties when they would hinder the actor's free movement. In the comic dance *The Tea Box*, for instance, much of the action is concerned with a fairly large wooden box containing tea and a struggle for its possession. The box is equipped with a harness so that it can be carried on the back. At one point the rival claimants to its ownership each put an arm through one side of the harness and dance with the box between them. Here the stage assistant holds the box up from beneath so that for the actors it is weightless and therefore does not interfere with their dance movement. A rather curious example of the stage assistant helping with dance movement occurs in the play *Flowers at Ueno*; the child Botarō is engaged in rhythmical fencing with two adults; to show his victory over them at the end of this scene, Botarō is held up by a stage assistant and, standing on one foot on the knee of one of the prostrate fencers, strikes an impressive *mie*. In these functions, since the stage assistant's movement must be synchronized with the dance movement of the actor, the stage assistant himself must have considerable ability in the dance. Unless particular dramatic significance is attached to the activity, the actor does not open or close the sliding doors of the Kabuki setting himself; ordinarily the actor performs the gesture of manipulating the door, but actually it is moved by the stage assistant.

The stage assistant is the manipulator of a variety of 'stage-effect' properties whose use is also closely coordinated with the movement of the actor. These properties consist basically of a bamboo pole, painted black, some six feet long (*sashidashi*), at the end of which is attached a 'theatrical' object. For example, in *Twenty-four Dutiful Sons*, when the heroine Yaegaki-hime has removed a helmet from a shrine, she is come upon by two warriors who would take the helmet from her. At this point a stage assistant attaches the helmet to the bamboo pole and raises it above the heads of the warriors. Dramatically, the helmet has shown its mystical powers. There ensues a dance in which the helmet engages in a conflict with the warriors and at the end defeats them. Throughout the dance, the helmet is moved by the stage assistant in an intricate pattern. In *Lion Dance*, as well as in other dances, paper butterflies are attached to the ends of two poles and the butterflies are fluttered about the dancer. Frequently in plays dealing with supernatural doings, burning tapers are attached to the end of the poles and waved about the stage; these represent *kitsunebi* (fox-fires) and indicate the presence of the spirits of the dead. In *Snowbound Pass* a bird flies in on the end of such a pole bearing a message in its mouth. The *tsura-akari* ('face-light') of the pre-Meiji theatre was essentially this same instrument; with a candle attached at the end of the pole, it was used for the purpose of lighting the actor's face. Although any practical necessity for this device has disappeared, the use of the *tsura-akari* survives in certain plays because of its striking effect. In *Mitsukuni and the Sorceress* the supernatural heroine Takiyasha-hime makes an entrance rising on the trap-lift in the *hanamichi*, and two stage assistants carrying *tsura-akari* advance from the stage and kneel on either side of her. As she postures at the *shichi-san*, they move the candles about her creating a kind of contrapuntal design to the actor's movement.

The stage assistants also prompt. In former times, during the first three days of a new play, the authors (there were usually three) dressed in the black costume of the *kurombo* and took positions directly behind the actors, script in hand. Today the author no longer performs this function, but since the Kabuki program is changed monthly and there are seldom more than three days rehearsal of the eight or ten plays that constitute the program, during the first several days of the month prompting is one of the stage assistant's most important activities. The stage assistant crouches upstage of the actor; from this position prompting can be done more efficiently than, as in the Western theatre, from the wings or from a prompter's box at the front of the stage.

In all these activities the stage assistant makes himself as inconspicuous as possible. He enters the stage quietly and swiftly, sometimes at a run; he takes a position behind the actor, or behind a screen, a tree, or a platform. When the stage setting offers no place of concealment, he kneels facing upstage, a position which, in the aesthetic of the Kabuki, makes him nonexistent; when he can do so, he makes his entrances and exits behind the actors. He is meant not to be seen; and so efficiently is his work done that even the foreigner after seeing a few Kabuki performances becomes unaware of his presence.

The stage assistant in the Kabuki does not efface himself because he is a nonrealistic intrusion into the stage picture. He does so in order that he will not detract from the total design—a design which, by his arrangement of the actor's costume and his skilful manipulation of properties, he has assisted in creating. He is indispensable to the Kabuki on both utilitarian and aesthetic grounds, for without him the actor would be obliged to arrange or change his own costume, to procure his own properties at the appropriate moment, and would thus lose, to a damaging extent, his expressiveness. The stage assistant in freeing the actor of these obligations enables the actor to perform his true function—that of acting.

A man dressed in black work clothes, known as the *kyōgenkata*, appears as he is needed during the course of the performance in the extreme down-left corner of the stage. He is equipped with a flat board, about eighteen inches wide and two feet long, and with two clappers made of oak, about nine inches long and three inches thick, which are called *ki* or *hyōshigi*. Placing the board on the stage floor and kneeling before it with a clapper in either hand, he performs complicated rhythmical patterns as accompaniment to certain parts of the play. This performance of the *kyōgenkata* is known as *tsuke-uchi*.

The striking together of resonant pieces of wood has been an attention-getting device in Japan since ancient times and is used, outside the theatre, throughout the country today. A Buddhist priest chanting sutras accompanies himself rhythmically by beating wooden clappers together. The night watchman in every city and town goes his rounds beating wooden clappers, and the sound has a multiple message: It advises others that he is on the job, it reminds them to be careful of fire, it is a warning to any burglar in the vicinity to be off. In the Kabuki the *tsuke-uchi* is similarly used as a device for attracting attention (for example, when a scene change takes place in sight of the audience), but it is also used as a rhythmical means of underlining the actor's movement. When a running entrance is made onto the stage, it is almost invariably accompanied by a rapid beating of wooden clappers, beginning fortissimo and ending pianissimo. When a running exit is made from the stage, the dynamic pattern is the opposite. At these entrances and exits, which are of relatively short duration, the *tsuke-uchi* quickly and sharply draws attention to them and in addition points up the excitement of the actor's movement. The *tsuke-uchi* is sometimes used to accompany the movement of the actor on the *hanamichi* as he approaches or leaves the *shichi-san*, particularly when that movement shows a cumulative increase or decrease in tempo. In the scenes known as *tachimawari*, ballet-like scenes of fighting, the *tsuke-uchi* is indispensable; here it creates no simple rhythms, but a richly syncopated pattern of sound which is frequently contrapuntal to the actor's movement. The *mie* is always accompanied by the *tsuke-uchi*, the method of usage varying with the nature of the *mie*; in some instances the clappers are beaten rapidly in a general crescendo as the *mie* reaches its climax, in others a few rather widely separated beats mark the introduction to the climax. But the climax of the *mie* is invariably announced by a single sharp beat of the clappers.

It is difficult to describe the emotional effect of the *tsuke-uchi*. The sound is sharp, crisp, clear, and immediate. It is relatively high pitched and thin, yet resonant. There is in it nothing of the thickness of the sound of the drum, although it has the same pulse-quickening quality. The *tsuke-uchi*, like the sound of the samisen, is rather sharp-edged and biting; although it draws immediate attention, the sound does not impose itself on or overpower the movement of the actor. With the *tsuke-uchi* a structure of purely theatrical sound, nonrepresentational and nonmusical, is erected about the actor, taking its form from his movement, frequently contrapuntally, and drawing a precise aural outline about his movement.

The wooden clappers, beaten against each other and not against a board (this technique is known as *kikkake*), are also used behind the scenes preparatory to drawing the curtain. Before the beginning of an act, the wooden clappers are beaten together first at intervals of about ten seconds, then at increasingly shorter intervals, principally to indicate to the actors and backstage workers that curtain time is approaching. The drawing of the Kabuki curtain is always accompanied by the beating of wooden clappers, but they are never used with the drop curtain. With the opening and the closing of the curtain, the pattern of sound is the same: The beating begins slowly and is gradually accelerated. Here, as elsewhere, the sound not only attracts attention to the opening or closing of the curtain but also creates a certain excitement and anticipation in the audience; the sound invests the movement of the curtain with the same dramatic emphasis as the *tsuke-uchi* creates about the actor. This pattern—a gradual acceleration of the tempo to a climax, rather like the building up of a wave as it moves toward the shore—is a basic pattern of the Kabuki; it is utilized in musical accompaniments and appears in the actor's movement.

The whole of the Kabuki performance is surrounded with music and with what, for lack of a better phrase, can be called musical sound effects; they are seldom literal and usually have a strong rhythmic quality. The Kabuki began as dance, and, as we shall see, has never moved far from it. The Kabuki actor, essentially a dancer, is the genesis of the performance. The music and the sound derive, therefore, from his movement, underlining it and sharpening its effect. Kabuki music rises about the body of the actor. It does not impose itself upon the actor, but instead gives musical and rhythmic expression to his movement, and in doing so increases the flow of theatrical expressiveness toward the audience.

The general term for the musicians and singers who appear on the stage is *degatari*, a word written with two Chinese characters meaning *to come out* and *to declaim*. They are to be distinguished from the sound-effects men and the musicians who occupy the *geza* (the 'music' room on stage-right). It is significant that the word *degatari* is used, for it suggests the intrinsic quality of most Kabuki music. The music is essentially narrative or descriptive; in the majority of plays the singing of narrative or descriptive passages to the accompaniment of the samisen is one of the most important elements of the production. This is particularly true of plays of doll theatre origin (*maruhommono*) whose musical narration, *chobo*, is usually performed by a samisen player and a narrator-singer; but in no Kabuki play is the element of musical narration entirely lacking. The *chobo* performers always appear at stage-left, as they do in the doll theatre, seated on a small revolving stage. The samisen player sits downstage of the narrator (*tayū*),[1] who has before him a handsomely lacquered stand, two large

---

[1] According to Okuni-legend, Nagoya Sanzaemon, Okuni's lover, used the word *tayū* to designate the chief actor. However, *tayū* was the fifth grade in social rank, a grade granted temporarily to performers so that they could appear before the Court. The continued use of the term probably derives from this practice.

tassels suspended from the front of it, on which he places the script of the play. Both are dressed in *kamishimo*. At the front of their platform are two tall candlesticks, a reminder of earlier days, now equipped with electric bulbs.

In addition to the word *chobo*, the words *jōruri* and *gidayū* are also used to describe the musical-narrative element of the doll theatre play in a way that is rather confusing to the foreigner. At the beginning of the seventeenth century, Sawazumi Kengyō, a performer associated with an Ōsaka doll theatre, first used the samisen, a three-stringed instrument played with a plectrum, to accompany the recitation of the metrical romance *Jōruri Jūnidan Zōshi*, the heroine of which was a Princess Jōruri. The rhythmical recitation of historical romances such as *The Tale of Heike* and *The Tale of Hogen*, both appearing toward the end of the twelfth century, had long been common, but these had been accompanied by an ancient stringed instrument, the *biwa*. The use of the samisen in Sawazumi's recitation was a popular innovation and was quickly taken up by other doll theatre performers. This new style of recitation became known as *jōruri*. Rival schools of *jōruri* sprang up in Ōsaka under Uji Haganojō and Inoue Harima, but when Takemoto Chikugo Gidayū (1651–1714) opened his doll theatre in Ōsaka in 1685 and later collaborated with the playwright Chikamatsu Monzaemon (1653–1724), he became undisputed master of this new form and the name *gidayū* was generally applied to his style of *jōruri*. *Jōruri* was brought to Edo by a pupil of Sawazumi, Toraya Jirōemon, who later took the name of Satsuma Jōun. Satsuma brought with him his wooden dolls made in Kyōto, and in 1635 opened his theatre in Edo. The *chobo*, the musical-narrative accompaniment to Kabuki plays of doll theatre origin, therefore, is *jōruri*, while *gidayū*, strictly speaking, is a style of *jōruri*, although the terms are scarcely differentiated today in popular use.

Although a variety of musical instruments are used in the Kabuki theatre, the samisen is basic and indispensable. The samisen was introduced into Japan between 1558 and 1569, having been brought from the Ryūkyū islands to the port of Sakai. This three-stringed instrument, called *jamisen* ('snake-skin; string') because the sounding box was covered with snake skin, was played with a bow. It came into the hands of a certain Nakashoji, a player of the *biwa*, a four-stringed plucked instrument of ancient origin. Nakashoji used the plectrum in playing the *jamisen*, changed the snake-skin to cat-skin, and the instrument became the *samisen* ('three-string') in much the same form in which it exists today. The popularity of the samisen was immediate; it was first used in the Kabuki about 1624 and it remains today the chief musical instrument of Japan, the indispensable accompaniment of native singing and dancing.

The strong narrative element of the Kabuki derives from the Japanese love of story-telling, a form of amusement deeply rooted in Japanese life. Story-telling, accompanied by *biwa*, rhythmical taps of a folded fan on the narrator's desk, or later by the samisen, is of ancient origin. In the thirteenth century it was customary for blind Buddhist priests to recite long romances, accompanying themselves on the *biwa*. At the beginning of the seventeenth century, reciters of the *Taiheiki* (a long historical work of the years from 1318 to 1368, written toward the end of the fourteenth century) appeared on the streets of Edo, set up booths, and immediately attracted large crowds of listeners. These performers were called *kōdan-shi*, and their repertoire was confined to romances of historical or pseudo-historical nature. A subsequent rival school of story-tellers called *rakugo-shi* used the less formal material of contemporary event, love stories, frequently of a highly erotic nature, and humorous, at times obscene, anecdotes. The originator of this form of entertainment, according to tradition, was Fukai Shidōken (1682–1765), who told his stories in the vicinity of the Kannon Temple in Edo. His fame increased until he came to rival the popularity of the Kabuki actor Ichikawa Danjūrō II, and after Ichikawa's death in 1758, Fukai became indisputably the greatest entertainer in Edo. The first hall devoted to story-telling was built in Edo in 1795. In 1815 there were seventy-five of these *yose* in Edo; ten years later there were one hundred and twenty-five. The government, not approving this manifestation of public frivolity, reduced the number of *yose* to seventy-six and finally closed them altogether. But the *yose* had become a necessary part of the citizens' amusement and continued to thrive both in private homes and on street corners. The crowds gathering in the streets to listen to the story-tellers became so large that the passage of traffic was made impossible. Finally realizing that this entertainment could not be eradicated, the government in 1851 repealed the laws restricting the number of *yose*. With the appearance of the silent film in Japan a new field of endeavor opened up for the storyteller. He became a *benshi* (a speaker), a man who stood at one side of the screen, telling the story in detail, commenting on the acting, and delivering the supposed lines of the actors. So popular did certain of the *benshi* become that audiences often went to hear a particular *benshi* rather than to see the film. The *benshi* have disappeared, but the halls of the storytellers survive today in the cities and towns of Japan. Their number is somewhat smaller than formerly, but their continued existence, as well as the radio appearance of *kōdan-shi* and *rakugo-shi*, testifies to the Japanese devotion to this traditional narrative form of amusement.

Today the narrative element is the chief characteristic of the Japanese child's first acquaintance with 'theatre.' This 'theatre' is a form of entertainment which is built upon the use of narration and dialogue to explain and interpret a picture. It is known as *kamishibai* ('paper-play'). The performer is in actuality a candy salesman who entices children to buy his wares by performances of paper-plays. His theatre consists of a small cart, with a wooden frame on one end, in which the illustrated scenes of the play are displayed one by one while the narrator tells the story of what is happening. The pictures are printed on pieces of cardboard measuring about twelve by eighteen inches, and a given play consists of some fifteen or twenty cards. The cards and the 'continuity' are commercial products and in this day of standardization the narrator is required neither to improvise nor to learn his lines. When the card on display is removed from the front of the pack, it is placed at the rear of the pack of pictures, and on the back of this card is printed the dialogue and narration to accompany the card which is now revealed. So popular and widespread is this form of entertainment among children that during World War II it was completely controlled by the government and given over to propaganda purposes.

Despite the importance of musical narration to the Kabuki performance, this element of the production is not permitted to detract from the central position of the actor. This is clearly demonstrated in the difference between the relation of *chobo* and actor in the Kabuki performance of doll theatre plays and the relation of *jōruri* and the dolls in the doll theatre. In the Kabuki the actor is the point of departure in the performance, and the narrative and descriptive element, although it is not relegated to an obscure position, is nevertheless subordinate to the field of dramatic influence effected by the actor; in the doll theatre the genesis of the performance is the *jōruri*. In both the Kabuki and the doll theatre the narrator symbolizes his respect for the script by the traditional gesture of raising it up in both hands to his forehead before he opens it at the beginning of a performance and of repeating this gesture at its conclusion. This gesture states a literal

116

attitude in the doll theatre; in the Kabuki it is empty convention. In the doll theatre everything derives from the script. The narrator does not attract attention to himself, even though his delivery of the lines and of the descriptive passages is much more impassioned than that of the narrator in the Kabuki; the dolls are the visual center of interest, but their movement is derived directly from the script. In the Kabuki the actor takes over lines from the *chobo* when it is convenient to his purposes to do so and allows the narrator to speak them when he wishes to engage in more expressive activity. Thus in the Kabuki not only is the role of the narrator considerably reduced, but the dynamics of the performance are shifted from the script to the actor. It is probably for this reason that the plays of the doll theatre have somewhat greater literary value than those of pure Kabuki origin; in the West the theatre similarly dominated by the actor has at times produced only second-rate playwrights.

The unique function of the *chobo* in the Kabuki has led some writers to suggest that it is analogous to the chorus of Greek tragedy. In some respects the analogy can be drawn. As with the Greek chorus, the *chobo* consists of words and music; the narration sets the scene, comments on the action of the play, moralizes about it, and in doing so guides and gives voice to the sentiments of the audience. In the same fashion as the Greek chorus, the *chobo* has its individual attitude toward the characters in the play and their actions, approving this one, censuring that, and throughout reacting intellectually and emotionally from a frame of reference in common with that held by the audience. But other than in these respects, the *chobo* and the Greek chorus have nothing in common. The performers of the *chobo* are not actors or dancers in the performance but are separated from it aesthetically and spatially. They occupy their conventional positions at stage-left and wear conventional costumes. Only musically and vocally do they participate in the events taking place on the stage. The Greek chorus, on the contrary, was an active participant in the performance. Having a generalized dramatic character, wearing costumes indicating age and sex, it was supplied with logical reasons for taking part in the action of the play, and it existed visually and psychologically within almost the same aura of theatricality as the chief actors in the play. Although the *chobo* is intimately related to the actor on the stage, it occurs on a different aesthetic plane, being a purely formal theatrical element existing midway between actor and audience and aesthetically differentiated from both of them, as the

Greek chorus was not. The narrator's lines also frequently differ in subject matter from those of the Greek chorus, for the narrator sometimes speaks the thoughts of a character as they pass through the character's mind with an omniscience never granted the Greek chorus. What corresponds to the long narrative passage of the Greek messenger is also a part of the *chobo*, appearing particularly in the scenes known as *monogatari* (tales) in which the actor pantomimes a succession of past events while the narrator describes them vocally. As has already been noted, the narrator on occasion takes over the lines of the actor, a function which the Greek chorus never performed.

In the performance of plays derived from the doll theatre, the actor's voice, the voice of the narrator, and the music of the samisen, whose range is that of the human voice, form an aural continuum. The actor's line reading is highly formalized, and, particularly at climaxes, begins to move, by the prolongation of vowels, in the direction of recitative. The narrator employs the same manner of line reading as the actor, but in the narrative passages and in those which reveal the character's thoughts he moves into what can only be described as song or chant. These English words, however, do not convey, because of their associations, a correct impression of the quality of the narrator's voice. Takemoto Gidayū wrote in his book on *jōruri*, 'The words in *jōruri* should not be sung or chanted but declaimed. However, they should be declaimed or narrated with a melody.' Except that it has less variation in pitch, the quality of *chobo* speech has more in common with the *sprechstimme* of Arnold Schönberg's *Pierrot Lunaire* and of Alban Berg's *Wozzeck* than it does with other forms of Western vocal expression. It employs the quarter tones and intermediate tones of conversational speech, and the vocal pattern arises out of a prolongation of the words rather than out of a melodic pattern imposed upon the words. There is nothing in it which resembles melody, either in the popular or technical sense of the word, nor which, at least to Western ears, can be called a tune.

The samisen, however, plays short melodic passages, both in accompaniment to the narrator's voice and as interludes and introductions. The music of the samisen is closely related to the characteristic qualities of Japanese speech, which is distinguished by strong consonants, frequent glottal stops, sharp and almost equal stress on every syllable. There are consequently almost no syllables which are unstressed. Although the Japanese language possesses many of the consonants of European languages, it has only five vowel sounds, and even when these are combined in diphthongs their duration is less than it is in most European languages. The great majority of Japanese syllables begin with a consonant, and this characteristic, together with the sharp stress of the syllable, produces a generally staccato quality which is frequently greatly exaggerated in the theatre. The samisen, being plucked, produces the same sharp attack to every note and the consequent lack of legato quality. It is also capable of producing the intermediate tones of the human voice. In scenes of weeping, for example, the samisen underlines the movement of the character's body as he weeps and then, musically, takes over the sound of 'weeping,' although this sound is in no sense a literal representation. There is the greatest freedom of movement between the actor's voice, the narrator's voice, and the music of the samisen. The narrator, like the samisen, can take over the weeping or the laughing of the actor without pause, and the actor similarly begins with no break between his speech and that of the narrator. And since this triad of expression moves within the same range of pitch, and since each has the vocal qualities of the other two, they produce a strong sense of aural continuity. The sound moves, with no break or division, from the stylized line reading of the actor to the more musical style of the narrator to the music of the samisen, which frequently performs, as in the case of 'weeping,' the function of an abstract human voice. The fluid movement between speech, vocal music, and instrumental music has no parallel in the Western theatre unless perhaps in the aural effect that was produced in Greek tragedy. There is no resemblance between this and the use of incidental music in the contemporary Western theatre. There the incidental music always remains music, the actor's voice always produces speech, and the two exist on separate aural planes, the actor's voice either dominating the music or being dominated by it.

Although the word *chobo* is used generally to describe only the accompaniment of plays of doll theatre origin, narrators and samisen players are also used in plays written for the Kabuki and are employed in exactly the same manner. The position of the musicians on the stage in these plays, however, may vary according to their importance to a given scene or according to technical considerations of staging. If the curtained stage-left entrance is to be used in a given scene, the platform for the narrator and samisen player cannot be used since it blocks this entrance to the stage. In this circumstance, the narrator and samisen player occupy the second-story room on stage-left. If they figure prominently in the action, the bamboo curtain at the front of this room is raised; if not, they perform behind the curtain. If the stage-left entrance to the stage is not to be used and the musical-narrative element is not predominant, the narrator and samisen player do not occupy the platform on stage-left but take positions behind a bamboo curtain within the room on the stage level.

Incidental music corresponding in use to that of the Western theatre is performed by the musicians in the *geza*. The principal instruments are the voice, the samisen, the *shakuhachi* (a bamboo traverse flute), the *fue* (a small flute played laterally), gongs, bells, and drums of various sizes. Less frequently used instruments are the *koto*, a thirteen-stringed instrument of harp-like quality plucked with the fingers, and the *kokyū*, a three-stringed instrument played with a bow. The music from the *geza* is generally employed to create a mood, to state in introductory fashion the nature of the scene to follow, and to accompany scenes performed in pantomime. In this function, the use of *geza* music closely resembles that of the sound-track music of the film or that of the early *mèlodrame*. In characteristic Kabuki fashion, the *geza* music has been acquired from a variety of sources—from the Nō, from dance music, from folk tunes, from the popular songs of all periods of Kabuki history. The music for a given play is traditional and new incidental music is never written for an old play. Consequently, the associative value of the music is very strong and the mere statement of a phrase of music is sufficient to establish clearly the characteristic quality of a scene for the audience. The *geza* music is somewhat thin and fragmentary; even when it is used continuously throughout a scene as an accompaniment to panto-mime it never takes on the character of an independent composition in its own right, but on the contrary is subordinate, as good theatre music should be, to the dramatic intent of the scene. It should be noted that the samisen used in the *geza* performs a different function from that of the samisen in the *chobo*. The *geza* samisen merely performs passages of incidental music, and not infrequently in the performance of the doll theatre plays, the samisen in the *geza* is heard alternately with that of the *chobo*. The musical accompaniment from the *geza* is almost constant throughout Kabuki plays; only when a dance piece, or a piece which is predominantly dance, is being performed, and the musicians appear on the stage, is the *geza* music omitted.

The men in the *geza* are also employed in the production of what can be called sound effects although these are not the literal reproductions of sounds, except in those cases when a musician in the *geza* doubles for the actor who is supposedly playing a flute, a samisen, or some other instrument on the stage. Ominous passages, such as the appearance of a supernatural being either on the stage or through the trap-lift in the *hanamichi*, the movement of a would-be suicide to a river, or a murderer approaching his victim, are accompanied by the rapid beating of a drum which is somewhat more resonant than the Western bass drum. Battles are indicated by drumming and by the clanging of metal; there is no shouting or hubbub of voices. The single note of a large temple bell is not used to represent literally the sound from a nearby temple but rather to create the feeling of the coming of night and its attendant loneliness, a mood much prized in Japanese artistic expression. Similarly, the desolate sound of the crow cawing in the fourth act of *The Loyal Forty-seven Rōnin* (which later is used dramatically as a signal between the forty-seven *rōnin*) is not a literal reproduction of the sound but a theatricalization of it. In one scene of *Through the Iga Pass* the mother kneels in the snow clutching her baby, a palpable, freely displayed doll, and the sound of the child's crying issues from the *geza*. The sound here is as conventionalized as the baby. Except in those infrequent instances when sounds are heard from the rear of the *hanamichi*, they come from the *geza*, and in either event, as in the case of the crying child, they are not meant to be conceived of by the audience as having a realistic origin. Sound from the *geza* does not have the purpose either of literal reproduction or of an extension of the psychological field of the performance beyond the observable limits of the stage or *hanamichi*. The only attempt to use sound literally and thus project the play beyond the confines of the playing areas occurs in those plays influenced by Western models, such as those of Okamoto Kidō, which have been written within the last fifty or sixty years, and which are not, strictly speaking, Kabuki.

The musicians who appear on the stage as a kind of orchestra and chorus are called *debayashi*, a 'coming-out orchestra,' as distinguished from the orchestra of the *geza*. When they appear for the accompaniment of dance pieces which are of Nō origin and use the Kabuki adaptation of Nō setting, they sit on a two-tiered platform, covered with red cloth, at the rear of the stage, and the dancers perform in front of the orchestra as in the Nō theatre and in the early Kabuki theatre. This ensemble usually consists of ten samisen players, ten singers, six drummers (who use the finger drum, hip drum, and large drum of the Nō theatre), and the player of the *fue*, the flute of the Nō theatre, which in range and quality of sound is rather like the piccolo. If the dance piece does not use this conventional setting, even though it is of Nō origin, the position of the musicians on the stage as well as their number varies according to the plan of the stage setting and the technical requirements of the staging. The musicians always sit on a raised platform, which may be placed on the right or left side of the stage facing the audience, or the musicians may be divided into two groups, one placed on stage-right against the *geza*, the other in the corresponding position on the opposite side of the stage. One or the other of these positions is also used by the musicians in pieces which are not purely dance but which contain considerable dance movement and are essentially lyric. In these, and in the dances which do not use the conventional Nō setting, the musician's platform is decorated so that it ties in visually with the rest of the setting. In *Izayoi and Seishin*, for example, when the scene is a stone-walled river bank, the musician's platform is similarly painted with stones: at the end of *The Three Kichiza's*, the scene a winter one with snow, the musician's platform is painted white. On certain occasions, as in *Yūgiri and Izaemon* and *Sukeroku*, the musicians are placed in an up-stage area of the setting, such as an alcove, which is visually an architectural part of the setting.

The musicians, like the *chobo* performers, wear *kamishimo*, but the color of their costume is often related to the color of the setting. Thus in the scene of *Izayoi and Seishin* just mentioned in which the setting is painted in pastel greens, blues, and grays, the musicians wear green *kamishimo*; and in the winter scene of *The Three Kichiza's* their *kamishimo* are white. The decoration of the musicians' platform and of their *kamishimo* in colors or designs matching the setting is not done for the purpose of establishing the musicians within the same frame of reference as the actor. In *Izayoi and Seishin* the musicians are not conceived by the audience as a group of men who happen to be sitting along a river bank playing and singing; on the contrary, their relation to the play is the same as that of the Western opera orchestra to the action taking place on the stage. But they are visually related to the rest of the stage simply because the Kabuki is concerned with pleasing visual effect, and the repetition of the design and the colors of the setting on the musician's platform and on their *kamishimo* creates visual, not psychological, continuity. The platform on which the musicians invariably appear distinguishes them aesthetically from the area of the actor-dancer. Here, as elsewhere in the Kabuki, aesthetic differentiation is achieved through clearly defined spatial areas. Visual continuity between platform, *kamishimo*, and setting is not established when the piece is being performed in a Nō setting. Here, as with the *chobo*, the *kamishimo* and the musician's platform have a purely formal quality.

The position of the musicians, the color and design of their costumes, the decoration of their platforms, are determined, as are many other elements of the Kabuki, by tradition. Thus the feeling is that when the play is derived from the Nō and uses, in the main, Nō music and movement based upon the patterns of Nō movement, the setting should be the Kabuki adaptation of the Nō setting, and the musicians should be placed in front of the rear wall of the set as in the Nō theatre. However, even when the play is of Nō origin, but shows in its music and dance movement more of the Kabuki than of the Nō, the conventional Nō setting is not used, and the musicians are placed where they can be best related visually to the stage. *The Girl at Dōjō Temple* is a dance play of Nō origin, but it is thoroughly Kabuki in movement and music; although the Nō setting is not used, the musicians are placed on a platform in front of the rear wall of the setting. In the final scene of *Kokaji*, another of the Nō plays completely converted to Kabuki, the musicians are divided into two groups; the samisen players, singers, and a *kokyū* player are placed in the position of the *chobo* on stage-left, while the drummers and the flutist are in a corresponding position on stage-right. In those plays and scenes of plays which are not pure dance, but in which lyric and dance predominate, the orchestra is seldom placed upstage of the actor, but is either on the right or left of the stage. In this circumstance, the number of musicians is much smaller than that used for the pure dance pieces and the group consists generally of three or four samisen players and an equal number of singers. Whether the musicians are placed on one side of the stage or the other is determined by the convenience of the actor. Actually, the convenience of the actor may not be that of a given actor today, but that of an actor in former times, whose method of staging a given piece has now become an unbreakable tradition.

When the musicians are seated on the platform at the rear of the stage the impact of the music upon the audience is as strong, both acoustically and aesthetically, as that in the conventional physical arrangement of the performance of Western symphonic music, and the dancer who appears downstage of the musicians is approximately in the same position physically, and in the same position aesthetically, as the soloist in the performance of a concerto. The presence of the musicians behind the Kabuki performer, like that of the Western symphonic orchestra behind the soloist, has the effect of projecting the dancer's sphere of performance toward the audience. Thus the psychological sequence is that of audience–dancer–music, as opposed to that of audience–music–dancer which occurs in the performance of Western ballet. When the Kabuki musicians are placed on the right or left sides of the stage, their platform is set along the line of the 'inner-proscenium,' and in this position, which is also the position of the *chobo*, the musicians are at an obtuse angle both to the line of the actor's performance, which is parallel to the front of the stage, and to the auditorium. In this arrangement, the position of the musicians reinforces the strong downstage plane of the stage.

The words and music of the Nō dances, of those of Kabuki origin, and of scenes which are predominantly dance, bear the same relation to the actor's movement and speech as the words and music of the *chobo*. Most Kabuki dance ideologically consists of acting out the words of a song. In the dance pieces the singers describe the moods, thoughts, and passing emotions of the character, and these the actor mimes. There is a similar aural continuity as with the *chobo* between the samisen, the singer-narrators, and the actor's voice (for speech occurs in the dances) and the same fluid, uninterrupted flow of sound from one of these elements to another. The music used to accompany the pieces is of three principal varieties: *nagauta*, used to accompany the Nō dance; *tokiwazu* and *kiyomoto*, used to accompany the pure Kabuki pieces. These are practically indistinguishable to Western ears except after long study. Even the uninitiated, however, can determine which of these styles of music is being performed by observing the kind of music stand used by the musicians, for each style requires the use of a distinctively designed stand.

Like the stage assistants, the musicians and narrator-singers are placed on the stage for both utilitarian and aesthetic reasons. The physical proximity of the musicians to the actor-dancer permits them to accompany his movement as a group; there is no 'conductor' who in the Western theatre acts as a controlling link between the dance movement on the stage and the orchestra in the pit; in the Kabuki it is, in actuality, the actor-dancer's movement which is the conductor.

Since the musicians respond directly to his movement, there is no necessity to interpose a conductor to act as a control at a point midway between the actor-dancer and the musicians. The musicians are placed, therefore, where they have a good view of the actor and are able to follow his movement directly. They are brought upon the stage where they can do their work more efficiently and more economically than if they were required to perform at some distance from the actor-dancer, in the manner of the orchestra of the Western ballet and the property man of the Western theatre.

The Kabuki theatre draws the productional elements on to the stage as they become important to the flow of the performance. The *kyōgenkata* appears at his corner of the stage to perform the *tsuke*; the *chobo* performers are seen or are hidden behind a bamboo blind according to the importance of the *chobo* to a given scene; the stage assistant appears when he is needed, disappears when he is not; the stagehand brings on pieces of scenery as they are needed and removes them when they are no longer required. The performers of incidental music are hidden from the audience in the *geza*; however, when the music is not incidental but an intrinsic part of the performance, the musicians appear on the stage. Similarly, the sound effects of the Kabuki are directed, aesthetically, toward the stage rather than away from it. The frank recognition of the theatricality of the performance and the consequent acceptance of workers in the theatre, other than the actor, upon the stage, is a basic principle of the Kabuki. The workers are of course distinguished from the actor by costume, by placing the musicians on platforms, and, probably more important, by the audience's 'being used to' this convention. But the presence of the workers on the stage, far from distracting the audience from the actor, increases the essential theatricality of the performance by throwing the actor and the sphere of his acting into higher relief. The musicians, stagehands, and stage assistants by the very fact that they are not actors bring with them onto the stage the world of actuality, and against this background the theatricality of the actor's performance is intensified. The same principle requires that men play women's roles; a man impersonating a woman separates the performance from actuality and in so doing moves the performance into the realm of pure theatricality.

This quality of the Kabuki offers a striking contrast to the practices of the Western representational theatre. As the Western theatre moved toward representation, the productional elements were gradually concealed from the eyes of the audience. The musicians of the Shakespearean and Restoration theatres who at first performed in sight of the audience were at last hidden away. The stagehands of the Restoration theatre disappeared from the stage as the forestage decreased in size and the actor moved into the more representational area behind the curtain line. At Bayreuth, Wagner concealed a whole symphony orchestra from the eyes of the audience. The sound effect flourished with the rise of representationalism, became more and more literal, and culminated in such phenomena as the offstage cries of women in labor. Theatre reality came to exist only when the illusion was complete, and any immediate evidence of the presence of a worker in the theatre other than the actor destroyed the illusion. Similarly, this movement required that the actor be less the actor and more the real person, and for the West, the absence of theatricality was requisite to the sense of theatre reality. The division between the actor and his role, in the mind of the audience, became less and less, until finally, in the film, the two became almost indistinguishable. The antithesis of these characteristics of the representational theatre is found in the Kabuki.

CHAPTER VI

The Stage

THE Kabuki stage is a decorated area, not a disguised one. Stage decoration serves the purpose of indicating place, rather than representing it, and of providing a background against which, rather than in which, the actor plays.[1]

The original Kabuki stage floor, that of the Nō theatre, was a dancing floor, and this floor, always undecorated, opposed both the body of the actor and the set pieces of nonrepresentational design that were placed on it. Today, the stage floor of the Kabuki maintains this original characteristic despite an increase in scenic materials. Actually, two stage floors are used. One is the permanent floor consisting of thick unpainted boards about ten inches wide, nailed down at right angles to the front of the stage; the other is the *shosabutai* (dance stage) which is used both for pieces which are purely dance and also for those which, although they are not pure dance, contain

[1] The reader who has examined the photographs of stage settings may doubt this statement. But he should bear in mind that most of these photographs were taken in the 'flat' lighting of the Kabuki stage. Consequently, there is not much feeling of plasticity in the actors' figures, while at the same time the flat, painted backgrounds and cut-out pieces appear almost three-dimensional. As a result, both actors and settings seem to have a common dimensionality. In actuality, this is not so, for setting and actor are clearly opposed.

A clear sense of spatial and dimensional relationships in the theatre is apparently exceedingly difficult to obtain in photographs, for even in the plastic lighting of the representational theatre, few photographers seem able to capture these qualities. It is doubtless for this reason that sketches and drawings give us a stronger sense of the 'feel' of the *mise en scène* than do photographs.

considerable dance movement. The *shosabutai*, which appeared at the end of the seventeenth century, consists of platforms about five inches high made of highly polished Japanese cypress (the same wood that is used for the Nō stage) which are laid down on the permanent stage floor and on the *hanamichi*, completely covering both areas.

Neither of these floors ever loses its identity as a literal floor on which the actor performs, even when a floor cloth (*jigazuri*) is used. The scenic elements are 'set upon' the stage floor and are opposed to it; the relation is the same as that which exists between the stage floor and the body of the actor. The Kabuki floor cloth differs in function from the floor cloth of the Western theatre, which is used primarily to deaden the sound of the actor's shoes on the stage floor and to provide him with a surer footing than that possible on bare boards. In a very literal sense, the Western floor cloth aids in negating the impact between the actor's body and the stage floor. The Kabuki floor cloth, on the contrary, is only a scenic indication, and since it is made of thin material and lies loosely on the floor, the opposition between the actor's body and the stage floor is not lost by its use. The floor cloths, as we have mentioned before, are white, blue, and gray; the white is used to indicate snow, the blue to indicate water, and the gray to indicate earth. They do not represent these qualities in any literal sense. When the white floor cloth is used it serves only to indicate the presence of snow; it is not bunched up to represent drifts nor is it painted so that it gleams like snow. 'Snow-quality' is only lightly sketched in a preliminary fashion by the floor cloth, but it is actually conveyed theatrically by the actor's movement as he walks upon it. The white floor cloth does not, therefore, disguise the stage floor either for the actor or for the audience; the stage floor exists beneath the floor cloth.

On some occasions the whole of the stage area as well as the *hanamichi* is covered with a floor cloth, but, more frequently, only a part of these areas is covered and the uncovered area is either the floor of the permanent stage or that of the dance stage. A Kabuki pool is created by laying blue cloth on the stage floor, the rest of the stage being undisguised boards. Similarly, an interior is indicated by putting down the rice-straw mats which cover the floors of Japanese homes, the area thus covered becoming an interior while the uncovered boards of the stage are conceived to be the ground outside. In a setting showing simultaneously a snowy exterior and an area within a garden separated from the rest of the setting by a gate (such as the

'Okazaki' scene of *Through the Iga Pass*), the white floor cloth is used to define the area outside the garden. The area within the garden, although the garden is also an exterior, is not covered with a white floor cloth nor a gray one, but is the bare boards of the stage. In this circumstance it is not assumed by the audience that the snow has been removed from the garden or that the garden is roofed. The two areas are defined for theatrical, not realistic, reasons. Since Kabuki usage has established the convention that an area whose quality is not indicated by a floor cloth is earth, the gray floor cloth is not often used.

No effort is made to attach the floor cloth or the straw matting to the stage floor, either in the literal sense, by nailing or tacking it down, or in the aesthetic sense of making it appear to be realistically related to the stage floor. The Kabuki 'pool,' for example, is not conceived to have literal depth; it simply lies loosely on the surface of the stage floor. It can, however, be made to have theatrical depth in a scene in which a character drowns: A stage assistant lifts the upstage edge of the cloth and the actor disappears beneath the cloth and exits through a trap-door. Cut-out pieces, such as those indicating stone lanterns, trees (either flat or round), bushes and grasses, are set upon the stage floor, and like the floor cloth, show a similar non-representational opposition to it. A tree is not made to look as though it were realistically, or even theatrically, growing out of the stage floor; it is held up by two or three small stage braces, plainly in sight. Rocks, whether they are built in the round or are flat painted cut-outs, are not constructed in a manner to suggest that they are imbedded in the stage floor. Both the rock and the tree are indicatory elements existing not in a representational relation to the stage floor, but set upon it and opposed to it. In general, the boards of the stage floor are more often seen than not, so that the presentational quality of the Kabuki performance is reinforced by the visual reminder that the floor of the stage and of the *hanamichi* is an undisguised acting area. The Kabuki actor literally 'treads the boards' in a manner which the Western actor in modern times has forgotten.

Since the stage floor is aesthetically opposed both to the body of the actor and to the scenic elements which are set upon it, the stage floor exerts a force which is stronger than that of the scenic elements and which creates, by its antagonistic strength, a field against which the barefooted or lightly shod actor plays. The genesis of Kabuki movement and of Kabuki staging is thus the field of force exerted by the stage floor. The actor is thrust up into this field of force on the trap-lifts in the stage or in the *hanamichi*, or he disappears below the stage floor by the same means. The area below the stage and below the *hanamichi* is not thought to be localized; sometimes supernatural beings appear from below, but the regions below, in this circumstance, no more represent the netherworld than they do when a group of twenty or so musicians are similarly brought up on to the stage on a trap-lift. There is no psychological extension of the playing area below the level of the stage, as similarly there is no psychological extension of the *hanamichi* beyond the *agemaku*, the curtain which separates it from the auditorium.

Although in the settings for plays written after 1868, Kabuki scene painting shows the influence of late nineteenth-century painting in the Western theatre, the settings for the large majority of the plays now performed have resisted this influence. As the boards of the stage floor continue to exhibit the strength of a dancing floor and to refuse to be converted into a representational locale, so do the walls and backdrops of the setting. This characteristic is clearly shown in the treatment afforded the flat placed in front of the *geza*, the 'music room' on stage-right. The *geza* in many instances is not concealed, but when a flat[1] is placed in front of it, whether the flat is painted to resemble trees, a stone wall, or the side of a house, the flat is perforated with a number of rectangular openings at the level of the screened opening of the *geza* so that the men in the *geza* can see the actors and so that the music and sound effects can be clearly heard. The rear backing of an exterior is neither the plaster dome nor the carefully sewn, painted, and lighted backdrop of the representational theatre. Instead, it consists of a series of flats nailed together side by side, the cracks between them obvious, the lower part of the 'backdrop' usually painted with a distant scene, the two flats on stage-right and stage-left angled in to mask the backstage area from the eyes of the audience. This backing does not extend into the wings nor does it extend upward out of sight. At the top it is cut off sharply with a black cloth border (*ichimonji*), ten or twelve feet above the stage floor. The material is hung straight, not in folds. The cloth border is not used to create a literal sense of nothingness, as black velour draperies are sometimes used in the Western theatre; it is

---

[1] The Japanese flat, like the Western one, has a wooden framework, which, however, is covered not with cotton material but with sheets of newsprint, one pasted on top of another, to a thickness of between an eighth and a quarter of an inch.

frankly a conventional, nonillusionistic means of defining the upward limit of the setting. Black is used frequently on flats painted with trees; the background is entirely black, not as an indication of night, but as an indication of nothingness beyond the trees. The difference between the nothingness of Western 'space' staging and Kabuki scene painting is that the Western audience accepts generally the 'nothingness' of blackness if it cannot see the means by which it is produced, that is, if it is not aware that the 'nothingness' is produced by black curtains on which no light is permitted to fall. But the Kabuki audience accepts blackness, whether in paint or cloth, both clearly visible, as the indication of 'nothingness.' The upward limits of the Kabuki setting are clearly and sharply marked. A painted tree stops arbitrarily some twelve feet above the stage, its upper branches existing neither in paint nor in the imagination of the audience. The *tsurieda* (the floral decorations indicating cherry or plum blossoms, or, less frequently, pine branches) which are hung above the stage directly behind the Western proscenium, are not conceived of as representing the lower branches of invisible trees, but as frankly theatrical decorations sharply defining the upper limit of the stage setting.

These characteristics of Kabuki scene decoration do not arise out of ineptness, caprice, or the mysteriousness of Eastern ways, but out of a serious and defensible view of the function of the theatre. The Kabuki stage is utilitarian. Scenic elements are valuable, but they cannot be allowed to interfere with the smooth functioning of the performance. For this reason the flat in front of the *geza* is pierced with holes. Scenic elements indicate place, but they do not represent it literally. Therefore there is no need to erect a *kuppel-horizont* or plaster cyclorama at the rear of the stage or even to conceal the cracks between flats. An agreeably painted background adds to the visual delight of the play (as does a blue cloth indicating water), but it is not, as any member of the audience can plainly see, a means of convincing him that he is witnessing actuality. The Kabuki performance is concentrated on the stage and on the *hanamichi*; therefore any extension of the sky or the tree upward or into the wings would expand the psychological area of the performance beyond the limits within which it actually exists. The performance evolves from the actor. An extension of the performance beyond the observable limits of the stage would detract from the force of the actor; he would have to become oriented in these directions and such a division of his energies would weaken his impact upon the audience. The setting, by its concentration on the stage and its indifference to investing, even by implication, the unseen parts of the stage with theatrical significance, reinforces only the area with which the actor is aesthetically concerned. In this way, the setting, like the sound effects and music of the Kabuki, projects the performance in the direction of the audience.

The Kabuki exterior backing, like the stage floor, opposes the body of the actor in much the same way that the backdrop of the vaudeville theatre opposed the body of the actor who was playing 'in one.' The three-dimensionality of the actor is emphasized by his being placed against a flat surface which is painted in a suggestive rather than a literal manner. The techniques employed in the painting of most Kabuki backings are in general those used in the *ukiyoe* prints which made their appearance in the Genroku period (1688–1704). In these and in Kabuki scene painting the artist is concerned primarily with design rather than naturalism. There are no shadows (a general characteristic of Oriental painting) and therefore shapes are defined by drawn contour and not by the chiaroscuro of Western painting. The effect of the actor against this kind of background differs from that of the Western actor against the sky cyclorama. Both in Kabuki and in the Western theatre the body of the actor is defined against the background, but in the Western theatre, by careful lighting and painting, the actual surface of the cyclorama is made to appear nonexistent; an illusion of infinity is created so that the 'sky' becomes as visually three-dimensional as the body of the actor. With the Kabuki background the actual painted surface is always apparent. Although the painting indicates depth, it does not represent it illusionistically. And so although the theatrical advantage is gained of indicating a vista behind the actor, the opposition between the actor's body and the background is not lost by the background being made illusionistically three-dimensional. The aesthetic purpose of the Kabuki painted background is not to penetrate the space behind the actor illusionistically, but to suggest such a penetration theatrically in two dimensions, thus creating a visual force which will emphasize the plasticity of the actor.

About the middle of the eighteenth century, when the stage proper had already become the area in which interiors were set, painted flats were placed upstage of the sliding doors which marked the rear of the room, so that when these sliding doors were opened a vista (*tōmi*) would be revealed. The circumstances under which the doors were opened to reveal the distant view were probably much the same as those under which this vista is revealed today. This nonrepresentational use of the painted scene is significant of the general relation between the actor and the setting. The scene of the most important act of *Strife at Uji* is the war camp of Moritsuna; the setting consists of a large platform almost three feet high indicating an interior, while the rest of the stage is exterior. When the act begins, the six sliding doors at the rear of the platform are closed, but as the act progresses they are opened for entrances and exits, and it can be seen that the backing behind the doors consists of flats painted white. During the greater part of the act, no more than three characters use the platform at any given time, but toward the end of the act it is necessary that the commander-in-chief, Hōjō Tokimasa, and his six retainers be seated on the platform while Moritsuna and the three women of the play take positions on the stage floor in front of the platform. Although the area on the platform in which Hōjō Tokimasa and his retinue is seated is some nine by fifteen feet, the crowding together of six actors in this space, together with the presence of the four actors downstage of the platform, creates, to the Japanese theatrical sense, a confusing and intolerable concentration of actors. The problem is solved in this way: When Hōjō Tokimasa enters with his retainers, four of the sliding doors at the rear of the platform are removed by the stage hands and there is revealed not the white wall previously seen upstage of the doors but painted flats showing a pine tree, an expanse of water, and distant mountains. The effect is visually striking and would have been equally so if it had been used earlier. But the painted landscape is introduced at this point in the action so that, both by opposing the bodies of the actors and by suggesting nonillusionistic depth, it will create a greater sense of space than if the actors were seen against the sliding doors. The Kabuki conception of the relation of the actor to stage space will be discussed later; but it should be observed that the Kabuki actor requires, and is given, considerably more actual and aesthetic space in which to perform than is allowed the actor in the representational theatre. The use of the painted scene behind the actors in the present case illustrates the utilitarian and purely theatrical way in which the suggestion of nonillusionistic space is created around the actors' bodies. An exactly similar use of the painted scene occurs in the 'Kumagai's Camp' scene of *The Battle of Ichinotani* in which, toward the end of the play, it is necessary that eight actors appear on a similar platform simultaneously; the upstage sliding doors are removed and a painted scene appears in place of the white flats used previously in this position. In *The Famous Tree at Sendai* and in *The Loyal Forty-seven Rōnin*, the upstage sliding doors are similarly removed, when a large number of characters appear on the stage, to reveal interiors painted in perspective.

The painted scene, then, is a theatrical indication of depth, not an illusionistic representation of it. In general, the effect aesthetically is that space is not illusionistically extended behind the actor but that the theatrical indication of space is drawn toward, and into, the playing area. This principle is illustrated in a somewhat atypical but nevertheless significant fashion in a scene from Chikamatsu Monzaemon's *Yūgiri and Izaemon*. Izaemon has come to see his courtesan-love Yūgiri. Since Yūgiri, unfortunately, is engaged with a patron of the house, Izaemon must wait until the patron has left. Izaemon tries unsuccessfully to while away the time, hesitates between going and staying, and finally, feeling that he has been too much put upon, decides in anger to go to the room where Yūgiri is entertaining. Izaemon moves to the rear of the stage and stands before two sliding doors. He opens them, and another pair of sliding doors, reduced in size by perspective, is revealed only a few inches upstage of the first pair. Izaemon continues to open sliding doors, each pair smaller than the previous one, each pair set directly upstage of the other, until he has at last opened five sets of doors. The visual effect is as though an actor had moved into a Serlian perspective setting; Izaemon does not become smaller, but the doors do. This effect is in no way disturbing aesthetically to the audience, for the use of space on the stage is governed by the theatrical advantage to which it can be put and not by the conception that its dimensions must correspond to those of actuality. In this scene actual space is contracted, and concurrently theatrical space is expanded, as it was in the Western perspective setting. But the purpose of the early perspective setting was to create an illusion of actual space behind the actor, and this illusion could not be maintained if the actor were to move into the area of the perspective setting. The area in which the actor moved was therefore carefully separated from that of the setting. But since, as we have seen, perspective is not used in the Kabuki to create illusion, the disproportion between Izaemon's body against the series of smaller and smaller doors does not create an aesthetic dichotomy. The doors serve the purpose of indicating a progression in theatrical perspective, not a progression in actual space. The staging of this scene serves as a further illustration of the unwillingness, in the aesthetic of the Kabuki, to extend illusionistic space beyond the playing area of the actor; on the contrary, when the idea of an extension of space is to be conveyed to the audience, it is created by a kind of diagrammatic perspective, such as the doors which Izaemon opens, and this area is drawn into the same plane as that in which the actor moves. A somewhat more subtle use of this same device occurs in the second act of *The Battle of Ichinotani*. The scene is a seashore; the background is painted with sky at the top and waves at the bottom, and in front of it is a low flat, a *nami-ita* ('wave-board') on which are painted stylized waves. One of the heroes of the play, Atsumori, first appears on his horse, which is swimming out at sea. This effect is created by the actor moving in the area between the backdrop and the 'wave-board.' However, in order to state in theatrical terms that Atsumori is a considerable distance from the shore, both the horse and Atsumori are reduced in size. This feat is accomplished by using a child actor and, instead of the conventional two-man Kabuki horse, a proportionately small figure of a horse worn about the child actor's waist. The child-actor-Atsumori moves across the stage and disappears into the wings, and presently the man-actor-Atsumori, costumed in the exact manner of the child actor, appears from the downstage wings and takes a position in the downstage area. It might be thought that a child actor and a horse reduced in size are used so that the mounted Atsumori appears in perspective conformity with the 'wave-board' and the backdrop, but this is not so. In the case of Izaemon's opening of the perspective doors, there can be no doubt in the mind of the audience, because of the temporal sequence of the door-opening, that Izaemon is moving, in theatrical terms, farther and farther from the audience. In the case of Atsumori, who must be conceived by the audience as first appearing far out at sea and not merely splashing about in the breakers near the shore, it is necessary to reduce actor and horse in size as a diagrammatic indication of their distance from the shore. In other words, the figure of Atsumori and his horse are reduced in size by the same principle that reduces the size of the doors which Izaemon opens. In both instances perspective is used not to create illusionary depth but to indicate purely theatrical distances.

The painted scenic backgrounds for exteriors are of two general types: those which are panoramic and without a central vanishing point, and those which have either a single vanishing point or a central point of predominant interest. In the first category are the backgrounds showing the sea, an unaccented expanse of landscape, or a river and its bank on which there is a row of generally undifferentiated houses. The second type consists of views of countryside in which there is a central object, such as Mount Fuji; a street with houses on either side of it; or the walled compound of an estate culminating in a single vanishing point and employing simple perspective. Interior backgrounds are almost inevitably a single large room painted in simple perspective. In all painted backgrounds in which a vanishing point or an object of greatest interest is used, the vanishing point or the important object is placed on a line at exactly the center of the stage, and, in most instances, this point is placed at about the level of the actors' heads.

Consequently, there are no complicated axes in the scene painting. The scene is always painted as though it were parallel to the front of the stage and the central vanishing point is constructed on a line which is at a right angle to the front of the stage. Even in this non-representational style of scene painting there is no introduction of oblique or multiple vanishing points which would set up lines of force suggesting penetration into the space of the wings of the stage or upwards above the proscenium, such as those which appeared in Baroque scene painting. Instead, the composition of the painting simply reinforces the line of the front of the stage, or it sets up a single axis at a right angle to the front of the stage, thereby creating a line of force through the auditorium parallel to the *hanamichi*. In both cases, the scene painting holds the attention of the audience strongly to the stage.

In the painted backgrounds there is no concern with establishing a strong middle ground. The foreground of an exterior setting in which the actor moves is frequently decorated with a half-round or flat painted tree or rock, or with three-dimensional grasses or bushes which are placed directly in front of the backdrop. The interior painted background is placed directly behind an opening in the setting. Strictly speaking, the painted background itself may have a middle ground in the form of a river with mountains behind it, or a clump of trees set against a distant forest, or in the gradually diminishing size of the walls of a room. But judged in relation to the actor's body and the scenic objects placed before the background, the actor occupies the foreground and the painting creates a background with no strong theatrical sense of a middle ground existing between the two.

136

After the middle of the eighteenth century the stage proper of the Kabuki theatre became the area in which interiors were indicated, and more frequently than not a platform was placed on the stage proper so that it was differentiated by height from the forestage. The use of a platform was brought about by several considerations. Platforms were occasionally introduced onto the stage of the Nō theatre to show a spatially differentiated area. The use of the platform was probably also suggested by the relation between exterior and interior in Japanese architecture. The usual Japanese home is raised not more than a few feet above the ground, and its outer 'wall' consists of a series of sliding doors which during most of the year are kept open. Therefore the spatial relation between the platform on the stage proper, indicating an interior, and the forestage, which in juxtaposition to the platform becomes exterior, is that which exists outside the theatre. Since in an interior Japanese usually sit on the floor, the actors seated on the stage proper, previous to the use of a platform, could not be very well seen. The height gained by the use of a platform in this area was therefore a means of flattening out the stage picture by visually projecting the actor seated on the stage proper toward the stronger playing area of the forestage. A similar technique of bringing figures separated in distance into a closer plane by placing one figure above another without perspective diminution in size appears in Japanese graphic art.

Except when the piece is predominantly dance, or when the whole set is a single room, Kabuki stage decoration at present normally uses platforms both in interior and exterior settings. The platforms are used scenically and thus differ in function from those on which the musicians sit. They are invariably placed parallel to the front of the stage, never at an oblique angle to it, and they are always placed well upstage, at a distance of some eight or ten feet from the footlights. Because of the simple axes of the Kabuki stage—those created by the painted backgrounds and by the arrangements of the platforms —the basic spatial patterns of the stage settings are relatively few, and although the surfaces of the settings are variously, and at times, even gaudily, decorated, the spatial arrangement of the architectural and scenic elements has been reduced to formula and to formality.

The 'stock' set of the Kabuki is the Kabuki adaptation of the Nō stage, which is used for pieces which, although they have been translated into the idiom of the Kabuki, show strongly the influences of their origin. Pieces such as *The Subscription List, Ibaraki the Demon,*

A Substitute for Meditation, and *The Tea Box* are invariably performed with this setting. It corresponds to the box set of the Western theatre, a straight wall at the rear parallel to the front of the stage, the side walls angled in sharply following the line of the inner proscenium. There are two entrances. In the upstage-left wall is the 'hurry'-door, a sliding door about three feet high, used principally for the entrances and exits of the stage assistants, but also for unobtrusive exits and entrances by an actor. In the stage-right wall is the principal entrance, an opening approximately seven feet high and four feet wide, hung with a curtain of vertical bands of purple, yellow, red, green, and white. For an entrance, the curtain is raised from the bottom and lifted up offstage by bamboo poles attached to the lower corners of it. The whole surface of the set is painted to suggest the wooden wall at the rear of the Nō stage, and on the rear wall is the Kabuki exaggeration of the stylized pine tree (*matsubame*) of the Nō, painted in greens and browns. The right and left walls are painted with a few stalks of bamboo, this design deriving from the left wall of the Nō theatre. The musician's platform, covered with red cloth, is placed, as we have seen, directly in front of the rear wall. This is the most formal of Kabuki settings. It is not only a stock set; it also gives no indication of place or time whatsoever. During a performance the idea of the place and time of the play is conveyed by the actor and by the musicians. The properties and the scenic elements introduced into this setting are extremely few. In *The Subscription List* three small stands with gifts placed on them are brought in and later two sake bottles and a sake cup. In *Ibaraki the Demon* a small gate is used and a box containing the arm of a demon. In *A Substitute for Meditation* a small stand with a tray of food is brought in, and in *The Tea Box* the only property is the tea box about which the action of the play revolves.

The exterior setting has two possible spatial arrangements. In the first, one or more scenic elements—rocks, grasses, trees—are placed just downstage of the painted background; in the second, platforms extending the width of the stage are placed in front of the background, parallel to it. The flat stage floor is used primarily in pieces which are pure dance or largely dance, and the decoration just in front of the background may consist, as it does in the dance *The Wisteria Girl*, of a single large tree placed up center, or, as in the *michiyuki* scene of *The Loyal Forty-seven Rōnin*, of a ground row and several cut-out trees. When the upstage platform is used, its downstage surface is painted, so that it becomes a hill, a pathway, an eminence, and so forth. In *Just a Moment* the upstage platform is a walled embankment upon which the opponents to the hero are seated, with steps at stage center connecting the two areas. Throughout most of *Izayoi and Seishin* an upstage platform is used as a river bank, the river existing downstage of it in the substance of a blue cloth, and a ramp at stage-right leads up to the platform. In what seems to be the great majority of exterior settings, the upstage platform, with one or two willow trees placed upon it, is used as a river bank. This practice may arise from the fact that in former times most Japanese roads and pathways ran along rivers, but the use of this setting is so frequent that one suspects there must be more deep-seated reasons for the Japanese predilection for it.

In exteriors, the whole setting may be placed behind the inner proscenium, the inner proscenium left undecorated. If the inner proscenium is decorated, the decoration consists of two large flats, one placed against the onstage surface of the *geza*, the other on the opposite face of the inner proscenium. Whether these two surfaces are covered with flats depends principally upon whether the formal, curtained, down-left entrance to the stage is to be used. If it is to be used, the downstage flats are dispensed with, for the one on stage-left would obstruct the use of this entrance.

The simultaneous setting showing both interior and exterior has four standard patterns of arrangement. If the platforms are used to indicate the raised floor of only a part of a rather large house, the platforms are placed in the area extending from the left side of the stage to a point about one-half the distance between stage-center and the right wing. In this arrangement the downstage area in front of the platform and the area to stage-right of it become exterior; a gate is usually placed on a line with the stage-right edge of the platform, downstage of it, and the character coming to the house makes his entrance on the *hanamichi*, moves to the stage, and then enters into the area in front of the house through the gate. Since the interior setting is principally on stage-left, the area outside the gate is opened up so that the actor approaching the gate can play in this area. Therefore in this arrangement the spatial relation between the *hanamichi*, the forestage, and the platform is the same as that which existed when these three elements were first used. The platform is usually divided into two rooms, the one at stage-center being the more important acting area and having an upstage entrance to it. The room on stage-left is distinguished by being surrounded with *shōji*, sliding doors covered with translucent paper, which are placed on its front edge and also on the line between the two rooms, so that entrances can also be made from the stage-left room into the center room. When the secondary interior is to be used briefly as a playing area, the *shōji* are opened by a stage assistant and closed at the conclusion of the scene. In 'Kumagai's Camp' this room is used to display for a few moments the battle dress of Atsumori to his mother; in 'Moritsuna's Camp' the *shōji* are opened so that the boy Kōshirō can be seen watching the action taking place in the downstage area.

One or more steps, depending upon the height of the platform used, placed at stage center, are the means by which the actor moves between the upstage platform and the downstage area. Trees, rocks, pools, and so forth, are placed in the downstage area in front of the platform only when they are necessary to the action of the play but never for sheerly decorative purposes. This practice repeats the Kabuki pattern of placing the actor against the setting, not in it. In 'Anniversary Celebration,' three trees, a pine, a plum, and a cherry, represent the triplet sons of Shiradayu and figure largely in the action; they are placed within a bamboo-fenced enclosure directly in front of the secondary room on stage left. In 'Moritsuna's Camp' a maple tree is used on stage-left in front of the secondary room so that an arrow can be shot from the *hanamichi* to lodge in the tree. (This is a stage effect, not a display of skill in archery.) The area to stage-right of the platform, also exterior, is likely to be decorated simply for the sake of decoration. This area usually has a painted background, with trees and bushes, either cut-out or three-dimensional, set in front of it in the same manner as in the usual exterior setting. The edge of a roof usually defines the top of the interior platform, but a complete roof is seldom shown in this arrangement. A black cloth border is used to define the upward limit of the set.

When the whole of a small building, usually having but one room, is depicted, a large platform is placed directly at stage-center, the area in front of it and to either side of it being conceived as exterior. The small building does not occupy the area at stage-right and therefore does not interfere with the movement of the actor to and from the *hanamichi*. In *Mitsukuni and the Sorceress* the building is a small temple with high walls on either side of it; in *The Arrow Maker* it is the workshop and home of the arrow-making Soga brother, Gorō, and is set against an exterior backing.

A third arrangement of simultaneous exterior and interior setting is that in which platforms are placed on either side of the stage, each showing a room or a part of a house, the exterior area existing in front of them and between them. This arrangement is used in the 'mountain' scene of *Mount Imose* in which the area between the two houses is a river, part of which is painted on a backdrop, its foreground indicated by blue cloth, painted with stylized waves, and by three-dimensional rocks. Yet another arrangement is that in which platforms are placed across the whole width of the stage, as they are in the exterior 'embankment' settings, the platforms being the area of an interior, the downstage area below them an exterior. This setting is used when it is necessary to show three rooms in the same dwelling, either simultaneously or one after another. In a scene of *Twenty-four Dutiful Sons* the hero Katsuyori is seen in the center room, his lover, Yaegaki-hime, is in the stage-left room, while the 'other woman,' Nureginu, is in the stage-right room. The stage-center room is used as the principal acting area and the rooms to the right and left of it are surrounded with *shōji*, which, as in the case of the secondary room of the arrangement previously described, are opened to show the interiors when they figure in the action and closed when they do not. In this scene Katsuyori appears in the center room, which is not enclosed with *shōji*. Presently the *shōji* are opened by stagehands, and Nureginu is revealed seated in the stage-right room. When her part of the action is ended, the *shōji* are closed, and shortly afterwards, the *shōji* on stage-left are opened to show Yaegaki-hime at her prayers. When the three characters become involved with each other as the scene progresses, the *shōji* are removed from both of the side rooms, and the whole platform becomes a continuous area. Here again, steps are placed at the center of the stage connecting the platform with the downstage exterior plane. On rare occasions, the stage-left area may be an exterior and the stage-right area an interior, as in one act of *Mirror Mountain*, but this arrangement is used when the action requires that a character entering upon the *hanamichi* move directly into the house without prolonged activity outside its entrance. In this circumstance, the stage-left exterior area is purely decorative and is not played in.

In all the simultaneous interior-exterior settings the downstage area in front of the platforms is conventionally conceived to be exterior, whether or not there are scenic evidences of its being so, and the center room is always the strongest acting area. However, when two interiors are placed on opposite sides of the stage, they are almost equally balanced in strength.

The standard arrangement of an interior showing a single room and occupying the entire stage is like that of the uncomplicated Western box set and follows the lines of the formal Nō setting. The rear wall consists of some eight or more *fusuma*, sliding doors with a wooden interior framework, their surfaces covered with opaque decorative paper. Above the *fusuma* is a painted surface indicating the upper part of the wall above the doorway. The stage-right and -left walls of this setting are very sharply angled in toward stage-center. Two *fusuma* are in each of the side walls and can be opened so that entrances can be made from both sides of the stage. The 'returns,' those downstage flats of the interior setting which continue offstage parallel to the front of the stage in the Western box set, also consist, respectively, of two *fusuma* and the heading above them; these are used as supplementary entrances. The floor in this setting is not raised on platforms. The upstage part of it is covered with the straw matting used in Japanese interiors, the downstage area is the bare boards of the stage. It is this type of setting which is used in the third and fourth acts of *The Loyal Forty-seven Rōnin*. Platforms are used in interior settings both to indicate separate rooms and, theatrically and practically, to flatten out the stage picture so that characters seated upstage, in the presence of a large number of characters, can be better seen. In *The Courier of Hell* Chūbei must hide himself in another room and yet be seen by the audience while his rival attempts to win the attention of the courtesan Umegawa whom Chūbei loves. The room in which Chūbei hides is a platform at stage-left, in the position of the secondary room, and, like the secondary room, it has walls of *shōji* which are pulled aside to show Chūbei listening within. The room is a high platform, and on the stage-right side of it are five steps down which Chūbei moves when he quits the room. Usually, however, when platforms are used within an interior setting, they are placed upstage. In *The Soga Confrontation* a high platform extends across the width of the stage; at the beginning of the act, eight of the principal characters of the play are seated in this area, and the subordinate characters are in the downstage area. Soon these positions are reversed; the important characters move to the downstage area, the others seat themselves on the upstage platform during the rest of the play. This arrangement is as common in interior settings as it is in the exterior 'embankment' setting. The side walls of the interior settings are invariably a flat surface, set at the angle of the line of the inner proscenium. This angle is somewhat more acute than that of the right and left walls of the Western box set; but unlike the walls of the box set, the Kabuki wall is never broken up by a jog or by a succession of jogs. The line thus created is along that of the perspective painting of the background, and the establishment of this line in the side walls reinforces the simple perspective of the painted background.

The use of platforms provides for multiple areas of interest. Upstage and downstage are clearly differentiated into river bank and river, a hill and the area below it, two parts of a single room; or there may be two or three rooms parallel to the front of the stage with an exterior area to the front and side of them. Thus in its almost constant use of differentiated areas and levels, the settings, like the *hanamichi* in its relation to the stage, create a sense of 'things happening' at various distances and levels from the audience and induce considerable physical movement on the part of the audience. The platforms are, it must be remembered, always some eight or ten feet upstage. In this position they allow the upstage actor to be easily seen, and they diminish the effects of natural perspective by visually projecting the actor at the rear of the stage into the downstage plane. Aesthetically, the platforms reinforce the strong line of the downstage playing area. The Kabuki unwillingness to penetrate space in the painting of backgrounds is also apparent in the use of the platforms.

But the platforms have another equally strong ideological force: They are used to show degrees of social differentiation, a preoccupation which runs through Japanese civilization. The West also uses a scale from high to low to show social relationships. God, kings, certain amusements are 'high'; the Devil, the peasant, other amusements are 'low.' But in Japan the hierarchical sense is developed to a much more intense degree and pervades every aspect of daily Japanese life. The Western tradition of kneeling and bowing before a superior, inherited from feudal times, exists today only in attenuated form, but the Japanese tradition, inherited from similar times, remains the basis of a complicated choreography which informs the social ballet. The Japanese bow is of infinite variety, running the gamut from a slight inclination of the head to kneeling prostration on the floor, each degree of obeisance clearly defined. In Japan one does not 'give' something to another, he 'raises' it to the recipient. The 'god-shelf,' the small Shintō shrine of the Japanese home, is placed high on the wall above the heads of the occupants of the house. The word used during the Edo period for the leading actor who played the role of the hero was *tachiyaku*, the 'standing' actor, because, being more important, he stood when others knelt.

The platforms introduced to the stage in the eighteenth century soon came to be used to show a proper concern for the social hierarchy. At last they were constructed in three heights, a convention which is still retained. The *tsuneashi* ('ordinary legs'), one foot three inches high, is used for the homes of ordinary citizens; the *chūdaka* ('medium height'), two feet one inch high, is used for the homes of samurai; the *taka-ashi* ('high legs'), two feet nine inches high, is used for palaces and temples. Therefore, in interior settings, the platforms may be used, in addition to the uses described above, to show degrees of social differentiation.

A superior social position may be conveyed to the audience by the actor's sitting on the high stools called *aibiki*. In the suicide scene of the fourth act of *The Loyal Forty-seven Rōnin*, the setting is a single room with an unraised floor. The two government officials who come to see that the suicide is carried out as ordered are easily differentiated from the other characters on the stage, all of whom are kneeling, by being seated on *aibiki*. On other occasions, a small dais may be used, as it is on stage-left in *The Soga Confrontation*, as a seat for the person of highest rank in the scene. However, in most scenes in which a person of high rank is to appear for an extended period of time in an upstage area, platforms are placed in this area.

The relation of the strength of the downstage area to the raised upstage area is rather curious. In general, all important action in the Kabuki takes place downstage, and no matter how high the rank of the person seated in the upstage raised area, the downstage area never loses its proportionally greater strength. In the 'Hamamatsu-ya' scene of *Benten the Thief* an official (he is really an impostor) seats himself in stern judgment on the upstage platform while the thief Benten Kozō is seated below him in what is, theatrically, the same room. Benten Kozō is disguised as a woman, and as the scene progresses he is gradually forced by the official to reveal his true identity. This he does with a great show of bravado, flinging off his woman's clothes and revealing the tattooed body of a professional thief. But although this revelation is brought about by the official who is seated in the raised, upstage, socially superior position, there is no

144

moment in the development of the scene when that area is equal in strength to the downstage area. Near the end of 'The Village School' Midai-sama makes her appearance; she is the nominal head of the house to which every other character on the stage owes his loyalty, and she takes her position, with her son Kanshūsai, on the upstage platform, while the other characters remain downstage of her. These are Genzō and Matsuōmaru and their wives. Before this point in the play, Matsuōmaru and his wife sacrificed the life of their only son to save the life of Kanshūsai, and Genzō was forced to be the murderer of their child; the greater part of this action took place in the downstage area, and the conclusion of the action is also confined to this area. Thus although Midai-sama and Kanshūsai are in the upstage area, the downstage one is the stronger. Under certain circumstances the downstage plane of the representational theatre may also exhibit much greater strength than the upstage area, but only, and this is the important point, when it is invested with this significance by the grouping and positions of the actors. To a certain degree the Kabuki actors similarly strengthen the downstage plane, but the area, by custom, tradition, and the whole history of the Kabuki theatre possesses an innate strength of its own.

To the Westerner the interior setting seems at first sight to show comparatively greater realism than the exterior. It is frequently raised above the stage floor as the Japanese house is raised above the ground. The floor of the interior is covered with straw matting. The upstage wall consists usually of sliding doors or has a single entrance in which may be hung a *noren*, a curtain covering the upper part of the doorway. In general, these rooms seem to exhibit the characteristic qualities of a Japanese interior. However, on closer examination it is found that these interiors are less realistic and more theatrical than they first appear. The strips of straw matting on the floor, about three feet wide, are laid side by side parallel to the footlights; they are not arranged in the conventional six foot by three foot pattern of rectangles which is used in the Japanese home. The sliding doors are smaller in height and width than those in the Japanese house so that the actor will look larger against them. A chest of drawers in a recess in the upstage wall, or a cabinet with sliding doors, is painted on the wall if it is sheerly decorative but is built in three dimensions if it has to be opened and closed during the action of the play. The wooden supports of the interior wall are invariably painted, not built in three dimensions. The *shōji*, the exterior paper-covered sliding doors of a house, are in real life placed so that the wooden ribs of the framework face the interior of the house and the paper-covered surfaces face the exterior. Seen from outside, the *shōji* thus present an uninteresting flat, white surface. In the Kabuki the placing of the *shōji* is reversed; the more interesting design of rectangles of white paper and dark wood is seen from the exterior, that is, from the audience. *Shōji* would never be placed thus in a Japanese home, but here as elsewhere the Kabuki is less concerned with imitating actuality than with pleasing the eye.

The Japanese domestic interior is in itself austere, uncluttered with furniture, having almost no curved lines, and in the theatre the interior is further simplified and theatricalized so that the actor plays against the interior setting rather than in it to the same degree that he plays against the exterior setting. The Kabuki actor cannot lose himself visually in a profusion of chairs and sofas, in window draperies and cushions, in a welter of properties, in angled walls, or, in brief, in the 'soft' environment that is frequently set up about the actor in the representational theatre. Instead he plays against the flat upstage wall which is always parallel to the front of the stage. He sits on the floor, sometimes on a flat rectangular cushion. There is no 'furniture' not required for the business of the play, and the most elaborate 'furniture' to appear on the stage is a low table and perhaps an arm rest or a low screen. Properties come and go as needed in the hands of the stage assistants. The interior is purely functional and offers a 'hard' environment which emphasizes the plasticity of the actor. Here as elsewhere in the Kabuki, the spectator is constantly aware of the strong theatricality of the performance projecting itself through the visual surface created by scenic indications of place.

Although the Kabuki setting is as functional as the constructivist setting, it does not convey the impression of cold angularity. On the contrary, its interior surfaces are decorated with painting on the upstage sliding doors, or the doors may be covered with glittering gold and silver. In the second scene of the third act of *The Loyal Forty-seven Rōnin* the sliding doors are covered with gilt, and on this surface are painted stylized branches of pine trees in rich greens and browns. In one of the settings for *The Famous Tree at Sendai* the sliding doors behind the central platform are gilded and painted with a bamboo design in brilliant greens, while on the rear walls on either side of the center platform are painted seascape murals in blues, browns, and greens. Even when a humble dwelling is shown and the scene painter must be less lavish in his use of colors, he still manages to create, by the careful use of low toned hues, the effect of agreeable color harmonies. In 'The Village School' the home of Genzō, who is presumably not very well off, has soft gray walls, a pastel blue curtain hung over the upstage entrance, and a lattice-work of unpainted wood on the stage-right side of the room; the effect is that of quiet, pleasant color. Even when it is necessary to convey the idea of a dilapidated house or temple, the scene painter does not produce literally the cracks in the plaster, the smoke-discolored walls, and the torn paper of the sliding doors; he shows instead the effects of weathering and creates the beauty that arises when colors are softened by age. In short, the scene painter is less concerned with creating a literal sense of actuality than he is with providing for the actor a rich, lavish, colorful background having that quality which the Japanese call *karei* —magnificence, splendor, brilliance. In exterior settings he paints clouds of cherry blossoms against the deep green of pine trees, the scarlet of maple leaves against green fields, snow against gray skies and the sharp black lines of trees. If the division were not clearly drawn between the actor and the setting, the actor would disappear in all this color, as the actors in *The Girl of the Golden West* were probably diminished into relative insignificance before Belasco's elaborate sunset. But since the difference between the plasticity of the actor and the comparative flatness of the setting is firmly established, the brilliantly costumed actor can exist simultaneously with an equally brilliant setting, both performing their appropriate functions, with the color of the setting clearly subordinate to, though complementing, the color of the actor's costume.

There are, however, moments when the setting is allowed to perform brilliant solo passages, and the actor at these times relinquishes his superior position. The earliest Kabuki stage used little scenery, but throughout the eighteenth century scenery and machinery increased. In 1794 when a play with twenty-four different settings was played in Ōsaka, critics protested the elaborateness, complaining that they had come to see the actors, not settings. Their protests had apparently little effect; two years later the Nō roof was removed from the Kabuki stage so that the stage designer could have unobstructed room in which to rear up his increasingly vivid scenes. The war between scene designer and playwright, epitomized in the Western theatre by that between Ben Jonson and Inigo Jones, was never fought in the Kabuki because the playwright, from his first appearance, was

the unrebelling slave of the actor. The only possible conflict, therefore, was that which might arise between the actor and the scene-
designer, but the actor, his position established, was quick to seize
upon any innovation in scenic technique or machinery and adapt it to
his own purposes. To a much greater degree than the Shakespearean
actor, he had always carried considerable scenery on his back in the
form of his elaborate costuming and on his face in the form of stylized
make-up. After the first trap-lift appeared in the stage floor for the
purpose of raising set pieces up from below, the actor quickly appropriated it to his uses so that he too could make startling entrances and
exits; and in due time the actor required his own trap-lift in the
hanamichi to be used only by the actor and not by the scene designer.
But the actor-manager realized that catering to the universal love of
spectacle is commercially profitable and for that reason he permitted
the scenic designer his bravura passages.

The characteristic quality of Kabuki stage effects is rapid, startling
revelation or change. In their lavishness they are reminiscent, both in
intent and in some of their techniques, of the theatre of Inigo Jones.
The drawing off of sliding doors to reveal the interior of a secondary
room or a painted background has already been mentioned. Frequently
an upstage platformed area is hung with bamboo blinds, as in the
second act of *The Famous Tree at Sendai* or in *Thunder God*, and these
are drawn up to reveal a group of actors; or a pack of hinged flats, like
a folding screen hung from one end (*ageshōji*), is folded up for the
same purpose as in *The Arrow Maker* and *The Soga Confrontation*. A
more startling effect is that of the *furiotoshi*, which is reserved for the
sudden revelation of a colorful setting, usually an exterior. When the
Kabuki curtain is drawn there is revealed a plain, undecorated curtain
of light blue (*asagimaku*) hung without folds. A short prologue,
called *shidashi*, usually takes place in front of this curtain, involving
four to eight porters, servants, or other supernumeraries, who give
some intimation of place and time. After they leave the stage, a
crescendo of drumming comes from the *geza* and stops abruptly at a
climax. There is a moment of silence, a sharp click from the wooden
clappers, and the curtain falls shimmeringly to the stage floor and is
rapidly pulled off by the stage hands. The setting thus revealed may
be, in *Sukeroku*, what is called the 'gay quarters' of Edo, the elaborately coiffured and costumed crowd of courtesans sitting in front of
their establishment, or, in *The Girl at Dōjō Temple*, the stylized
blossoming cherry trees painted on the background and the great

green bronze temple bell hung over the downstage area. The *furiotoshi* is used frequently and always produces the effect of strong theatrical excitement; there is no contemporary device in the Western theatre, either in lighting or in the use of the front curtain, which has as sharp an impact.

A black curtain (*kuromaku*) or less frequently a gray one, hung upstage, sometimes indicates night and sometimes nothingness. Most of the action of *The Forest of Suzu* takes place before this black backdrop; at the center of the stage is a large monument with several rows of bamboo grass on either side. Shortly before the end of the act, as the two heroes are about to set off for Edo, dawn comes, theatrically and instantaneously, by the black curtain being dropped to the floor to reveal a painted landscape. Musicians are similarly quickly revealed either by the quick lowering of flats hinged to the front and side of their platform or by the removal of a cloth held up by stagehands in front of their platform, which is dropped to the floor and pulled offstage. The cloth in this circumstance is most likely to be a white and blue one with a stylized pattern of clouds on it (*kasumimaku*).

Change of setting by means of the revolving stage (*mawari-butai*) is less immediate but no less spectacular. The lights are kept up on stage while the scene change is being made, except in the performance of plays written under the influence of early twentieth century Western stage practice; in these, both the stage and the auditorium are darkened, and a row of small green lights in the front edge of the stage is turned on while the scene is being changed. This is a very dull proceeding compared to the scene changed before the eyes of the audience. At the end of the first scene of the fourth act of *The Loyal Forty-seven Rōnin*, for example, the faithful retainers of Hangan, within his house, decide to avenge their dead master, and the scene ends as they are seated on the revolving stage laying plans to accomplish their revenge. Stagehands come on from stage-right and -left, pick up the ends of the straw matting which covers both the surface of the stage proper and the revolving stage, and throw it onto the revolving stage. As the stage begins to turn counterclockwise, the conversation and the pantomime of the *rōnin* continues. The stagehands remove the side flats in front of the inner proscenium and replace them with flats painted as exterior walls. Meanwhile a steady drumming, the same kind that is used to accompany ominous passages of acting, comes from the *geza*, as the *rōnin* disappear from view, still acting their roles, and the new set, showing the exterior of the house, appears from the right. The stagehands pull out the floor cloth which has been bunched up on the revolving stage in front of the exterior setting, spread it over the stage floor, two additional flats are lashed to the right and left sides of the flats on the revolving stage, the drumming stops, and the action of the play begins. The *rōnin* who have been within the house emerge through its front gate and are met by others of their group entering from the *hanamichi*. If a scene ends in a static tableau, rather than one in which the action is continued as the stage revolves, the actors do not move out of the tableau until they have disappeared from sight. More frequently than not, when the revolving stage is used, the action of the play from one scene to another is continuous. Toward the end of *Through the Iga Pass* the stage revolves three times in quick succession to reveal 'another part of the battlefield'; the action is continuous, with the swordsman hero, Masaemon, appearing in all the scenes. In this use of the revolving stage, as in its previously described use in *The Loyal Forty-seven Rōnin*, a flow of continuous action is made possible. The visual and psychological effect of the actors on the revolving stage moving away from the strong downstage plane and then being brought back into it in another setting is much the same as that produced by the fade-out and fade-in of film technique. In this use, the revolving stage performs a function similar to that of the *hanamichi* which also, in only a slightly less literal sense, fades the actor in and out of the realm of the performance.

No more than two settings are ever placed on the revolving stage; in this respect its use differs from that of Western practice in which three or more wedged-shaped settings are sometimes placed upon it. The necessity in the Kabuki to establish a scenic line parallel to the front of the stage prevents the use of settings which are constructed in triangular form. These settings may, as in the instances described above, indicate two spatially related though disparate areas with the actor disappearing in one of them and then reappearing in another. But the technique is also employed of having the actor walk on the stage as it turns and thus move before the eyes of the audience into a new setting which is a spatial continuation of the previous one. This technique is known as *idokorogawari*, literally, 'change of one's whereabouts.' In the 'Okazaki' scene of *Through the Iga Pass*, the curtain is opened on the conventionally arranged interior-exterior setting with a center room and a secondary room on stage-left, a gate parallel to the stage-right edge of the interior platform, an exterior in front and to the stage-right side of the interior. After a spy has entered and concealed himself within the house, the stage revolves one-quarter counterclockwise to show the area at the side of the house. The hero, Masaemon, enters from the *hanamichi*, moves to the stage, is soon set upon by nine swordsmen, and in an extended scene of stylized fighting he subdues his enemies. During the fight the old man who lives in the house comes through the gate, which is now on stage-left parallel to the front of the stage, and after the hero's adversaries have fled, Masaemon and the old man begin to move to stage-left; as they do, the stage revolves clockwise. They pass through the gate into the exterior area in front of the house, and the stage stops turning when the platform of the interior is parallel to the footlights. In *Scarred Yōsaburō* as the two villains of the piece move away from the entrance to a house, the stage revolves counterclockwise as they walk on it clockwise and move into a new exterior setting. The visual effect is similar to that produced in the film when the camera follows an actor as he moves through a succession of visual planes.

The revolving stage is also used to shift the point of view of the audience for purely spectacular effect rather than to show an actual change of place. In both Chikamatsu Monzaemon's *The Girl of Hakata* and in Nakamura Gyogan's *The Eight Camps*, there are scenes in which the setting is a ship at sea; the side of the ship is parallel to the front of the stage and the stage floor is covered with a blue cloth painted with stylized waves. At the end of both these scenes, the stage is revolved one-quarter so that the ship is at a right angle to the footlights, the prow of the ship downstage. In Chikamatsu's play, the pirate captain Kezori mounts to the prow of the ship, towering above the audience, and the curtain closes on this striking tableau.

Two techniques are used to change the side flats in front of the inner proscenium when the stage revolves to a different setting. The first, and more frequently used, is that of the stagehands removing the original flats and bringing on new ones. In the other, the side flats are built with another flat, half the height of the complete flat, hinged to the complete flat on a middle line parallel to the stage floor. The half flat is hooked to the top of the complete flat. At a scene change, the top of the hinged half flat is unhooked, its upper edge falls to the stage floor in the manner of a page falling when a book is held suspended by one cover, and a new painted surface is revealed.

The trap-lifts (*seridashi*) are used for a variety of spectacular effects and scene changes. Usually scenic units are raised or lowered on them, but the trap-lift is sometimes used, as it is in *A Substitute for Meditation*, to raise the twenty musicians from below to above the level of the stage floor. In *Mitsukuni and the Sorceress* the walls and the roof of the old temple at the center of the stage are placed on a trap-lift. Toward the end of the scene the hero Mitsukuni realizes that the beautiful Takiyasha-hime, with whom he has been engaged in conversation and dance, has supernatural powers and has come here bent on destroying him. At this point six samurai rush in to protect him; Takiyasha-hime fights with them and then suddenly disappears within the temple. The structure, with the exception of the steps in front of it and the narrow railed veranda about it, descends into the stage floor, and the roof is brought down to within five feet of the stage. Over the ridge-pole appears a great toad, Takiyasha's familiar, and soon Takiyasha-hime takes her place beside it in an attitude of defiance. Mitsukuni appears on the lower part of the roof, sword drawn, the other warriors on the stage floor raise their spears toward Takiyasha-hime, and the curtain closes on the tableau. It should be pointed out that the temple sinking into the floor of the stage is not intended to indicate a supernatural occurrence; it is merely a scenic device which will enable the audience to see the characters on top of the roof in a striking pyramidal tableau. This use of the trap-lift also represents the Kabuki characteristic of drawing the setting down into what is visually a relatively long, low, horizontal band rather than drawing the eye of the audience upward; it is the same characteristic which requires that the upper limit of the setting be sharply defined.

An opposite movement with the use of the trap-lift occurs in *The Famous Tree at Sendai*. The whole setting is an interior, the upstage area consisting of low platforms about six inches high. It is necessary to the purpose of the play to show the area beneath this room. At the conclusion of the interior scene, bamboo blinds fall on the raised area, stagehands come on and remove the straw matting on the stage floor in front of it, a trap-door opens in the center of the downstage area; simultaneously, both the whole of the upstage area and a small trap-lift bearing the warrior Arajishi, a large rat beneath his foot, are raised upward. In this instance the new setting revealed is felt to be spatially continuous with the previous interior setting.

22. Setting for *Kasane*, typical of the exterior setting using a raised upstage area.

On stage-left a river is indicated by blue cloth laid on the stage floor. The principal acting area is the undisguised floor of the stage. [*Shochiku.*]

23. A scene from *The Loyal Forty-seven Rōnin*, with the usual arrangement for showing two separate interiors, the downstage area being exterior.

[*Shochiku.*]

24. A scene from *Hiragana Seisuiki*.

Upstage is the *nami-ita* ('wave-board'), which is the conventional indication of ocean. Seated in front of it are *hana-shiten*, the brilliantly costumed 'flower-warriors.' The stage-floor is covered with a gray floor cloth. The line of the revolving stage can be seen at the lower edge of the photograph. [*Shochiku.*]

25. *The Soga Confrontation*.

The upstage wall is brilliant gold and blue. Above the stage is a *tsurieda* of plum blossoms. [*Shochiku.*]

26. *The Subscription List*, which is played with the Kabuki version of the Nō setting.

Togashi, played by the late Uzaemon, stands at stage-left, Benkei, played by the late Matsumoto Kōshirō VII, at stage-right. [*Haar: Tuttle.*]

27. The Hamamatsu-ya scene of *Benten the Thief*.

Benten Kozō, played by the late Kikugorō VI, has been disguised as a woman but now reveals himself. The pseudo-official, played by the late Matsumoto Kōshirō VII, is seated on the upstage platform. [*Shochiku.*]

28.   (a) & (b) *The Famous Tree at Sendai.*
   At the conclusion of the scene shown at the top of the page, the entire
   upstage platform is lifted up and the scene shifts to that shown below.
   [*Top, Haar: Tuttle.   Bottom: Shochiku.*]

28 (b).

29.   (a) & (b) *Benten the Thief.*

The photograph at the top of the page shows Benten Kozō fighting on the temple roof in a scene of *tachimawari.* At the conclusion of this scene, the roof is pulled over, as shown in the lower photograph, and at the same time a temple rises through the stage floor on a trap-lift. This is the scene change called *gandogaeshi.* [*Iwanami.*]

29 (b).

30. (*above*) The final tableau of 'The Village School.'
The Genzō and Tonami are at stage-right, Matsuōmaru and Chiyo at stage-left dressed in white, Midai-sama and Kanshūsai on the platform. The setting is typical of *sewamono* interiors. [*Shochiku.*]

31. (*next page top*) *The Loyal Forty-seven Rōnin*, Act IV.
At the end of the act, in order to theatricalize Yuranosuke's departure from the House, this entire façade is slowly moved upstage as Yuranosuke exits on the *hanamichi*. [*Shochiku.*]

32. (*next page bottom*) The opening scene of *The Loyal Forty-seven Rōnin*.
The painted background, the upstage platform, and the spatial arrangement of the characters are typical of exterior Kabuki settings. [*Shochiku.*]

33. Setting of *The Arrow Maker*, an *aragoto* piece, one of the 'Eighteen Best Kabuki Plays' of the Ichikawa troupe.

The arrow maker is at center and the arrows, greatly exaggerated in size, are upstage of him. [*Shochiku.*]

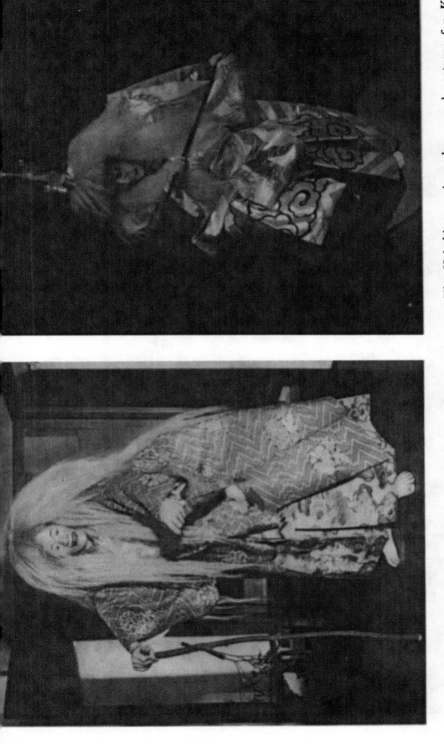

34. The Nō actor in costume, wig, and mask.
[*Haar: Tuttle.*]

35. The Kabuki actor in make-up and costume for *Kokaji*, a Kabuki dance adapted from the Nō theatre.
[*Haar: Tuttle.*]

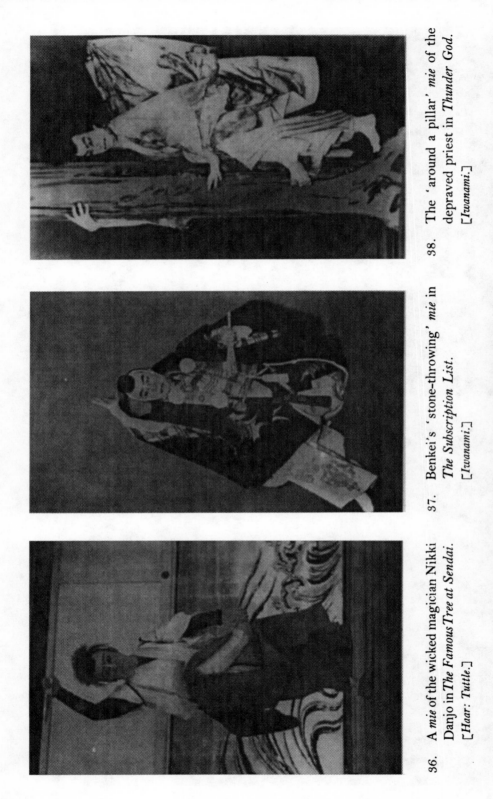

36. A *mie* of the wicked magician Nikki Danjo in *The Famous Tree at Sendai*. [*Haar: Tuttle.*]

37. Benkei's 'stone-throwing' *mie* in *The Subscription List*. [*Iwanami.*]

38. The 'around a pillar' *mie* of the depraved priest in *Thunder God*. [*Iwanami.*]

SOME OF THE VARIETIES OF *MIE*

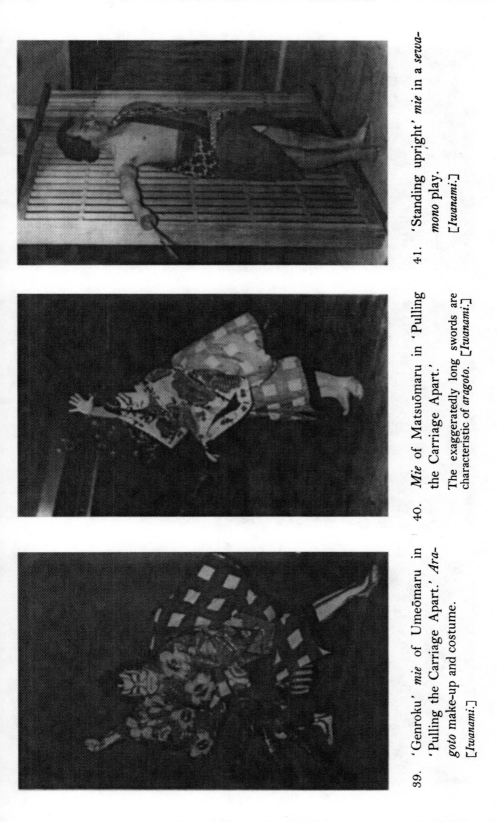

39. 'Genroku' *mie* of Umeōmaru in 'Pulling the Carriage Apart.' *Aragoto* make-up and costume. [*Iwanami.*]

40. *Mie* of Matsuōmaru in 'Pulling the Carriage Apart.'

The exaggeratedly long swords are characteristic of *aragoto*. [*Iwanami.*]

41. 'Standing upright' *mie* in a *sewamono* play. [*Iwanami.*]

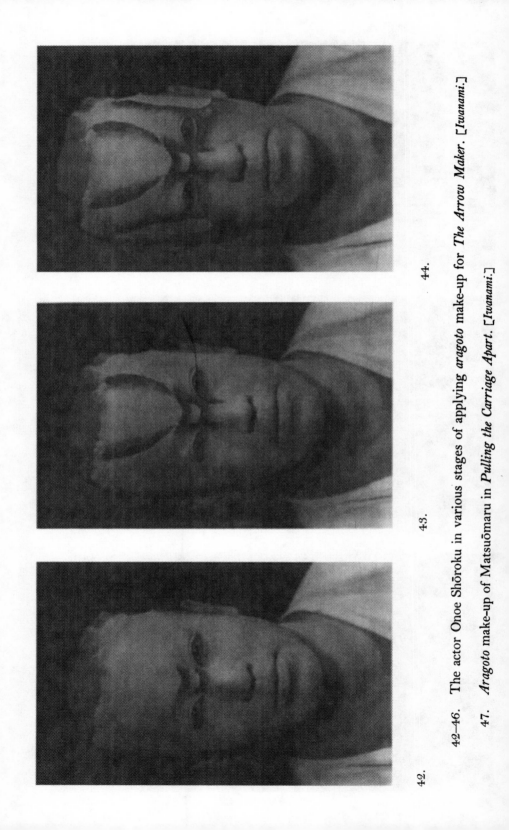

42.

43.

44.

42–46. The actor Onoe Shōroku in various stages of applying *aragoto* make-up for *The Arrow Maker*. [*Iwanami.*]

47. *Aragoto* make-up of Matsuōmaru in *Pulling the Carriage Apart*. [*Iwanami.*]

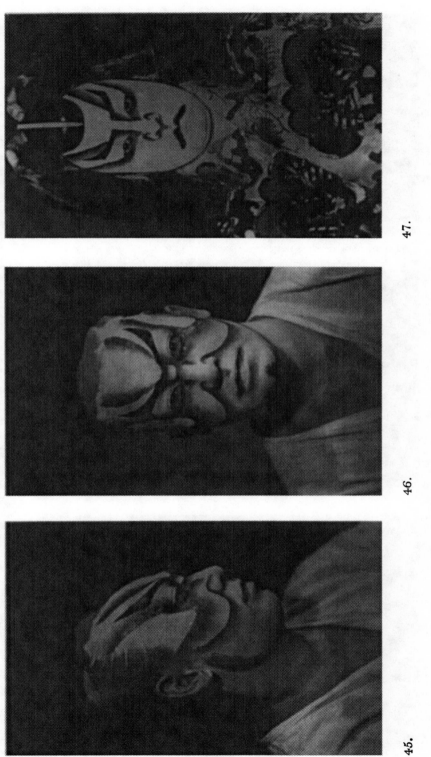

45.

46.

47.

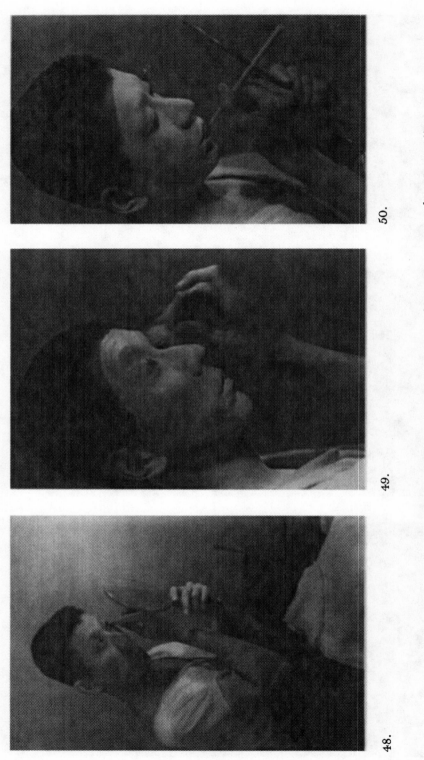

50.

49.

48.

48–53.　The actor Nakamura Utaemon preparing to play an *onnagata* role. [*Iwanami.*]

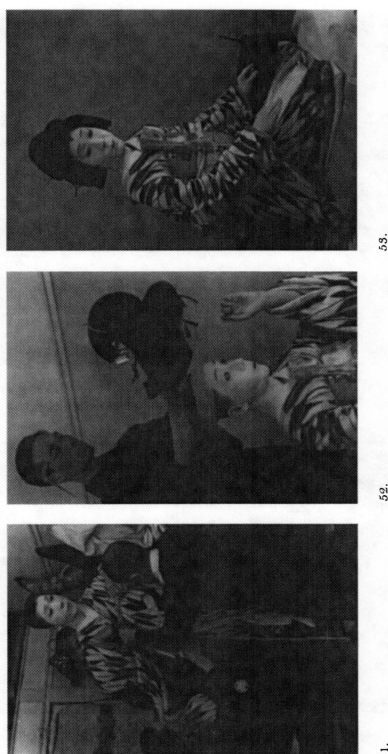

51.

52.

53.

54. Nikki Danjo disguised as a rat and quelled by Arajishi, in *aragoto* make-up and costume, in a scene from *The Famous Tree at Sendai*. [*Haar: Tuttle.*]

55. A *tengu* (long-nosed demon) in *Takatoki*. [*Shochiku.*]

56. The dog in the comic dance *The Blind Masseur*. [*Shochiku.*]

A somewhat different change of setting using the trap-lift occurs at the end of the second scene of *Benten the Thief*; the scene is a mountain exterior set entirely on a platform about two feet high, the whole contained within the inner proscenium. At the end of the scene, stagehands appear and attach a cloud-curtain (*kasumi-maku*) to the front edge of the platform. The whole setting rises upward until it is out of sight and the cloud-curtain attached to it covers the opening of the inner proscenium. The cloud-curtain is then dropped, like the *furiotoshi*, and another mountain scene is revealed.

On occasion two trap-lifts, both bearing scenery, are used for spectacular effect. The final scene of *The Three Kichiza's* is a winter exterior; at the center of the stage is a high wooden watch-tower, surrounded by a fence, a bell hung at the top of it. Along the rear of the stage are several one-story buildings; behind them hangs a black curtain, which in this case indicates nothingness. The play concerns three thieves who have become blood brothers and have taken the same name—Kichiza. Two of them, Obō-kichiza and Ojō-kichiza, have met here and await the arrival of the third, Oshō-kichiza. But before his arrival, the pair is discovered by the police and engages in a fight with them. Ojō-kichiza climbs the watch-tower to strike the bell and warn the missing thief, while Obō-kichiza disappears offstage followed by the greater number of the police. At this point, the trap-lift on which the watch-tower and the high fence are placed descends out of sight and simultaneously the upstage area of houses ascends. The black curtain is dropped revealing a painted background showing the roofs of the city. Obō-kichiza at the same moment appears on the roof of one of the upstage houses where he engages in a fight with his pursuers. He is at last defeated and is taken off stage-left by the police. The upstage houses descend, the watch-tower area ascends, revealing Ojō-kichiza also captured, and the setting returns to its original form. Here, as in *The Famous Tree at Sendai*, the trap-lifts are used to show contiguous vertical planes.

Probably the most spectacular of all Kabuki scene changes using trap-lifts is that which occurs toward the end of *Benten the Thief*. The scene is a temple roof, the upper part of the roof rising sharply, the forepart almost flat; the downstage edge of the roof is about three feet above the level of the stage floor and directly in front of it and below it is a cloud-curtain extending the width of the stage. The thief Benten Kozō has been driven to the temple roof by his pursuers, and having conquered them in a long ballet of fighting, he ends his life by *seppuku*.[2] Cables are attached to the two downstage corners of the roof, and by means of these, the whole roof is pulled over backwards away from the audience, until the under surface of the roof, which is painted as an exterior background, is in a vertical position. This is the method of scene change called *gandogaeshi*. Meanwhile a trap-lift, extending the width of the stage, has been ascending; on it is a two-storied temple with another of the thieves of the play, Nippon Daemon, seated on the upper story. The underside of the roof becomes the background behind the temple, and two large flats are carried on and attached to either side of it so that the painted background extends the width of the stage. When the upper story of the temple is in sight, the lift stops, and Nippon Daemon fights with two pursuers; he conquers them and they disappear. Then the temple ascends again and simultaneously a small trap-lift in the downstage area is brought up bearing three men standing on a bridge which is conceived to be on a level with the first story of the temple.

The uses of the revolving stage and of the trap-lift as means of changing scenery complement each other: The revolving stage produces a scene change on a horizontal plane while the trap-lift does it on a vertical plane. But both are of equal force in creating the feeling that the scene change is being projected toward and into the stage area. Both are used to produce spectacular effects. Although similar machines are used in the Western theatre, their use is almost always confined, in the representational theatre, to rapid scene changes either in darkness or while the front curtain is closed; only in the musical comedy and revue are they used for the same visual delight as in the Kabuki. The effect in the Kabuki differs somewhat from that for which machines were used in the theatre of such men as Sabbatini and Inigo Jones. In the Renaissance theatre the desire was to produce an instantaneous, magical scene change; sometimes the audience was blinded by sudden light or distracted by a contrived commotion so that the method of changing the scene would not be perceived. In the Kabuki the actual mechanics of change of scene is more impressive than the feeling that the scene change has been effected by mysterious, carefully concealed techniques. It is the operation of the machines themselves which delights the audience, not the feeling that the machines produce illusion. Even when the scene change shows successive areas which are spatially contiguous, the concern is not with

[2] *Seppuku* is suicide by cutting into the belly. Foreigners usually, Japanese seldom, call it *harakiri*.

showing a representational continuity between these areas but with the display of the resources of theatre machinery. Thus in its use of machines the Kabuki also exhibits its basic theatricality and its desire to display frankly the means by which its effects are produced. There are, to be sure, certain 'tricks' in the Kabuki, such as that of *haya-gawari* in which the actor conceals himself, makes a rapid change of costume and make-up, and appears in an unexpected quarter of the stage, but such effects are relatively few.

The small wagon stage (*hikidōgu*), which was introduced into the Kabuki at the beginning of the eighteenth century for the purpose of facilitating the handling of small pieces of scenery, was another of the scenic devices which the Kabuki actor took over for his own purposes. These small platforms could be used, he found, to move the actor onto the stage with as striking effect as that produced when towers and temples were brought on. Today the use of movable platforms bearing the actor is confined almost entirely to those pieces which are dance or largely dance. When the curtain opens on the dance *The Seized Armor*, the musicians, seated on a two-tiered platform at the rear of the stage, play and sing an introductory passage; at its conclusion, their platform is divided into two sections, the right half of it being pulled off to the right, the left half to the left, and through the opening thus effected between the two halves, a small platform bearing the two dancers, a woman and a warrior, is pushed downstage by stage assistants. In *The Arrow Maker* the elder brother of the arrow maker appears to him in a dream; the arrow maker sleeps at stage-center, and the elder brother Jūrō, standing on a platform, is pushed onto the scene from stage-left on a line parallel to the front of the stage; when the dream is over, the platform is pulled off into the wings. In *The Miracle at Tsubosaka Temple* the goddess Kannon appears briefly on a similar platform. In the last scene of the dance *Kokaji* two platforms are pushed into the downstage area, a small one bearing one of the dancers, a larger one bearing Kokaji and the anvil on which a sword will be forged. These platforms are in every instance moved on a straight line. In *The Seized Armor* the platform is pushed from up-center to down-center; in *Kokaji* the larger platform is moved on this same line while the smaller one is moved down on a parallel line to stage-left of it. In *The Arrow Maker* the movement of the platform is parallel to the front of the stage. In other pieces in which platforms are used in this fashion they are moved on these two lines, and there-fore, moving at a right angle to the front of the stage and parallel to it, they move along the two strong axes of the Kabuki stage and project the actor into its strong downstage plane. Their use in this respect suggests comparison with the Greek *eccyclema*, but whereas the *eccyclema* was a conventional means of showing an interior, the movable platform of the Kabuki very rarely carries with it the idea of a disparate area. In *The Arrow Maker* the appearance of the absent brother does not convey the notion that he is now transported into this area but rather that he is visible evidence of the dream of the sleeping arrow maker. The movable platform is used for pure stage effect rather than, as the *eccyclema*, a means of imposing a comparatively representational interior plane on an exterior plane.

The scene designer did not entirely relinquish the use of the wagon stage to the actor; it is still used for moving large architectural scenic units. However, the wagon stage is not now used as a means of changing the setting but merely for rearranging it, and the rearrangement is always made in order that the movement of the actor will be enhanced. In 'Shio Temple,' the most frequently played act of *Flowers at Ueno*, the setting is the conventional interior-exterior arrangement, with the house placed on the stage-center and stage-left areas, the exterior in front of it and to stage-right of it. In the stage-right area is a well. The action of the first part of the act uses the interior, in which the principal characters are seated, and shifts to the exterior area in front of the platform when the old nurse Otsuji runs in to protect the child Botarō who has been roughly handled by the villain of the play, Moriguchi. The other characters presently quit the stage, and Otsuji and Botarō are left alone. Botarō, in order to escape death at the hands of his father's enemies, has pretended to be deaf and dumb; his nurse, Otsuji, knowing nothing of this deception, has been fasting and praying so that Botarō's affliction will be removed. She now decides to kill herself so that her prayers will be answered by the god Kompira. The boy tries to prevent her, but she entangles him in her outer kimono, runs to the well, and theatrically, not actually, pours water over herself in the gesture of purification. As Otsuji goes to the well, the interior platform is pulled offstage to stage-left. The reason for this is that a greater area is thus opened up stage-left of the well and that Otsuji is consequently given more space in which to perform her ballet of death; there is also revealed an exterior backing against which Otsuji appears in greater relief than against the interior platform. After the action at the well is completed and Otsuji has stabbed herself, the interior is again moved onto the stage and characters enter through the upstage doors of the interior.

At the end of the fourth act of *The Loyal Forty-seven Rōnin* the movement of scenery on a wagon stage in synchronization with the movement of the actor is used in a slightly different fashion. Yurano-suke, the chief of the *rōnin*, is left alone on the stage. He stands before the house of his dead master and silently bids farewell to it. He carries a paper lantern bearing the crest of the house; he blows out the candle, and it is as though the light of the house had gone out forever. A crow caws; the desolate sound hangs on the air. Yuranosuke weeps, then turns and walks toward the *hanamichi*. As he does so, the great facade of the house is slowly pulled upstage. Yuranosuke pauses at the *shichi-san* and the movement of the house is stopped. Then as he moves to the rear of the *hanamichi*, the house also moves upstage. This rather unusual piece of Kabuki staging is of recent origin, but the technique employed is less illusionistic than a description of it would suggest. The growing distance between Yuranosuke and the house is less an illusionistic device than it is a theatrical means of underlining the poignance of the scene—that of Yuranosuke's separation from the House and his becoming a masterless man. The withdrawal upstage of the house is not meant to decrease it visually in size and thus suggest a possible infinite progression in space toward the rear of the stage, but rather to create a purely theatrical emphasis of the growing distance between Yuranosuke and the house. If the Kabuki conception of stage space were a realistic one, the house could not be moved at all; but since space is used theatrically, both the house and Yuranosuke can move away from each other. Until about twenty years ago, the painted facade of the house was not moved upstage; the house was painted on two flats of equal size which were hinged together on a line parallel to the stage floor. When Yurano-suke reached the *shichi-san*, the upper flat was folded down over the lower one, and there was thus revealed a new surface, half the height of the former one, on which the facade of the house, correspondingly reduced in size, was painted.

Among all the machines described, it will be noticed that none provide for lowering scenery from above the stage. A small cloud, signifying the presence of a god, is used in certain plays. Snow, in the form of bits of white paper, is scattered from above in winter scenes, but this device is used sparingly and, like the white floor cloth, serves only as an introductory visual indication of snow; the presence of falling snow is more strongly conveyed by the movement of the actor. Less frequently the petals of cherry blossoms fall to the stage. In *Thunder God* rain is indicated by lowering into the first border position a border about two feet wide consisting of vertical silver wires. Otherwise, there is no projection downward of scenic elements. The presence of the Nō roof in the early theatre may have deterred the development of machinery above the stage, but had there been any substantial desire to lower scenic objects from above, the Japanese inventive genius that created the revolving stage and the trap-lift would have triumphed over the presence of the roof. As it was, the roof remained until the increasing height of the scenery dictated its removal. It seems, then, that the absence of the development of machinery over the stage was the result of a natural disinclination to regard this area as one for scenic exploitation. Instead, machines were developed which derived their strength from that of the stage floor and which projected scenery and actors into the downstage plane of the stage. The stage floor and the downstage plane today retain their original vitality, which would be correspondingly weakened by the use of machines to lower scenery and actors from above the stage, for this use would involve dissolution of the line which arbitrarily cuts off the upward limit of the Kabuki setting. The setting, like the movement of the actor, evolved from the stage floor, and the machinery was designed to project scenic elements and the actor through the floor and back into it; there was no impulse to establish an opposite line of movement from the area above the stage. A disinclination to exploit upward line is to be seen in the historical development of Japanese architecture; native architectural forms tended to be earthbound, and it was not until Chinese architecture had been introduced into Japan, in such forms as the pagoda, that there was a strong upward line in Japanese buildings.

The only occasion in which the actor makes an entrance suspended above the stage floor is when the device known as *chū-nori* ('riding in mid-air') is used. This machine, by which the actor enters suspended from a rope, appeared toward the middle of the nineteenth century along with the development of ghost plays, of which *Ghost Story of Yotsuya* is one of the best known. It is used principally in such plays today so that the legless Japanese ghost can float above the stage. It is said that the actor Ichikawa Kodanji (1812–1866) made frequent use of *chū-nori* in dances. In *Takatoki* (1885) long-nosed demons, *tengu*, make their entrances by swinging in from the wings on ropes.

Rapid 'trick' appearances and disappearances of the actor are relatively few and are held in low esteem by the Kabuki connoisseur, who refers to them as *keren* (playing to the gallery). When they are used they involve the setting rather than trap-lifts. Toward the end of the first scene of *Kokaji*, the goddess Inari, in the guise of a human being, makes a rapid and startling disappearance behind a section of painted fence and shrubbery; this section of the fence, parallel to the front of the stage, is painted with the same design on both sides and is constructed so that it can be revolved on a central axis parallel to the stage floor. As the dancer leaps into the air, the section is revolved to a position in which its surface is parallel to the stage floor, the dancer's movement carries him over the top of it, the revolution of the section is completed so that the upstage surface faces downstage, and the dancer is concealed behind it. In one scene of *Tadanobu the Fox* a fox in the form of a man makes a series of rapid and acrobatic entrances and exits through various parts of the setting, appearing and disappearing suddenly through sliding panels and revolving sections of the upstage wall. In *Takatoki*, the demons vanish through the upstage wall which consists of flats arranged so that each revolves on its vertical axis.

Stage tricks involving properties are also rather sparingly used. The hero of *Stone-cutting Kajiwara* shows the power of his sword by testing it on a huge stone basin which obligingly splits down the middle. The fall from grace of the priest Narukami, as a woman's lips touch his, is pointed up by the sudden consumption by fire of the sacred scroll painting which hangs above his altar. In *The Spirit of a Courtesan* the hero, to show his skill as an artist, draws a picture on the upstage side of a stone basin; so powerful is his drawing that it penetrates through the stone and is revealed to the audience on the downstage side. The fox-fires, previously noted, which are managed by stage assistants, are similar trick effects. But on most occasions tricks of this kind are used with comic rather than serious intent. In *Stone-cutting Kajiwara* a dummy is cut in half, its viscera shown as red cloth. In *Just a Moment* the hero swings his sword over the heads of a circle of enemies; each of the men covers his head with a piece of red cloth and runs from the stage, while a stage assistant pushes a dozen or so dummy heads downstage, all of them tied together on a long string for the purpose of quick retrieval. Several small dragons mount a painted waterfall in *The Golden Pavilion*. In *Political Story of Tenichibō*, a fish which has been served up on a platter comes to life and wiggles about. Almost the entire fighting scene of *The Forest of Suzu* consists of amusing tricks involving properties. A man has his arm cut off and carries it with him as he leaves the stage; when another's leg is cut off, he hops from the stage on one leg while the severed leg, in the hands of the stage assistant, hops along after him. Another fighter has his face cut off: He is wearing a double mask, hinged at the chin, so that it can be made to fall down and reveal a surface of red cloth. All these effects are used to get laughs; in most of the serious scenes of death and destruction, in the scenes of *seppuku*, there is rarely any theatrical evidence of blood, except in the violent plays that developed during the nineteenth century. The severed head which must be identified in the scenes called *kubijikken* is a conventional property, not a realistic one, and bears no relation to the head of Jokanaan in *Salomé*. It comes into theatrical being not of itself, but in the way in which it is handled by the actor, and thus has, visually, a purely formal quality; whereas in the trick effects involving properties, the properties are allowed to exist in their own right independent of the actor.

The properties in the majority of plays in general resemble real objects. There is the charcoal brazier, the pipe with its long stem and very small bowl, lacquered trays and stands, the squares of silk in which all portable objects are wrapped; the two swords, a long and a short one, which the warrior always wears, and so forth. The appearance of Kabuki properties is rigidly controlled by the principle of allowing no property on the stage which does not contribute directly and immediately to the import of the scene. The isolation and controlled appearance of the properties surrounds them with an atmosphere comparable to that of the properties which are occasionally invested with special dramatic significance in the representational theatre—properties such as Hedda Gabler's pistols and Lovberg's manuscript. In *sewamono* pieces there is an observable tendency to introduce a few properties, not required by the actor, whose only purpose is to suggest the nature of the people living in the house— books and scrolls in the home of the poet or artist, brooms and pails in the houses of the poor—but these too are rigidly selected and are never as profuse as the books, the table lamps, the magazines, the vases of flowers, the potted plants of the representational theatre, all of which are as carefully selected as Kabuki properties, but which are intended to create their effect compositely. Even the 'atmospheric' properties of the Kabuki retain a certain austere individual isolation from each other and produce their effects singly in the manner of the images of the *haiku*.

The folding, ribbed fan (*sensu*) is a property of a very special nature; it does not display its theatrical characteristics in *sewamono*, being in such plays a literal object, but in all other plays it is transmutable and becomes the most utilitarian of Kabuki properties. Closed, it can become a whip, a dagger, a pipe, or any other long, thin object; half-closed, it is a bottle, a head-dress, a lantern; opened, it can be transmuted into a tray, a piece of paper on which a poem is being written, a rising moon, a battle flag, or any object with a flat surface. This characteristic of the Kabuki fan was derived from the Nō, in which the fan is almost the only property the actor uses. As in the Nō the fan is also used in a less literal fashion and can be made to suggest the blowing of the wind, the ripple of water, the fall of rain. In all instances, the theatrical form which the fan has assumed is clearly stated both by the actor's movement and by the music. Again, the fan can exist merely as a fan, purely decorative or used to enlarge visually a gesture of the hand or arm. The fan is the most used Kabuki property and is without doubt its most theatrical one.

In *sewamono* plays the *tenugui*, an oblong strip of cotton cloth approximately two feet long and ten inches wide, is used as a personal property to about the same degree that the fan is used in the other plays. The *tenugui* undergoes none of the theatrical transformations of the fan, but it does perform all the functions to which it is put in daily Japanese life. The *tenugui* seems indispensable to the Japanese, particularly to those of the lower and middle classes, with whom *sewamono* is concerned. A workman seems unable to undertake any task without folding it lengthwise and tying it about his head; it hangs perpetually from a rear pocket of the student; a man leading an ox-cart places it on his head and ties the ends under his nose; sometimes a truck driver puts it over his head, holding a corner of it in his mouth; it is towel, kerchief, and sometimes advertisement for a commercial company whose name it bears. In the Kabuki it is put to all these uses. Tied over the head and beneath the nose it becomes a disguise for the thief; it is a glorified purple headband for Sukeroku, showing both that he is a man whose sympathies are with the commoners and that, since it is tied on the left instead of the right, he is ill. A characteristic pose of the Kabuki heroine is that in which she holds one end of the *tenugui* in her mouth, pulling tightly on the other end, an attitude which shows that she is preventing herself from giving way to tears. In the *mie* it is hung about the neck, seized with both hands, or used in a variety of other postures. The *tenugui* in its literal and suggestive uses displays something of the broad versatility of the fan. It is so peculiarly Japanese that there is no comparable object in the Western theatre.

Properties in dance and in *aragoto* are more freely theatrical, that is, less literal, than those in other plays. The warriors opposed to the hero in *michiyuki* scenes, such as those in *The Loyal Forty-seven Rōnin* and *The Thousand Cherry Trees*, are dressed in kimono of a floral design, and their weapons are not swords but flowering branches of the cherry or other trees. They are called flower warriors (*hana-shiten*). Since exaggeration is a basic characteristic of *aragoto*, it is manifested in the properties used. In 'Pulling the Carriage Apart' one of the heroes wears three swords instead of the conventional two, and these are larger than those ordinarily used. In *The Arrow Maker* the arrows being sharpened are as long as the arrow maker is tall. In *Snowbound Pass* the villain wields a great axe some four times larger than life-size.

Since during the greater part of its history the Kabuki could not use lights, it evolved conventional means of indicating time of day or state of the weather, and these are largely retained today in the same form in which they existed when a given play was first produced. The lighting problem of the Kabuki, until modern times, was how to get the greatest possible amount of light onto the stage. Modern lighting instruments solved this problem and today, generally, Kabuki lighting of pre-Meiji plays consists of uncolored light directed on the stage from positions in the auditorium, from the footlights, and from a first border position behind the proscenium. Strip lights are used behind the headings of interiors or behind ground rows to light an exterior background. There is little cross-lighting; consequently most Kabuki lighting is flat rather than plastic, although the downstage area is more strongly lighted than the upstage one and the lighting of backgrounds is to some degree independent of the lighting of the area occupied by the actor.

When the black backdrop is used to indicate night, the actor appears in front of it well lighted and fully visible. This practice was no doubt adopted from a convention of the graphic arts during the Tokugawa period in which night scenes were indicated by placing clearly visible figures against a black background. In interior settings, the coming of night is indicated by bringing on the stage one or more *andon*, standing lamps two to three feet high containing a candle; the intensity of the stage lighting is not changed when this is done. A candle in a circular box placed behind a translucent backdrop to give a moon effect appeared in the Kabuki theatre about the time of the first perspective backgrounds and is used today in certain plays, an electric lamp substituted for the candle. These conventional practices give introductory indications of night; the quality of darkness is definitely established by the miming of the actor, who, like the English actor in the Renaissance public theatre, moves slowly as though he were unable to see the others around him or approaches the lamp in order to read a letter. In scenes of fighting at night, such as those in *The Forest of Suzu* and in *Umekichi the Fireman*, the dances of conflict are slowed down so that the movement resembles that in the slow motion film. This technique is used even in those scenes in which a painted background is used instead of the black cloth. The Kabuki has overcome the problem, which the representational theatre has not, of making action taking place at night clearly visible.

The temptation to use modern lighting instruments to produce sunsets, sunrises, moonlight, and so forth, has been rather rigidly resisted in the performance of plays written before the middle of the nineteenth century, although there is an observable tendency at the present time to change slightly the intensity of the lighting, not its color or quality, in distinguishing between night and day, and in time it may well be that the purely formal stage lighting of pre-Meiji Kabuki plays will give way to the atmospheric lighting of the representational theatre. It seems a strong temptation to resist because startling, colorful effects are of the essence of Kabuki and also because in the lighting of twentieth century plays most of the effects possible with modern instruments are employed. In Okamoto Kidō's *The Tale of Shuzenji*, a play thoroughly under the influence of the representational theatre, the effect of moonlight on a rippling stream is projected against a painted background; this projection of light has nothing to do with the development of the plot of the play but is used merely as an 'effect.' In the pre-Meiji *Izayoi and Seishin*, on the contrary, the moon, projected on the background, appears and disappears arbitrarily, and its use is related theatrically to the love affair between the hero and heroine.

CHAPTER VII

The Actor

IT is recorded both in the *Kojiki* (712) and in the *Nihongi* (720) that when the Sun Goddess, Amaterasu, was incensed by the rude behavior of her brother Susa-no-wo, she entered the Rock Cave of Heaven, closed the entrance with a stone, and refused to come out. Darkness descended upon the earth. Though the other gods brought gifts before the cave and sang litanies, Amaterasu was not moved. Then Ame-no-uzume-no-mikoto, the 'heaven-alarming-female-augustness,' decked her head with vines, exposed her breasts, lifted her skirts, jumped onto an overturned tub, and there danced and sang so indecently that the heavens shook with the laughter of the gods. When the curious Amaterasu moved the rock to see what was causing the laughter, one of the gods quickly pulled the rock door open and light was restored to the world. The heaven-alarming-female then became the maid-servant of Amaterasu and comforted her in times of affliction. Today she is one of the chief of the pantheon of gods which are worshipped under the name of Inari, whose temples are guarded by stone foxes. The heaven-alarming-female is the patron deity of all professional actors, for, as she does, they lighten the hearts of men, comfort them in distress, and make the sun shine again. An Inari shrine, large or small, is installed in every Kabuki theatre, and, of course, in all Japanese film studios.

The original dramatic impulse found expression in Japan, as it did elsewhere, in the dance. When the Nō was crystallized into a unique dramatic form toward the end of the fourteenth century, its creators, Kannami (1333–1384) and his son Zeami (1364–1443) drew upon existent dance forms. The principal of these were the *sarugaku*, which seems to have been more or less comic in character at that time and was flexible enough to absorb new materials; the *dengaku*, a somewhat more rigid form and therefore less influential upon the Nō than *sarugaku*; the *ennen no mai*, a dance performed by old men and boys particularly in the temples of Kyōto and Nara; and *bugaku*, the ancient court dance which survives today under the protection of the Imperial household and from which came the 'five-movements' into which the principal Nō dances are divided. Certain of the Nō scripts have literary value, but according to competent Japanese authorities, the majority do not; they are merely the unrealized basis for the performance of a musical dance drama whose artistry arises out of the dance rather than the words and whose chief effects are visual rather than auditory.

Okuni danced the *nembutsu-odori*, a dance of Buddhist origin which by the end of the sixteenth century had been so much influenced by folk dance that it had lost its liturgical character. Her legendary companion, Nagoya Sanzaemon, being a samurai, was acquainted with the Nō and, according to legend, taught her adaptations of Nō dances. To these was added the influence of contemporary popular dance, but evidence is lacking today to show just what form the dances of Okuni and the other performers of Women's-Kabuki took. We know that in Okuni's troupe men played the parts of women, the women played the parts of men, and that the songs to which they danced, judging by the few examples which remain, were largely romantic, if not erotic. The following excerpts from three of the Okuni-Kabuki songs indicate the general tenor of their subject matter:

'Abandoning ourselves to the urgency of Nature,
We sing and dance.
There is no past, no future,
But only the present.'

'The world is a dream;
Let us lose ourselves in it.
The reality of thunder
Cannot destroy the dream between us.'

'How lonely it is to sleep alone!
I have not even anyone to talk to.
Come, my dear pillow,
I will talk to you.
My pillow is silent.'

It is no great exaggeration to say that the majority of the actresses and actors in early Kabuki were prostitutes, and the dances they performed seem to have been principally concerned with girls meeting samurai or *rōnin* and then repairing to a tea-house or other convenient spot. This simple plot was expressed in dance movement rather than words, but there is no evidence that the movement was realistically suggestive like that of the heaven-alarming-female. Troupes composed entirely of men performers appeared as early as 1617, and when Women's Kabuki was prohibited in 1629 there was no break in the Kabuki tradition which had been established, for the Young Men's Kabuki continued to perform the same kind of dances, with the same subject matter, as the women's troupes. This form of Kabuki, however, developed a new dance form called *saruwaka*, distinguished from the earlier forms by its more literal pantomime. Not until after the prohibition of Young Men's Kabuki in 1652 was there any great development of plays with a well defined plot. At this time the actors could no longer, as the Japanese put it, 'sell their pretty faces.' The troupes found it necessary to provide something in the way of dramatic interest to compensate for this loss, and the result was the development of plays rather than dances in 'Male' Kabuki. But for the first fifty years of its existence the Kabuki was almost purely dance.

The first creative artist to appear in the Kabuki, other than the actor, was not the playwright but the *furitsuke-shi*, the choreographer and dance teacher. Many schools of Kabuki dance were developed, and their founders taught not only within the theatre but outside it —among the nobility, among the sons and daughters of the rising middle class—so that the dance forms evolved within the Kabuki theatre came to have a fairly wide popular circulation.

Dance remains in Japan today a communal form of expression, closely associated with the work movement of daily life and with religious observance. The pulling in of a net from the sea, the planting of rice, the felling of timber, the installation of a telephone pole— these and other forms of group work are resolved into rhythmical movement and chanting. A worshipper at a Shintō shrine during a religious festival pays a sum to have a dance, the *kagura* ('a dance to console the gods'), performed by the priestesses of the shrine. The men and boys of the town or the neighborhood twice annually dance through the streets bearing a shrine on their shoulders, chanting as they go. The *bon* festival, a Buddhist celebration for the souls of the dead, involving a circular dance around a drum tower, is participated in by the young men and women of the community. The chief merit of the geisha is that she is a dancer, or that, as a musician, she can play the accompaniment to a dance. The constant association in Japan between rhythmical dance movement and the business of daily living probably accounts to a considerable degree for the physical dexterity of the Japanese. Rhythmical movement is not made a special, detached form of social expression, as it has tended to become in the West, but remains an integral part of mundane existence. It is not an activity restricted either to the professional performer, to rural districts, or to those of a particular age group. The child of six and the man of sixty are both participants. The use of rhythmical movement as a primary means of expression in the Kabuki reflects a national preoccupation with dance that has continued to this day. There has never been in Japan the growing disparity between the physical vocabulary of expression of the professional performer and that of the member of the audience which has appeared in the West with ballet or with the forms known as modern dance. The most uneducated Japanese peasant recognizes at once the artistry of the Kabuki dancer, for he himself has had personal experience of a similar form of physical expression.

The conception of Kabuki as being primarily dance was deeply imbedded in its tradition, and thus dance was not only a point of departure in the development of new means of expression, but the preoccupation with dance also dictated the inclusion of new rhythmic elements developed outside the Kabuki, such as those of the doll theatre.

The movement of the dolls, since it was controlled by strongly rhythmical music and chant, was and is patterned movement. Even before the doll theatre of Ōsaka had been crystallized by the genius of Chikamatsu and Takemoto, the puppet theatre had exerted an influence upon the Kabuki. The style of acting called *aragoto* ('rough business'), the invention of Ichikawa Danjūrō I in 1673, was first used in *Four Faithful Bodyguards*, a play written for the puppet theatre by Sakurai Tambanoshōjō. The recitative of this play was performed in a much more violent manner than that characteristic of the usual *jōruri*, and it was probably because of its rhythmic violence that Danjūrō chose this particular play for the genesis of a manner of acting that was acrobatic, muscular, and heroic. The evidence indicates that the Edo Kabuki theatre, because of its development of *aragoto*, with its stylized movement and rhythmical line reading, was closer to the form of the doll theatre than was the Ōsaka Kabuki theatre which, probably to preserve its identity, had evolved a somewhat less stylized form of expression. The result was that when the Kabuki found it necessary, about the middle of the eighteenth century, to perform the plays of the doll theatre (called *maruhonmono* when adapted for the Kabuki), there was relatively little change required in the Edo style of acting, but a considerable readjustment was necessary on the part of the Ōsaka and Kyōto actors. The Ōsaka and Kyōto actors looked with horror on the nonrealistic stylization of *aragoto*, and one of them, Onoyama Ujiemon, wrote indignantly, 'It's ridiculous to appear on the stage painted red and blue, looking like a boiled lobster.' But the well bred and restrained audiences of Ōsaka and Kyōto eventually welcomed a style of playing which was vigorous, masculine, and stylized.

The three greatest influences upon Kabuki dance movement were the Nō, folk and popular dance (*zokkyoku*), and the movement of the dolls in the doll theatres. At present it is possible to distinguish between that movement in the Kabuki which can be called, for want of a better term, pure dance, that rhythmical movement which has been derived from the doll theatre, that which derives from the Nō, and that which is characteristic of *aragoto*. Pure dance, if such a phrase can be used to describe Kabuki dancing, is apparent in the pieces called *shosagoto*, such as *The Girl at Dōjō Temple* and *The Wisteria Girl*. The movement of the dolls appears particularly in the performance of plays taken from the doll theatre, as well as in the very special form known as *ningyō-buri* ('doll movement') in which the actor plays the part of a doll and is moved about by stage assistants in exactly the manner of the dolls in the doll theatre. *Aragoto* movement is used in such pieces as *Just a Moment*, *The Arrow Maker*, and 'Pulling the Carriage Apart'; while the influence of Nō dance is seen in *The Subscription List*, *Benkei at the Boat*, *Ibaraki the Demon*, and in all the dances which are performed in the Kabuki version of the Nō setting. But in the other forms of Kabuki plays, in *sewamono*, the plays of the commoners' life, and in *kizewamono*, the 'living' plays of humbler life, the distinction between the various forms of dance movement is more difficult to make. The forms of movement have not been compartmentalized but have tended to borrow one from the other and to exhibit a synthesis of all elements. As a generalization, it can be fairly said that all Kabuki movement shows the qualities of dance movement, although dance movement is less pronounced in the *sewamono* and *kizewamono* pieces; but even in these, the climax is revealed in strong rhythmical movement.[1]

It is interesting that the heaven-alarming-female danced on an overturned tub which gave resonance to her stamping upon it. The floor of the Nō stage has clay pots placed at certain spots beneath it to give resonance to the stamping of the actor. The Kabuki dancing stage, *shosabutai*, not only provides a smooth surface for dancing but also, since the low platforms are not nailed down, provides greater resonance for the actor's stamping than the ordinary stage floor. The early dance of many countries seems to have grown out of stamping upon the earth, either to quell the spirits beneath its surface or to invoke them. The original impulses of Japanese dance are lost in antiquity, but it seems that to the early Japanese, demons beneath the earth were more clearly conceived than spirits in the air, an attitude not strange in a land of frequent earthquakes, and that the early unknown dances were designed to keep the demons in their proper sphere, or to invoke their aid at the time of rice-planting, which was attended, from earliest times, by music and dancing. Dancing in the fields, *tamai*, seems to have been of very early origin, as was the *dengaku* ('music of the farmhouse'), which was accompanied by drumming. Western dance, except in some relatively recent forms, has moved away from the dance floor and, particularly in ballet, has sought to negate the existence of weight, but Japanese dance has never tried to minimize the contact between the dancer's feet and the floor on which he dances. Instead, by the use of a resonant platform, it has emphasized the opposition between the dancer's body and the dancing floor and has used the sound of the dancer's stamping upon the floor as a means of rhythmically punctuating the dance, with a sharp, clean sound not unlike that produced by the wooden clappers of the Kabuki. Perhaps this desire for sharp physical contact between the dancer's body and the dance floor has been more or less unconsciously preserved from ancient times; but even in contemporary Japan, the genesis of movement is from the floor. The Japanese sleeps on the

[1] The Japanese distinguish three forms of native dance: *Mai* is slow and dignified (this term was used for all dance until the end of the fourteenth century); *odori* is rapid, free, and pronouncedly rhythmic; *furi* is dance of dramatic expression. *Mai* and *odori* are performed only to instrumental music; *furi* is in essence the dancing of the meaning of the words of a song. Kabuki dance is primarily *furi*.

floor and sits on the floor. He has never known, until modern times, the chair, the sofa, or the bed; and the floor, although it is covered with thick mats of rice straw and is thus not a hard wooden surface, is the beginning and end of physical movement. It is not unnatural, then, that in the Kabuki, as in other forms of Japanese dance, the floor has continued to be the source of movement. It should not be inferred, however, that Kabuki dance consists of constant stamping on the stage floor. Such percussive movement is relatively infrequent. The stage floor provides, rather, a continuous counterpoise to the movement of the actor upon it.

The use of the word 'dance' to describe Kabuki movement is perhaps misleading, for there is little about it that resembles the Western forms suggested by the word. In general Western dance, whether square dancing, tap dancing, ballet, or folk dancing, has tended to express itself in more or less abstract movement, in movement whose source in the movement of real life is not immediately evident; and the 'ideas' expressed in it, if they exist at all, are general rather than specific. Western dance may 'tell a story,' but it does so in the main by the cumulative effect of a series of nonspecific movements. In this respect it differs from the movement of the actor in the representational theatre whose movement, at any given moment, is required to be as literal as possible so that it can be immediately identified as representing a certain gesture or attitude occurring in actual life. Kabuki dance movement never enters the realm of 'pure,' nonrepresentational movement such as appears in the waltz, the square dance, or the Lindy Hop, nor does it ever become the more or less literal reproduction of movement taken from actuality. In essence it is the rhythmical ordering of movement taken from actuality and presenting to the audience a series of clearly defined, specific, though nonrepresentational images. Aesthetically it stands at a point about midway between the abstract movement of Western social dancing and the surface realism of the movement of the representational actor. Kabuki dance movement is as precise in its meaning as the rhythmic movement of workers in the rice fields or on the seashore; and like the movement of the workers it is movement taken from actuality and submitted to a rhythmical pattern. Movement from real life is its point of departure, and Kabuki dance reduces the multiple movements of human existence to their essential forms by narrowing, and thus intensifying, the visual impression of the movement, not by broadening it so that it no longer has precise meaning. The images of

Kabuki dance are always as literal as those of the *haiku* and show the same economical rhythmical selection, the same concern for a clear-cut visual impression, the same unwillingness to deal with abstract statement. Because of its strict rhythm and design, dance movement, like the *haiku*, is not representational. The Japanese desire to reduce a natural object to a design, as with the dwarf tree, and to regard the design as the most important aesthetic element is the principal artistic consideration in Kabuki dance.

All Kabuki dance gestures are not, however, rigidly cast in a single inflexible design, for within the preestablished area of the defined form considerable variation is permitted. The Kabuki dancer distinguishes three degrees of literalness in his gesture. Most literal is *shinsho*, the 'precise' style which the student of dance is first taught. In *gyōsho*, details of the gesture are contracted, while *sōsho* is a cursive style, the least literal of the three. Analogous styles are used in the writing of Chinese characters.

The representational theatre is, of course, concerned with taking the raw materials for its gestures and attitudes from actuality and, by rhythm, design, and selection, giving them a sharper, less diffuse form than that which they have in actuality. But however designed and rhythmical the movement of the actor in the representational theatre may be, he is obliged not to allow the rhythm to become too pronounced, the design of his movement too obvious, for if he does, these qualities will break through and destroy the surface of realism which he must maintain. Henry Irving may have 'danced'; but his doing so was carefully concealed beneath a comparatively realistic pattern of movement. Kabuki dance movement also begins with the raw material of human movement, but it is not obliged to maintain a surface which convinces the audience of its theatre reality by its mundaneness. Movement taken from life and transmuted into Kabuki movement need no longer correspond to an observed reality. Rhythm and design, the essential qualities of Kabuki movement, are as frankly displayed as the other elements of production.

Most Kabuki dance movement is in actuality the 'acting out' of the words of the narrator or the singer. In *shosagoto*, the plays which are principally dance, in the pantomimic scenes of *monogatari* and *sawari* of the doll theatre plays, in passages in *aragoto*, the actor mimes the words of the music. In *shosagoto* pieces his movement is in general smoother and less energetic than it is in *aragoto* or in the doll theatre plays; the musicians sing of Mount Fuji, the actor creates the outline of the mountain with his hand; they sing of shooting an arrow, and this he mimes in stylized gesture. At times the music and the gesture may simultaneously express different ideas, in contrapuntal or antiphonal fashion. However, there is no possibility of vagueness in Kabuki movement, for words, gesture, and attitude always remain specific.

The movement both in *aragoto* and in the doll theatre plays was based upon the sharp, clear movement of the dolls, and the actor today retains the form of this movement. Although it is somewhat less fluid than that of *shosagoto* because it breaks continuous movement, such as that of the bow, into small units, the degree of its stylization as well as the artistic principles which prompt its use are basically the same. The movement of the doll is similarly designed rhythmically to show not the movement of a human being but a stylization of that movement which will create a greater sense of theatre reality, to a Japanese audience, than the reproduction of a human gesture.

The mode of manipulation of puppets and marionettes in the West differs considerably from that of doll theatre production in Japan. Japan also developed the string-operated marionette, but it was apparently less popular than the doll which was manipulated by three men. This form of manipulation was the one employed in the theatre of Chikamatsu and Takemoto and survives today in the Bunraku-za of Ōsaka. Two of the men wear the same costume as the *kurombō* of the Kabuki; the chief manipulator is dressed in *kamishimo* and his face is uncovered. As in the Kabuki, there is no concealment of the means of production. Usually this technique is at first disturbing to the Westerner, who experiences a certain visual confusion, but as he watches the performance the manipulators become less obvious as the dolls become more so. Although their faces are completely expressionless, the manipulators do not visually cease to exist, and there is good reason that they should not, for against this background of flesh and blood the movement of the dolls is set off in relief, so that the stylized quality of their movement is enhanced by its juxtaposition to the human beings who operate them. The result is not a loss of expressiveness (as would occur if the Western marionette operator were visible) but an increase of it. In his adaptation of movement from the doll theatre, the Kabuki actor plays at once the part of the manipulator and of the doll. In the performance of these plays he does not move throughout in the sharp, jerky patterns of the doll, but reserves his use of these pronounced movements for the most expressive moments so that, by contrast to his other movement, his action is thrown into the same trenchant relief that exists between the doll manipulator and the doll. He has also learned from the doll the value of complete immobility; the doll does not move, gesture, or come to life except when it has something to express; consequently, against this ground of inanimateness, gesture and movement are increased in significance.

It can be argued at some length, on the lines laid down by Gordon Craig, that the actor is most expressive when he becomes an *über-marionette* and sacrifices the literal gesture and attitude. This phenomenon occurs in the Kabuki, both in the movement which is basically dance and that which derives from the movement of the dolls. The movement is specific, sharp, clear; it is not even momentarily lost in a flow of other movement; it eschews the literal gesture for one that is at once stylized and of supranormal significance. Utilizing the unavoidable theatricality of all movement in the theatre, it proclaims the superior expressiveness of movement which is based frankly on design and rhythm.

Since the Kabuki retained dance movement as the underlying force of its performances, the distinction between actor and dancer that exists generally in the Western world at present was not made in the Japanese theatre. It is true that certain Kabuki actors show greater skill than others in some of these forms of dance movement, although occasionally an actor, like the late Onoe Kikugorō VI, may be equally proficient in all of them. But the Kabuki actor is nevertheless essentially a dancer and the whole of his performance, both his movement and line reading, is expressed in strongly rhythmical terms which are intensified by instrumental music, singing, sound effects, and the sound of the wooden clappers.

The English word 'dance' also conveys the notion of a continuing fluid pattern of movement closely related to the line of the accompanying music. Kabuki dance movement, though fluid and graceful, tends finally toward a posture; its most significant moments are thus not realized in movement but in the achievement of a static attitude. The word used to describe the pieces which are primarily dance, *shosagoto*, literally means 'posture-business'; and the dance resolves itself, in visual effect, into a succession of striking postures. In this respect, the movement exhibits the characteristic pattern of the Kabuki performance at large, which is realized, not in a cumulative, symphonic form, but in a single line of progression which at certain intervals solidifies into a significant tableau. In the representational theatre, comparatively speaking, movement is more expressive than the static pose, while in Kabuki dance the pose is more expressive than the movement which precedes it. Therefore, although there is considerable vigor in some Kabuki dance movement, the total impression is one of a series of concrete visual images rather than the continuing progression of movement in time and space characteristic of Western dance. As a result, a characteristic quality of all Kabuki acting is that it is not much concerned with depicting subtle and fluid transition from one emotion to another; instead, the actor tends to present the character in a succession of unrelated, detached moments.

The static poses may or may not be in the form of a *mie*, and they may involve several characters, but they are always the highest point of audience interest and are preceded by increasingly rhythmic movement which reaches an equilibrium in the pose. In this respect Kabuki dance has much in common with that of the Nō. The Kabuki broadened and to some degree vulgarized the line of Nō dance, but in its essential pattern of generally slow, stately movement (a characteristic of all Japanese movement on formal occasions) and in a climactic static attitude, it has retained the characteristic quality of the Nō dance.

The rhythmical design of physical movement is repeated in the line reading. As with movement, the rhythm of the line reading becomes more pronounced as the play moves toward a visual climax. Japan has no complicated or subtle verse forms; the open syllables, the almost equal stress on every syllable, and the lack of rhyme make the language unsuited to the development of any but the simplest forms. Both the *haiku* of seventeen syllables and the *waka* or *tanka* of thirty-one syllables are an arrangement of alternating lines of five and seven syllables. In the dialogue of the *jōruri* of the doll theatre plays, the same metrical form (*shichigo-chō*) was used, and this form influenced to some degree the writing of lines for the Kabuki. But it can be said, not unfairly, that the poetry of the Kabuki is not its strong point and that literary value is to be found rather in the doll theatre plays than in those of Kabuki origin. The line reading in the Kabuki shows a considerably wider inflectional pattern than colloquial speech and it has, to the Japanese ear, certain delicate and subtle rhythmical intonations; but as Sir George Sansom observes, the Japanese language 'is a graceful but not a noble instrument,' and its rhythms, as they appear in the Kabuki, are less expressive than the movement of the actor. There are no purely vocal climaxes; the reading of a line may accompany climactic movement, but when it does, the pattern of line reading is clearly derived from the actor's movement and dependent upon it. This characteristic of Kabuki line reading is almost the antithesis of line reading in the representational theatre in which, even in plays written in verse, the actor seeks generally to avoid identical physical and vocal movement. In the Kabuki, since movement is a relatively more important means of expression than the words, the movement of the actor dominates the rhythms of the line reading. The pattern of line reading as a visual climax is approached is the same as that of the gradually accelerated beat of the wooden clappers accompanying the opening of the curtain or the movement of an actor on the *hanamichi*. The rhythm is gradually speeded up toward the climax.

We have already observed that the Kabuki setting is arranged so that it will enhance the expressiveness of the actor. Similarly, all movement on the Kabuki stage and all groupings of characters are determined by the principle of providing for the complete physical expressiveness of the actor. The medium in which the actor of any country performs physically is space, and in the Kabuki a basic consideration is to give the actor the greatest amount of theatrical space possible in which he can display the design of his movement.

Japan is a small and crowded country; in its walled gardens it has attempted to create a feeling of extensive space in a small area. The same impulse is apparent in the ideal visual world of its theatre. Whether the Japanese show a lack of interest in broad, limitless expanses because of some deep national characteristic or because their natural scenery shows little of this quality is a matter for speculation. But in the Japanese garden, as in the Kabuki, the sense of space is created within a limited and well-defined area. The background of the Japanese garden is in most cases a wall; there are gardens which are arranged so that distant trees behind the wall provide a background for the composition of the garden, but these trees stand in the same relation to the garden as does the painted backdrop of the Kabuki. The foreground, represented by the garden, is the field of greatest interest as is the downstage plane of the Kabuki stage. There is no inclination to suggest an infinite penetration of space, but rather to create the sense of space within a sharply defined area. The composition of the Japanese garden on this principle suggests that the unwillingness of the Kabuki stage to penetrate space is based on a similar aesthetic consideration.

The human body in daily Japanese life moves on a longer vertical line than it does in the West, and this line is exploited in the Kabuki. The actor begins, as we have seen, with the stage floor, as does the Japanese in daily life, who lies on the floor and derives his upward movement from it. The actor sits on the floor with his legs folded in front of his body or beneath it. He bows almost prostrate on the floor, he bows in the sitting position, he bows when standing. He raises his arms above his head in the *mie*. He gains added height by movement up steps to a platform, or, as sometimes happens at the end of a dance, by mounting a small platform brought on by a stage assistant. In the representational theatre the actor's usual sphere of expressive movement is that which is defined by a bottom line at about the level of the seat of a chair, and an upper line at about the top of the actor's head. This horizontal band of playing area is reinforced by the design of the setting, by the lighting, by the placement of properties and furniture, to the end of keeping the attention of the audience more or less constantly attracted to this area. There are relatively few occasions when the actor is permitted to raise his hand above his head. The floor of the stage has little immediate dynamic power, for the actor's footwork is in general important only in that it contributes indirectly to the expressiveness of the upper part of his body. The representational theatre on some occasions provides platforms or flights of steps for the actor's use, but these must be used as representational architectural objects and only rarely as theatrical objects. The Kabuki actor utilizes a vertical line extending from the floor to as high as he can reach as a sphere of expressive movement and therefore has approximately twice as much vertical space in which to move than does the representational actor. The surprise expressed at Judith Anderson's using a long vertical line in *Medea* is some evidence of the fact that audiences in the representational theatre are not accustomed to its use. Since the Kabuki actor is not restricted to realistic gesture and attitude, he can be equally expressive with every part of his body along this vertical line. The movements of his feet and legs are as expressive as those of his arms and head, while the representational actor's physical expressiveness is confined largely to his face and hands. In *Sukeroku* the hero insults his rival Ikkyū by offering him a pipe which he holds between his toes.

Since he must be expressive in every part of his body, the Kabuki actor is a lithe figure. His education in the theatre begins not only with dance but also with the more strenuous forms of acrobatics. He must be capable of performing the backward somersaults that show defeat in a scene of fighting; he must be able to perform as a fox, a part of a horse, a rat, or a tiger. In *aragoto* there is created the impression of sheer muscularity. But in the greater part of the Kabuki the skill of the actor is demonstrated by delicate and subtle muscular control; this is an attribute shared by the Japanese people at large who in the mere process of writing the language acceptably must develop a muscular control of the hand and arm which in the Western world is achieved only by the artist. The great Kabuki actors all exhibit more than normal skill in painting and calligraphy; their hands and fingers are exceedingly supple. The fine points of Kabuki acting consist in this delicate control, and the crucial test of the actor's skill is his ability to handle properties with consummate grace and ease. His ability is no more than a refinement of that shared by all Japanese, whose common etiquette includes a concern for handling chop-sticks, rice-bowls, and most of the objects of daily use in a highly formalized and graceful fashion. Since the Kabuki actor is basically a dancer, this skill extends to every part of his body.

The competent actor in the representational theatre takes care to surround himself with space, to keep, whenever possible, another actor from approaching him and thus occupying the spatial and psychological area which is rightly his. But there are heroines to be kissed, hands to be shaken, blows to be struck, and all of these acts require physical contact. The Kabuki actor is equally aware that he loses his sphere of expressiveness when he is in physical contact with another actor, and he sets up about him, whether he is a bit player or a star, an area which is never invaded by the other actors on the stage. The whole of the love scene between Izayoi and Seishin, which culminates in their decision to commit suicide, is acted out with no physical contact between them other than a touch of their extended hands. Love is expressed by a conventional attitude in which the woman kneels at the side of the man, who is standing, and the two exchange glances. The only physical contact between Hangan and Moronao, in *The Loyal Forty-seven Rōnin*, before Hangan is driven to strike him with a sword, is that which occurs when, to detain Moronao, Hangan sits on the long train of Moronao's kimono. When the blow is struck, there is no actual physical contact; no actual blows ever occur in the Kabuki. In the scenes of fighting (*tachimawari*) and of murder (*koroshiba*) there is no contact between bodies or between swords. A characteristic 'fighting' pattern is that in which the hero moves across the stage parallel to the footlights while his opponents approach him in a line from the opposite direction. When they meet the hero, the opponents move, alternately, to the right and left of him as he waves his sword in their direction. It is characteristic of the Kabuki to present to the audience not the thing itself, but the designed impression of the thing, and this principle dictates that 'real' conflict be avoided. But the almost complete absence of physical contact in the Kabuki also appears to be the result of the unwillingness of the actor to forfeit any part of his expressiveness to another actor. This characteristic is inherent in the nature of the self-contained Kabuki gesture and attitude. The actor's torso is the axis of the design and his arms and legs are moved with reference to this central line. Gesture away from the body does not establish a continuing line outward, but the movement is completed by a return to the central axis of the torso.

The *mie*, as the ultimate physical expression toward which all Kabuki movement tends, is a synthesis of the patterns of characteristic Kabuki movement. The *mie* bears so clear a resemblance to certain figures of Buddhist sculpture that it is difficult to believe that the pose was not directly derived from them. The god Fudō, who is the Japanese manifestation of the Hindu god Acala, has the power to ward off devils. His large eyes stare defiantly, the corners of his mouth are drawn down in a forbidding expression, he is surrounded with fire, in his right hand he holds a sword and in his left a rope with which to bind the demons. The Niō, the two gods that stand at either side of the entrances of the larger Buddhist temples, are similarly engaged in warding off evil; in one hand they carry a mace; the other hand is extended, palm vertical; the eyes are crossed, and all the muscles are tense. These gods, and others of similar attitude, were introduced to Japan in the early ninth century. They possess, in common with the *mie*, these qualities: Their attitudes are balanced and self-contained in the use of the antagonistic muscles, so that tension and intensity of expression are their chief characteristics; since the movement is self-contained, the attitude is defensive rather than offensive; the crossing of the eyes, according to the Japanese, concentrates the line of the eyes in a single direction and thus intensifies the expression; the drawing down of the corners of the mouth (which is accentuated in the Kabuki by make-up) creates a grim expression which intimidates the aggressor. The legs, hands, and arms of the *aragoto* hero are made-up in stylized designs in red and white to indicate the tension of muscles and veins. It has been maintained by certain Japanese scholars that a basic Japanese attitude in conflict is the defensive one. In view of recent world history, this notion may perhaps be questioned, but at least throughout the Tokugawa period, which the Kabuki reflects, the basic pattern of Japanese political thought was that of self-enclosure, self-containment, defense rather than aggression. In the classical forms of Japanese conflict—fencing, jūdō, and wrestling—the philosophy of movement is that aggressive movement is weaker than defensive and that the aggressor invariably loses. This philosophy is borne out in Kabuki sword fighting in which the hero is almost invariably attacked and his attitude throughout the scene is defensive. The first, and traditional, movement of the Edo fireman when attacked by an opponent was that of slipping his clothing from his shoulders, striking a defensive attitude, and revealing an expanse of tattooed flesh which would intimidate the aggressor. In large things and small, Kabuki attitudes display the characteristics of tension, self-containment, and isolation in space.

The *mie* is, of course, not a realistic pose. In the type known as the 'stone-throwing' *mie*, the right hand is raised above the head, fingers and thumb extended tensely, while the left hand grasps a sword hilt or fan. This *mie* does not suggest the throwing of a stone but is a position after the act of throwing has been completed. In the 'around a pillar' *mie*, the actor poses around a tree or around the supporting pillar of a house or gate; not infrequently in this attitude his right arm is extended around the pillar at about the level of his head; his left hand, palm downward, is held against the side of the pillar about level with his waist; his left foot is raised with the sole flat against the pillar. In the Genroku *mie*, supposedly invented by Ichikawa Danjūrō I for use in *aragoto*, the right arm is extended outward and upward, the right hand is clenched in a fist, the left hand is on the sword hilt, and the feet are wide apart, the right leg bent and the left leg straight. The position of the legs in this *mie* is similar to their position in the 'separated feet' *mie*, but in this variety the right hand holds a sword vertically behind the back while the left hand is extended in front of the body, palm outward, in the tense fashion of the guardian deities. In the 'standing upright' *mie* the feet are close together, a sword in the right hand is held outward to the side of the body about parallel to the floor. In many of the *mie* used at the end of a scene, the 'close of the curtain' *mie*, a frequent pose in that in which a sword is held over the head. Technically, female characters do not perform *mie*; their poses are called *kimari*.

These are only a few examples of the various forms that the *mie* may take. In all of them the essential quality is one of balanced tension, and the effect is sculptural; to realize this effect, the actor must be given considerable space in which to perform. Space around the actor is maintained more religiously in the Kabuki than in any form of Western theatre except possibly the ballet.

The composition of scenes involving a relatively large number of characters is determined by two considerations: the strength of the downstage plane and the provision of a sufficient spatial playing area around each actor. As a result, a characteristic arrangement is that in which the less important characters are placed on a single line upstage, always equidistant, usually kneeling rather than standing, while the important characters are arranged on a similar line, parallel to the footlights, on the downstage plane. A Kabuki 'crowd' always acts as a unit; and there is seldom any differentiation made between its members either in costume, make-up, or characterization. Its visual composition is always regular and the movement and attitude of its members is almost as similar as those of the chorus line in the Western revue. As in the revue, the same visual relation prevails between the upstage line of actors and the downstage plane of the principals, so that the frieze of richly costumed upstage actors at once partakes of the nature of a decorative background and also projects the downstage actors aesthetically toward the audience. However, unlike the chorus line, the members of the Kabuki upstage group are never placed closely together. The lesser characters are not used in the Kabuki to produce a sense of mass, and because of the regularity of their spacing they create no feeling of weight. Mass is established always by the stance, the *mie*, the elaborate costuming of the individual central characters, while the regular grouping of the subordinate characters prevents them from detracting from the mass of the central characters. The lesser characters may at some times be arranged in groups on stage-right when an interior-exterior setting is used, or they may be divided into two equal groups placed on either side of the stage, but their usual position, other things being equal, is the upstage one.

The strong downstage plane pulls the actor into it, and his basic position is facing the audience. It is for this reason that lesser characters are placed behind him. When two or more important characters are in the downstage plane on a single line parallel to the front of the stage, they do not as a rule turn toward each other in their dialogue. When two of the characters are more important than a third, the third one takes an upstage position between them. The result is a triangular grouping. The triangular formation is the basic emphatic form in the representational theatre, but there the upstage character at the apex of the triangle is generally in the strongest position. In the Kabuki the reverse is true: The downstage characters are in the stronger position. The triangular formation is frequently employed in the Kabuki, sometimes with a single downstage character, the lesser characters taking the upstage positions. This arrangement is that of the 'inverted' triangle of the representational theatre which is, however, relatively infrequently used. When a socially superior character is seated on an upstage platform and two less socially important characters are seated, or stand, below the platform, the triangle grouping is thus visually made a vertical one and becomes pyramidal in form. In this formation the emphatic position may or may not be the top of the pyramid. If the central character takes his position at the top of the pyramid and lesser characters, such as opposing warriors, are on the stage floor below him, then the central character is clearly in the most emphatic position. But when a character is seated at the top of the pyramid solely because of his social importance, the characters placed below him are more frequently than not in the stronger positions. In 'Moritsuna's Camp,' for example, Yoshitsune, socially the most important character, is seated at the top of the pyramid; Moritsuna, the hero, is seated on the stage floor, to Yoshitsune's right, while the three women are seated on the stage floor to his left. The strongest position is at first that of Moritsuna who inspects a head, supposedly that of his brother. But then the boy Kōshirō moves into the women's corner of the pyramidal formation and commits suicide by stabbing himself; with this, the emphasis shifts to the women's side of the formation. Throughout the scene, the downstage corners of the pyramid are stronger than Yoshitsune's upstage position.

The pyramidal form is also created without the use of upstage platforms. At the end of certain dances when a small platform is brought on stage for the chief dancer to stand upon, as in *The Love Affairs of Six Poets*, lesser characters below him are grouped on either side of the platform. *The Girl at Dōjō Temple* ends with the heroine atop a large temple bell, the group of priests, hands raised toward her, kneeling below. At the conclusion of the *michiyuki* in *The Loyal Forty-seven Rōnin*, the comic character Bannai ascends a pyramid consisting of the bodies of his followers and looks, through an improvised telescope, at the departing hero and heroine on the *hanamichi*. And in the fourth act of the same play, after Hangan has struck Moranao, a group of courtiers rush in to restrain him; as the curtain is drawn, they kneel in a circle about him and lift him upward in standing position. A reverse of the pyramid formation is that in which a character kneels between two or more who are standing and in this the central position is usually the strongest one.

The triangular formation is invariably shallower than that normally used in the representational theatre, and the pyramidal formation is in actuality no more than a visual flattening out of the depth of the triangle so that, in effect, the upstage apex of the triangle can be projected into the strong downstage plane and the sense of depth minimized. At the same time it is a method of uniting visually the raised upstage area with the stage floor so that they do not become disparate areas and thus suggest penetration of depth. Almost always the pyramidal formation is constructed on the stage-center axis which is often reinforced visually by the single vanishing point of the perspective background and by the angling in of the inner proscenium, and this grouping consequently produces a purely formal effect. However, within the outlines of the pyramid or the triangle there is very seldom absolute symmetry; the sides of the pyramid are usually not equilateral, and there is usually an attempt to complicate the design by an irregularity in the groupings at the three points.

In general Japanese art abhors bilateral symmetry, although this kind of design sometimes occurs, particularly in the art produced previous to the flowering of Zen Buddhist art in the fifteenth century. The Zen artists felt that too much symmetry in design hindered the spontaneity and imaginativeness of the work, and the influence of this belief has to a large degree permeated the Japanese aesthetic consciousness. In one type of flower arrangement, the flowers are placed so that they occupy a spatial area which is half a sphere, the straight side of which is vertical. The flowers do not fill up the curved side of the sphere so that its geometrical outline is clearly indicated, but merely suggest the existence of this half-sphere by touching it at three points. The vertical line is established not by a straight branch or stem, but by a curved one, so that the strongest line of the composition, about which the rest of the arrangement is built, is not stated but only suggested. In this sort of flower arrangement the existence of a complete sphere is implied, but visually only one half of the space is utilized.

In the Kabuki the triangular and pyramidal formation, the frieze of subordinate characters (or musicians) placed equidistant from each other upstage of the principal characters, and the inclination to place characters on a line parallel to the front of the stage constitute the formal lines upon which the grouping of the figures is composed. This symmetrical balance is established upon the forces of the down-stage plane and of the central axis of the stage. But within these large symmetrical designs the chief actors seek to establish the kind of off-center, or as it has been sometimes called, 'occult,' balance such as occurs in flower arrangement and obtains both in the relation between the stage and the *hanamichi* and in the arrangement of interior-exterior setting in which the interior is placed on stage-left. The groupings on the stage therefore are a combination of symmetrical and 'occult' balance, the latter shown most frequently in the pose of the individual actor. It is equally true that the grouping of actors on the stage of the representational theatre is a similar compromise between a balanced geometrical design based on the central axis of the stage and the avoidance of a purely geometrical pattern by the readjustment of the attitude of the individual actor within it. But the difference lies in the fact that while in the representational theatre an effort is always made to conceal the geometrical form upon which the grouping is based, in the Kabuki the geometrical form is clearly and exactly stated; against this form, as against the setting and the painted background, the 'occult' balance of the individual actor is thereby set in greater relief. The actor appears in spatial isolation from the others on the stage, and by the design of his individual pose he also acquires a certain aesthetic isolation from the others which is similar to that obtained by his refusal to place himself in physical contact with another actor. In groupings, therefore, as in the *mie* and elsewhere, the individual expressiveness of the actor is maintained.

The same isolated quality appears in the general pattern of line reading. Only in certain parts of domestic plays does theatre speech resemble the give and take of colloquial dialogue. Most of the time the individual line is a self-contained unit, and every speech concludes with a downward inflection. Therefore in general the dialogue conveys little sense of moving forward in vocal progression or of an actual vocal interchange. Even in the scene known as *kakeai*, such as that in *Chivalrous Gorozō*, when two opposing groups address each other alternately, the effect is less that of vocal conflict than of an antiphonal series of isolated speeches. This characteristic appears also in the recitation of 'divided lines' (*wakizerifu*) in the performance of which one character is on the *hanamichi*, the other on the stage, and they declaim their lines alternately. Even when the convention of *watarizerifu* ('extended lines') is used, in which a sentence or a speech is broken into phrases and each phrase is recited by a different character, the effect is that of relatively isolated phrases rather than of fluid continuity.

The costume, the make-up, and the movement of the actor create a sculptural quality which is both enhanced by and fills up the space with which he surrounds himself. The most gorgeous and complicated costumes are those worn by the heroes of *aragoto* and by the *onnagata* in the roles of courtesans. The kimono of the *aragoto* hero and the *obi* about his waist are padded with cotton, the sleeves of the kimono are larger than normal (as in *Just a Moment*), his wig increases the height and breadth of his head, his nonrealistic red and blue make-up is designed to show strength, and all of this creates about him what the Japanese call a 'square-form.' The courtesan wears a high wig decorated with long tortoise-shell hair ornaments, her costume consists of several kimono one on top of another and having a considerable train, her *obi* is a large one tied in front, she walks on wooden clogs six inches high. The *kamishimo*, the standard formal male costume of the Tokugawa period, emphasizes the horizontal line of the shoulders and also thickens the lower part of the body. Only in domestic plays is the costume a relatively simple one consisting of a kimono of simple line tied about the waist with an *obi*; but in this the simplicity of line is in itself sculptural. Because of the wide kimono sleeves of all costumes, all movements of the arm are not only emphasized, but when the arm is held up the material of the sleeve increases the size of the figure considerably. The actor holding a fan or a sword further increases the extent of the spatial area he inhabits. Thus the isolated solidity of his pose, greatly contributed to by the costume and make-up he wears, is one of the means by which, in the extensive playing area of the Kabuki stage, he is enabled to attract and to hold the attention of the audience.

He has other means of visual emphasis. When he moves into the downstage plane, he is in so emphatic a position that when he turns his back to the audience he ceases to exist theatrically; he takes this position so that his costume can be rearranged by a stage assistant, the perspiration wiped from his face, a cup of tea drunk. There being no requisite to 'look real,' the normal attitude of the Kabuki actor is absolute immobility, and against the ground of immobility his gesture and movement gain increased emphasis. In crowd scenes, when the downstage actor is usually set against the upstage frieze of actors, the expressionless faces and static attitudes of the upstage actors emphasize the downstage movement.

The Kabuki scene is generally lavish in its combination of colors. In *The Soga Confrontation* the back wall of the setting consists of golden doors with blue crests painted upon them. In front of this on a platform sit a group of retainers dressed in metallic cloth; below them are four courtesans richly dressed in a variety of colors, while on stage-left on a small platform sits Kudō, the antagonist, dressed in black and gold, with two colorfully dressed attendants. The Soga brothers, who bear no love for Kudō, appear on the *hanamichi* dressed in pale blue, and as the play progresses they move gradually from the *hanamichi* to the center of the stage. Gōrō is the more aggressive of the two brothers, and his brother Jūrō attempts to calm him. The pale blue costumes of the brothers stand out against the metallic richness of the setting and the costumes. As Gōrō moves closer and closer to Kudō, his anger increases, and this movement is accompanied by changes of costume which emphasize both his anger and his visual importance. He first removes his right arm from his outer kimono revealing a bright red kimono beneath; there is almost no red in the other costumes or in the setting. After a time he removes the left arm so that the upper part of his costume is entirely red; later he removes the upper part of the red kimono to display a brighter red one beneath it. A partial change of costume, such as this, to increase the emphasis upon a central character is used throughout the Kabuki.

But violently contrasting color is not always used to emphasize the important character. In the *michiyuki* of *The Loyal Forty-seven Rōnin*, the hero Kampei, when about to engage in fighting, slips off the upper part of his kimono to reveal a scarlet under-kimono. His opponents are not dressed in contrasting colors, but wear the pink and red costumes of floral design of the 'flower-warriors,' and these complement the red of the hero's costume. In the scene of Hangan's suicide in the same play, the colors used are pale blues, silver, white, and grays suitable to the solemnity of the occasion. After Hangan's death, the importance of the character Yuranosuke is shown visually not by contrast but by his being dressed in a costume of black and dark gray.

A change of costume, particularly on female characters, is one of the standard methods in the representational theatre of renewing audience interest; but in the Kabuki the change is more often than not made before the eyes of the audience and consequently is much more impressive than that which takes place behind the scenes. It concentrates the attention of the audience on the actor at the time the change is being made and thus, like the change of scenery before the eyes of the audience, obeys the Kabuki principles of displaying frankly the means by which its effects are produced and of creating sudden changes. In addition to the business of removing only the upper part of the kimono (*hada wo nugu*) there is also the complete removal of the outer clothing to reveal another costume beneath it, by this means showing a change of mood or attitude on the part of the character. In 'Kumagai's Camp' the hero removes his battle costume to show himself clad in the robe of an itinerant priest. At the end of 'The Village School' Matsuōmaru and Chiyo remove their outer kimono and show themselves dressed entirely in white, the color of mourning. In *Snowbound Pass* the harmless appearing woodsman is converted into a demon by his change of costume. In the costume change called *hiki-nuki* ('pulling-out') the parts of the outer kimono are basted together and when the threads are pulled out by a stage assistant the outer costume falls from the body of the actor. This change, usually employed in dances, shows a change of mood rather than a change in character. In the dance *White Heron Maiden* the heroine changes costumes four times in this fashion to show the passing of the seasons of the year. The quick change (*hayagawari*), unlike the others, does not take place before the eyes of the audience but is done offstage, and it is for this reason regarded as a somewhat vulgar trick by Kabuki purists; the actor disappears as one character and almost immediately reappears as another with different costume and make-up. However, in the surprise which it occasions, the emphasis it throws upon the actor, the rapid change lies close to the characteristic forms of Kabuki expression. This trick change seems to have appeared in the beginning of the nineteenth century and was particularly the forte of the first Onoe Matsusuke. In 1804, in *Tokubē's Tale of a Foreign Country*, a play by Tsuruya Namboku IV, Onoe in one scene committed suicide by jumping into a pool on the stage as one character, and then appeared almost immediately as a different character at the rear of the *hanamichi*. So startling and rapid was his transformation that he was summoned before government officials who suspected, since he had this presumably magic power, that he might be a Christian, and Christian belief had been forbidden to the Japanese after 1638. Playwright, actor, and audience in the early nineteenth century seem to have delighted in these rapid changes in character. Onoe Kikugorō III played three different roles in Tsuruya's *Ghost Story of Yotsuya*, and Tsuruya wrote one play—*Osome and Hisamatsu*—in which seven quick changes occur.

The relation of the actor to other actors, the fluidity of the setting and of the properties are further evidence of the actor's being aesthetically superior to and consequently unencumbered by the forces which these elements of production set up. The actor in the representational theatre is always, to some degree, 'pulled into' the representational milieu by which he is surrounded. He must relate himself psychologically as a character to the illusory world of walls and doors that look solid, of palpable chairs, tables, and windows. He is almost constantly engaged in psychological rapport with the other actors on the stage. He is also oriented toward the upstage area and to the wings by the car arriving outside, the footsteps on the stair, the knock on the door. He is related to the *mise en scène* not only psychologically but also visually—so much so that were he to move any considerable distance downstage he would be 'out of the picture' and in that downstage limbo which in the representational theatre is neither stage nor auditorium. But although the whole representational world of the stage draws the actor inward, he must at the same time be placed in a position from which he can speak his lines more or less directly to the audience and from which, since his face is more frequently utilized as a visual means of expression than any other part of his body, a sufficient quantity of facial expression will be shown to allow the audience to understand the nature of the emotions he is expressing. The movement and attitude of the actor is thus subject at any given moment to two opposing forces: that which will move him into a 'facing front' position in which he can be seen and heard to best advantage, and that which pulls him in toward the setting and the other actors. So complicated were the problems created by this phenomenon that they could not be solved by the actor alone and necessitated the appearance of the director in the representational theatre. The director did not appear in the Kabuki theatre until after 1926; he was needed at this time to cope with the problems that arose when the Kabuki experimented with certain Western theatre conceptions.

We have seen that the Kabuki actor does not involve himself with the other actors in realistic groupings, that he addresses himself to the downstage plane of the stage, and that he is not oriented toward the extra-proscenium areas of the stage. He is similarly free from physical, and consequently aesthetic, involvement with settings and properties. The setting at all times opposes the actor's body, and parts of it, such as a gate or a platform, remain on the stage only so long as they are requisite to the actor. As described earlier, a whole setting may be moved to allow the actor greater space in which to play. Properties, managed by the stage assistant, assert their dramatic value only at the point where they are necessary to the actor's expressiveness and therefore do not set up centers of interest in rivalry to the actor. The Kabuki *mise en scène* does not involve the actor, except momentarily, in its milieu. Since it is created to invest only the observable limits of the stage with theatre reality, and since the actor is not oriented psychologically and physically toward the extra-proscenium areas, his basic impulse of movement toward the downstage plane is unrestricted. Every part of the downstage area is used except that in which the footlights are installed. The actor feels no compulsion to remain 'in the picture' because the 'picture' already exists in essential opposition to him; he moves as close to the audience when on the stage as when on the *hanamichi*. He is, however, involved in a certain psychological rapport with the other actors, but this he minimizes by avoiding physical contact with them, by maintaining a relatively large sphere of space about him, and by placing himself on a parallel line with other actors. In brief, the whole of his technique of acting is directed outward toward the audience; he is not forced to compromise between relating himself both to the *mise en scène* and to the downstage plane. The result is that he is immediately expressive; his communication with the audience is not the indirect one of the representational theatre but is realized in immediate contact.

In a variety of ways, then, the Kabuki actor maintains within his figure and his movement means of expression which in the representational theatre are shared with or taken over by the other elements of production. The idea of *night*, for example, can be conveyed by the Kabuki actor alone, while in the representational theatre this idea must be stated primarily by the lighting, only secondarily by the actor. The actor moving in a representational milieu thus forfeits certain areas of expressiveness, and it may be as compensation for this loss that the contemporary Western actor has concerned himself increasingly with the projection of psychological subtleties of character which, except in the theatre of expressionism, the setting is incapable of communicating to the audience. The Kabuki actor, on the other hand, relinquishes no part of his expressiveness for the aggrandizement of what he regards as the subordinate elements of production.

To the end of increasing his expressiveness, the actor makes use of three varieties of theatrical time. The first is what may be called nonactive, for in it the movement of the play does not actually go forward. During this 'time' the actor faces upstage to have his costume arranged, to drink tea, or to wipe the perspiration from his face. He may make an arbitrary cross to the other side of the stage or up to a platform so that he will be in a proper position for the scene to follow. He may seat himself on a high stool. In other words, he separates during the performance the time which is devoted solely to functional theatrical use and that which is the 'active' time of the progression of the play. This division is of course not made in the representational theatre, where theatre time must correspond more or less exactly, within a given act or scene, to the time which passes in the auditorium, and in which the actor on the stage must arrange his costume, if necessary, or move from one area of the stage to another within a single plane of more or less realistic time.

But the 'active' time of the Kabuki, that during which the action of the play progresses, shows a greater correspondence to that employed by Greek tragedy and by Shakespeare than it does to the relatively literal use of time in the representational theatre. It is only audiences of the representational theatre who notice that Agamemnon's return follows surprisingly quickly upon the fall of Troy or that Shakespeare manages to have a night pass, in *Othello*, in less than 400 lines. The Kabuki actor uses time, as he uses the other elements of productions, purely theatrically, suspending it, speeding it up, slowing it down, as it suits his purposes. Time is considerably expanded during the soliloquy, as it was in the Shakespearean theatre, and during the passages in which the narrator describes the actor's thoughts while the actor relates them in pantomime. Certain entrances on the *hanamichi* become soliloquies expressed in movement during which time is suspended. During Sukeroku's extended

189

posturing on the *hanamichi* at his first entrance, time stands still while the actor's pantomime reveals the character. When Benkei in *The Subscription List* makes his triumphal exit on the *hanamichi* he does so on a plane of time not measured by the ticking of the clock. The *mie* similarly exists on a timeless plane. The actor speeds up time, for example, by his changes of costume on the stage and by his freedom from the necessity of walking about the stage in order to lay hands upon a property required in the action. Time is slowed down and reduced to slow motion so that individual movements can be better communicated to the audience. At the conclusion of *A Substitute for Meditation* and of *The Tea Box* and in night scenes of fighting, the movement is reduced to about half of normal speed. The 'time' of Kabuki movement in this respect is not unlike the relatively free time of Western dance which does not create a strong sense of the passage of actual time.

The Kabuki also makes use of time which corresponds on the whole to that of the representational theatre, with, however, the possibility of an immediate suspension of this time if it is necessary to prolong a certain action or attitude so that it can be made more effective. In the 'Shio Temple' scene of *Flowers at Ueno*, after the villain Horiguchi has kicked the child Botarō from an upstage interior platform, he draws his sword, holds it aloft, and sits on the platform in a menacing attitude. At this point the nurse Otsuji runs in to protect the child. She comforts Botarō and talks to him, and her movement onto the stage and her conversation with the child are played in actual time. But for Horiguchi time is suspended; he remains in the same pose, immobile, until after Otsuji has persuaded the child to apologize, and in this static position he assumes a constant ideological force in his timelessness against the actual time in which Otsuji and the child move. As a result, the expressiveness of the three characters is increased over what it would be if all moved in actual time. A somewhat more complicated use of the division of time is employed in a part of 'Moritsuna's Camp.' In order to prove to Yoshitsune that the head before him is that of his father, the boy Kōshirō decides that he will kill himself. Kōshirō has been seated in the upstage secondary room observing the action that has been taking place in the downstage area. He now jumps down from the platform, sits beside his grandmother, is assisted in getting out of the upper part of his kimono by a stage assistant, and then stabs himself in the bowels. During this action, time stops for the other characters on the stage;

only after the boy has stabbed himself do they react to his deed. The boy's decision to kill himself, his heroism in taking this action (for he knows that the head is not really that of his father) are thus clearly defined against the immobility of the other characters in a way that they could not be if the others were to be aware of his intention and to try to stop him.

The onlooking actor in the Kabuki does not 'react' until his reaction is necessary to clarify a dramatic point. In the scene described above the audience is given the opportunity to examine in detail the action of Kōshirō and also the reaction of his uncle, aunt, and grandmother. In the representational theatre the two would have to occur almost simultaneously and the impression of the scene would be conveyed through the totality of the action of all the characters on the stage. In the Kabuki, with its visual fragmentation of time, the series of actions which in real life would occur simultaneously are held up before the audience separately so that the single impression of each of them is stated unambiguously. The technique employed—that of the complete immobility of the other actors until the boy's action is completed— is similar to that used in the film when a group reaction is broken into smaller units (and actual time is thus expanded) by the camera's recording a series of close-ups of individual characters reacting to a common stimulus.

Temporally, the Kabuki tends to 'take one thing at a time' both for the sake of clarity and also for the purpose of freeing the actor from a total, simultaneous reaction in which his individual expressiveness would be weakened. This consideration extends even to subordinate, undifferentiated characters. In the scenes of fighting, the hero is pitted against some ten or more warriors; usually at the beginning and the end of the scene he engages in dance movement with the entire group, but during the greater part of the scene he 'fights' with one or two at a time, the others waiting in the upstage area, so that each of the warriors is given his moment of unqualified attention.

The technique of dividing an action temporally into its component parts again reflects the Kabuki concern for the isolated expressiveness of the individual actor. An immediate group reaction to a given stimulus is a requisite of the representational theatre and arises logically out of the character's psychological and physical involvement with the *mise en scène*. The Kabuki, since it does not involve the actor with setting, properties, and other actors, also logically frees him, when necessary, from the demands of the immediate reaction in which the force of his reaction would be diffused. The immediate reaction would tie him in with the other characters as would close physical contact.

The aura surrounding the Kabuki actor—contributed to by the space with which he surrounds himself, the sculptural quality of his figure, his noninvolvement with the *mise en scène* or the immediate reaction—can best be described as one of detachment.

His detachment is not that of indifference or lack of intensity; it is rather the artistic detachment such as exists between the pianist and the music he is playing or the ballet dancer and the dance he is performing. In neither of these cases is the performer involved to any great degree in immediate emotionality. The virtue of his performance lies in the demonstration of technical skill and discipline acquired during years of study, and whatever emotions are aroused in the hearer or spectator, it is the surface of technical excellence which produces them, not the emotion which the performer as an individual may be experiencing at the moment. It is equally true that the competent representational actor probably does not, in a given performance, feel to any significant extent the emotions he is called upon to display. But the theatre reality of the performance for the audience depends entirely upon its acceptance of the emotions displayed by the actor as being those genuinely felt by the actor. Although the audience may to some degree be aware of the technical skill of the actor, it is the representational surface of the performance which establishes rapport between stage and auditorium, and beneath this surface the technical skill of the actor is concealed. The texture of the surface is so constructed out of immediate reactions to stimuli (ignoring them, as in the 'double take,' produces an incongruity resulting in laughter) and a more or less exact correspondence of the passage of time in the auditorium and on the stage that it gives rise to what has been called the illusion of the first time. Unless this illusion is carefully maintained, theatre reality does not exist. But one does not expect this illusion in the performance of a concerto, nor in a performance of *Les Sylphides*, nor even in a performance of *La Bohème*. The audience derives satisfaction, primarily, from the technical skill of the performer and conceives a certain detachment between the effects he produces and his relation to them as an individual. The representational actor usually distinguishes between his own personality and that of the character he is portraying, but the line between the two can be drawn only in his own consciousness, for during his performance it is necessary that the audience be unaware that he makes this distinction. The whole of the theory of representational acting, summed up in the work of Stanislavsky, is that the genesis of character portrayal should arise out of an identification of the basic qualities of the character with those of the actor; this concept is the one on which representational theatre reality is posited. In the Kabuki the actor detaches his own personality from that of the character he is portraying, so that the audience finds its aesthetic satisfaction not in an illusionistic identification of actor and character, but rather in the technical skill of his performance.

It should be mentioned in passing that the detachment between actor and character and the primary concern of the audience with his technical skill does not reduce the immediate emotional impact of the performance. There are few Americans who weep at a performance of ballet; there are many who are deeply moved in the representational theatre. It would seem that a high degree of stylization in the American theatre, at this point in history, cannot arouse strong, immediate, nonintellectualized emotions. But in the Kabuki the audience's reaction to the performance and to the display of the actor's technical skill is immediate and vital; probably more tears are shed at the Kabuki theatre during a performance of *The Subscription List* than are shed at the Orpheum during the showing of a film displaying the woes of Olivia de Havilland. Although the language in which the Kabuki speaks is basically nonrealistic, the emotions aroused are as strong as those provoked in an American by a performance of *Death of a Salesman*.

The approach of the Kabuki actor to the character is summed up in this practice: In the small room at the end of the *hanamichi*, there is a large mirror; when the actor is fully prepared for his entrance, he sits before the mirror and studies his figure so that he can absorb the nature of the character he is to play by concentration on its external appearance. He does not base the character on something within himself but derives from the visual image an inward significance. In doing so he follows the theory and practice of Japanese art. The poet Bashō's advice to his pupils was 'Feel like the pine when you look at the pine, like the bamboo when you look at the bamboo'; in other words, truthful artistic expression can arise only with the complete surrender of the artist to the nature of the object before him, a surrender uninhibited by the artist's intellect or emotions. The late Kikugorō shaved the hair from his hands when playing a female role, not because the audience would be aware of, or disturbed by, the incongruity, but so that he himself could believe whole-heartedly in the theatrical figure he animated. The practice, taken from the Nō theatre, of the actor studying his image in a mirror, is symbolic of the method of training the Kabuki actor.

He makes his first appearance on the stage at the age of five or six, playing children's roles under the watchful eyes of the older actors. His education in the theatre, like that of most learning processes in Japan, is based not upon an understanding of principles nor the application of theory, but upon exact and unquestioning imitation. The gestures, movements, and attitudes which have been transmitted from one generation of actors to another for centuries, he must learn by rote. So formidable is the body of skills he must acquire that only after he has reached the age of fifty or so is he accepted as a finished actor, and it is not until this time that there is any considerable opportunity for him to make substantial changes in the traditional method of playing a certain role. In the past and at present it has been only the unskilful Kabuki performer who, being incapable of absorbing traditional modes of expression, has dared to substitute novelty for skill in acting. The weight of tradition lies heavily upon all Japanese artisans, who, like the actors, feel obliged to continue the use of the techniques of their forefathers. This practice arises out of the Japanese concern for continuity of a family and also out of the propensity to respect precedent rather than investigation. The process is time-consuming and, judged by Western standards, wasteful, but it results in an exquisitely perfected craftsmanship and artistry based upon an almost religious regard for the traditional means of expression. Perhaps it is only under such conditions, which equate solid traditional style and the freedom permitted the mature artist, that the evanescent form of expression called acting can be seriously considered an art form. The Kabuki actor does not 'create' roles in the manner of the contemporary Western actor; he rather, in his training, gradually disciplines his body in the inherited patterns of expression. The personality of the actor emerges, but only through the medium of the conventional forms which interpose between the personality of the individual and the role. The Kabuki actor, in brief, does not impersonate. He acts. And as with other productional elements of the Kabuki his performance is based upon its uncompromising theatricality.

This concept of the function of the actor appears most clearly in the practice of men playing the roles of women. The *onnagata* came into the Kabuki because of practical necessity when women were prohibited from appearing on the stage. But even in 1629, the essential stylization of the Kabuki permitted the convention to be quickly established. In modern times a few actresses have essayed to play Kabuki roles, imitating the manner of speaking of the *onnagata* and their movement, but they have never achieved success. Both Kabuki audience and actors feel that a woman playing a woman's role brings the performance too close to reality; the distinction between actor and character is lost and with it the *raison d'être* of the performance. Yoshizawa Ayame (1673–1729), a famed player of women's roles, wrote in his book *Ayame-gusa*, 'If an actress were to appear on the stage she could not express ideal feminine beauty, for she would rely only on the exploitation of her physical characteristics, and therefore not express the synthetic ideal. The ideal woman can be expressed only by an actor.' From the point of view of the design of the production, the *onnagata* is necessary because, according to the Japanese, although the surface of the woman portrayed should be soft, tender, and beautiful, beneath this surface there should be a strong line which can be created only by a man. A man of eighty plays the role of a girl and, because of his mastery of the vocabulary of Kabuki acting, creates before the audience a stronger theatre reality of her essential qualities than could any woman. This phenomenon could not exist unless the division between actor and character were clearly marked and unless the purpose of the theatre were to view realism as less expressive than stylization.

Because the line of detachment is clearly drawn between actor and character, the actor is not in any way dependent upon physical beauty, or even attractiveness, for success in the theatre or for the ability to play certain types of roles. His theatrical beauty is provided solely by the materials of the theatre, not by any physical attributes he may bring to it. He can therefore at the age of eighty play a girl of sixteen, since his projection of the role is not dependent upon the audience's esthetic identification, within the confines of the performance, of his individual being and that of the character, but upon the audience's recognition of the theatricality of the theatre and their appreciation of technical artistry.

The detachment of the actor from the role is further marked in his make-up. The face of the actor onstage is a compromise between the human face and the mask. The mask-like quality is created both by the make-up and by the propensity of the actor to reserve facial expression for only the most significant moments. As a result, all facial expression is thrown into high relief against the ground of facial immobility; it is not obscured in a succession of realistic facial 'reactions.' The make-up (*kumadori*) tends always toward conventionalization of the face according to the standard types of roles which were created during the Tokugawa period and shows little concern for realism except in certain *sewamono* and *kizewamono* pieces and in the horror plays which appeared in the early nineteenth century. In *The Ghost of Yotsuya* the facial disfigurement of the unhappy heroine is shown in her make-up. Otherwise, except in *aragoto*, the usual make-up is a dead white for men, women, and children. On this surface the eyebrows are painted in black, higher on the forehead than the actual eyebrows; the eyes are lined with black for men and red for women; lip rouge is used to produce a thin line of downward curvature for men's mouths and a small mouth in which the thickness of the lips is minimized for women. Peasant types wear a darker make-up; but even thieves such as Benten Kozō or Yōsaburō (in *Scarred Yōsaburō*) wear white make-up. The use of white make-up for the well-born and well-to-do can be explained on a logical basis, for such folk did not expose themselves to the sun's rays and therefore a white skin has always been prized in Japan as evidence of social superiority; the geisha and the Japanese woman in native costume continue to use this make-up. But that thieves and other important low characters should wear it as well arose out of practical theatre necessity: There was little light in the Kabuki theatre before modern times and the white make-up was a means of minimizing the effects of darkness and of projecting the expression of the actor's face.

The dramatic forms which preceded the Kabuki made use of masks, and the Nō and the Bugaku, the classical court dance, continue to use them at present. It is not strange that the Kabuki, which was in its beginnings a modern and startling form of theatre, should have avoided the use of conventionalized expression represented by the mask. But the instinct for stylization, which until modern times has informed all Japanese artistic expression, soon asserted itself in the Kabuki, most strongly in the make-up devised for use in *aragoto*. The origins of this type of make-up are obscure. The Kabuki legend is that Ichikawa Danjūrō II (1688–1758) devised it after studying a tree peony petal. A more likely original influence was that of the faces of the polychrome Buddhist statues of the Shingon sect whose attitudes bear a close resemblance to the *mie*. These figures had their origin in China, and so, indirectly, *aragoto* make-up may have had Chinese origins; but there seems to be no verifiable evidence that the make-up was imported directly from the Chinese theatre.

In addition to increasing the visibility of the face of the actor, the purpose of *aragoto* make-up, from its first use, was to create the effect of violent tension both on the face and on the body. On the arms, legs, and chest, red make-up is used to make a stylized outline of veins, sinews, and muscles, while the face is painted in red and blue in a nonrealistic design which, in general, outlines the muscular construction of the face, increases the height of the nose, draws down the corners of the mouth, and, most important, emphasizes the eyes. All *aragoto* make-up falls into two classifications: the 'one-line' and the 'two-line.' The 'lines' are those which are drawn upward on the face from the corners of the eyes, and the 'two-line' variety is the stronger. In a scene of Chikamatsu's *The Battles of Coxinga* the hero Watonai appears with 'one-line' make-up, but in a later scene in which he is angry, he wears the 'two-line' variety.

The influence of *aragoto* make-up spread to other Kabuki characters outside the plays which were pure *aragoto*, so that as a rule *aragoto* make-up is used today in all plays, except domestic ones, in which it is necessary to show great strength of character. The essential quality of 'Pulling the Carriage Apart,' for example, is confrontation and conflict between Matsuōmaru and his two brothers, and Matsuōmaru uses the 'two-line' *aragoto* make-up. But when Matsuōmaru appears in 'The Village School,' where he is not a defiant character, he wears the usual dead-white make-up. The demons who appear in the plays taken from the Nō, such as *Benkei at the Boat* and *Earth Spider*, also wear make-up derived from *aragoto*, and these in particular show considerable variety in color, using, in addition to red and blue, brown, black, green, gray, purple, and orange.

The change of make-up during the course of a play or within a single act from one variety to another is based on the same impulse toward sudden change that characterizes the change in costume or in setting, as well as the impulse to regard the actor as a technician rather than a 'personality.' The Matsuōmaru of 'Pulling the Carriage Apart' and that of 'The Village School' (two acts of the same play) are completely different in nature, and that difference is made apparent in the make-up used. In the Nō demon plays adapted to the Kabuki, the chief actor generally appears first in customary dead-white make-up and then changes both his costume and make-up to appear as a demon in the latter half of the play. These make-up changes are made offstage, but on some occasions the change may be made in sight of the audience. In *Snowbound Pass* the woodman's make-up is changed, along with his costume, onstage; the materials of make-up are concealed in a small compartment within the blade of the gigantic axe he carries, and he holds the blade before his face while, in a very few moments with the help of the stage assistant, his make-up is changed to that of a demoniac character.

Since the individual character is surrounded by an aura of detachment, to which costume, make-up, and the use of theatrical space contribute, the communicative flow of the performance is not realized in a simple totality of expression of all the productional elements, but these elements state their effects through, and are concentrated upon, the individual character. He is normally an isolated figure visually and aesthetically; only in the case of lovers, brothers, father and son, mother and daughter, and so on, when a very intimate bond exists between the characters, do they share the same spatial area and contribute to a common communicative flow toward the audience. In general, the characteristic movement of the actor is away from the other elements of production and toward concentration of theatrical expressiveness within his own figure. Therefore even the image of dramatic conflict is not expressed by the actor by directing it outward toward another character but by containing it within his own figure. A case in point is the scene between Hangan and Moronao in the third act of *The Loyal Forty-seven Rōnin*. Hangan is socially inferior to Moronao, who has been attempting to seduce Hangan's wife. In this long scene Moronao repeatedly insults Hangan until at last Hangan is driven to the unpardonable crimes of drawing a sword within the palace and of striking an official of the Shōgun. In the realistic theatre this scene would normally increase in intensity to the point at which the blow was struck, the climax of the scene, and Hangan would show greater and greater agitation and increasing involvement with Moronao as he approached the point. This is not the case in the Kabuki. In the first part of the scene Hangan's agitation is pronounced; he forces himself to bow before Moronao, his whole being rebelling against the movement; he can barely prevent his hands from reaching for his sword. But as the scene progresses toward the blow, Hangan's movement becomes less violent, he appears calm, and when the blow is struck it comes dramatically almost as an afterthought. The external mechanics of playing the scene would perhaps be possible in the representational theatre, but the important distinction is that the blow, to the Kabuki audience, is of secondary importance to the impact of the situation upon Hangan. The dramatic conflict is not expressed in terms of shared conflict between Hangan and Moronao, but arises entirely out of and is communicated by the figure of Hangan. The blow, which of course involves no physical contact, is not really the climax of the scene; the climax is that which has taken place within Hangan and which is revealed through his figure.

This scene illustrates the characteristic textural surface of Kabuki acting; it is constructed of what can be called secondary effects. The overt act, such as the blow, has little dramatic validity or interest in itself. Translated into terms of the Western theatre, the assassination of Caesar would be of little importance; the drama would lie in 'Et tu, Brute,' which in the Kabuki would be expressed in a *mie* rather than in words. It is true that in Western tragedy, as opposed to melodrama, the effect of events on character are relatively more important than the events themselves, but this feeling arises when the play is read, or when the performance is remembered, not within the theatre while the play is being performed, for there, in the representational production, the actor is bound to a strict sequence of immediate responses to dramatic stimuli and the surface of the play moves in general from one state of shared and immediate tension to another. In the Kabuki since the actor is not bound by such considerations and since he is the focal point of expression, it is not the blow itself which is important but the effect of it upon him.

Concern with the effect of the act rather than the act itself is apparent in large things and small; it rises basically out of the fact that the actor is the principal means of expression, that dramatic communication is concentrated in and expressed through the individual character rather than in the total effect of the *mise en scène*, and that the actor achieves his greatest communication visually. The effect of conflict in the scene of fighting, for example, is not conveyed by a clashing of swords: Actual contact is omitted, and the dramatic idea of being struck is not expressed in the blow but in the stylized pattern of movement (a somersault, for example) which follows it. In similar fashion, the *mie* does not indicate immediate participation in an event, but a concentrated visual synthesis of the attitude of the character toward the event. The usual pattern of acting at the *shichi-san* on the *hanamichi*, at which point the actor shows the adjustment of the character to the situation existing on the stage, is not expressed in immediate reaction to the dynamics of that situation (which would require that the character move onto the stage or away from it almost at once) but in the relatively slow and explicit demonstration of the interplay between the character and the situation stated in terms of the character. Properties, as well, are rarely used so that they have immediate dramatic validity; instead of having significance in themselves, they are merely a visual point of departure for the expressiveness of the actor. The papier-maché head which figures in the scenes of 'head-identification' (*kubijikken*) does not possess theatrical vitality of its own, but its effect is expressed on a secondary plane through the actor. The folding fan seldom has a literal surface of theatrical form but becomes in the hands of the actor a variety of objects on a plane once removed from its immediate image.

The division between the personality of the actor and the role was not always as marked as it is today. The *onnagata* wore the clothes of a woman and moved with feminine grace in private life (at least one actor's wife objected strongly to this), while the player of leading male roles attempted to lead a luxurious life offstage so that he would be capable of demonstrating the same elegance of manners and deportment in the theatre. The identification between individual and character is not to be wondered at considering that the actor was forced to live his whole life within the physical and spiritual confines of the theatre and was prohibited association with people in the outside world.

Identification of the actor and the role was also strengthened by the organization of the troupe, and this in turn influenced the playwright. During the Edo period the troupe consisted of eight principal actors and the plays were constructed on an eight character basis. The roles were an amplification of the three roles of the Nō theatre: the principal character (*shite*), the subordinate character (*waki*), and the 'companion' (*tsure*). The eight Kabuki categories were the hero (*tachiyaku*), the villain (*katakiyaku*), the elderly woman (*kashagata*), the young woman (*wakaonnagata*), the young man (*wakashūgata*), the old man (*oyajikata*), the comedian (*dōkegata*), and the child (*koyaku*). With the exception of the last, who grew up, the actor tended to play one of these roles throughout his life; the fact that Ichimatsu Sanokawa I (1722–1762), an *onnagata*, took up the playing of villains in later life caused contemporary amazement, as did the abandon-

57. A scene from *The Famous Tree at Sendai.*

A typical 'pyramidal' arrangement of characters, the highest ranking seated on the platform. [*Haar: Tuttle.*]

58. Nakamura Tokizō waiting to make his entrance upon the *hanamichi* in the 'woman's' *Just a Moment*. [*Iwanami.*]

ment of feminine roles for those of heroes by Onoe Kikugorō (1717–
1783). There were subordinate divisions within each of the roles, all
carefully defined, and these are preserved today. Among the young
women's roles, for example, are those of the young daughter, the
young princess (called *akahime*, 'red princess,' because her costume is
invariably red), and, the most difficult to play, the courtesan (*oiran*
or *keisei*, literally, 'castle-destroyer'). The older women's roles
include 'respectable' women of high rank, middle-class wives, old and
dignified women, and *onnabudō*, an infrequent role in which the
woman behaves rather like a warrior and is more important than the
hero of the play. There are of course supporting roles, such as that of
the *sabakiyaku*, a male character who aids the hero in overcoming the
villain, and such roles are usually played by the younger or less
accomplished actors.

Today the actor in most cases no longer restricts himself to one
type of role. It is not unusual to see in a single day's performance a
first-rate actor playing four different roles, both male and female,
serious and comic, young and old. Apart from the quick changes of
costume and character, there are occasions when, during the course of
a single play or act, the actor may perform two or more roles. A case
in point is Chikamatsu's *The Courier of Hell* in which the great,
recently deceased Kabuki actor, Kichiemon, played Chūbei, an errant
son, in the early part of the play and Chūbei's father at the end. In a
single act of *The Plains of Adachigahara*, Kichiemon first played the
role of an erring and disowned daughter who returns to seek entrance
to her father's house, and in the latter half of the scene, after the
daughter, being refused entrance, has died in the snow, Kichiemon
played the role of her stern, unforgiving father. Such transformations
of costume, character, and make-up are so common that they excite
no great show of enthusiasm on the part of the spectators; the
applause that greeted the appearance of Helen Hayes in the last scene
of *Victoria Regina* would scarcely be understood by a Kabuki audience.
Plays are seldom staged in their entirety, but on the rare occasions
when they are, it is not unusual to see one actor playing a certain
character in one act of the play while another plays the same character
in a subsequent act. In 1947 when *Sugawara's Secrets of Calligraphy*
was played in its entirety for the first time in some forty years, one
actor played the role of Matsuōmaru in the act called 'Pulling the
Carriage Apart,' another played Matsuōmaru in the act called
'Anniversary Celebration,' while a third played Matsuōmaru in 'The

Village School,' the final act of the play. The Matsuōmaru in 'The Village School' is a more substantial role than it is in the other acts and was, in this production, reserved for the ablest actor.

The rapidity with which roles are changed and the number of roles the actor is called upon to perform during the course of a day make any immediate emotional identification between actor and character very unlikely. There is, to be sure, an intense concentration of the actor upon his performance and the ultimate projection of the personality of the actor, not the man, through the stylized means of expression he employs; the actor does not move through the performance like an automaton. At the same time, his point of departure is not an inner identification of himself as an individual with the character he is to portray. The actor performs through the medium of the theatrical figure in much the same way that the accomplished pianist performs through the medium of the piano; however close he approaches to complete control of his medium, he never identifies himself with it.

Rehearsals, except for newly written plays, extend no longer than six or seven days, and during this time the entire bill for the following month is prepared, consisting usually of seven or eight pieces with a total playing time of eight to ten hours. Certain well known pieces, such as 'The Village School' and *The Subscription List*, are not rehearsed at all; the actor is always prepared to play these at a moment's notice and would regard a rehearsal of them as a confession of his shortcomings as an actor. With less frequently performed plays, a day or two is devoted to reading the script while seated (*honyomi*), two or three days to rehearsal with movement (*tachi-keiko*), one day to a general rehearsal with music (*sōzarae*), and one day to dress rehearsal (*butaigeiko*). The present active Kabuki repertoire consists of some three hundred pieces which can be called plays and about one hundred which are largely dance. The competent actor is capable of performing roles in any of these during a week or less of rehearsal. His repertory is therefore considerably greater than that of the Western opera star, but his ability to assume a role with little rehearsal shows a similar command of technical skill.

Obviously the Kabuki actor is one of the hardest working actors in the world. He is on the stage from six to eight hours a day, seven days a week, and most of his waking hours are spent within the theatre building. A new bill opens on the second or third of every month, and if a new play is to be performed, rehearsals must be scheduled between his performances during the day. If he is a star he may receive a month's vacation during the summer, but if he is a young actor he is likely to receive no vacation at all. He is not as well paid as a film star, and any substantial increase in salary must wait upon his being given a new name and thus being promoted in rank. He does not retire from the theatre in his last years unless he is bedridden; the late Matsumoto Kōshirō continued to play the athletic role of Benkei at the age of seventy-nine, even though at the end of the performance he was too exhausted to leave the theatre and slept in his dressing room.

The actor's devotion to the Kabuki is colored by a deep respect for the theatre traditions he has inherited and for the actors who have gone before him. The program for February, 1952, at the Tōkyō Kabuki-za was dedicated to the commemoration of the fiftieth anniversary of the death of Onoe Kikugorō V by the members of the Kikugorō troupe to 'comfort his soul.' The actor's dedication to the theatre is based less upon a personal desire for fame and fortune than it is upon a sense of personal obligation to preserve its traditions. Ichikawa Danjūrō VII (1790–1855) was the greatest of his line, and his son had already inherited his name; but the year before his father's death, the son, realizing that he would never be as great an actor as his father, committed suicide 'to save his father from reproach.'

Although the actor is no longer segregated from the rest of society and has indeed in recent years been decorated by the Emperor, the mere physical requirements of the Kabuki allow him little time outside the theatre, and most of his life is enclosed by its walls. The theatre is therefore, in a very concrete sense, his life. And his dedication is strengthened by the fact that he is not an actor as an individual but as a member of a theatrical troupe, a self-contained historical unit, which may have had a continuous existence for two hundred and fifty years. As has been frequently observed, the social unit in Japan is not the individual but the family, and the Kabuki troupe (*gekidan*) is the theatrical equivalent of a family. Outside the theatre the family preserves its continuity by adoption, if there is no male heir to carry on the name, and within the theatre the same practice is observed. When a great actor either has no son or his son shows no great promise as an actor, he does not hesitate to adopt a promising young man to inherit his name, and this young actor may well come from another troupe. When this happens the adopted son no longer has any ties with his original troupe but is bound by strong moral obligations to the new troupe. Although there have been occasions when an outsider, one who was not a member of a theatre family, has succeeded as an apprentice, no matter how popular he was with the audience there was no possibility of his receiving an increase in salary unless he was adopted into the troupe and given one of the traditional names. Adoption and name-giving continue to be rigidly controlled by the elders of the troupe.

At present there are five first-rate Kabuki troupes composed of some ninety-six actors, whose skill is recognized by their having names of historical significance, in addition to several hundred apprentices. And between these troupes there is considerable trading back and forth so that suitable actors can be obtained to bear the great names of the theatre. Ichikawa Danjūrō IX died in 1903, and at present no actor is of sufficient stature to assume this greatest of Kabuki names which dates from 1700. Because of their adoption from one troupe to another, some actors have extremely complicated genealogies. For instance, the eldest son of the late Matsumoto Kōshirō VII is a member of the Ichikawa troupe with the name of Ichikawa Ebizō, the ninth actor to hold that name; Kōshirō's second son inherited his father's name and is now Matsumoto Kōshirō VIII in the Kichiemon troupe; his third son became a member of the Kikugorō troupe and is now Onoe Shōroku II. The process of adoption assures the maintenance of the important names by skilful actors as well as a high degree of artistic inbreeding, both of which contribute to the almost mystical sense of devotion which the actor shows for the theatre. The system of training, the actor's complete absorption in his work, and his respect for tradition have resulted, after a period of almost three centuries, in a highly refined, rich technique of expression that has not been equalled in the Western theatre.

CHAPTER VIII

Plays and Characters

THE Japanese have a great love of classification. In the Kabuki this is demonstrated by the division and subdivision of plays into categories which are generally not based upon a conception of the play as a type of dramatic composition—such as tragedy, comedy, farce, or melodrama—but upon traditionally defined areas of subject matter. A few of these classifications indicate the exact quality of the play: In the *shosagoto* dance pieces, such as *The Girl at Dōjō Temple* or *The Wisteria Girl*, there is less plot than in the *jikyōgen* dance pieces, such as *The Tea Box* or *A Substitute for Meditation*; the short pantomime scenes, now rarely performed alone but as a kind of interlude in a long play, are called *dammari*.[1] The other classifications are less indicative of the nature of the play. For instance, an important category of plays is that known as the 'Eighteen Best Kabuki Plays' (*kabuki jūhachiban*), which Ichikawa Danjūrō VIII selected in 1840 and which became the traditional property of the Ichikawa troupe. Today only seven of these plays—among which are *The Subscription List*, *Sukeroku*, *The Arrow Maker*, and *Just a Moment*—are performed. Although they all include *aragoto* acting, as befits the Ichikawa

---

[1] *Dammari*, a dumb show accompanied by music, was a form evolved to introduce the members of the troupe in the November opening of the Kabuki season and was used as a curtain raiser in these performances. The scene of the typical *dammari* was before a mountain temple, and the action involved the appearance of all the members of the troupe elaborately costumed, with the chief actor making his entrance on the trap-lift in the *hanamichi*. The plotless action included *mie* by the principal members of the troupe and a fighting sequence. Kawatake Mokuami, the last great Kabuki playwright, frequently made use of *dammari* as an integral part of the action of his plays.

troupe, and are all one-act plays, they show no other common qualities. *The Subscription List* is an adaptation of the Nō play *The Barrier at Ataka* and has a well-knit plot; *The Arrow Maker*, improvisational and almost plotless, is simply an opportunity for the chief actor to display his skill; *Sukeroku* is both comic and serious; *Just a Moment* is lavish vocal and visual display. There is also a list of 'New Eighteen Best Kabuki Plays' chosen by Ichikawa Danjūrō IX and a list of 'Ten Plays Old and New' selected by Kikugorō V, both of which are equally eclectic and show a preoccupation with excellent roles rather than a conception of types of drama. Nevertheless these classifications are regarded as important by both actors and audiences. Plays which deal with historical events prior to the Tokugawa period are grouped under *jidaimono*; most of these are concerned with the period of civil war from 1490 to 1600. In point of historical fact, *The Loyal Forty-seven Rōnin*, which belongs to this classification, deals with events that in reality occurred during the Tokugawa period; the government forbade the use of contemporary material and therefore the playwrights set the time of their play in the Kamakura period (1192–1333). From a logical point of view, *The Subscription List* would belong to this category since it takes place in the civil war period; but *The Subscription List* is not thought of as *jidaimono* but as one of the 'Eighteen Best Kabuki Plays.' The *jidaimono* classification is subdivided into *ōdaimono*, plays which deal with very ancient events, and *ōiemono*, plays concerning the fall of a great house. *Sewamono*, domestic plays, deal generally with scenes of the commoners' life, whereas *jidaimono* are concerned with the aristocracy and with high deeds in palaces. But at the same time, *sewamono* characters and situations have been introduced into *jidaimono* and in some instances constitute a major part of the action. The kind of play called *kizewamono*, the 'living' domestic play, was given this name to distinguish it from *sewamono*, for it too deals with nonaristocratic characters, even more humble than those of *sewamono*. This classification came into being during the first quarter of the nineteenth century to designate plays, such as those of Tsuruya Namboku (1755–1829) and later, those of Kawatake Mokuami (1816–1893), which dwelt upon thieves, ghosts, cruelty, and bloodshed. Another category is that of 'traditional congratulatory plays' (*kichirei no kotobuki*) such as *The Soga Confrontation* and *Ceremonial Prelude*, which have ceremonial significance for both actors and audience. *The Soga Confrontation* is frequently used as a framework for the ceremony of giving a new name to an actor, while the *Ceremonial Prelude*, a dance based upon ancient fertility rites, is of a felicitous nature; during the Edo period lesser actors were frequently called upon to perform this dance at about three in the morning in order to bring prosperity to the theatre. Plays written after the beginning of the twentieth century are grouped together under the name of neo-Kabuki. Most of them show strongly the influence of the Western theatre in staging and in lighting effects, but the majority of them are set in the Edo period or in earlier periods. None are set in the contemporary scene.

The majority of these classifications therefore reveal little about the form of the play. They indicate a concern with the kind of costume and setting, with traditionally defined fields of subject matter, and they show the importance of the actor in the theatre. The classifications also reveal that the play as a form of literature capable of existing outside the theatre has not been a concern of the audience or the actors.

The greater number of plays of the Kabuki repertoire are those written during the Edo period and they naturally reflect the tastes of the audiences during that time. Throughout its history, the Kabuki theatre never made any attempt to change, direct, or influence the manners, morals, or thoughts of its audiences; on the contrary, its audience was given exactly the kind of theatrical fare it wanted. The playwright on occasion voiced a higher view of the function of the theatre, but, caught between the demands of the audience, the actor, and the government, he was forced to submit to their collective desires.

The audience wanted, primarily, to escape the restrictions imposed upon it in daily life, restrictions that were issued and reissued in much the same form throughout the period. The Kabuki, in its escapist function, resembled the dress of the townsmen: The *chōnin* were forbidden to wear handsome and extravagant silks, and so they wore kimono of an unprepossessing and sombre exterior, lined with rich, expensive, and colorful silk. The world of the Kabuki, in its lavish display, color, and excitement, provided, like the lining of the kimono, a sense of secret daring and fulfillment difficult to gratify in the strictly regulated world outside the theatre. The Kabuki from its beginnings had catered to a desire for striking, novel effects in costume, dance, and subject matter; it dealt with sensuous pleasure, high living, assignations between courtesans and samurai, and the whole realm of their betters that the townsmen came finally to emulate. By 1700, the townsmen had become, at least economically, stronger than the warrior class; but although they had devised their own pleasures and their own tastes so that their culture constituted a different one from that of the samurai, who at that time clung to their more austere tastes and arts, the *chōnin* never ceased to try, in *nouveau riche* fashion, to penetrate into the world of the nobility. This they were at last able to do factually; by about the middle of the nineteenth century the fee for the adoption of a commoner into a samurai family had been standardized. But in the early Edo period, the townsman could only ape his social superiors.

With Tsunayoshi (1680–1709) the Nō had its last interested patron who was a *shōgun*; he had a passion for the Nō, appeared on the stage himself, and worked up considerable enthusiasm for it among his courtiers. After his death the Nō lost its official prestige and never regained it to quite the same degree, but the townsmen, impressed by this display of fashionable interest, took up the patronage of the Nō, dispatched their sons and daughters to learn Nō singing and dancing, and thus laid the foundations for the extensive adaptation of Nō plays into the Kabuki, which remained, in spite of the temporary mania for the Nō, their true love. Kabuki plays throughout the seventeenth century reflected the townsman's insatiable curiosity about the aristocracy, the feudal lords (*daimyō*), their loves, intrigues, and revenges. This glowing world never lost its interest, for it summed up all that the *chōnin* aspired to, mirrored in the historical pieces. The townsman's closest daily contact with this world was in the person of the *rōnin*, the masterless samurai, the 'wave-man' set adrift in the society of the commoner. The *rōnin* brought with him the aura of glory, the code of behavior, the sense of honor and loyalty of the realm of the aristocrat, and, being a romantic figure, he quickly became a stock figure in the Kabuki. He was almost always depicted as a character seeking justice and righting wrongs, and as such vicariously satisfied the feelings of the townsmen who were subject to confiscation of all their property if the authorities believed they were living too luxuriously. The *rōnin* entered into the lives of the commoners not only in the theatre; they became the backbone of the townsmen's organizations known as *machi-yakko* which protected the commoners from attack by the bands of samurai attached to a lord and instilled in these groups the same spirit and the same sense of honor that motivated the samurai.

The Kabuki was also a means, in days when dissemination of news was difficult, of learning the latest gossip. About 1688 there was introduced into the theatre a new form of play called *kiri-kyōgen*, a kind of living newspaper which dramatized current events. This kind of play was dealt a blow in February 1703, the month in which the forty-seven *rōnin* revenged themselves on Kira. Apparently fearing a portrayal of this affair on the Kabuki stage before the authorities could decide upon the intricate problem of ethical right and wrong that it created, the government forbade the dramatization of current affairs. Thereafter playwrights resorted to the device of setting current happenings in the past (when they involved the samurai), as was done in *The Loyal Forty-seven Rōnin*. A minor but significant point concerning the presently played dramatization of this story, that of Takeda Izumo, is that the audience was more titillated by the opening act in which the villain attempts to make love to the hero's wife than it was concerned with the unfolding of a plot now already familiar. The first act was based upon a current happening in high society and thus delighted the audience both with its topicality and with the portrayal of scandalous doings among the warrior class.

The Shōgunate had little objection to the dramatization of current events other than those which concerned the aristocracy or political affairs. In *sewamono*, the domestic play, the latest piquant occurrence in the world of the commoner was used without the necessity of disguise. The rise of *sewamono* at the beginning of the eighteenth century was in part due to its being a substitute for the larger realm of forbidden dramatic material, but it was more largely due to the townsman's increasing sense of his importance. During the Edo period, the commoner was never able to assert directly political and economic rights. Indeed, such a concept was unknown to him. But within the narrow confines of his own world, he came to have greater and greater confidence, and within the theatre, in *sewamono*, it was possible to create an idealization of the townsman which must have only infrequently existed outside the theatre. A playwright such as Chikamatsu took care to surround his *sewamono* characters with the aura of everyday life, but beneath this familiar surface the commoner appears as a heroic figure, moving in a realm of ethics and acting according to a code of behavior scarcely distinguishable from that of the samurai in the historical plays. When, however, the *sewamono* character behaves in a manner not befitting a warrior, he is usually quick to notice it. Jihei, for example, the hero of Chikamatsu's *Love Suicide at Amijima*, upon leaving his sword behind at an inn, remarks,

'A commoner isn't upset by such forgetfulness, but a warrior would probably commit suicide.' In general, the chivalrous commoner (*otokodate*), the Edo fireman, the wives and daughters of the towns-men behave in the *sewamono* plays with as great dignity and essential nobility as the well-born characters of the historical plays. Frequently the characters of the domestic plays could be distinguished from the samurai only by their speech and by their costumes, but even the costumes of *sewamono* were not made to resemble those worn by con-temporary townsmen until the middle of the eighteenth century. The appearance of *sewamono* represented an almost complete theatrical assimilation of the elevated world of the samurai into the world of the commoner.

Kizewamono, the 'living,' or in a certain sense, 'realistic' domestic play, developed at the beginning of the nineteenth century, shows no change in the ethical standards of the audience, but it reflects the social unrest, the vague feelings of dissatisfaction, the desire for shock that have resulted in the demand, in other countries and at other times, for cruelty, suffering, and bloodshed in the theatre. This kind of play was brought to its highest development by Kawatake Mokuami (1816–1893) who chose his characters from the lowest stratum of society and wrote with most success about thieves. In their historical environment, but not otherwise, his plays suggest certain parallels with those of Euripides: In technical construction, Kawatake returned to the earlier 'classical' form of the Kabuki play; he dwelt upon pathetic scenes of personal suffering; he invested his characters with a morbid psychology; his plays have a *fin du siècle* air and show a deeper pessimism than any others in the Kabuki reper-toire. His contemporary characters are all, in a limited sense, rebels against society, and when he looked to history for characters he found them in such men as Sakura Sōgorō, who, in 1655, had dared to appeal to the Shōgunate over the head of his lord and was subsequently crucified, along with his wife, after his children had been decapitated before him. Kawatake's thieves, like the gangsters of the American film during the depression years, are the wicked yet fascinating super-men of their day, the rebels against the status quo, and they vicariously provided an outlet for the emotions of an audience which was part of a society in ferment and yet was incapable of taking specific measures to rectify social conditions. It seems significant that at present Mokuami's plays are enjoying a wide popularity.

The audience's wants in the theatre were few and easy of gratification. It wanted escape into a world of color, excitement, and romance, and this desire was at first satisfied by plays concerning courtesans, samurai, and high doings among the nobility. It had an insatiable appetite for titbits of gossip within its narrow society, and this taste was indulged. It wanted to see itself raised into the same ethical atmosphere as the samurai, and with *sewamono* the commoner became almost as romantic a figure as the noble. It wanted vicarious release from the injustices imposed upon it by the government, and this it found in the derring-do of *aragoto* heroes, *rōnin*, chivalrous commoners, and, toward the end of the period, in the thieves and murderers of *kizewamono*.

It did not want new ideas or a new view of life. The ready-made code of ethics and morality of the samurai which the commoners finally adapted to their own uses was a satisfactory and complete ideological realm. The townsman frequently chafed and fretted under government restrictions, taxes, and interference in his affairs, but he never questioned the hierarchical structure upon which the authority of the government was based and which constituted its reason for being, nor did he view the injustices, which at times he keenly felt, as inherent in the social system. Injustices, on the contrary, were conceived as isolated events, to be remedied by specific measures appropriate to the particular situation. Almost the only overt social criticism of the townsman was his occasionally honoring executed criminals. The restoration of the Emperor to the position of titular head of the state in 1868 was not, in the Western sense of the word, a revolution, for its genesis was not in new and different political notions of authority but in an unworkable economic system. To be sure, the development of the idea that the Emperor rather than the Shōgun should be head of the state was at last an excuse to push over the toppling Shōgunate, but ideologically the restoration of the Emperor involved nothing new and was based on the feeling that this was a return to a traditional form of government. Even the peasant uprisings which increased in number and frequency during the last one hundred years of the period were not motivated by revolutionary ideas but were simply protests against specific economic distress. A curious but significant aspect of these uprisings is that although in many cases measures were taken to meet the demands of the peasants, the leaders of the peasant groups were almost invariably punished, as was Sakura Sōgorō, even if the demands were granted, and the peasants apparently accepted this practice as painful but unavoidable.

Although the rising merchant class finally developed its own artistic standards, which were somewhat at variance with the early austere tastes of the samurai class, it never formulated a political philosophy of its own, and the Kabuki, insofar as it expressed a social philosophy, reflected the unquestioning acceptance of the status quo. The theatre dwelt frequently upon the unhappiness that the social system inflicted upon the Kabuki heroes, but at no time did it suggest that the social system was possessed of inherent faults. The audience came to be composed increasingly of wealthy townsmen chiefly because of economic conditions: Toward the end of the eighteenth century the price of a first-class ticket was one *ryō*, two *bu*, a sum that would buy enough rice to feed two adults and a child for half a year. The theatre in these circumstances catered to the tastes of its wealthy and relatively secure audiences, and it is to be seriously doubted whether after the middle of the eighteenth century the Kabuki audience was a socially representative one and whether it was a 'popular' theatre. The financial plight of the farmer, for example, was never given dramatic form, nor was the farmer a member of the audience.

During the latter half of the Tokugawa period the majority of the audience was women, the wives of the townsmen, the wealthier of whom in Edo would travel 350 miles to Kyōto to attend a fashion show. Toward the end of the eighteenth century it was no longer the ladies of the nobility that set feminine fashion, but the Kabuki actor; he was idolized, imitated in dress and bearing, with the enthusiasm that women everywhere lavish upon matinée idols. While the wealthy commoners amused themselves with geisha and in brothels and imitated the increasingly impoverished nobility by taking mistresses, their wives had only the theatre as entertainment, and it became the focal point of their social lives. It is therefore not strange that the Kabuki, bent on pleasing this audience, turned more and more to display rather than to the cultivation of literary excellence in the plays.

The actor was the Kabuki's first playwright; it was not until about 1661–1672 that the names of playwrights, as distinguished from actors, began to appear on Kabuki programs. Miyako Dennai, of Edo, and Fukui Yagoemon, of Ōsaka, are the first known playwrights. By this time the position of the actor as the center of interest in the theatre had been firmly established. The playwright came into being after the prohibition of Young Men's Kabuki in July 1652 for the purpose of fashioning plays with plots—*mono-mane-kyōgen*[2] ('plays imitating things')—which would arouse interest in the audience now that the 'pretty faces' of the young men were forbidden. The first two-act play was written in 1664 by Ichimura Takenojō IV. The actor was also confronted with the problem of pleasing the audience by his technical skill in acting rather than by his physical beauty, and the playwright's aid was enlisted to provide scenes which would show him to best advantage. Although the playwright became an increasingly skilful fashioner of plots of greater intricacy and length, he was less a literary artist than a technician skilled in providing 'vehicles' for the actor. His plays increased in length and complexity by a process of accretion, some of them having as many as thirteen acts, so that effect could be piled upon effect for the enhancement of the actor. His plays 'told a story,' but the story was told novelistically rather than dramatically, and the movement of the plot was dictated not by inner necessity but by the necessity for striking effects. The lack of concern for large architectural forms in Japanese art is reflected in the work of the Kabuki playwright; his plays never developed an inner coherence nor yet a consistent outward form. (Even though the Kabuki plays are casually constructed, it should not be inferred that the performance is diffuse and formless. The conventional use of the acting areas, the stylized expression of the actor, and the traditional techniques of production give rise to a form lacking in the scripts of the plays.) The plays of the doll theatre, although they never achieved to a tightly knit structure, were at least not subject to the whims of the actor, and, as a result, have something of literary merit; but even these, when taken over by the Kabuki, were cut and refashioned to suit the actor. Toward 1868 the plots ceased to be of concern to either actor or audience. As today, only parts of plays and even parts of acts were performed, and many members of the audience had very little or no idea of the 'story' of the act or scene they were witnessing.

This condition was not altogether due to the domination of the actor; it was also inherent in the system of composing plays. The playwright learned his craft as an apprentice to the leading playwright of a given theatre, and, like the young actor, the promising apprentice might finally achieve to the name of his master; consequently among the Kabuki playwrights there are lines of Namiki's, Chikamatsu's,

---

2 The word *kyōgen* ('wild-words'), a generic term for *play*, is derived from the Nō theatre, where it refers principally to the short comic pieces performed as interludes between the serious plays.

Tsuruya's, Kawatake's, and so forth. The playwright was always attached to a certain theatrical troupe and never existed as an author outside the theatre, selling his plays to the theatre management. The usual arrangement was that each theatre had its leading playwright, *tatezakusha*, who was assisted by two lesser playwrights and from five to seven apprentices. When a new play was to be fashioned, the leading playwright outlined the plot. He and the other two playwrights decided upon a division of labor, each undertaking the writing of certain acts, while the apprentices were given the task of drafting the less important scenes of the play. Although the leading playwright supervised the work and was responsible for the finished product, each of the other two playwrights was relatively free to create both the acts entrusted to him and the characters involved in them according to his own notions. The play, consequently, was rather a collection of acts than a unified composition, and a character appearing in a given act of one playwright's composition sometimes bore little resemblance to the same character in the hands of another playwright in another act. But the chief playwright was not the final judge of the play's excellence; when the play was completed the chief actor decided upon its merits. Very rarely did the playwright rebel against the judgment of the actor: It is said that Sakurada Jisuke (1734–1806) so resented the criticism of his new play in 1770 by the actor Nakamura Denkurō that he left the theatre and remained away from it for a year. Sakurada's attitude was not, however, a typical one; a contemporary playwright, Nagawa Tokusuke (1764–1824), frankly conceded in his book *A Writer's Inheritance* that the actor was more important than the playwright. During most of the Tokugawa period, the salary of the average playwright was the same as that of the costumer and considerably less than that of the chief actor.

At the time when the Kabuki playwright first appeared, as distinct from the actor-playwright, the Shōgun was Ietsuna (1641–1680), who kept a sharp eye on literary activities. During his incumbency a large number of authors were either imprisoned or banished. In this atmosphere it is not strange that the first Kabuki playwrights contented themselves with bland and inoffensive dramatic material; further, they saw themselves not as students of the social scene or as authors concerned with commenting on the world in which they found themselves. They existed in the isolated world of the theatre to almost the same degree as the actor, and most of them had no very high view of the playwright's profession. (In fact many of the early playwrights were ashamed to have their names appear on billboards or programs.) Many of the plays of Chikamatsu Monzaemon, particularly the *sewamono*, show criticism of social conditions of his day by indirection, but he is the only Kabuki playwright who seems to have recognized that the social system was responsible for much of the unhappiness visited upon individuals. However, after Chikamatsu, who was a *rōnin* and keenly felt the plight of the socially dislocated, the playwright scarcely concerned himself with serious examination of the contemporary scene, for such a concern would not have pleased government, audience, or actor. The government, in spite of its constant vigilance, never found occasion to object to any of the moral or political ideas expressed in the theatre, for these, by and large, mirrored those which the government approved. The only view that the Kabuki playwright expressed generally concerning the function of the play was that it should 'encourage good and rebuke evil' (*kanzen chōaku*). This moralistic concept arose entirely out of Confucian ethics; it does not appear in pre-Tokugawa literature. Tamenaga Ichō in his book *A Primer of the Kabuki* (1762) expresses a view that sums up the ideological attitude of the playwright toward his craft:

> In general, Kabuki plays should be a mirror reflecting good and evil. Seeing a play performed on the stage, the audience should be aware that a subject should work hard for the sake of his feudal lord, a child should be obedient to his parents, a woman should be loyal to her husband, a mother-in-law should be kind to her daughter-in-law, a stepmother should be kinder to her stepchild than to her own child, a stepchild should be obedient to his stepmother, brothers and sisters should have friendly relations, friends should be frank and avoid hypocrisy. Thus the audience should learn how to live by seeing plays performed on the stage by skilful actors. But nowadays most people consider plays only as entertainment and forget their true function. Spectators discuss the beauty of things on the stage and actors think it most important to display their beauty.

In *Battle of the Geisha* (1796) the playwright Namiki Gohei expressed a similar idea through the speech of one of his characters:

> ... No matter how young you are, you should not consider a play only as entertainment. The theatre aims at encouraging good and rebuking evil. In other words, it is a way of studying life. You should appreciate the moral points of view expressed in a play and apply them to your activity in daily life.

The Tokugawa regime could scarcely find anything objectionable in this view of the function of the Kabuki, but the view was one that was shared neither by the actor nor by the audience who not even indirectly conceived the theatre to have a moral purpose. The restrictions of the government upon the playwright, considerably fewer than those upon the actor, were not directed against the ideology of the plays, which was above reproach, but against certain kinds of subject matter. In May 1655 the government prohibited the performance of plays dealing with 'luxurious matters' and courtesans, even when the actors were performing in the homes of feudal lords. Nine years later plays about the world of the courtesans (*keiseigoto*) were again forbidden. In 1723 after a wave of double suicides swept the country, largely inspired by a play of Chikamatsu, the government forbade printing books or presenting plays that dealt with this subject; it was in this same year that government officials confiscated thousands of books containing pornographic drawings. In the following year the regulation against performing plays that dealt with double suicide was reissued, and in 1783 it was repeated in strong terms. The Shōgun Yoshimune in 1736 forbade plays which dwelt at any length upon love affairs; and throughout the Edo period there were constant admonitions against the performance of love scenes. As late as 1866 the government issued an order to theatre owners stating that the plays of recent years had shown too many 'low emotions' and thus were a threat to public morality and that in the future as few love scenes as possible should be presented. During World War II, the authorities forbade the performance, among other plays, of *Thunder God*, a play which shows a priest being seduced from his duty by a woman; and on at least one occasion during the War a Kabuki samisen player was taken to a police station and kept there overnight until he was able to remove the 'erotic' quality from his performance of samisen music.

All these restrictions were made on moral grounds, but the commonly accepted Japanese notions of morality during the Tokugawa period, and to a great extent at present, differ so considerably from Western moral concepts that they require a brief explanation. The morality fostered and promoted by the Tokugawa regime was entirely political in intent: Any social manifestations which contributed to the maintenance of the status quo and the strict division of classes were moral, while those which would contribute to a weakening of the hierarchical structure were immoral. The social structure required that the individual be subordinate to the group in which he existed and that he feel keenly the importance of social duty over individual inclinations. The Japanese never had a strong sense of abstract Good and Evil, and the Western concept of sin was unknown to them. Good and Evil were almost entirely a matter of social ethics, not of religious or personal conviction, and this concept was greatly strengthened during the Edo period. Women's Kabuki was not forbidden because a large number of the women were prostitutes: Prostitution was and is accepted as a normal, necessary trade. But the Bakufu saw in this form of theatre something new, different, and, consequently, troubling. The simple dances showed a world of individual passion apart from social duty. Young Men's Kabuki was forbidden not because of moral objections to homosexual practices, which were widespread among priests and warriors during the period of civil wars, but because the samurai pursuit of, and quarrels over, the favors of the actors reflected a breakdown of social barriers between these widely separated classes. Courtesans had a high position in Edo society out of all proportion to their social class, and therefore plays dealing with these public figures and surrounding them with further glamour were inappropriate. The depiction of luxurious living on the stage might well encourage the already wealthy townsman as well as the less wealthy member of the warrior class to further extravagance at a time when the government hoped to create economic stability by exhortations to frugality. The official concept of 'morality' was to preserve, intact and eternally, the social hierarchy which had been established at the beginning of the seventeenth century.

The Shōgunate seems to have sensed that the world of the individual was the most dangerous threat to its well being. Suicide in Japan remains today an honorable and, indeed, laudable death. The waves of double suicide in the eighteenth century were not 'sinful,' but they were dangerous in that they represented the commoners' adopting what was a prerogative of the aristocracy and asserting the power of individual emotions over social duty. The governmental strictures against love scenes on the stage were prompted by the same concepts as those with which the contemporary police state sets about the destruction of the private emotional world of the individual. When the government censors forbade the performance of *Thunder God* during World War II, they did not forbid the performance of *Sukeroku*. In *Thunder God* the priest is seduced by the woman and is destroyed; in *Sukeroku* the hero, although he is the favorite of the courtesan Agemaki, does not languish in her arms but, having a keen sense of his social duty, sets out to regain a sword which is a family heirloom. The attitude toward the theatre of the police state of Japan during World War II did not greatly differ, ethically, from that of the Edo period; 'immorality' consisted in both instances in the performance of plays in which private emotions were glorified, as they were in the *sewamono* of Chikamatsu, and in which social duties were forgotten. The apparently natural antipathy of both actor and audience toward 'ideas,' the subjugation of the playwright to the actor, constant government surveillance of the theatre—all these forces contributed to limit the intellectual inquiry of the playwright and at last to reduce him to the position of a mere hack who played eternal variations on well worn themes, his only creativity that of devising new twists of plot and new theatrical effects.

The Kabuki playwright never succeeded in creating precisely defined forms of drama, as did the Western playwright, nor did he even achieve the formality of the Nō theatre with its strict division between serious and comic pieces. In the Kabuki repertoire there are few 'pure' comedies, and the majority of these are dance pieces (*jikyōgen*) adapted from the Nō comedies. All are one-act plays, excessively simple in plot, moving the audience to amusement but not to hilarity. In *Three Odd Ones* a lord employs three people, one lame, one deaf, one mute, in the hope that their physical deformities will prevent them from drinking his wine while he is away from the house. After he has left, it is revealed that the servants are in perfect condition physically; they get drunk and the lord returns to find that he has been duped. *The Tea Box* is built upon the simple incident of a thief who claims to be the owner of a wooden box containing tea. A lord attempts to decide which of the two claimants it belongs to, always questioning the real owner first. During the questioning the thief eavesdrops, and when he is questioned in turn, he repeats the answers of the owner. Finally the thief makes off with the barrel, the owner in pursuit. *A Substitute for Meditation* concerns the attempt of a husband to escape from his overvigilant wife and to spend the night with his mistress. He informs his wife that he intends to practice Zen meditation, sitting up all night with his head covered by a priest's robe. After his wife is reconciled to this, the husband has a servant take his place beneath the robe and goes off to his mistress. Before he returns, the wife has discovered the deception, driven away the servant, and placed herself under the robe. When the tipsy husband returns, he describes his night's adventure, in glowing and detailed terms, to the robed figure who at last reveals herself and pounces on the unhappy husband. Other plays of this variety, such as *Dropped Coat* and *Tied to a Pole* are equally simple in plot; their chief charm is not in the unfolding of the story but in the dancing ability of the actors.

A number of one-act comic dances of pure Kabuki origin are based on equally simple incidents. *Blind Masseur* is a two-character piece in which a blind masseur's dog plays a series of tricks upon his owner. In *Returning Palanquin* two palanquin bearers discuss in dance the respective merits of the women of their native towns. *Dumpling Selling* shows a dumpling peddler and his wife on the streets of Ōsaka. Dramatically, both the pieces adapted from the Nō and those of Kabuki origin are theatrical jokes rather than comedy.

The short play *Camel* is one which is not primarily dance, which is thoroughly comic throughout, and which arouses rather hearty laughter from the audience. A gambler, thoroughly disliked in the neighbourhood, has died during the night; with him has been living Hanji, who, although he bore the gambler no great love, feels morally obligated to conduct a wake for him, but he has no money with which to provide wine for the occasion. Hanji prevails upon the garbage-man, Kyuroku, to go to the home of a wealthy neighbor, Sahei, to ask for a contribution, threatening Sahei with the prospect of having the corpse of the gambler brought to his house to perform a 'ghost dance' if he does not contribute. Kyuroku, a meek little man, delivers the message to Sahei, but returns to Hanji with the information that Sahei will give no money and that he would welcome the performance of a 'ghost dance' in his house. Thereupon Hanji loads the corpse on the frightened Kyuroku's back; they go to Sahei's home where Hanji dances the corpse about, so upsetting Sahei and his wife that they give Hanji money to take the corpse away. The play then undergoes a sudden shift in plot, a characteristic of Kabuki playwriting. Hanji and Kyuroku return to Hanji's house with the corpse and with considerable wine. They begin drinking, and slowly a transformation of their characters occurs. The meek and frightened Kyuroku under the influence of the wine becomes bolder and more assertive while the domineering Hanji becomes meek and frightened of Kyuroku. When the original nature of both the characters is reversed, the play ends abruptly.

A number of Kabuki plays can be described as comedy not because they are particularly humorous but because they do not end unhappily. Their plots are few and involve such matters as the reunion of long separated lovers or parents and children, or the person who is saved from suicide or misfortune by the timely arrival of money or by a curious twist of the plot. But in the majority of instances the plays with these well worn plots turn out unhappily, in grief, sacrifice, or suicide, preceded by greatly prolonged scenes of suffering.

It appears curious that a people as generally cheerful as the Japanese and as willing to laugh at their own and others' misfortunes should have failed to develop true comic characters and the comic spirit more extensively within their theatre. The last scene of *Camel* is a rare example of Kabuki comedy developing out of character; elsewhere the amusing and the laughable are more frequently than not the result of situation rather than character. The comedy *On Foot to Kyōto*, based on a famous novel by Jippensha, has two heroes who show some differentiation in character. Yarobei is the cleverer of the two, Kitahachi the duller, who is almost invariably put upon by Yarobei. But the humor of the play, here again, arises out of the situations imposed upon the characters during their foot journey from Edo to Kyōto, and the piece consists of a series of picaresque incidents bound together only by the presence of the two central characters. There are no Falstaffs, no Volpones, no Lady Bracknells among the Kabuki characters. There is no trenchant satire, only the slightest hint of comedy of manners, and no high comedy. It is doubtful whether true comedy exists at all; the comic pieces are much closer to farce.

The reasons for this are complex and can be only briefly noted. The great Western comedies are based on honest criticism of the contemporary social scene and a willingness to laugh at the inconsistencies which it represents. Aristophanes held up to good-natured ridicule political figures, warriors, and gods. For the Edo period Japanese to have laughed at corresponding figures in their civilization is as unthinkable as Hitler Germany laughing at a play about Hitler. The superiors of the commoner were not and could not be figures of fun, for such treatment of them would not have been tolerated by the government. Further, the commoner admired and wished to emulate the behavior and ethics of those above him. The whole area of fruitful comic material in those with intellectual and social pretensions was unacceptable to the majority of an audience which never developed its own standards of education and etiquette but accepted those of the samurai ready-made. The social climber, of whom Molière made capital, would not have been amusing to the large number of wealthy commoners' wives in the audience. Comedy requires a willingness to speculate about the society in which one lives and this speculation necessitates a certain detachment from society. The commoners were incapable of either of these attitudes; consequently, the field of their comedy was restricted to 'low' characters from whom they felt sufficiently removed to allow the detachment that would permit laughter. Thieves, peasants, servants, and logically enough, the deformed, the deaf, and the blind are the usual humorous characters of the Kabuki stage.

An examination of Kabuki comic pieces reveals a society constructed on a different basis than that which the Bakufu officially sanctioned; the government wished to preserve the hierarchical arrangement, in order of importance, of warrior, farmer, and townsman. The comic pieces show that this arrangement was changed about in the mind of the townsman; he viewed himself in much the same position as the warrior and relegated the peasants, who, historically, began to decrease in numbers after 1725, to the realm of the low comics. The picture of the social structure that can be gained from the slight evidence of the humorous pieces is a truer one than that which existed in the minds of government officials; it shows the increasing economic importance of the townsman, the clear division of society into haves and have nots, and the complete absence of a true bourgeoisie.

Only rarely are members of the warrior class made comic figures. Izaemon, the hero of Chikamatsu Monzaemon's *Yūgiri and Izaemon*, is an impoverished samurai in love with a courtesan; the short play is largely concerned with Izaemon's comic behavior as he is forced to endure the indignity of waiting in an anteroom for the courtesan until she has finished entertaining a wealthy guest. Izaemon is scarcely a heroic figure as he wavers between pride and petty jealousy. In *The Drum of Matsuura* the hero is a lord who, although rather a gentle soul, constantly complains that his retainers are not as loyal and devoted to him as the forty-seven *rōnin* are to their dead master. The willingness of his retainers to show their loyalty to him is reduced to absurdity when snow falls from the branch of a pine tree on the lord's head, and the retainers, having only this opportunity to show their loyalty, rush to their master to brush the snow from his clothing.

The strongest influence upon Kabuki comic pieces was the *kyōgen* of the Nō theatre, which are short one-act plays. It is almost technically impossible to draw true comic characters within so narrow a form; the comic character, like the tragic one, must have sufficient space in which to be developed. Falstaff cannot be created in thirty minutes of playing time. But, as noted previously, the Japanese have never evolved extended, internally coherent forms of artistic expression; even the greatest and perhaps the longest of Japanese novels, *The Tale of Genji*, is structurally a collection of incidents. Within the theatre this characteristic of Japanese literary expression was exaggerated by a system of playwriting which did not permit a single intelligence to create the play. The comic pieces continued to be, as they were in the Nō theatre, little more than interludes between the acts of serious plays. Since these short plays do not permit the creation of true comic characters, they are, of necessity, based simply upon a humorous situation, not upon a situation that grows out of the character. They therefore are technically farce, and the Japanese refer to them in English by that name. But the sole purpose of farce in the Western theatre is to provoke laughter, the more immoderate the better, and this phenomenon does not occur in the Kabuki.

The serious plays are also less compact dramatic forms than they are an accretion of details, but long serious plays exist in large number while long comic pieces are rare. Among the Confucian ideas that received wide acceptance among the townsmen was that of the unsuitability of laughter as impolite, undignified, vulgar, and not to be indulged in, at least publicly, by the educated. This notion still exists in Japan; hearty laughter prevails among film audiences and among the devotees of the musical revue; but an audience of college students and intelligentsia will express its amusement at *The Merry Wives of Windsor* or Pagnol's *Fanny* only in the politest of titters, and a well-bred young lady still simpers like a little maid of *The Mikado*, a hand held delicately over her mouth. The social inappropriateness of public laughter accounts to some degree for the relative absence of comic plays in the Kabuki repertoire. It is almost entirely in plays written after 1868 that the foreigner finds what can be described, in Western terms, as comedy. The humor of the Edo period was not revealed in the theatre, where it could not be properly appreciated because of social taboo, but in novels, in thirty-one syllable satiric poems (*kyōka*), in the seventeen syllable *senryū*, and in pornographic pictures (sometimes called in Japanese 'laughing-pictures'), all of which could be enjoyed in private. Tokugawa Confucian ethics equally deplored the public tear, but this could be, and is, more easily concealed in the theatre than the laugh.

The great preponderance of serious plays over amusing ones is also to be explained on the basis of the predilection of the Japanese for the romantically melancholy. Whether this taste is natural or acquired is a difficult problem to decide, but there is little question of its existence throughout Japanese culture. The first foreign novel to be widely read after 1868 and the first to be translated directly into Japanese without changing the locale to Japan, or the motivations of the characters to Japanese ones, was Goethe's *The Sorrows of Werther*. A romantic view of life does not promote humor; the Byrons are the exception rather than the rule; romantic, sentimental attachment to people, places, and things allows no room for the detachment which is the prerequisite to a comic view of life. Perhaps to some degree the trend toward the melancholy play was accelerated in the Kabuki when, toward the end of the eighteenth century and following, the number of women in the audience increased and became larger than the number of men. This notion is put forward with some hesitation, for no very great differences in artistic tastes according to the sexes can be distinguished during the Edo period. But the nature of the plays in the latter half of the period suggests that the playwrights were concerned with manufacturing plays which, like the American soap-opera, would represent an ideal world of escape for women rather than men. A *senryū* of the time, written by a man, is

> *Shibai mita ban wa*
> *Teishu ga iya ni nari*
>
> The night she's been to the play,
> She's sick and tired of her husband.

The verse merely points out the temporary, though apparently universal, dissatisfaction of women with their husbands after looking at actors. But at the same time a great number of plays from this period concern women who are long-suffering, wise, and forbearing, while their husbands are fickle, imperceptive, and intolerant.

Besides the mildly satiric treatment of low characters, both in the short humorous plays and in brief scenes in the long serious plays, the only field for satire was that of the Kabuki theatre itself, and much of the humor of the Kabuki is unintelligible to one who does not recognize the parodies of line reading, of the *mie*, and of dance movement. The Kabuki, like Japan at large, became inbred during its centuries of almost complete isolation, and particularly in the nineteenth century it tended to feed on itself, producing plays in which other plays were referred to, plays which were variations on older plays, plays whose language was in part unintelligible without knowledge of the Kabuki repertoire, plays about actors. The strict design of rhythmical speech, dance movement, doll theatre movement, and the *mie* lent themselves to satire in the same way that the *chorus*, the *deus ex machina*, and the *eccyclema* were attractive comic material for Aristophanes. In the dance piece *Blind Masseur*, mentioned above, the dog is not primarily amusing because he acts like a dog; he is funny because he satirizes the conventional movements and attitudes of the travelling lovers in the scenes known as *michiyuki*. One of the most amusing sequences in *On Foot to Kyōto* is that in which the Kabuki is satirized in a provincial performance of *The Battle of Ichinotani*: The *jōruri* performers are raucous and incompetent, the horse bearing Kumagai falls on the stage, its tail comes off when pulled by the irate actor, who in the confusion loses his wig. The inept actors who play the horse run out on the *hanamichi* and sit there, much amused at the untoward events taking place on stage. In the midst of the profoundly serious 'The Village School,' the stupid schoolboy makes an appearance brandishing a broom and performing a mock *mie*, while in *Through the Iga Pass* and *Benten the Thief* there are extended dance scenes satirizing the serious ballet-like scenes of fighting which occur elsewhere in the plays.

Comedy is used most frequently in the Kabuki in scenes of comic relief in the serious plays. Comic relief is employed in two general ways as it is in the Western theatre: Comic scenes having no dramatic relation to the rest of the play are used, as well as scenes which, like the Porter's scene in *Macbeth*, are intimately related to the play itself and have the effect of heightening, both by contrast and by apposition, the serious scenes against which they are played. In certain plays, comic scenes of the latter variety can be distinguished from similar scenes in Western plays in two ways: The actors concerned in the serious movement of the play do not leave the stage but remain there immobile and uninvolved in the scene, and the comic relief scene is a direct and obvious parody of a serious scene which has preceded it. The essential quality of this variety of comic relief is that it becomes a sudden, and at times almost shocking, projection of comedy into a profoundly serious dramatic situation; but this usage is of a piece with the over-all 'sudden change' pattern of the Kabuki performance. In 'The Village School,' for example, the touching scene of the mother parting from her child is followed immediately by a comic passage in which this scene is parodied. Contrary to the general practice of the Western theatre, comic relief is imposed directly upon the serious scene and not separated from it either visually or dramatically. Comedy serves its most important function in the Kabuki not in extended and purely comic pieces, but in providing both a sudden change from, and an impact upon, the serious scene.

The serious Kabuki plays, even those written in the late nineteenth and early twentieth centuries, exist entirely within the intellectual framework of the official ethics of the Tokugawa period. This code of ethics, which had been in pre-Tokugawa Japan a loosely applied code of behavior for the warrior class, became at last the governing ideology of all classes. The involved complications of the code need not concern us, but the serious Kabuki play is unintelligible without some understanding of the ethical background from which it derived.

Roughly stated, the intellectual climate of the Tokugawa period was derived from three main sources: the *Buke Hatto* (*Laws of the Military Houses*), which is sometimes referred to as the Tokugawa Constitution; the Japanese adaptation and version of Confucian ethics; and the cult known as *bushidō*, the 'Way of the Warrior.' All of these had been in existence, in some form, before the seventeenth century, but under the Tokugawa regime they were gradually combined into a fairly rigid ethical code. Ieyasu (1542–1616), the first Tokugawa Shōgun, was fully aware that disloyalty was the disintegrating force that had led to war and political confusion in the past. He and his councillors therefore set about to create a code soundly based on the principle of abiding loyalty in the *Buke Hatto*. His successors implemented and strengthened this code, converting it into ethical propaganda in the hope of maintaining their regime in perpetuity. (The actual document of the *Buke Hatto* did not circulate freely among all members of the warrior class; it was available only to lords facing a difficult ethical decision.) Until after the middle of the seventeenth century, the masterless samurai, the *rōnin*, were troublesome; they were, economically, a group of unruly unemployed, and partly in order to inspire them with a code of behavior, the Shōgunate encouraged the development and general acceptance of the concept of loyalty to a master, which eventually broadened into the cult of *bushidō*. Following the luxurious excesses of the Genroku period, the Shōgun Yoshimune, who, during his tenure from 1716 to 1745, wished to re-establish the austerity of Ieyasu's reign, encouraged the study of various schools of Confucianism, all of which recognized the hierarchical structure which had been implicit in Japanese society from the seventh century, when Chinese conceptions of law were first introduced into the country. Throughout the eighteenth century the ethical code hardened into strict and unswerving dogma. In 1795 the Confucian scholar Hayashi Jussai was able to persuade the Bakufu to allow only those who subscribed to Confucian philosophy of the Chu Hsi school to hold government positions; this order was called the *Prohibition of Heresies*, a title which indicates the official view taken of intellectual deviation. In the last half of the eighteenth century and in the nineteenth, official Confucian thought (as well as other salutary doctrine) was popularized in *shingaku*, a preceptive philosophy which finally gained adherents among both feudal lords and servant girls. Ironically, it was at last the strict interpretation of Confucian principles which demanded that the Shōgunate be destroyed and the Emperor restored as head of the state. In general, as economic conditions worsened, increasingly oppressive measures were taken to insure an intellectual uniformity which might preserve the regime.

The concept that social duty, rather than religious principles, individual rights, or abstract notions of Good and Evil, determined the whole of ethical behavior had many centuries of acceptance before it was codified under the Tokugawa regime. And it has left such a deep mark upon Japanese consciousness that, in spite of recent surface changes in the Japanese political structure and modes of thought, the average citizen in his daily life continues to act according to its dictates. The center of this system was loyalty and obedience, both of which imply neither change nor progress, but the eternal maintenance of a static society. Social duty did not consist in a sense of obligation toward society at large but toward the social unit into which one was born or adopted. The group to which one owed his loyalty was not the blood relation nor the family but a somewhat larger social unit known as the House, which came into being out of the necessity of continuing ancestor worship perpetually. When the House failed to provide male issue, or when the males of the House seemed incapable of managing its affairs properly, men of ability were adopted into it, whether blood relations or not, and they thereafter owed perpetual allegiance to the House to the exclusion of all other human ties. During the Edo period, the political structure of Japan theoretically consisted of a number of Houses, the heads of which owed feudal loyalty to the Shōgun. Within the Houses, all members owed unquestioning loyalty and obedience to its head. The system did not allow for the development of an economically powerful townsman class, and therein lay its weakness; but as the townsman came into economic importance, he willingly accepted the system, and, in effect, established his own House, which was organized along the same lines as that of the nobility. Within the House was the same feudal structure characteristic of the nation at large, based upon precise notions of the duties of a wife toward her husband, a child toward his father, a stepchild toward his stepmother, and so forth. The system was both a moral and a political one, the two constituting a single doctrine as they have always in China and Japan. It contained no notion of individual rights; when this concept was introduced into Japan in 1868 a Japanese word had to be invented to describe it. It contained no idea of Good and Evil, as these exist philosophically in the West; good consisted entirely of the performance of social duties, evil, in the Confucian ideology, of 'disorder,' 'disarrangement,' the failure to fulfil one's obligations. There was no allowance for individual interpretations of right and wrong and consequently no freedom of thought within the ideological confines fixed by the Shōgunate.

So far as the individual was concerned, his sense of obligation toward his superior and toward those below him within the social unit was based upon their mutual welfare. During the Edo period the relations between apprentice and actor, as well as similar ones in other low social groups, became indistinguishable from those which prevailed between a feudal lord and his inheritor. In practice, the relationship was not of advantage only to the superior. The actor fed, clothed, and housed the apprentice, taught him his trade, and if the apprentice was skilful he could one day inherit the name of his master. The obligations of the apprentice to the actor were just as binding as those of the actor to the apprentice. So strong was this feeling of mutual obligation that it came to permeate and dominate all Japanese social relationships, even those that were not based upon the hierarchical structure. If one was given aid in distress by a complete stranger, not only did the recipient incur a debt of obligation toward him which must sooner or later be repaid, but at the same time the doer of the good deed was required to accept a certain obligation toward the one he had aided. The Samaritan, in this context of thought, having stopped by the roadside and administered first aid, would thereafter be bound by strong moral obligation to pay the bill at the inn, to guarantee the payment of further expenses, to perform of necessity all those acts which he had undertaken out of the goodness of his heart. This concept continues today to influence Japanese behavior, and it accounts for the Japanese unwillingness to give aid to those who have been injured in public places.

Since the House was the ultimate social unit, its preservation was of prime importance no matter what sacrifice this required from the individual; and since loyalty to this House was the highest and greatest good to which the individual could attain, virtue lay in the act which would maintain the unblemished character of the House. This line of reasoning led logically, in the Confucian code, to the idea that revenge upon those who had committed what the House conceived to be a wrong against it was the highest duty of the vassal and that, consequently, no member of the House could 'live under the same heaven' with one who had murdered a member of the House. Therefore the individual engaged in righteous revenge became a synthesis of all that was laudable in human conduct.

From these generally accepted social attitudes was derived the dramatic material of the serious Kabuki play. Its theme is loyalty: to the lord, to the House, or to the one to whom one owes a debt of obligation, a debt either natural, deriving from the Confucian code of personal relationship, or acquired. Loyalty manifests itself dramatically either in carrying out a revenge or in sacrificing for it either oneself or those to whom one is closely bound by emotional ties. Not only does this theme inform the whole of the primary dramatic situations of the Kabuki, but its influence continues to be felt throughout the majority of contemporary Japanese films and plays.

To describe the serious Kabuki play in terms of its thematic material or in terms of its plot must of necessity convey a false impression of the effect of the play in the theatre upon an audience. The Kabuki repertoire does not pretend to be literature, nor does the audience go to the theatre with the intention of witnessing the unfolding of a story. The script of the play is merely the point of departure for the actor, and it is he whom one goes to see. Therefore the mere listing of the stock situations of the Kabuki drama, which, like those of Western opera, scarcely enter into the consciousness of the audience, invests them with an importance which they do not enjoy in the theatre. It throws into undue prominence the murders, suicides, and other gory events, which, in actual performance, are relieved of horror by the stylized mode of production. Further, brief summaries of the plots make them sound as ridiculous as those of opera and cannot convey the impression which these plays create in performance. Nakamura Kichizō, the author of a work on the Kabuki play, writes that Kabuki scripts are not worthy of analysis 'apart from the technique of acting them on the stage,' but he proceeds to discuss them, remarking that 'even a dead tree has a kind of beauty.'

Even within the confines of the script itself, apart from its performance in the theatre, the interest of the playwright was not in the constantly repeated theme but in the effects of the workings of this code of behavior upon the characters he had created. And this conflict between social duty and individual inclination, between painful fulfilment of the code and personal felicity, is the basic dramatic conflict in both the historical and domestic plays. In the same way that in the performance the actor is concerned with 'secondary effects,' with presenting not the immediate total reaction but the detached attitude of the character toward the event, so the playwright was occupied with showing the cruel impact of the inexorable code upon warmhearted human beings. The code in itself needed no dramatic exploitation, for it existed as an omnipresent background to life outside the theatre. In the dramatic foreground stood the pitiable character in the web of forces over which he could exercise little control, and it was upon him, rather than the ideological background, that the playwright concentrated his attention.

Loyalty to the House which has come upon evil days constitutes the subject matter of many of the plays concerning 'great Houses' (ōiemono). Plays of this sort were attractive both to the masterless samurai, who found in them both nostalgic charm and vicarious satisfaction, and to the townsmen, who dearly loved high deeds in high places. Two of the most popular of all Kabuki pieces belong to this category—The Loyal Forty-seven Rōnin and Sugawara's Secrets of Calligraphy. In both plays the House, as an entity, is destroyed, but its honor is vindicated by faithful retainers.

The historical plays dealing with the conflict that arises when the central character feels simultaneously a debt of gratitude toward two opposed individuals have a special name; they are 'plays of divided loyalties' (matatabimono). Divided loyalties confront Matsuōmaru in 'The Village School.' Matsuōmaru's father is a retainer of Lord Sugawara, he has been greatly indebted to Sugawara throughout his life, and two of his triplet sons have entered, like their father, into Sugawara's service. But the third, Matsuōmaru, has transferred his allegiance to Sugawara's rival, Shihei, whose machinations have caused the innocent Sugawara to be sent into exile in disgrace. Matsuōmaru comes to realize that he has conflicting obligations:

first, to Sugawara who has greatly befriended his father, and second, to Shihei to whom he has sworn allegiance. His conflict reaches its climax when Shihei requires that Matsuōmaru bring about the death of Sugawara's only heir, his young son, and Matsuōmaru must make the choice of betraying one or the other of those to whom he owes loyalty. In 'Moritsuna's Camp,' the chief character Moritsuna is in the service of Hōjō Tokimasa, while Moritsuna's younger brother, Takatsuna, is allied with Minamoto Yoriie. These rival chiefs are at war; consequently Moritsuna is pitted militarily against his brother Takatsuna. Moritsuna's conflict comes to a climax when his commander, Tokimasa, brings to him for identification a head purported to be that of Moritsuna's brother. Just as Moritsuna begins the ceremony of identifying the head, his brother's young son, Kōshirō, who is being held prisoner in the house, rushes forward crying, 'Father, I will follow you,' and kills himself by committing *harakiri*. Moritsuna is for the moment confused; he knows that this is not the head of his brother and he knows that the boy Kōshirō must also have been aware of the fact. But almost at once he realizes that the boy has committed suicide in order to convince Tokimasa that this is really the head of his father and that his act is part of an involved strategy by which his brother Takatsuna hopes to win the war. Moritsuna therefore must choose between loyalty to his lord, which will require that he announce that this is not the head of his brother, and loyalty to his brother so that the sacrifice of the child will not have been in vain. The heroine of *Three Shōguns of Kamakura*, Tokihime, must choose between loyalty to her father and to her lover, who are opposing each other in battle. Her lover insists that she kill her father to prove her love, while her father has sent word that she must kill her lover's mother.

Although in the Japanese classification plays of divided loyalties are confined to those with an historical setting, the same conflict is generally characteristic of those of the domestic type. In these there is perhaps a greater inclination for the principal characters to permit themselves to follow the dictates of their hearts, while in the historical plays the characters tend to suppress their individual inclinations in order to carry out their social obligations, at least in token form. Matsuōmaru in 'The Village School' resolves his conflict by sacrificing his own son in place of Sugawara's; but, on the contrary, Moritsuna deceives his lord and announces that this is the head of his brother. However Moritsuna is eventually made to suffer the consequences of his act and is, even at the moment of performing it, prepared to commit suicide in apology. Tokihime, after her lover's death, dies, at last, to save the life of her father. In the *sewamono* pieces, the superior loyalties tend less to be toward a politically superior individual than toward the person to whom the character is bound by more intimate ties, while in *kizewamono* the ultimate loyalty tends to be toward the sworn blood-brother, in most cases to the extrasocial group, for example, Mokuami's recurrent bands of thieves, who have sworn allegiance to each other. But in the domestic plays, as inevitably as in the historical ones, the code of behavior eventually triumphs over and destroys the character who attempts to follow the dictates of his emotions. The system remains impervious and unchallenged, and the individual is a sacrifice to it.

In the *sewamono* pieces of Chikamatsu Monzaemon the conflict between individual inclination and social duty, and the sympathy of the playwright for the unfortunate individual, is perhaps more clearly stated than in the *sewamono* plays of later authors. In *The Courier of Hell* the conflict arises in the character of Magoemon, a simple farmer, whose son, Chūbei, embezzles public funds in order to buy the freedom of the courtesan he loves. The son and the courtesan have determined to commit double suicide, but before doing this they feel it necessary to visit Chūbei's father to apologize for their misbehavior. By embezzling the money Chūbei has not only broken his allegiance to his employer but has also, in the process, brought shame upon his father in his old age. When Chūbei and the courtesan visit the father's village, the father is torn between loyalty to the code of social behavior which requires that he never again see the son who has disgraced him and his natural inclination to forgive his son whom he loves dearly. This scene of anguish is considerably prolonged, but at last the father gives way to parental emotion, meets his son, and finally gives the lovers money so that they can travel on in an attempt to avoid the arresting officers. They are, of course, eventually seized. In *Love Suicide at Amijima* Chikamatsu constructed what is probably the most complicated set of conflicting debts of obligation in any of the *sewamono* plays. The play concerns three principal characters— Jihei, a commoner, Osan, his wife, and Koharu, a courtesan with whom Jihei has fallen in love. At the beginning, Jihei and Koharu have agreed to commit double suicide, and at the end they do so. The action of the play consists in the revelation of the various social forces which motivate and inhibit the central characters, and it is made more involved by the fact that the two women are not, in actuality, rivals fighting for Jihei's love. On the contrary, the women mutually recognize certain debts of obligation and are greatly concerned that these obligations be fulfilled. The wife is willing to give money and her clothing to Jihei so that he can 'ransom' Koharu, and at the end of the play the courtesan, ever mindful of her obligation to the wife, insists that their manner of death be such that she and Jihei do not appear to have died as lovers. In addition to the intricate social relationships between the three central characters, there are also tremendous external social pressures. The courtesan has responsibilities to her mother and to the brothel. The wife has responsibilities to her children and to her parents. Jihei has responsibilities to an elder brother and to his mother- and father-in-law, while at the same time he feels keenly the necessity of adhering to the social code of the small business world in which he moves. His family ties are further complicated by the fact that his wife is also his cousin. The web of social obligation surrounding Koharu and Jihei is so intricate and ramified that suicide becomes the only avenue of escape.

In the *kizewamono* plays, particularly those of Kawatake Mokuami, the characters, usually thieves and gamblers, are actively opposed to the social system about them, and frequently, like the character Benten Kozō, they extort money from the rich. But within their own group they are as loyal to one another as the most faithful of the samurai, and their code of behavior is in no way different from that which motivates the characters in the historical pieces. The thieves of Kawatake's *The Three Kichiza's* and *Benten the Thief* live and die within a world of their own, painstakingly patterned on that of the larger social structure, like the socially superior heroes of the historical plays. Characters of this sort represent the greatest exploitation of the rebel against society in the Kabuki drama; they are attractive individuals theatrically and appear, within the context of the plays, somewhat more honest, honorable, and warmhearted than those in the society which they oppose. But although during the course of the play they are extrasocial individuals, at the end society closes in upon them and demands its due. They are either imprisoned or commit suicide. The *kizewamono* plays not concerned with thieves, gamblers, and other low characters are for the most part occupied with unhappy love affairs somewhat more lurid than those of *sewamono* and frequently enlivened with scenes of murder. Typical of such plays is Kawatake Mokuami's *Izayoi and Seishin*, in which the unhappy lovers, having been rescued from an attempt at double suicide by drowning, pursue a life of thievery and murder until at last they are punished; or Kawatake Shinshichi's *Sashichi, Son of Edo*, in which an Edo fireman, Sashichi, falsely believing that Koito, the geisha he loves, is no longer in love with him, murders her. In these plays the code of ethics of the Tokugawa period is pushed so far into the background that it is almost forgotten in the display of lurid and bloody event, but at the final curtain, the code inevitably asserts its authority.

Throughout the serious Kabuki plays, the working of the code of behavior permits the characters only two possible courses of action: revenge or sacrifice.

Revenge, sanctioned by the Japanese interpretation of Confucian ethics, was the final avenue to justice. For this reason the affair of the forty-seven *rōnin* at the opening of the eighteenth century created a knotty political and moral problem. Their revenge of their lord was clearly a responsibility and a duty according to Confucian principles; but on the other hand, their lord had committed an offense against the Shōgunate by drawing his sword within the palace and striking a government official. After a year's discussion among high authorities, it was apparently somewhat reluctantly decided that, since the *rōnin's* behavior had flouted the power of the Bakufu, they should be ordered to commit suicide. The decision showed, in part, the increasing power of the Shōgunate; but it changed in no way the popular opinion that personal revenge to right a wrong was the ultimate means of obtaining justice, and the deification of the avengers in the theatre both in *The Loyal Forty-seven Rōnin* and other plays, as well as in actuality, is evidence of the popular strength of this opinion. Plays concerning revenge against those who have brought about the fall of a House constitute the larger forms of revenge plays. But frequently the honor of the House is symbolized in a sword which has been lost or stolen and which the hero attempts to regain. Plays with this theme are legion. Among them are such pieces as *Sukeroku*, in which the hero, a chivalrous townsman, is engaged in the recovery of a sword which is now in the possession of a samurai, or *Bloodshed at Ise* in which the hero Mitsugu, having recovered the sword, murders almost the entire cast: The sword, having tasted blood, turns its wielder into a murderer, and Mitsugu is greatly pleased at this event for it proves the authenticity of the sword. It is not always a man who is the avenger. In *Mirror Mountain* the maid of the heroine kills the villainess who had driven her mistress to suicide, while in *The Vow of Rokusuke* the heroine, Osono, is a stronger character than the hero and more determined upon revenge.

Revenge is carried out by the living in the majority of plays up to the nineteenth century, although occasionally, as in the final act of *Sugawara's Secrets of Calligraphy*, now never performed, an avenging spirit returns to punish his enemies. With the rise of *kizewamono* after 1800, the avenging ghost became a stock character. An early typical play of this variety is Tsuruya Namboku IV's *Ghost Story of Yotsuya* (1825) in which the greater part of the action is concerned with the ghostly revenge of the unfortunate wife O-Iwa upon her cruel husband and his accomplices. In *Sakura Sōgorō* the ghosts of the Sōgorō family return to punish the man who had killed them and are at last placated. Sometimes the avenging spirits are simply demons, as they are in *Takatoki*. The character Takatoki has a somewhat extraordinary love of his dogs and bestows upon them honors and privileges more appropriate to human beings. When one of the dogs bites the mother of a samurai, the samurai kills it, and Takatoki orders that mother and son be killed. He is at last with difficulty persuaded to rescind this order, but that evening he is visited by a swarm of long-nosed goblins who, by giving him a severe drubbing, convince him that his arrogant love of his dogs should be superseded by a greater love for human beings.

The sacrifices demanded by the code of behavior are either of one-self or of those with whom one has intimate ties. In the historical plays the sacrifice is usually for the lord, while in the domestic pieces it tends to be made for members of one's own family, but both kinds of sacrifice are to be found in all the plays. Gonta, one of the heroes of *A Thousand Cherry Trees*, out of loyalty to a superior substitutes his wife and child for those of Koremori so that Koremori's family may escape death. In *The Battle of Ichinotani* the hero Kumagai, because of a complicated web of obligations, comes to kill his son and substitute his son's head for that of another in order to repay an obligation incurred by his lord. The child Senmatsu in *The Famous Tree at Sendai* eats the poisoned cakes intended for the young prince Tsuruchiyo, thus saving the young lord from death. Sacrifice of this kind does not necessarily involve death. Perhaps the most subtle of all sacrifices is that of Benkei in *The Subscription List*. So that his lord, Yoshitsune, may escape recognition and consequent death, Benkei is required to treat the disguised Yoshitsune as a servant and to beat him. This act, in terms of the ethical code, is unthinkable; it is the most unforgivable of all acts of disloyalty and every part of Benkei's being rebels against it. Nevertheless, in order to save Yoshitsune's life, Benkei beats him, with the full knowledge that he is thereby sacrificing what is to him the only reason for being, his loyalty to Yoshitsune. The moment at which Benkei strikes his lord is probably the most poignant of all sacrificial acts for the Kabuki audience.

Those who sacrifice themselves for their blood relatives are usually children and wives. Kotarō, the son of Matsuōmaru in 'The Village School,' goes calmly to his beheading at the request of his father, and we are told that he smiles and stretches forth his neck at the moment of decapitation; and Kōshirō of 'Moritsuna's Camp' cheerfully disembowels himself so that his father's strategy for winning the war may succeed. The large number of sacrificed children can be attributed, in part, to the necessity of providing roles for the child actors, but the child cut off in the bloom of youth also has the same poignancy for the Japanese as that of the fragile, soon destroyed cherry blossom. The vast majority of Kabuki women sacrifice their happiness for that of their husbands or lovers. Typical of these is the long-suffering wife Osono in *The Love of Hanshichi and Sanshō* who, although her husband has gone off with a courtesan, bears him no ill will and insists that she must have been at fault for not having sufficiently amused her husband at home. Satsuki, the wife in *Chivalrous Gorozō*, leaves the husband she loves in order to acquire, from a rival for her affections, a sum of money with which the husband can repay an obligation to his former lord.

The failure to perform social duties required by loyalty, either because of divided loyalty or because of some error of judgment, is in most instances atoned for by suicide. After Moritsuna has deceived his lord into thinking that the head he has examined is that of his brother, Moritsuna is determined to kill himself by way of apology to his lord, and he is saved from suicide only by the complicated workings of the plot. But one of the heroes of *The Loyal Forty-seven Rōnin*, Kampei, when he realizes that he has been negligent in carrying out his revenge, performs *harakiri* in shame and in apology to his dead master. The case of Sakuramaru in 'Anniversary Celebration' is similar. Sakuramaru, earlier in the play, had innocently arranged a meeting between Sugawara's daughter and the crown prince. The assignation becomes known, and it is used as the basis of a plot against Sugawara which results in his exile. When Sakuramaru comes to the realization that he was instrumental in setting this series of catastrophes in motion, he is driven to the conclusion, to which his aged father agrees, that he must kill himself in apology for having failed in his duty.

Generalizations about the serious Kabuki plays apart from their performance in the theatre are of little value except in that they demonstrate the degree to which the plays mirrored the attitudes of the audience which attended them. The common characteristic of the plays is that the social status quo is accepted unquestionably as stable, necessary, and eternal. Revenge, the ultimate means of obtaining justice, is carried out within the confines of the code for the purpose of correcting an immediate, isolated injustice, in the same manner that the agrarian uprisings were not conceived in the spirit of true political revolution but with the intent of remedying a specific evil. The social code remains inviolate throughout, and, particularly in the plays concerning the fall of a House, the series of misfortunes, piled one upon another, have their genesis in a rather casual and seemingly insignificant infringement of the code. In *Sugawara's Secrets of Calligraphy* the clandestine meeting of the crown prince and the daughter of Sugawara, although innocent in intent, is a breach of the code which releases a flood of catastrophe. The eleven anguished acts of *The Loyal Forty-seven Rōnin* arise out of the unrequited and illicit love of the villain, Moronao, for Hangan's wife. The implication is that any violation of the code, however minor and unintentional, will result in vast and uncontrollable misfortunes, visited even upon the innocent, until by means of sacrifices social equilibrium is restored. But although the code remains, it is to some degree circumvented by sacrifice. The behavior of Matsuōmaru in 'The Village School' is typical of that of the Kabuki hero; he must, according to the code, fulfil his obligation both to his master, Shihei, and to Sugawara toward whom he also feels a debt of obligation. Shihei has demanded the head of Sugawara's son; Matsuōmaru resolves the problem by substituting, through a complicated pattern of indirection, the head of his own son, and by identifying it as that of Sugawara's child. He has thus saved the life of Sugawara's heir and at the same time satisfied his obligation to his master. That he has actually deceived Shihei in substituting his own child does not constitute a problem in this play, although the logical implication is that Matsuōmaru must thereafter commit suicide in order to apologize to Shihei. A somewhat similar situation is that of Togashi, the guardian of the barrier in *The Subscription List*. Togashi is in actuality not deceived by the disguised

Yoshitsune; the suggestion is subtly made that Togashi is aware that the man he has allowed to pass through the barrier is the one that he has been ordered by his lord, Yoritomo, to apprehend. But being thoroughly imbued with the code of loyalty himself, Togashi is so moved by Benkei's loyalty to Yoshitsune that he allows the party to pass. The clear implication at the end of the play is that Togashi will then kill himself to apologize to his lord for his transgression. In the domestic plays the demands of the code are also both circumvented and fulfilled by an ultimate sacrifice, usually suicide. The lovers of *Love Suicide at Amijima* die together both to be joined in death and also to apologize to those whom their love has brought sorrow. The thief Benten Kozō at last performs *harakiri* as apology for having unwittingly murdered the son of a lord to whom Benten's father was indebted.

Since the basic conflict of the serious play resolves into that between *giri*, social (and therefore 'moral') obligation, and *ninjō*, human feelings, throughout it is the man of passion, of deep sensitivity, and of humanitarian impulses, who suffers; for his emotions impel him in an opposite direction from that required by the ethical code. Hangan, in *The Loyal Forty-seven Rōnin*, unable to control his anger toward Moronao, strikes him, and in that act performs a violation of the code which demands his life. Chūbei, the clerk of *The Courier of Hell*, unable to bear the taunts of a rival for the courtesan he loves, embezzles public funds so that he can ransom her. The priest in *Thunder God* gives way to lust and is seduced from his duty. Human feelings, in short, give rise to the great evil of the Confucian code, 'disorder' and 'disarrangement.' The scenes in which the individual is caught, immobile, at the point where social duty and human feelings erect their opposing fields of force are those toward which all serious Kabuki drama moves; and these static scenes of anguish—realized most frequently in partings from loved ones—are the essential substance of the plays. It should be observed in passing that the Japanese are a people of great emotionality, probably as intense in their loves and hates as any people in the world. The Confucian notion that the display of emotion was vulgar required that emotion be repressed, and the repression resulted in states of violent tension, seen both in the behavior of individuals and in much of Kabuki acting, and the consequent channelling of repressed emotion into an opposite overt expression. Not a rare occurrence in 1945 was that of a Japanese telling a foreigner how all his family was killed in an air raid, laughing the while. A few instances of this sort would do much toward creating in the imperceptive the idea that the Japanese lack all human feeling, but one need only see Kabuki actors performing to realize that, freed from social restrictions upon the display of emotion, the Japanese are strongly inclined to tear a passion to tatters with an Elizabethan violence of emotion.

The external world of the Kabuki hero is dominated by the social code which demands its due, laying its implacable mechanical force upon human sympathies, imposing an ultimate defeat upon all who seek to oppose it. And as the exterior world of the Kabuki hero is almost mechanically fixed, so, to a similar degree, is his inner world of individuality. Confucian ethics shapes the world about him and a popular Buddhist concept shapes that within him.

During the Tokugawa period the establishment of the ethical code and its ultimate penetration into all aspects of Japanese thought contributed to the decline of the power of Buddhism, which had previously been widely influential. Despite this decline, Buddhism survived in popular form in the consciousness of the individual and constituted what little private world the state allowed him. He lived, as do the majority of the characters in the serious Kabuki plays, a Confucian, but he died, like them also, a Buddhist. The first half of the act of *The Loyal Forty-seven Rōnin* in which Hangan kills himself in the presence of government officials is devoted to the strict etiquette of this social procedure, but the latter half of the act is concerned with solemn Buddhist rites for the dead; only after these are completed do the characters move back into the world of the ethical code and of revenge. Similarly, Kumagai, in *The Battle of Ichinotani*, having sacrificed his son and satisfied the code, removes his armor and becomes a Buddhist monk, 'having realized the vicissitudes of earthly life.' So far as the effect of Buddhism upon the serious Kabuki drama is concerned, it is apparent, as it was in society at large, within the inner life of the character, mostly apart from his duties as a social being. At only one philosophical point do Confucian ethics and Buddhist belief meet insofar as they affect the drama: Neither of them conceives of an ideological separation between man and his environment. In the Confucian code virtue lies in the wholehearted absorption of the individual in the performance of his social duties; he does not question the hierarchy, his station in it, nor his precisely defined relations to others; he is inseparable from the social milieu. Buddhist thought, on an emotional rather than a social level, does not distinguish between man and other living things, between 'the man who sees the world and the world that he sees.' The individual is as thoroughly undifferentiated from the flow of life as he is inseparable from the social mechanism of Confucian ethics.

But more important so far as the drama is concerned is the popular and unphilosophic belief in the Buddhist idea of *karma*, or, as it is called in Japanese, *inga*. This is the 'chain of causation' by which the individual is reborn to suffer or to be rewarded according to his conduct in a previous existence. Death is but a temporary cessation of the workings of this force, which is without beginning, although it may eventually end. So widespread is the acceptance of this idea that at present a criminal may make the plea in court that he himself is not responsible for the crime he has committed because it is the result of his *inga*. It is true that philosophical Buddhist belief puts forward the notion that an evil *inga* is to be fought against and that only by good deeds can the individual triumph over it, but in popular thought there is little emphasis upon this aspect of Buddhist teaching. Instead there is the cultivation of what has been described as fatalism, the simple acceptance of misfortune as the unavoidable result of an evil *inga* over which the individual can exercise no control.

Thus the events of the individual's life are as rigidly controlled by the character's *inga* as his social life is dominated by the workings of the ethical code. When Genzō and his wife Tonami in 'The Village School' contemplate the murder of an innocent child as a substitute for the heir of Sugawara, Tonami muses, 'How cruel is the law of *inga*! Can it be the sins of the mother or the sins of the father that have sent him here to us on this day?' As it turns out, the child is making the sacrifice willingly, but Genzō and Tonami think immediately, as do most Kabuki characters when confronted with misfortune, that one is punished because of his inescapable fate. Significantly, it is usually *inga* that is blamed, not the ethical code. The hero is therefore walled about with forces over which he can exercise little control, and so strong are these that they permit him movement only in a few well-trodden paths. He is caught up and suspended by these forces as inevitably as the hero of the Western naturalistic novel is caught between the forceps of heredity and environment.

From the point of view of Western drama, the Kabuki plays have more of the melodramatic than of the tragic. There is, primarily, the fact that the situation in which the hero finds himself is largely thrust upon him arbitrarily and that he is not permitted to create his own destiny to the degree to which the tragic hero is allowed to create his. The field of the Kabuki hero's activity is so narrowed down by the forces about him, he is so molded within the form wrought out of his social duty and his *inga*, that he seems less an individual than a stereotype. Since they all come from the same mold, it is difficult to recognize the Kabuki heroes as individuals; the wide differences of personality that exist between Medea and Antigone or between Othello and Hamlet do not obtain in the Kabuki. There are no characters of complex, ambiguous personalities. The situations in which they are placed are extraordinarily involved, but the characters themselves remain singularly uncomplicated. The forces which set these heroes in motion are as obvious and straightforward as those which spin the hero of melodrama through one external literal event to another. It is conceivable that a Coriolanus or an Iago could exist within the Kabuki drama, but a Hamlet is unthinkable not only because of his incapacity to revenge immediately but, more particularly, because of the depth and richness of his interior life. The simplicity of the Kabuki hero is also in large part due to his being essentially a 'good' man, like the usual hero of melodrama. His evil is largely external to him and does not exist, in the form of a tragic flaw, as an essential part of his being, making him the involved personality, neither too virtuous nor too vicious, which Aristotle described. And even his relatively simple character lacks consistency. This lack of consistency is not of the sort which at times arises out of the organic complexity of the tragic hero. It is possible that the abrupt changes of Kabuki characters have their prototype in those Nō play characters who undergo complete transformations in personality in the second half of the play. But the lack of consistency is also the result of the system of playwriting whereby different playwrights composed different parts of the play. Thus the Matsuōmaru who appears in other acts of *Sugawara's Secrets of Calligraphy* bears no resemblance to the hero who sacrifices his son in the last act of the play, 'The Village School.' It is true that the author of the last act, Takeda Izumo, felt obliged to make some attempt to rationalize Matsuōmaru's actions and to explain his irreconcilable patterns of behavior. But the Kabuki hero is not a personality who is sustained, who lives and grows, over an extended period of dramatic time. As a result, his personality, insofar as the script demonstrates it, is realized principally within single acts or scenes. There is little feeling of the character's nature being shaped and changed by a sequence of temporal events; instead, the character is stated in terms of the significant, isolated moment. A sense of the character evolving out of a complex of time in which the past contains the seeds of the present, in which time exists as a continuum, is almost entirely lacking. This is true both within the character of the hero and within the entire texture of the play.

Enclosed within his narrowly restricted field of activity both by his ethical code and by popular Buddhist thought, the Kabuki hero never achieves to as strong a sense of opposition as that which the tragic hero feels between himself and the society which surrounds him. Every tragic hero is to a certain extent a rebel against his environment, standing off from it, viewing it critically, and determined to refashion his external world in some respect. The Kabuki hero shows little of this revolutionary quality. He seems undifferentiated from society, for all who surround him are motivated by the same notions and live within the same ideological realm. Both Benkei and his opponent Togashi in *The Subscription List* share a common attitude toward reality. In his effort to achieve his ends the tragic hero uncompromisingly wages war against the status quo and to an appreciable, meaningful degree obtains what he desires. The movement of his life across society has profound and far-reaching effects; society is changed by Antigone's or Hamlet's necessary sacrifice. But the Kabuki hero is uncompromising only within the limits which society has set for him; he does not break through these limits; he does not question the world which surrounds him. He performs, in fact, his necessary sacrifice not that the essential nature of his world may be changed but that it remain exactly as it always was. He does not challenge or condemn, but accepts. Although the tragic hero at times displays a similar fortitude, it does not constitute the sum of his being. The extreme willingness of the Kabuki hero to submit to the strict requirement of the ethical code overlays him with what, from a Western point of view, is an extreme fatalism. His sacrifice appears, when compared with that of the tragic hero, to be almost pointless; it lacks the sense of victory in defeat, of the heart which 'bursts smilingly' in tragedy. And the end of the Kabuki hero, viewed through Western eyes, is deeply pessimistic. For the Kabuki hero endurance is all. He does not seem to take arms against a sea of troubles. He appears to be fixed on a sharp sword of circumstance, and he can do not more than struggle and suffer aimlessly before he is destroyed.

Since nothing is essentially changed by his sacrifice and since all the characters of the play share a common view of the nature of reality, the Kabuki hero does not move among the worlds of multiple reality which the heroes of tragedy inhabit. Consequently the Kabuki hero does not appear to achieve to any significant 'recognition.' He is not seared to the depths of his being by the recognition of a new and ultimate reality such as that which flames through Oedipus, nor does he experience the irreconcilable worlds of reality which surround Macbeth.[3] He not infrequently 'recognizes' debts of obligation which he had not formerly been aware of, but these realizations are usually thrust upon him in mechanical fashion by the workings of the plot and do not arise out of his own being. The only recognition to which the Kabuki hero attains, either as he sacrifices himself or his loved ones, is his realization of the 'vicissitudes of earthly existence.' This Buddhist phrase echoes among the last lines of Kabuki characters as they die or, having sacrificed others, as they set out upon an 'aimless journey.'

The themes of these plays appear to the Westerner to have about them the triviality, the lack of magnitude, which he at times feels in the brief, unextended statement of other forms of Japanese art. The ultimate concern of tragedy with throwing light on the meaning and purpose of human existence does not seem to exist in the Kabuki drama; its final implication, philosophically, is that mankind must suffer so that the social pattern may endure. The plays are not based upon the relative and interacting forces of philosophical Good and Evil which form the foundations of tragedy; within the Kabuki drama good and evil are merely limited social, not philosophical, problems. Ultimate good consists in the performance of the character's social duties; evil in the social 'disarrangement' and 'disorder' of Confucian ethics. This limited field of activity appears in Western eyes to be more fertile for social drama or even comedy of manners than for serious consideration of the nature of man's existence. It further lacks, of necessity, the deep moral strain which runs through tragedy. The basic impulse of the tragic hero's action is to achieve what he conceives to be an ultimate moral good based upon clearly

---

[3] The film *Rashōmon* (1951), concerned with multiple worlds of reality, is thoroughly nontypical of Japanese dramatic expression. It was generally ignored in Japan until after it had achieved some reputation abroad. Japanese critics speculated in the press upon the reasons for its foreign popularity but were unable to determine the causes.

defined, though individual, interpretations of what constitute right and wrong. Even Othello, who bears some resemblance to a Kabuki hero in that his actions are motivated by a rigid code of honor, kills Desdemona not out of the mechanical workings of that code but that 'else she'll betray more men'; Othello's sacrifice of a part of himself is at last brought about by a deep conviction based upon his conception of moral right and wrong. But because in Confucian ethics the only morality is that which is dictated by the social code, the Kabuki hero cannot hold individual conception of right and wrong, for these are determined precisely and minutely in the world which surrounds him and of which he is an undifferentiated part. There is never any question in Kumagai's mind about the morality of killing his son; the code demands that he do so to repay a debt of obligation and therefore his act is morally correct. The failure to penetrate beneath the surface of existence, but to accept the status quo unquestioningly as the ultimate mundane reality, creates in the Westerner the feeling that the lives of the Kabuki characters are sacrificed meaninglessly, that the anguish of the plays is scarcely justified, and that the view of human existence expressed in the plays is singularly naïve.

But to compare the drama of the Kabuki with that of another culture serves no function except that of clarifying, to some extent, the bases upon which the Kabuki play and its characters are constructed. Although from the Western point of view the drama lacks much of what goes to make up tragedy, judged within the context of Japanese thought both of the Tokugawa period and of today (and no drama can be judged conscientiously except within the framework of the society which created it), the Kabuki drama reveals certain characteristics of tragedy. The world of the Kabuki play is not the almost limitless universe in which the characters of Sophocles and Shakespeare move. But within the limits set for them, the greatest Kabuki heroes are not merely the puppet figures of melodrama.

Because the Kabuki hero in his loyalty to the code of behavior epitomizes the highest, most laudable behavior to which man can achieve, he has great stature for his audience. These heroes are not merely types for the Japanese; existing within a closely knit, almost undifferentiated society, they appear types to the foreigner who does not see them in their complete relation to the background out of which they are evolved. The audience in this society carries within itself a part of the hero and this part the playwright need not state. In the fixed, stable world of Aeschylus, in order to convince the audience of their theatre reality, the characters were not required to be painstakingly delineated individuals; in the less certain world of Euripides, the detail of behavior, the subtle psychological convolution, needed projection. The character Benkei exists not only in the Kabuki theatre but throughout Japan, and this Benkei the audience brings with it when it comes to the play. Further, the outlines of his character are invested with vibrant colors by the skill of the actor who shares with the audience their common view of Benkei. The situation is not that at a contemporary performance of *Hamlet* in America where no audience in its entirety is convinced that this actor's protrayal of Hamlet is the authoritative one. In the Kabuki theatre, Benkei, presupposing his portrayal by an accomplished actor, becomes simultaneously both the individual and the synthesis——the two levels on which the tragic hero exists. Because of the essential nature of the Kabuki, the play cannot be judged apart from its performance in the theatre, and one characteristic of this performance, that of placing emphasis on the character rather than the event, minimizes the melodramatic elements of the play, for it allows the hero to exist, as he does in tragedy, in greater prominence than the mechanism of the play to which he is attached.

Since he is essentially a 'good' man (even the thieves of *kizewamono* are basically 'good'), and the evil is external to him, he is not possessed of that Western 'mole of nature,' the tragic flaw. But within the ethical framework, he has his *hamartia*. This is emotion, which in the Confucian code gives rise to the evil of 'disorder' and 'disarrangement.' The Kabuki hero is a man of strong and passionate feelings. If he were not, the necessary conflict between the performance of his social duty and his human feelings could not exist. The drama of all the Kabuki heroes has its genesis in their emotionality, and this brings them close to being composed of the same stuff as the tragic hero. Antigone, Macbeth, or Lear could not exist if they were not possessed of the ability to feel strongly, to be abnormally sensitive emotionally, to be 'finely aware.' Mere emotionality does not make a tragic hero, but it is a prerequisite to the demand of tragedy that the hero's suffering be not merely physical, as it frequently is with the hero of melodrama, but arise out of his keen and deep sensitivity to the situation of which he is a part. The Kabuki hero is as aware, as sensitive, within the limits set for him, as is the tragic hero within his larger world. In both tragedy and Kabuki drama it is the man of strong feeling who suffers, and it is the extreme sensitivity of his nature which sets him apart from other men and gives him dramatic stature.

The tragic hero allows no limits to be set on his uncompromising activity and he is prepared to destroy everything that stands in his way in order to gain his ends; therefore a character like Antigone, who would set the ways of the gods above the ways of men and overtly and deliberately oppose political authority, cannot exist in the Kabuki play. The Kabuki hero is permitted to move only to the limits fixed by the ethical code; here he must stop short, for the code cannot be transgressed, and he must at last compromise. But within these limits the hero stands opposed to the mechanical workings of the code, and to this degree, which was the utmost extent of revolutionary thought of which the Tokugawa mentality was capable, he is un-compromising in his desire to rectify social wrong as he, the indi-vidual, conceives the wrong. To this degree he is differentiated from society; and although the code remains at last inviolable, the hero succeeds, by an act of sacrifice, in preventing its application in a specific, isolated case. In so doing he exhibits as much strength, singleness of purpose, and unwillingness to compromise as the tragic hero, and with equal resoluteness he advances unflinchingly to meet his fate. To gain his ends, he must break the code, and this act is as significant and awe-inspiring within the society of the Kabuki hero as the rebellion of the tragic hero within his. Benkei breaks the code when he strikes his master Yoshitsune, Moritsuna when he lies to Tokimasa about the identity of the head before him, Matsuōmaru when he deceives his lord by substituting the head of his own child for that of Sugawara's heir. All these acts require a sacrifice. That of Benkei is purely psychological; Moritsuna is prepared to commit suicide to atone for his behavior; Matsuōmaru sacrifices the life of his son.

For the audience these sacrifices are of great moment, for they demonstrate the fleeting triumph of the human spirit over the slings and arrows of outrageous fortune. That the victory is not greater or more far-reaching in its effects, as it is in tragedy, does not lessen its significance for the Japanese, whose philosophy is not concerned with abstract Good and Evil but with social good and evil. The inter-dependence of these two in the Kabuki play is shown as rigorously as that between Good and Evil in tragedy. The tragic hero is unable to obtain what he considers his greatest Good without suffering a cor-responding Evil. The greatest Good for Oedipus, as a king, is to rid his country of the plague by finding the guilty man who is the cause of it; at the end of his uncompromising search for this man he attains his greatest Good and also his greatest Evil, the realization that he himself is the guilty man. In the final moment of victory and defeat of the tragic hero, that which exists as Good and Evil for him are shown to be the inseparable halves of a whole, mutually interdependent; no Good can be achieved (as it is in melodrama) without the ultimate sacrifice. It is about this fulcrum that the life of the tragic hero moves, and at last the opposing forces of Good and Evil are brought into equilibrium. The greatest good of the Kabuki hero is the performance of his social duty within the code (and in this respect Oedipus is not unlike him). For Matsuōmaru the greatest good is the repayment of his debt of obligation to Sugawara by permitting Sugawara's son to avoid death, but he cannot do this by simply allowing the boy to escape. The code demands its sacrificial victim, and if Matsuōmaru is to circumvent its workings he must provide the sacrifice. He achieves his greatest good, the restoration of Sugawara's son to his father, but in doing so he must suffer an equal evil, the loss of his own son. Precise interdependence of good and evil, a son for a son, is not always shown as exactly as it is in the case of Matsuōmaru, but whenever the hero violates the ethical code for the purpose of securing his individual social good, he is required to suffer a corresponding evil.

Tragedy reconciles man to life by demonstrating that although the tragic hero suffers greatly he attains an ultimate victory which more than compensates for the evil that befalls him, and his end is thus a curious mixture of both joy and pain. The Kabuki hero also achieves his important victory, but there is little in it that can be described as joy. Kabuki drama does not suggest, as does tragedy, that life is worth living; it suggests merely that life must be endured. But this view of life, however pessimistic it may seem to the Westerner, is not pessimistic for the Japanese. A willingness to accept adversity as unavoidable, to suffer uncomplainingly and stoically, to meet misfortune with the phrase, 'Shikata ga nai' ('Nothing can be done about it'), lies at the roots of the common Japanese attitude toward reality. The attitude does not arise out of phlegmatic indifference or a lack of sensitivity; the Japanese is acutely aware of the subtle currents of human existence. But he is inclined to accept rather than to change; and for him the endurance and suffering of the Kabuki hero is the valid statement of his view of life, neither pessimistic nor optimistic, but true, as true for him as the less fatalistic view of life expressed in tragedy is to the Westerner. The sole 'recognition' of the Kabuki hero, his realization of the 'vicissitudes of earthly existence,' is, within the context of popular Buddhist thought, a discovery of profound significance. All Buddhist philosophy tends toward the attainment of this experience, and when the Kabuki hero has gained it, he again represents, for the Japanese, an ultimate in human achievement. Since his experience is mystical and can only be hinted at, it lacks the communicability of the experience of the tragic hero when he comes to his ultimate reality. But for the audience the Kabuki hero's attainment is ample reward for the sufferings he has undergone. He has seen through and beyond the social code which hedges his life, through and beyond the meaningless motion on the surface of life, and achieving to an awareness of the unchanging eternal, he has won the ultimate victory.

CHAPTER IX

Kabuki and the Western Room

THROUGHOUT its history the pattern of Kabuki development was to absorb all new and attractive theatrical material created outside the walls of the theatre and incorporate this into the mainstream of Kabuki tradition. It utilized the Nō, the doll theatre, dances of all varieties and sources, history and legend, and, insofar as it was permitted, contemporary event. The casual, gradual absorption of these materials was easily accomplished aesthetically, for the general uniformity of attitude and taste throughout the country, as well as the limitation on material caused by the isolation of Japan, resulted in the evolution of forms which possessed certain basic common characteristics. Furthermore, at the time the process of assimilation was taking place, the Kabuki had already firmly established its aesthetic tradition. New elements could therefore be adopted into it without working any significant or essential changes in its form. Influences from the outside world penetrated into the Kabuki only after they had been generally absorbed into Tokugawa society, and by that time these influences had been made so thoroughly Japanese that they had ceased to be foreign. An occasional foreign novelty might be taken directly into the theatre, which constantly sought novel means of intriguing its audience; a telescope, for example, figures prominently in the first act of *Through the Iga Pass*. But during the Tokugawa period the Kabuki was entirely free from any direct influence of foreign drama. There is some evidence that a stage was built in the Kurishitan Church at Nagasaki and that mystery plays of the European kind were performed there. It seems likely that the Catholic missionaries would have utilized this method of religious instruction. However the church was closed in 1614 during the pursuit of an anti-Christian program by the Shōgunate; whether or not liturgical plays were performed in Japan during the late sixteenth and early seventeenth centuries, there was no possibility after 1614 of any influence of foreign theatre upon the Kabuki; consequently, it created its form of expression out of purely Japanese materials.

But after 1868 when there swept into Japan, as into a vacuum, a stream of foreign articles and ideas, there were also eventually carried into the country new, foreign, and eminently un-Japanese concepts of the theatre. The immediate effect of the Meiji Restoration upon the theatre appeared in the Kabuki. Danjūrō IX and Kikugorō V endeavored to present plays in the Kabuki idiom dealing with 'current history' and the 'ways of the new society,' but the movement was unpopular and consequently short-lived. The first obvious, though indirect, impact of the Western theatre upon Japan did not occur until about 1888. At this time there appeared, at first in Ōsaka, a theatrical movement known as *shimpa*. It arose not out of the efforts of the professional actors and theatre workers of the Kabuki, but was largely the creation of amateurs, including newspaper men and political enthusiasts, who although they had little firsthand knowledge of the Western theatre determined to create a new and vital contemporary theatre patterned, as they conceived it, on that of the West. They conceived the Western drama to be couched in colloquial language, as opposed to the stylized language of the Kabuki plays, to be concerned largely with the contemporary scene, and to be acted not in the strictly designed movement of the Kabuki but with an imitation of the movement and gestures of life. During the 'nineties *shimpa* enjoyed such a wide vogue that even the foremost Kabuki actors of the day felt impelled to play *shimpa* roles, and Morita Kanya, of an old Kabuki family, established a *shimpa* theatre. With this, the Kabuki began to influence the amateur *shimpa* performers, and their acting techniques came more and more to resemble those of Kabuki. Soon *shimpa* showed little difference, either in mode of production or in subject matter, from the plays of the traditional Kabuki performance. The roles of women in these 'realistic' *shimpa* pieces were played on the same stage during the same play by both men and women. Prints of *shimpa* actors show them to be performing, if not *mie*, at least an intense static pose that bears a close resemblance to the *mie*. The plays dealt, it is true, largely with contemporary event, but they also ranged into foreign countries, on one occasion into ancient

Greece, and such plays were performed in Japanese settings and costumes. Although certain of the plays were concerned with the Japanese interpretation of foreign political ideas, the majority, and the most popular ones, dealt with bloody and sexy happenings of the period. Consequently there was little difference, except that of artistry, between the thieves and murderers of the 'living' domestic plays and the detectives and murderers of *shimpa*.

Although he was not the chief figure in *shimpa*, Kawakami Otojirō (1864–1911) was so characteristic of the amateurs who brought it about that his career sums up the essential quality of the movement. Born a samurai of low rank, at the age of twenty he became a policeman. But feeling certain revolutionary inclinations, he resigned his position and began making public speeches attacking the government. This led to his frequent arrest, and at last he was forbidden by the police to make further speeches. He thereupon turned to comic story telling—*rakugo*—and at this achieved some success. Tiring of this profession he became a member of a group of provincial actors, and in 1891 at Sakai, a port town near Ōsaka, this group performed *The Beautiful Story of a Prosperous Country*, 'A Greek Historical Play,' which had political overtones. The play was a failure in Sakai, and when the troupe later attempted to stage it in Yokohama, the performance was forbidden by the police. But Kawakami succeeded, in August 1892, in renting a theatre in Tōkyō and avoiding police censorship. There the 'Greek Historical Play' was a great success and Kawakami's position in the contemporary theatre was assured. In 1899–1900 Kawakami went abroad. Although he had no training in its techniques of expression, Kawakami appeared in Kabuki plays in San Francisco, New York, and Paris, much to the bewilderment and dismay of the Japanese residents of these cities who were acquainted with the Kabuki. Kawakami apparently felt himself to be a theatrical missionary bringing the Kabuki to the West and conversely Western drama to Japan, for upon his return, he staged a production of *Hamlet* in which he played the leading role. The legend exists that in one scene of the play Kawakami, as Hamlet, made his entrance to the stage riding a bicycle. Legend or fact, the story embodies a good deal of truth about Japanese conceptions of Western drama at that time. In the same way that the American and European audiences who attended Kawakami's Kabuki performances were deceived into thinking that they were seeing Kabuki, so Japanese audiences were misled into thinking that Kawakami's production of *Hamlet* represented the Western theatre. Hamlet on a bicycle was not incongruous to the audience of that period, for both Hamlet and the bicycle were new and foreign and therefore logically belonged together. Similarly the audience was not disturbed at the characters of the 'Greek Historical Play' being dressed in Tokugawa period costumes and using contemporary oil lamps. In short, *shimpa* was based primarily upon what men of such dubious knowledge as Kawakami conceived the Western drama to be, expressed throughout in terms of Japanese life and attitudes.

Shimpa followed the same pattern as that used in introducing foreign literature to Japan. Whether the material was the novels of Bulwer-Lytton or Gray's 'Elegy,' translations into Japanese involved considerable effort to make the works thoroughly Japanese, if not in setting, at least in concepts and language. Even the scholar Tsubouchi Shōyō (1859–1935), who devoted some twenty years to translating the works of Shakespeare into Japanese (and who wrote popular historical plays in the early years of this century), felt it necessary to bridge the gap between Japanese and Western culture by using in his translations the tone and atmosphere of the Kabuki. The result was that his versions of Shakespeare bear at best only a passing resemblance to their originals. And it may be, in part, for this reason that the plays of Shakespeare have exerted little influence upon modern Japanese notions of dramaturgy; they appear in Tsubouchi's translations to be so close to Kabuki that they do not suggest to the young playwright the break with the past which he feels essential to the creation of contemporary Japanese drama.

The entire *shimpa* movement was a theatrical manifestation of the frenzied pursuit of novelty which has frequently characterized Japanese behavior and which was particularly uninhibited during the Meiji period. Between 1868 and 1903, according to Basil Hall Chamberlain, there were successive rages, among others, for rabbits, printing dictionaries by subscription, gigantic funerals, hypnotism, garden parties, and committing suicide by jumping into the Kegon waterfalls. The arrival of the first film in Japan in December 1896 created wonder and delight in a people dedicated to the new, particularly since the film was the new in a mechanical form. The tremendous increase in movie theatres following the end of the Russo-Japanese War in 1905 can be traced to the fascination exerted by the film upon *shimpa* audiences. These consisted in the main of workers from rural areas who, having little or no acquaintance with the traditional means of expression of the Kabuki, found it almost unintelligible. *Shimpa* was a movement toward representational theatre, but the film moved even farther and more satisfactorily in the same direction. In 1910 an effort was made to combine film and theatre in a form called *rensageki*, which was something of a nine-days' wonder but did not survive. The film had gained a constant and devoted audience. However, even in contemporary films, whose form of expression is generally representational, there are differences in acting between those which are 'period' pieces and those which are set in the present. The former show a rather strong influence of Kabuki acting, while the latter are more strictly realistic. Despite their surface representationalism, all contemporary films nonetheless reveal in their ideology and structure a great dependence on the Kabuki.

Shimpa did not survive as an influential form much later than 1905, and its effect upon the Kabuki disappeared at the same time. It had not worked any changes upon the traditional Kabuki form but merely involved certain of the Kabuki actors. *Shimpa* was succeeded by *shingeki*, a theatre movement which included the production both of contemporary Western plays and of Japanese plays based upon a study of Western models.[1] Various troupes were organized, the majority of them in Tōkyō, for the purpose of playing contemporary foreign plays in Japanese translation. The foreign plays were not performed in Japanese adaptations of the originals; a conscientious effort was made to costume, set, and act the plays in as nearly as possible the manner in which they were produced in the countries of their origin. The movement began in 1906 with the formation of the *Bungei Kyōkai* (Literature and Art Society) and the establishment in 1909 of the *Jiyūgeki Kyōkai* (Free Theatre Society) headed by Osanai Kaoru (1881–1928), who was the most influential figure in *shingeki*. In 1909 Osanai's group performed Ibsen's *John Gabriel Borkman*, Gorky's *The Lower Depths*, and Maeterlinck's *The Death of Tintagiles*. In the following year a troupe headed by Inoue Masao

[1] Technically, within Japanese theatre vocabulary, the word *shimpa* applies strictly only to the plays of the movement between, approximately, 1888 and 1905. The tradition of *shimpa* (chiefly that of having men play female roles) was carried on in attenuated form in 'New Life' *shimpa*. Although troupes can occasionally be seen performing in this manner, *shimpa* has long since ceased to be an influential or popular form of the theatre. The word *shimpa*, however, continues to be used, popularly and loosely, to describe plays as well as films with a more or less contemporary setting as opposed to those with a pre-Meiji 'historical' setting.

performed plays of Shaw and Chekhov, and in 1912 Kamiyama and his actress wife formed a troupe which played *Hedda Gabler*, *A Doll's House*, and other of Ibsen's 'middle period' plays. Other groups appeared, some succeeding in producing only one play, but none of the groups managed to survive for more than ten years. The intellectuals were interested in the performance of these plays, but the general public was not, and the number of intellectuals was not large enough to support the groups. Modern drama in Japan would probably have disappeared almost entirely if it had not gained the financial support of Hijikata Yoshi; at his own expense Hijikata built the Tsukiji Little Theatre in Tōkyō, a theatre seating 500, which opened in June 1924. The theatre was placed under the directorship of Osanai Kaoru and during the first five years of its existence produced 87 Western plays and 25 original Japanese plays. At no time in its history did the Tsukiji Little Theatre make its way financially; its debts were always paid by Hijikata. But the public was enabled to see, at moderate prices, a catholic variety of contemporary foreign plays, among others those of Ibsen, Chekhov, Tolstoy, Shaw, Gorky, Hauptmann, Suderman, Schnitzler, Wedekind, Kaiser, Strindberg, Maeterlinck, Brieux, Andreyev, and O'Neill. In 1930 dissension split the theatre into two groups. One group, to which Hijikata belonged, held that the theatre 'should be put to use as a weapon in the coming class struggle,' while the other expressed its belief in art for art's sake. Hijikata's group became the New Tsukiji Troupe, while the politically more conservative group became the New Society Troupe. Ironically, the leaders of both troupes were clapped into jail in August 1940, 'as offenders of the law for preservation of public peace.'

Certain of these plays had a considerable influence upon the young Japanese playwrights and exerted for them as powerful an attraction as new mechanisms from abroad—the telegraph and the train—had earlier excited the curiosity and interest of the public at large. Much of their interest in foreign drama was genuine, but part of it was dictated by the nation-wide desire, which at bottom was political in origin, to prove that Japan was in no way inferior to the West and that it could rapidly transform itself, at least on the surface, into a society based upon Western concepts. This impulse was succeeded by an eventual repugnance for Western concepts which reached its political climax in 1941, but by that time the form of the modern drama of Japan was firmly based upon the Japanese concept of the foreign plays performed during the first three decades of the twentieth century.

By far the most influential of these plays were those of Ibsen, Chekhov, and Shaw, playwrights whose work generally falls within the category of realistic theatre. Although the 'symbolic' plays of Ibsen, those of Maeterlinck, and those of the expressionists were performed, they produced little effect upon Japanese playwriting. The majority of the young men of the *shingeki* movement saw modern theatre largely in terms of the realistic play. The most important reasons for this can be briefly noted. It was somewhat easier for them to appreciate the wickedness of Hedda Gabler, the sentimentality of Madame Ranevsky, and the problems of Mrs. Warren, than it was to gain insight, for instance, into the vague, indecisive ways of Pelléas and Mélisande, whose behavior confused even the French. The characters of the realistic play, though Westerners, moved within a world of actuality, not within the remote world of a poet who had allied himself with a contemporary Western artistic philosophy. This quality of the realistic plays made them at once valid, interesting, and suitable, within the framework of Japanese society, for imitation. The characters of these plays were concerned in varying degrees with social problems, and so were the young Japanese intellectuals who wrote modern drama. Even the Kabuki before 1868 had moved toward a concern with shocking contemporary event, *shimpa* had dwelt upon similar subject matter, and therefore the movement in *shingeki* toward the literal imitation of life in the theatre showed some continuity with theatre tradition. But it had for the playwright the novelty of dealing with actuality in terms of the ready-made, and therefore laudable, form of the Western realistic theatre.

It should be pointed out that the 'ideas' of Ibsen, Chekhov, and Shaw exerted no observable influence upon Japanese dramaturgy; these were for the most part so far removed from those existing in Japanese society that they could have little significant meaning. It was perhaps possible for the Japanese to understand Hedda Gabler to some degree, for 'poisonous women' who destroyed the men around them were stock figures in the late Kabuki theatre and in novels; but it is difficult to imagine what the actress and audience made of Nora in *A Doll's House* in 1910. In 1946 this play was revived in Tōkyō because it demonstrated 'women's rights in a democracy,' and at that time Nora may have been somewhat more intelligible to the audience even though her solution to her difficulties was not.

With the obvious exception of the playwright who felt drawn toward Marxism (and in this he also showed a partiality for a ready-made pattern of thought) the 'ideas' of these plays were not what fascinated the playwright, the actor, and the technician. They were intrigued primarily by the mechanics of production of the realistic play. The playwright seized upon the obvious, surface construction of the plays. He did not concern himself with complicated dramatic characters. He could not follow Ibsen, for example, into the realm of the tragic characters of *Rosmersholm* and *The Master Builder*. He used colloquial speech, but he did not write tightly-knit dialogue. His 'social problems' were usually on a level with those addressed to Dorothy Dix. He saw in Chekhov not poetic insight into human beings but merely surface realism. The actor too was occupied with the literal imitation of reality; this represented a significant change from Japanese acting tradition and resulted in the exclusive use of women in female roles. But the greatest success in transplanting a foreign form of theatre into Japan was that of the scene designers and the technicians of the theatre. Since these men dealt with physical objects rather than ideas, they were on solider ground than the playwrights. The purpose of the stage setting was to look as much like reality as possible and to create on the stage an area illusionistically differentiated from that of the auditorium. Theatre workers set about this goal with an enthusiasm as great as that of Antoine. The proscenium was built, architecturally separating stage from auditorium; the stage was lit and the auditorium darkened. Objects supposed to be three-dimensional were not merely flat surfaces painted with light and shade but were built in the round. The sky drop was carefully painted and lighted so that it created the illusion of sky, and with the importation of new electrical lighting instruments the sky was flooded with sunsets, moonrises, and thunderstorms. Theatrical space was extended into the wings of the stage, and the director, who of necessity appeared in the Japanese theatre at this time, invested these newly penetrated areas with dramatic meaning by employing sound effects and by orienting the movement of the actors in these directions. *Shingeki* thus brought to Japan techniques of production which had nothing in common with the forms of theatre the Japanese had created before 1868.

Shingeki of itself did not attract large popular audiences, even though its realistic idiom was the same as that of the film. And it was through the film that representational expression, previously unknown to Japan, became widespread and popular. Confronted with this phenomenon, the Kabuki repeated its traditional pattern of attempting to absorb the new and popular form of theatrical expression. But formerly it had absorbed materials of native origin, and now it was faced with a form of theatre antithetical to its own. To combine these two forms required compromise, and the result was a bizarre collision of forces which the Japanese call neo-Kabuki. It is probably best represented in the plays of Okamoto Kidō.

The subject matter of the majority of Okamoto's plays does not differ greatly from that of pre-Meiji Kabuki; he turns a nostalgic eye upon the past and seems to long for its faded romantic glory. Like the *shingeki* playwrights, Okamoto was not interested in the ideas of foreign plays but in their techniques of production, and these he attempted to graft onto the established Kabuki form. In the performance of Okamoto's plays the auditorium is darkened and light is concentrated on the stage. Although the *hanamichi* is occasionally, and somewhat grudgingly, used for entrances, the actor does not use the space in the traditional fashion but merely as a means of reaching the stage. Instead of the flat, nonrepresentational lighting of Kabuki, the lighting is designed to produce the effects of time of day, season of the year, or, when possible, more elaborate effects: In *The Tale of Shuzenji* the audience is treated to a lighting effect of moonlight upon a rippling stream; this has little relation to the play, but the audience finds it pretty. Okamoto's plays are full of offstage sound effects which are designed to create a feeling that the play moves in a realm beyond the observable limits of the stage. There is offstage singing, conversation, playing of musical instruments, chirping of cicadas, most of which are made to sound as literal as possible. (The sound of the cicadas is produced with a mouth organ.) The effect of the offstage sound effects is reinforced by supernumeraries who move casually across the stage, as though it were a segment of a larger continuum of space, for the sole purpose of creating this illusion; in both *Night Tale of Shinjuku* and *Muromachi Palace* these strolling individuals, their movement reminiscent of that of certain of the characters in the last act of Chekhov's *The Three Sisters*, serve no other dramatic purpose. Okamoto is so intent upon creating strong offstage areas that he frequently has important action take place in them where it cannot be seen by the audience. In *Muromachi Palace*, for example, the unfortunate hero Ikeda Tango attacks his rival Mondonosuke within view of the audience; but after they have fought at some length, they disappear from sight, Ikeda kills his rival offstage, and then is afforded the opportunity of reappearing on stage by breaking through paper doors and revealing himself bloodstained and blinded. All these technical devices of the representational theatre are in direct opposition to the form of the Kabuki. The Kabuki is concentrated on the stage and on the *hanamichi*; it does not penetrate space in the upstage area or in the wings; it is not concerned with creating a representational locale about the actor which will attract attention to itself by its realism or, because of its visual and psychological force, influence the movement of the actor. The basic pattern of movement of the Kabuki actor is toward the audience and is not related to the setting nor, to a confining degree, to the other actors.

Despite the introduction of these devices into the Kabuki theatre, Okamoto did not succeed in converting the Kabuki to representational expression. The actor performing in these pieces does not use thoroughly realistic gesture and attitude, and the scenes of fighting are almost as stylized as those in pure Kabuki. The villain of *Night Tale of Shinjuku* is decapitated onstage, but he shows this, theatrically, by bending over backward. The roles of women are played by *onnagata* who speak in traditional semi-falsetto. The two-man Kabuki horse appears onstage in a scene which, for purposes of realism, requires the use of actual fire. The flat in front of the *geza*, the musicians' room, is pierced with the oblong holes of the Kabuki setting so that the music can be more clearly heard and the musicians can see the stage. Okamoto's plays, and others of the neo-Kabuki variety, are thus neither Kabuki nor representational theatre but exist at an unstable point somewhere between the two. They are of historical interest, but dramatically they are no more than a futile attempt to combine two antithetical forms of theatre. However, neo-Kabuki plays constitute the only substantial effort made in modern times to incorporate new material into the Kabuki.

With Japan's increasing militarism in the 1930's the Kabuki entered a period of trial from which it has only recently emerged. During World War II many of the younger actors were drafted into the armed forces; certain plays were forbidden because they were too 'luxurious' and therefore unsuited to the austerity of the times or because their characters showed too little inclination to set social duty over personal inclination. Finally, in February 1944 all the large Kabuki theatres in Japan were closed because they represented too frivolous an activity. The effort was made, however, to use the

Kabuki for propaganda purposes. A film was made of *The Subscription List* which pointed out that Benkei's loyalty to his master Yoshitsune symbolized the highest achievement of a Japanese citizen. Kabuki troupes were dispatched to factories manufacturing war materials to play pieces, such as 'The Village School,' which showed the virtue of unquestioning self-sacrifice. During the air raids on Japanese cities most of the Kabuki theatres were destroyed, so that at the end of the war few theatres designed for Kabuki performances remained and those planned for showing films and performing *shingeki* had to be used.

But the surrender of Japan did not mean the unimpeded resumption of Kabuki. Previously the Kabuki had been under the close censorship of government authorities; now it was subject to similar control by the Occupation authorities.

During the first three years of the Occupation, all public media of communication, including newspapers, radio, magazines, books, phonograph records, films, theatre, and mail, were subject to censorship by the Civil Censorship Detachment, a unit of G. H. Q. Censorship had two purposes; gathering information, particularly that revealing Japanese attitudes in their letters, which was of value to the Occupation; and suppressing the circulation of any material deemed inimical to the aims of the Occupation. One of the avowed and principal aims of the Occupation was the strengthening of democratic tendencies in Japan; therefore it was necessary that Censorship suppress any communication which would contribute directly to the weakening of democratic tendencies. At the same time that Censorship was exercising its negative control over Japanese thought and opinion, another organization, the Civil Information and Education Section, also a unit of G. H. Q., was designed to perform the positive function of revealing American practices to the Japanese in the field of communication and thereby inculcating in them a firsthand knowledge of the workings of democracy. Organizationally, there was no immediate communication possible between Censorship and Civil Information and Education, but in the early days of the Occupation those engaged in working with the theatre in both these units considered it advisable to work together, unofficially and almost clandestinely.

No one concerned with the theatre in either of these organizations was specifically trained for the performance of such duties. Some had been trained in the Military Intelligence Service Language School and therefore, although they had a limited knowledge of the Japanese language, possessed no knowledge of Japanese culture or history other than that privately acquired. Some had experience, professional and amateur, in the American theatre and had read the published material in English and European languages on the Japanese theatre, but no one at first engaged in these activities had ever seen the performance of a Japanese play before the conclusion of the war. American control of the theatre was therefore carried on, as Faubion Bowers, a recent writer, has remarked, in 'complete ignorance' of the Japanese theatre. G. H. Q. had no clear or precise notions of the specific aims of these organizations. The censors, being Americans, presumably knew what democracy was and therefore were capable of spotting and suppressing plays which were undemocratic. At last a code of censorship for the theatre was devised based on the provisions of the Potsdam Declaration; since the Japanese government had accepted the terms of this declaration, it seemed only fair that they abide by its provisions when translated into terms of the theatre.

It was assumed that the Japanese might make an effort to use the theatre as a medium for anti-Allied propaganda, but there were only rare and isolated cases of such occurrences. The problem that remained was that of preventing the performance of plays which showed an excessively feudal, and therefore 'undemocratic,' ideology. Following the general practice of other departments of Censorship, the censors required that no play could be performed unless the script had been approved by Censorship. By 1946 there were some 700 theatrical troupes performing in Japan, the large majority of them touring the provincial areas, and the censors, although they occasionally made tours, were principally confined to the cities of Tōkyō, Ōsaka, and Fukuoka. It therefore would have been quixotic of the censors to suppose that suppressed plays and, particularly, suppressed lines of plays would not be performed when there was no possibility of this being found out. However, as far as can be determined from Japanese informants and informers, there was little attempt to perform forbidden material. And it was somewhat dismaying to those interested in encouraging in the Japanese a slight independence of thought to see the actors, producers, and playwrights submit as undoubtingly, willingly, and fatalistically to American censorship as they had to that of the Japanese government from 1603 to 1945.

The state of mind of the first members of the Occupation engaged in reforming Japan can be stated roughly, but not unfairly, thus: Japan is to be made into a democracy. This is to be accomplished by removing habits, customs, and thoughts that are 'feudal' (it was these that had made the Japanese attack on Pearl Harbor possible) and substituting for them patterns of behavior, social organization, and thought which are democratic, that is, American. There was a minority among the Americans who did not believe that centuries of traditional attitudes could be wiped out in a few years no matter how well meaning, energetic, and intense the activity of the Americans; the validity of this point of view is becoming more and more apparent in recent developments in Japan. It was almost unavoidable that most Americans in the Occupation should have had no knowledge of or interest in Japanese civilization and that they should regard the imposition of American cultural habits on the Japanese as a highly idealistic undertaking. But it is regrettable that there were very few members of the Occupation who had sufficient knowledge of both Japan and America to encourage the pursuit of policies which, based solidly on foundations in Japanese culture, might have ultimate significance, rather than those that were totally foreign to Japanese thought and therefore trivial and ephemeral. Much was made of the superficial aspects of American society. Kissing, for instance, has never been a public act in Japan, but a member of the Occupation required that a kiss be incorporated into a Japanese film; this was done and resulted in great embarrassment for Japanese audiences, both for themselves and for the Americans. Square dancing was encouraged because it was highly democratic; it was not known that most group dancing in Japan is equally 'democratic' and that men, women, and children in the rural districts participate simultaneously in rhythmical work movement closely resembling dance. Radio was remolded in the image of commercial American radio with programs such as 'Twenty Questions' and soap operas closely patterned on American models. The score of Gershwin's *Rhapsody in Blue* was hurriedly sent for so that the Nippon Philharmonic Orchestra could acquaint its hearers with democratic music. Thornton Wilder's *The Skin of Our Teeth* and John Van Druten's *The Voice of the Turtle* were translated into Japanese and performed before small, bewildered audiences. None of these activities did any great harm, but neither, if the inculcation of the principles of democracy was the aim of the Occupation, did they do any great good. Baseball, although it had to be called by the Japanese name *yakyū*, continued to be the favorite Japanese sport throughout World War II. Perhaps common international wonderment at the juke box is not quite sufficient grounds for international understanding.

The Americans engaged in working with the Japanese theatre, the best prepared of them acquainted with the Japanese theatre only in print, of necessity regarded it through American eyes. Their view of the function of the theatre in a democracy was based not so much upon the existing American theatre (the Occupation was largely concerned with the ideal) but upon notions of the function of this theatre in a perfect democracy: The theatre should deal honestly and fearlessly with the stuff of life; it should be intimately related to the actual life of contemporary people. Its characters should be individuals rather than types. The theatre should not serve as a propaganda medium but as a free sounding board for all honest opinion. The theatre should not merely provide, like the average American film, anaesthetic escape into a world of unsubstantial fantasy but, on the contrary, sensitive perception of the meaning beneath the fact. The theatre should not be an evasion of reality but an intensification of it whether in comedy or tragedy.

The average contemporary American has relatively little faith in the theatre as a means of social expression; he has seen the professional American theatre decrease in size and importance with the rise of film, radio, and television, and he regards these media of expression as more popular and therefore more important than the 'legitimate stage.' But this is not the attitude toward the theatre in the Orient. The reasons for this difference in attitude are not easily determined; they do not consist exclusively in the fact that America possesses greater technical knowledge and more money than the Orient and can therefore produce and sell a greater number of film projectors and radio and television sets. The explanation may be partly that the theatre as a social institution is not firmly established in American tradition whereas it has centuries of acceptance in the Orient. But whatever the reasons may be, the fact remains that the theatre, despite films and radio, continues to be a vital institution in Oriental lives. It was not by chance or out of aesthetic considerations that the theatre was made to play an important role in the early years of the Soviet Union or that a large part of Communist propaganda was introduced to the Chinese through the medium of the theatre. Japan has a flourishing film industry which turns out an average of thirty-three films a month, and these are supplemented by American and other foreign films; radio programs reach every corner of the country, and television broadcasts have begun. But at the same time Japan supports some seven hundred professional troupes of actors, a larger number than existed in the American theatre before the coming of the film in the heyday of the 'legitimate stage.' It is true that the film, particularly the American one, attracts large numbers of the younger generation, but even so the day seems far distant when the professional theatre of Japan will attract as small an audience, comparatively, as that of the contemporary professional American theatre.

The members of the Civil Information and Education section were unfortunately not permitted, by the mysterious workings of the Army, to travel outside Tōkyō except on rare occasions, and they had little opportunity to carry their educational work to the outlying districts. Meanwhile it was to the rural areas and the fishing villages that Communist organizations sent troupes of trained actors. The plays they performed could scarcely be called Communistic from an American point of view, for they closely followed the pattern of ideas to which the Occupation subscribed at that time. They showed opposition to the *zaibatsu*, the large family corporations that the Occupation was in the process of breaking up (and which now are almost completely reestablished); they stated the principles of land reform which the Occupation was encouraging; and in general the plays demonstrated the revolution of the individual against the totalitarian state of war-time Japan. Most frequently the plays took the framework of Japanese legend, folk tale, and custom as a point of departure for the message and thus followed the old but eminently workable technique of spreading new ideas by grafting them onto native materials. (It was partially by the use of this technique that Christian belief was successfully introduced into Northern Europe.) The methods used by the Communists thus offered startling contrast to those of the Occupation in two principal ways: The Communists recognized the widespread popularity of the theatre in Japan, as differentiated from the film, and they hoped to achieve their aims by creating plays built upon elements already in existence in Japanese culture.

The activity of the Civil Information and Education Office concerned with the theatre had little influence on the country at large. Its program was apparently based on the notion that Japan could be democratized by the performance of American plays in Tōkyō. *The Skin of Our Teeth* is an interesting and unusual American play, but it is something less than meaningful to a Japanese audience. Lillian

Hellman's *Watch on the Rhine* is somewhat more straightforward in meaning and intent, but even this play is concerned with situations and values which, although they touch occasionally upon familiar strains in Japanese life, are yet so thoroughly Occidental that even though some Japanese found the play intellectually interesting they were unmoved by it. The substance of these and other modern plays had little rapport with Japanese life, for they were evolved out of a complex culture that bore little resemblance to contemporary Japanese culture. But the Occupation policy, so far as it can be judged by its tangible results, was to attempt to impose these remote ideas upon Japanese audiences by securing for them the latest and best in American drama. Meanwhile the Communists established a school of the theatre, trained actors and directors, and based their naïve plays on folk tales, legends, or native situations which were clear and unambiguous to the rural and provincial audiences before whom they were performed.

The Americans also brought with them other attitudes toward the theatre based on their conception of the function of the theatre in the West. Almost mechanically they related the representational play with the thesis play or 'social drama,' for the representational play in the Western theatre had become the principal medium through which the playwright—whether Ibsen, Pinero, Brieux, Shaw, or Odets—expressed his view of the society in which he lived. The outward form of the representational play had existed in Japan before the War, but the majority of the plays created in it were occupied with the trivial affairs of trivial characters. With the notable exception of one financially unsuccessful play, one could read all the plays being performed in Japan for a year after the end of the War without finding in them any reference to the surrender or to existing social conditions. The Americans realized that it was natural in those troubled times for audiences to seek escape in the theatre from a very painful reality. But even after the shock of defeat had lessened, eight out of ten plays which dealt with contemporary conditions were based solely on the simple, romantic plot of the soldier, thought dead, who returned to find his wife remarried. If the theatre was to 'strengthen democratic tendencies' in Japan, the Americans felt, it should deal with more substantial stuff than this.

The censors felt increasingly that mere suppression of 'feudalistic' plays could not result in a vital theatre unless it was supplemented by explanations of why the plays were suppressed, and more positively, of how the theatre should function in an ideal democracy. This seemingly obvious fact was pointed out in communications, through channels, to higher echelons. But no action was taken on the matter, and those in Civil Education and Information who presumably should conduct such an educational program continued to be immured in Tōkyō. Then certain of the censors, who were permitted considerable freedom of movement, decided that in their tours throughout the country they would explain in detail why certain scripts were not approved for production, answer questions from the Japanese concerning the principles on which certain plays were suppressed, and in the process point out the function of a democratic theatre. In this fashion the censors went to the majority of the provinces and before censorship ended some of them had been visited ten times. The undertaking was no more impractical than others in which the Occupation was currently engaged, but it was, for reasons not then apparent to the censors, as fruitless as the other idealistic attempts to impose American ideology upon the Japanese.

The Americans were acquainted with what can be described as the 'theatre of ideas' which includes the tragic ideas of Sophocles and Shakespeare, the social ideas of Ibsen and Shaw, the comic ideas of Aristophanes and Molière. No new ideas even remotely resembling these had entered the Japanese theatre since the middle of the seventeenth century. The conception of the theatre that the Americans described was so foreign to the Japanese theatre workers that no appreciable communication was possible. A few Japanese were politely interested in the curious views expressed by the Americans, but the great majority, even though they showed no hostility toward Occupation interference with their work, were naturally incapable of viewing their theatre and its plays from any other point of view than their own. Their theatre offered its audiences escape into an unreal world of romantic melancholy and therefore brought money to the box office. It became increasingly apparent that the possibility of changing this point of view was as remote as that of convincing the Hollywood executive that the quality and nature of his product should be improved. None of the Americans believed that exhortative lectures on theories of drama would produce immediate and revolutionary changes in the Japanese theatre, but they hoped that some meeting of minds, however tenuous, could be established with the Japanese theatre workers. But there could be none, for the Americans knew too little about the relation of the Japanese theatre to Japanese society and the Japanese knew too little about the Western theatre. Under these circumstances, superficial and ephemeral changes could be imposed upon the Japanese theatre by the Americans, and they were. But to bring about basic changes would require complete control for several generations, not only over the theatre, but over all aspects of Japanese life and culture.

The Americans were also unaware that despite the large number of the best foreign plays that had been produced by the Tsukiji Little Theatre during a period of sixteen years (on the average, two a month), the ideas contained in them, with the exception of those which put forward the pat and easily comprehended solutions of Communism to all human problems, rarely penetrated into the consciousness of the Japanese playwright. Had this fact been known it is possible that the Occupation would have placed less faith in the production of American plays in Japan and the attempt to teach democracy by reforming contemporary Japanese drama.

The censors felt no compunction about suppressing such plays of modern composition as those in which parents sold their daughters into prostitution to pay family debts (although this is a hallowed Japanese tradition) or those in which ruthless personal revenge was carried out in extralegal fashion. One play of the latter type was offered by a playwright who explained it as a document in democracy: To oblige a friend, the hero killed some half a dozen people in cold blood and then departed on an 'aimless journey.' Democracy lay in the fact that the murders were committed not out of selfish motives of revenge but in the democratic spirit of helping others.

But the Kabuki was a different matter. It was, so far as could be determined by reading about it, a highly developed art, much appreciated by some of the Westerners who had seen Kabuki performances. The feeling among Western writers seemed to be that it lacked the perfected formality and restraint of the Nō, since it was of vulgar origin, but that nevertheless it represented one of the high points of Japanese culture. The Occupation, although it hoped to work lasting changes upon Japanese society, was at the same time greatly concerned with the preservation of Japanese art works to the end of protecting itself against charges of artistic vandalism. There was set up in the Civil Information and Education Section a unit which drew up lists of art objects, historical structures, and museums for the purpose both of instructing the Japanese to preserve these treasures and of preventing the Occupation forces from injuring or destroying them. The Kabuki was not included in such lists nor were the Nō and the doll theatre, although these appeared to be cultural expressions of considerable importance. The censors saw no reason to concern themselves with the Nō; so esoteric a form of theatre could scarcely have a deleterious effect upon the inculcation of democracy. Although the doll theatre performed intensely 'feudalistic' pieces, it survived only in a single troupe playing in a small theatre before very limited audiences; initially as a matter of Army procedure the doll theatre was subject to censorship, but the practice was abandoned early in 1946. However, the Kabuki differed from the Nō and the doll theatre. Not only did it attract large audiences, but it was also known to have been used as a propaganda medium during the War. And the ideas expressed in the Kabuki plays, indubitably feudalistic, were those which the Occupation had set out to expunge.

Although they had received no instructions in the matter, the censors felt strongly that because of its cultural importance the Kabuki should be treated with care; but at the same time they were profoundly disturbed by the impact of its ideology upon large audiences. Pieces such as 'The Village School' had been described during the War as manifesting *yamato damashii*, the feudal spirit of the Japanese people. The censors were aware that certain plays had been forbidden performance by the government during the war, and it seemed likely these might be suitable for performance under the Occupation. Enlisting the aid of three prominent Japanese scholars, representatives of Civil Information and Education and of Censorship went over the plots of some three hundred Kabuki pieces and then compiled a list of plays which seemed, judged on the basis of the description of their plots, to be unsuitable for production. The list was regarded as temporary and subject to revision. But a certain general, hearing that such a list had been compiled, was with difficulty dissuaded from issuing a directive which would have prohibited the performance of all the plays listed. Plays which had been forbidden by the government during the War, because they showed characters unmindful of social duty, were now permitted performance, but the censors' objection to plays based upon feudal patterns of behavior resulted in a very much restricted repertoire. The greater part of the plays approved were dance pieces, which being almost plotless could scarcely have an undemocratic influence upon the audience. The Kabuki was presently subjected to further restriction by the Civil Information and Education Section. The Civil Information and

Education Section officers felt that the pernicious influence of the Kabuki could be somewhat mitigated by the performance on the same program of plays in modern settings, and they therefore required that one modern piece be played for every two Kabuki pieces on the program. None of the Americans was aware that this requirement was ludicrous; it was comparable, artistically, to requiring that a concert pianist play *Chopsticks* on his program as an antidote to the classicism of Bach.

But the Americans were fortunately not beyond education, and their education was gained by increased familiarity with the Kabuki and particularly with the relation that existed between the play and the audience in the theatre. It gradually became apparent that the ideas in the Kabuki play which loomed so large and dangerous to the censors did not have a similar impact upon the Japanese audience. The feudal background of the plays, after centuries of acceptance, had ceased to impinge upon the consciousness of the audience or to have more than a conventional value. The plots themselves were unimportant and, except for those who were scholars, very few of the audience were aware of the implications of the plot of the play they were seeing. The audience went to a thoroughly nonintellectual theatre to admire the technical skill of the actor, to weep, and less frequently, to laugh, to be dazzled by color and movement. They did not go there to think, even briefly. In spite of the efforts of the Japanese government to convert the Kabuki into a propaganda medium during the War, audiences refused to accept *The Subscription List* as anything but a Kabuki play, and they regarded the modern plays written to extol the war effort as dull, boring, untheatrical pieces. In short, the ideological influence of the Kabuki upon the Japanese was about that of the average Hollywood musical upon its audience.

The censors' knowledge of the effect of the Kabuki upon its audience was accompanied by the realization that Japanese patterns of thought were not likely to be changed significantly by the performance of American plays or even by the simpler plays which the Communists were producing. The method of the Communists was much more likely to produce results sooner than that of the Occupation, which seemed to be inspired partially by a desire to exhibit the superiority of American products, but even the Communist plays, based on materials close to Japanese life, could not bring about a sudden change in the habitual attitude of the Japanese toward the theatre. Today, the only avowed Communist troupe, the Zenshin-za, finds it necessary to play Kabuki pieces to support itself financially; its propaganda plays, couched in native idiom, do not attract a sufficiently large audience.

Japan has undergone profound industrial, social, and economic changes in modern times, but little of this has touched directly upon its inner cultural life. Its theatre and its film continue to derive their materials largely from the cultural patterns of the Tokugawa period, and the attitude of the audience to the play or the film also closely resembles that of the Tokugawa audiences. The Kabuki exerted strong influence upon its audiences before 1868, but its influence lay in introducing new fashions in hair arrangement, in design of textiles, or in physical deportment. Since it expressed so completely the view of life existing outside the theatre, this view, when repeated out of conventional necessity within the theatre, had no great vitality.

As the censors came to realize that the Kabuki lacked any immediate political significance, they restored plays that had been forbidden. The first of these was *The Subscription List*, then came 'Kumagai's Camp,' 'Moritsuna's Camp,' 'The Village School,' and others. Just before censorship of the theatre was discontinued, the censors permitted, over the strong objections of the Civil Information and Education Section, the performance of *The Loyal Forty-seven Rōnin*, the great revenge play of the Kabuki. The objection of the Civil Information and Education Section to the production of this play was based on the notion that since *The Loyal Forty-seven Rōnin* was a play of revenge it could not fail to excite ideas of revenge against the Americans. This attitude did not take into consideration the fact that at the moment Censorship came to an end, the first play to be staged by the Kabuki theatres would be *The Loyal Forty-seven Rōnin*.

With the end of Occupation censorship of the theatre in 1948, the Kabuki was free of government interference and censorship for the first time in its history. Police supervision of the theatre was ended at the beginning of the Occupation and it has not yet been resumed. At present there are indications of a resurgent desire in certain official Japanese circles to censor the foreign books, plays, and films brought into the country, but thus far governmental action on the matter has not been taken. Official restrictive activity against the theatre does not now involve the direct censorship of plays but is accomplished by preventing performances by Communist troupes. Government action against the Communist troupe, the Zenshin-za, has been based on its illegal distribution of handbills and pamphlets; the plays themselves have not been censored, but recently some of their performances have been effectively prevented. As yet there has been no attempt to restore the former nation-wide censorship of the theatre which included the installation of a special box in every theatre in Japan for the use of police officials who from this vantage point could detect subversive opinion. The Kabuki, at least for the moment, is permitted complete freedom in choice of plays and in their mode of production.

However, the position of the Kabuki remains somewhat insecure. It is not threatened by the film to the extent that the American professional theatre was, nor do the revues, based on American and European models, burlesque shows, and 'stage shows' of the large movie houses attract an audience which would otherwise attend the Kabuki. But the Kabuki seems now to have reached a point at which it can no longer move, in its historical pattern, with the times. It has attempted to combine the representational theatre with Kabuki in neo-Kabuki, and the few modern playwrights who have written for the Kabuki have shown no significant advance over the methods employed by Okamoto Kidō. The most touted new play performed by Kabuki actors in the 1951–1952 season was a three-part, twelve hour dramatization of the novel *The Tale of Genji*; its playwright showed greater respect for the Kabuki form than did Okamoto Kidō, but Kabuki scholars maintained that the play was not Kabuki. If the Kabuki continues to base its new plays on techniques derived from the representational theatre, it is inevitable that the traditional form of this theatre will disappear and that the Kabuki will have created its own destruction. There are few contemporary playwrights interested in writing for the Kabuki theatre. Their disinclination to do so stems partially from the fact that the Kabuki is dominated by the actor. On the occasions when the modern playwright has given his plays to the Kabuki he has seen them converted into vehicles for the actor and distorted from the purpose he intended. Further, he regards the Kabuki as a *fait accompli*, a static form in which, since it has already reached its ultimate refinement, nothing more can be said. The playwright therefore turns to *shingeki*, which to him represents the antithesis of Kabuki tradition.

Strictly speaking, *shingeki*, the modern theatre, is theatre which is distinguished by its means of expression from Nō, doll theatre, and Kabuki. It includes plays from foreign countries translated into

Japanese, or at times adapted to a Japanese setting. O'Neill's *Ah, Wilderness* is scarcely recognizable in the play *First Love*, set on the island of Kyūshū, its characters and situations changed to purely Japanese ones; a month after the film *All About Eve* was first shown in Japan, a play, *Naked Stage*, concerning an aging Japanese actress and her ambitious protégé, was performed in Tōkyō. Some Western plays are of course performed with the conscientious purpose of recreating their original manner of production. But at present considerably fewer such productions are presented than when the Occupation exerted strong influence for their performance. The modern plays set in Japan include both those with a contemporary setting and those set in the Tokugawa period. Rarely, a play by a modern playwright is set in a foreign country. The most popular play of the 1951–1952 season was a dramatization of the life of Van Gogh, *Man of Fire*; its extraordinary success was due to an excellent performance by the leading actor, the stress laid upon the idea that Van Gogh had been greatly influenced by Japanese color prints, and by the incorporation of an illustrated lecture on Van Gogh's principal paintings. The common quality of the large majority of modern Japanese plays is that they are designed to be representational; modern theatre is synonymous with realistic theatre and there is little discernible movement toward any other form of expression.

It seems curious, at first glance, that this should be so. A high degree of stylization is common to all Japanese artistic expression and the labored reproduction of reality has been generally avoided. But it is probably for just this reason that the contemporary playwright wishes to express himself in the form of the realistic theatre: It is modern for him because it represents a break with past practices. However, if he were to be completely 'modern' in the Western style, he would follow, as did his predecessors at the beginning of the century, the contemporary playwriting of the Western theatre which has gradually moved away from the more or less exact imitation of nature which appeared in the late nineteenth-century theatre. On the contrary, the increasing freedom from representation in the Western theatre which grew out of the French Symbolist theatre, expressionism, and the post-revolutionary Russian theatre has not influenced the Japanese playwright to any significant degree. He seems to have rejected the nonrepresentational theatre because theoretically it lies too close in mechanics and intent to the Kabuki. Typical *régisseurs* of the movement, such men as Fuchs, Meyerhold, Tairov, and Jessner, denied that realism was an expressive means of communication; their stage was frankly admitted to be a stage and not an illusionistic locale with realistic disguises. The dramatic idea was conveyed by linear and spatial relationships of actor and setting; the flow of emotion toward the audience was intensified by every means at the disposal of the physical theatre. Costume and make-up were imaginative rather than literal; time was expanded or contracted according to the needs of the play; the disparate 'worlds' of stage and auditorium were to be united into an aesthetic whole. Rhythm, either abstract or musical, was the unifying force of the production. These principal aspects of their theories had already been realized in the Kabuki and therefore suggested no forward movement in Japanese theatrical tradition. At only one point did the theory of the modern *régisseurs* fail to repeat the aesthetic concepts of the Kabuki: The modern movement was one toward abstraction. However far the Kabuki has moved in the direction of extreme selectivity, the reduction of a multiplicity of impressions of reality into an economical design, it has never advanced into that area known as abstraction in Western art, and in this it followed the form of the graphic arts, as well as the philosophy, of the Tokugawa period. From the point of view of Japanese theatre history, the lure of the representational theatre for the Japanese playwright at the beginning of the twentieth century was not without certain roots and was not entirely a pursuit of the exotic and unfamiliar. Throughout the nineteenth century the Kabuki had moved toward greater and greater 'realism.' Although it could not be compared to the realism of Ibsen or Hauptman, this 'realism,' within the confines of the Kabuki form, possessed parallel characteristics. Therefore when such plays as *John Gabriel Borkman* were first performed in Japan, although they displayed extremes of realism that the Japanese play-wright had never dreamed of, they nonetheless were technically related to the 'realistic' plays, such as those of Kawatake Mokuami, which the Kabuki had evolved. Thus to a certain degree the Japanese theatre was prepared to accept the realistic theatre in the same manner that the country at large was economically and temperamentally prepared to accept certain of the Western influences to which it was opened in 1868.

Besides the fact that the nonrepresentational theatre seems to resemble Kabuki too closely and that the Kabuki itself in its historical evolution was moving toward a kind of realism, there is another reason why the contemporary playwright clings devotedly to the representational theatre: In doing so he is conforming to a traditional pattern of Japanese cultural development, that of assimilating the foreign novelty and thereafter regarding it jealously as a part of the mainstream of Japanese culture. Early canons of Buddhism, for example, can be better studied in Japanese manuscripts than in those of the countries in which they originated.

In the Meiji period, Japanese with modern tastes built into their homes a Western Room, furnished in the late nineteenth-century style of interior decoration, and such rooms, although they have largely ceased to exist in the West except in museums, remain a necessary adjunct of the well-appointed Japanese home. Some of these rooms are today decorated in a style that can be described loosely as Swedish modern, but the majority repeat the doily, the antimacassar, the fringed table cover, the elaborate gilt picture frame, the floral carpeting, and the busy design of chair and table which characterized the Victorian parlor. It is difficult for the Westerner to be comfortable in this room; it is, of course, not authentic but derivative, and therefore lacks the possible charm or interest which the authentically reconstructed room might have. And for the same reason, the Westerner is uncomfortable in the presence of the majority of modern Japanese plays; these bear more than a surface resemblance to the Western Room. Therefore it is difficult for the Westerner to judge either the Western Room or the plays fairly. His theatre and his interior decoration have moved to other styles of expression, and the Japanese interpretation of these earlier forms can have for him at best only an academic interest, however necessary they are to the Japanese. The Western Room preserves the surface expression of a bygone age, and the modern drama preserves with equal insistence the outward literalness of the realistic theatre. As the Western Room represents the not quite accurate imitation of the Victorian interior, so, to the Westerner, most of the modern plays have about them the air of incomplete assimilation of a foreign form of playwriting. Both have the slightly incongruous appearance that accompanies the sudden dislocation of a particular aspect of one culture into a dissimilar one. Most Japanese are not really comfortable or at ease in the Western Room, nor, judging by attendance figures, are they really at ease in the modern theatre. But both have become so much a part of Japanese culture that they seem natively Japanese. Similarly, many Japanese will contend that the tune of *Auld Lang Syne* is a Japanese melody.

Although much of the modern drama is clearly imitative of the

Western representational theatre, the greater part of it cannot be that simply described; like the Western Room, it too has undergone subtle but important changes. The surface form of the plays is clearly derivative: Speech is colloquial; the actors move in an imitation of actuality; the stage and auditorium are conceived of as disparate psychological worlds; setting, lighting, and properties are designed to produce the illusion of actuality for the Japanese. But other than this the total effect of the production of a modern drama is that it is purely Japanese and owes nothing to the West. Judged by Western standards of realistic stage mounting, the settings show a greater influence of the Kabuki than of the Western theatre. The Kabuki convention of indicating a simultaneous interior and exterior setting by placing the interior on a raised platform is used; houses, temples, fields, and forests are painted on backdrops in a theatrical rather than illusionistic manner; three-dimensional objects such as trees and stone lanterns are frequently depicted in two dimensions in cut-out pieces. In performance the play does not seem to be conceived of as an architectural whole; scenes do not 'build' to a climax, and as a result neither the acts nor the play as a whole conveys a sense of complex forward movement. Instead, there is concern with the detail, the significant moment, and it is the succession of these moments that comprises the temporal movement of the play. This characteristic is particularly obvious to the Westerner when he sees the performance of a foreign play by a Japanese troupe. Because the performance dwells lovingly upon a succession of elaborated details, a play that would require no more than two and a half hours playing time in the American theatre cannot be performed in less than four hours in Japan. It is for this reason that a Japanese production of a Chekhov play seems more satisfactory to the Westerner than a production of *Watch on the Rhine*; in Chekhov the projection of mood and the revelation of character count for more than the progession of the 'story.' This characteristic quality of the performance of all modern drama, whether that of foreign or native plays, can be traced to its origin not in the foreign theatre but in the Kabuki. The actors in modern drama do not perform *mie*, nor does the production make use of the free theatrical time of the Kabuki, but in the actor's concern with the moment and the detail (which has the effect of detaching them from the fabric of the play itself), and in the consequent lengthening of the actual time of performance, the techniques of production are close to those of Kabuki. The modern Japanese actor studies Stanislavsky assiduously and avoids nonrealistic movement and posture; but except in the case of a very few contemporary actors, he does not escape entirely the subtle effect of centuries of Kabuki acting. In most modern acting there is the noticeable exaggeration, the somewhat uncontrolled intensity, which the Westerner associates with early film acting but which in Japan derives directly from Kabuki. Thus although the surface of modern drama bears a deceptive resemblance to the Western representational theatre, its inner flow and movement in performance is of purely native origin.

The subject matter of modern plays is in general more atavistic than the mode of performance. A rare play is occasionally concerned, as was *Man of Fire*, with foreign situations and characters or with an unorthodox approach to native material. But the great majority of contemporary pieces, unless they are unqualifiedly imitations of Western plays, are constructed out of the situations, ideology, and characters of the Kabuki. Here are the self-sacrificing wives, the unhappy lovers driven to double suicide, the Robin Hood thieves of the 'living' domestic plays, and the heroes torn between human sympathy and social duty of the historical pieces. Frequently the plays have, although not necessarily, a contemporary setting; and the one to whom a character owes loyalty becomes, instead of a feudal lord, a gangster or even the president of a corporation. It is for the social historian to decide whether the appeal that the Kabuki subject matter has for Japanese audiences is merely a matter of centuries of habit or whether it springs from deeper racial sources. But judging by box office receipts, one can only conclude that this subject matter attracts audiences while plays that are constructed out of other material are rarely financially successful.

As a generalization it can be fairly said that despite the adoption of representational techniques by modern drama, any play which deals with unromanticized contemporary material is not likely to appeal to a large audience. Both playwrights and theatre-goers shy away from plays which are seriously concerned with contemporary life and social conditions. When questioned closely the average theatre-goer will state that he objects to such plays because they are 'too real' and in this he reveals that his feelings about the theatre are the same as those of the Kabuki actor: Anything 'too real' is not appropriate for use in the theatre. The modern drama is therefore in a curious position. Although it hoped and hopes to break with Kabuki tradition and for that reason has patterned itself on an adherence to the outward form of the realistic play, nevertheless, in subject matter, in techniques of performance, and in the attitudes of the audience it remains close to the Kabuki. If the playwright wishes to deal with important contemporary actualities, and at the same time attract an audience, he must usually set his play in the past and surround it with the aura of the Tokugawa period or set it in a never-never land of folk tale and legend, the latter the principal device of the Communist theatre workers. In the first years of the Occupation, with officials insisting that new American plays be produced in Japan and that modern drama be encouraged, it appeared that in time the Kabuki would be reduced to a museum piece. At present that does not seem true. The Kabuki now has audiences approximately fifteen per cent larger than those before the War, while the modern drama has fewer productions, fewer theatres in which to play, and smaller audiences than it had under the Occupation. The most successful modern plays performed in Tōkyō, a city of some seven and a half million, cannot attract audiences for more than two months. The revival of interest in the Kabuki can be traced in part to the postwar interest of the older Japanese in their native culture as a revulsion to the forced feeding upon American culture during the Occupation; the Nō theatre is also enjoying something of a postwar revival. Even the younger generation, although it shows considerable interest in the American film and in revues, is more likely to attend the Kabuki than the modern drama. The workers of the modern theatre are to be greatly admired; they have great enthusiasm, they manage to live on comparatively small incomes, and they are genuinely concerned with creating a vital modern theatre. But since they lack popular financial support, it is difficult to predict an optimistic future for them.

Although the Kabuki is presently enjoying a wider popularity than the modern theatre, it is doubtful that this popularity will continue indefinitely unless its means of expression can be utilized by contemporary playwrights. If it continues to move in the direction of neo-Kabuki, it will of necessity end by abandoning its traditional means of expression and thereby cease to be Kabuki. It is possible that Kabuki no longer possesses an *élan vital*, that the form has reached its ultimate development, and that in the future it will be reduced to the position of the contemporary doll theatre. Some Japanese and most Westerners who visit Japan incline to this point of view. Americans in particular put forward the notion that Kabuki is like opera, a form in which no modern ideas can be expressed. In an article in the *Asahi Shimbun*, 14 March 1952, James Michener was quoted as saying that the Kabuki was a magnificent form of theatre and could be compared to performances at the Metropolitan Opera House. But as no American playwright would seek to gain fame by writing for the Metropolitan, no aspiring Japanese playwright should begin by writing for the Kabuki. He concluded, 'If I were a young Japanese playwright I would sell my shoes to go see the Kabuki, but I would sell my life to write a play for the modern theatre.' The idea that Kabuki is like opera has been frequently stated by Japanese at pains to relate it to a form of Western theatre. Certain similarities of Kabuki and opera exist: Both tend to be spectacular in costume and setting. Both are, in quite different ways, nonrealistic. Both use a repertory system. Both are less concerned with the development of plot and character than with theatrical effects. But there is no similarity in the relation of American culture and opera, a transplanted form of theatre in which an accepted 'American' opera is yet to be written, and the relation between Japanese culture and Kabuki, a form which has had its roots in the Japanese national consciousness for almost three centuries.

There is an important difference between the impact of opera upon an American audience and the impact of Kabuki upon a Japanese audience. An American goes to the opera to hear the music, even though he may find the other elements of production attractive. Unless he has rather peculiar tastes, he does not ordinarily go to see the acting. In the Kabuki, on the contrary, although music plays an important part in the performance, acting is the center of interest, and the force of Kabuki acting upon the audience is as strong to the Japanese as the performances in *A Streetcar Named Desire* and in *Death of a Salesman* are to the American audience. Without examining into the psychological and aesthetic differences, it can be granted that the effects of *Die Walküre* and of *Darkness at Noon* upon an American audience are somewhat different, that the opera seems, comparatively, removed from actuality while the play is immediate and vital. A similar immediacy and vitality characterizes the response of the Japanese audience to the Kabuki. It is a little difficult for an American to realize that a highly stylized form of theatre is capable of producing a vital impact which playwrights, actors, and theatre workers everywhere in the world throughout the history of the theatre have sought to establish. This direct emotional communication between stage and auditorium, between actor and spectator, constitutes theatre, regardless of the techniques used to bring it about. And if it is lacking, theatre does not exist, no matter what cultural improvement or intellectual satisfaction the audience may derive from the performance. It is precisely for this reason that the Kabuki is today a more vital form of theatre than the modern theatre. Despite its obscure language, the failure of some of the audience to understand certain of its conventions, its indifference to the contemporary world, the Kabuki continues to create a stronger and wider sense of theatre reality than modern drama.

The presentational technique of the Kabuki therefore remains a valid means of expression for the Japanese audience while the somewhat representational method of their modern theatre does not. From a purely utilitarian point of view it would seem that the contemporary playwright should utilize the exquisitely perfected means of expression of the Kabuki as a logical point of departure in the creation of the future Japanese theatre. In such an effort he would have to be aided by the Kabuki itself; the playwright would have to be capable of making a synthesis of existing theatre materials as Chikamatsu and Takemoto did in their time; the movement would have to be accompanied by certain changes in the thinking of the audience. Such a movement would require playwrights of greater skill than now seem to exist, those who are at once alive to the contemporary scene and thoroughly familiar with the Kabuki idiom. But unless some effort of this kind is made, the traditional form of the Kabuki will not survive, except perhaps as a museum piece, and Japan will have lost one of the most interesting expressions of its culture as well as one of the most highly developed forms of theatre that the world has produced.

List of Plays Mentioned in Text

(The English title is followed by the Japanese title or titles, the principal author or authors, and the date of first performance.)

'Anniversary Celebration':
 'Ga no Iwai.' An act of *Sugawara's Secrets of Calligraphy*
Arrow Maker, The:
 Yanone Gorō, Anon., 1729
Battle of Ichinotani, The:
 Ichi no Tani Futaba Gunki, Namiki Sōsuke, 1751
Battle of the Geisha:
 Sumida no Haru Geisha Tataki, Namiki Gohei, 1796
Battles of Coxinga, The:
 Kokusenya Kassen, Chikamatsu Monzaemon, 1715
Beautiful Story of a Prosperous Country, The:
 Keikoku Bidan, Yano Ryūkei, 1885
Benkei at the Boat:
 Funabenkei, Kawatake Mokuami, 1886
Benten the Thief:
 Shiranami Gonin Otoko; Aoto Zōshi Hana no Nishikie, Kawatake Mokuami, 1862
Blind Masseur, The:
 Zatō; Kaesugaesu Nagori no Bundai, Katsui Gempachi, 1826
Bloodshed at Ise:
 Ise Ondo Koi no Netaba, Chikamatsu Tokusō, 1796
Camel:
 Nemuru ga Rakuda Monogatari, Oka Onitarō, 1928
Ceremonial Prelude:
 Kotobukishiki Sambasō, Anon., 1856 (present version)
Chivalrous Gorozō:
 Otokodate Gosho no Gorozō; Soga Moyō Date no Gosho-zome, Kawatake Mokuami, 1864
Courier of Hell, The:
 Meido no Hikyaku, Chikamatsu Monzaemon, 1711

Dropped Coat:
  Suō Otoshi Nasu no Katari, Fukuchi Ōchi, 1892
Drum of Matsuura, The:
  Matsuura no Taiko; Shin-Butai Iroha no Kakizome, Segawa Jokō III, 1856
Dumpling Selling:
  Dango-uri, Anon., 1929
Earth Spider:
  Tsuchigumo, Kawatake Mokuami, 1881
Eight Camps, The:
  Hachijin Shugo no Honjō, Nakamura Gyogan, 1807
Exile of Shunkan, The:
  Heike Nyōgo ga Shima, Chikamatsu Monzaemon, 1719
Famous Tree at Sendai, The:
  Meiboku Sendai Hagi, Matsu Kanji, Takahashi Mohei, Yoshida Sumimaru, 1785
Flowers at Ueno:
  Hano no Ueno Homare no Ishibumi, Shiba Shisō, 1788
Forest of Suzu, The:
  Suzugamori; Banzuin Chōbei Shōjin Manaita, Sakurada Jisuke I, 1803
Four Faithful Bodyguards:
  Shiten-nō Osanadachi, Sakurai Tambanoshōjō, c. 1673
Girl at Dōjō Temple, The:
  Musume Dōjōji; Kyōga no Ko Musume Dōjōji, Anon., 1753
Girl of Hakata, The:
  Hakata Kojorō Namimakura, Chikamatsu Monzaemon, 1719
Ghost Story of Yotsuya:
  Tōkaidō Yotsuya Kaidan, Tsuruya Namboku IV, 1825
Golden Pavilion, The:
  Kinkakuji; Gion Sairei Shinkōki, Nakamura Akei, 1796
History of Azuma:
  Kanagaki Azuma Kagami, Anon., 1793
Ibaraki the Demon:
  Ibaraki, Kawatake Mokuami, 1883
Izayoi and Seishin:
  Kosode Soga Azami no Ironui, Kawatake Mokuami, 1859
Just a Moment:
  Shibaraku, Ichikawa Danjūrō II, 1714
Kasane:
  Iromoyō Chotto Karimame, Matsui Kōzō, 1823
Kokaji:
  Imayō Kokaji, Segawa Jokō III, 1852
'Kumagai's Camp':
  'Kumagai Jinya.' An act of The Battle of Ichinotani
Lion Dance:
  Renjishi, Kineya Katsusaburō, Kawatake Mokuami, 1861

Love Affairs of Six Poets, The:
Rokkasen Sugata no Irodori, Matsumoto Kōji, 1831
Love of Hanshichi and Sanshō, The:
Hade Sugata Onna Maikinu, Takemoto Saburōbei, 1772
Love Suicide at Amijima:
Shinjū Ten-no-Amijima, Chikamatsu Monzaemon, 1720
Loyal Forty-seven Rōnin, The:
Kanadehon Chūshingura, Takeda Izumo, Miyoshi Shōraku, Namiki Senyrū, 1748
Miracle at Tsubosaka Temple, The:
Tsubosaka Reigenki, Kako Chika, 1887
Mirror Lion:
Shunkyō Kagamijishi, Fukuchi Ōchi, 1893
Mirror Mountain:
Kagamiyama Kokyō no Nishikie, Yō Yōtai, 1782
Mitsukuni and the Sorceress:
Masakado; Shinobi Yoru Koi wa Kusemono, Takarada Jusuke, 1836
'Moritsuna's Camp':
'Moritsuna Jinya.' An act of *Strife at Uji*
Mount Imose:
Imoseyama Onna Teikin, Chikamatsu Hanji, 1771
Muromachi Palace:
Muromachi Gosho, Okamoto Kidō, 1913
Night Tale of Shinjuku:
Shinjuku Yobanashi, Okamoto Kidō, 1925
On Foot to Kyōto:
Tōkaidōchū Hizakurige, Kimura Kinka, 1928
Osome and Hisamatsu:
Osome Hisamatsu Ukina no Yomiuri, Tsuruya Namboku IV, 1813
Plains of Adachigahara, The:
Ōshū Adachigahara, Takeda Izumo, Chikamatsu Hanzō, Kitamada Shunichi, 1762
Political Story of Tenichibō:
Tenichibō Ōoka Seidan, Kawatake Mokuami, (two versions) 1854 and 1875
'Pulling the Carriage Apart':
'Kurumabiki.' An act of *Sugawara's Secrets of Calligraphy*
Returning Palanquin:
Modori Kago, Sakurada Jisuke I, 1788
Sakura Sōgorō:
Sakura Gijin Den, Segawa Jokō III, 1851; an act added by Kawatake Mokuami, 1861
Sashichi, Son of Edo:
Edo Sodachi Matsuri Sashichi, Kawatake Shinshichi III, 1898
Scarred Yōsaburō:
Yowa Nasake Ukina no Yokogushi, Segawa Jokō III, 1853

Secret Visit to Imagawa:
  Imagawa Shinobiguruma, Miyako Dennai, 1664
Seized Armor, The:
  Kongen Kusazuribiki, Anon., 1884
Snowbound Pass:
  Tsumoru Koi Yuki no Sekinoto, Takarada Jurai, 1784
Soga Confrontation, The:
  Soga no Taimen, Anon., 1676
Spirit of a Courtesan, The:
  Keisei Hangonkō, Chikamatsu Monzaemon, 1708
Stone-Cutting Kajiwara:
  Ishikiri Kajiwara; Miura no Ōsuke Kōbai Tazuna, Matsuda Bunkōdō,
  Hasegawa Senshi, 1730
Strife at Uji:
  Ōmi Genji Senjin Yakata, Chikamatsu Hanji, 1796
Subscription List, The:
  Kanjinchō, Namiki Gohei III, 1840
Substitute for Meditation, A:
  Migawari Zazen, Anon., 1910
Sugawara's Secrets of Calligraphy:
  Sugawara Denjū Tenarai Kagami, Takeda Izumo, Miyoshi Shōraku,
  Namiki Senryū, 1746
Sukeroku:
  Sukeroku Yukari no Edozakura, Tsuuchi Jihei, 1713, revised by Sakurada
  Jisuke I, 1771
Summer Festival:
  Natsu Matsuri Naniwa Kagami, Namiki Senryū, 1745
Tadanobu the Fox:
  Yagura Tadanobu, Takeda Izumo, Miyoshi Shōraku, Namiki Senryū,
  1747
Takatoki:
  Hōjō Kudai Meika no Isaoshi, Kawatake Mokuami, 1884
Tale of Shuzenji, The:
  Shuzenji Monogatari, Okamoto Kidō, 1925
Tea Box, The:
  Chatsubo, Okamura Shikō, 1921
Three Kichiza's, The:
  Sannin Kichiza Kuruwa no Hatsugai, Kawatake Mokuami, 1860
Three Odd Ones:
  Sannin Katawa; Kurikaeshi Kaika no Onna Mizuki, Kawatake Mokuami,
  1874
Three Shōguns of Kamakura:
  Kamakura Sandaiki, Anon., 1781
Thousand Cherry Trees, A:
  Yoshitsune Sembonzakura, Takeda Izumo, Miyoshi Shōraku, Namiki
  Senryū, 1747

Through the Iga Pass:
 Igagoe Dōchū Sugoroku, Chikamatsu Hanji, 1783
Thunder God:
 Narukami; Narukami Fudō Kitayamazakura, first version, 1684; present version, Tsuda Hanjurō, 1742
Tied to a Pole:
 Bōshibari, Okamura Shikō, 1916
Tokubē's Tale of a Foreign Country:
 Tenjiku Tokubē Ikokubanashi, Tsuruya Namboku IV, 1804
Twenty-four Dutiful Sons:
 Honchō Nijūshi Kō, Chikamatsu Hanji, Miyoshi Shōraku, 1766
Umekichi the Fireman:
 Mekura Nagaya Ume no Kagatobi, Kawatake Mokuami, 1886
'Village School, The':
 'Terakoya.' An act of *Sugawara's Secrets of Calligraphy*
Vow of Rokusuke, The:
 Hikosan Gongen Chikai no Sukedachi, Umeno Kafū, 1786
White Heron Maiden:
 Sagimusume; Yanagi ni Hina Shochō no Saezuri, Anon., 1856
Wisteria Girl, The:
 Fujimusume: Kaesugaesu Nagori no Ōtsue, Katsui Gempachi, 1826
Woman's Just a Moment:
 Onna Shibaraku: Arigatashi Yunzei Genji, Anon., 1755
Yūgiri and Izaemon:
 Yūgiri Awa no Naruto, Chikamatsu Monzaemon, 1711

Short Glossary of Theatre Terms

agemaku. 'Rising curtain.' In the Nō theatre, the curtain hung at the entrance to the 'bridge' and raised from the bottom. In the Kabuki, the curtain, hung by rings from a rod, at the rear of the *hanamichi*, opened by being slid to one side.

aibiki. A stool, about eighteen inches high, on which important characters may sit during a long scene. Characters so seated are conventionally assumed to be standing.

aragoto. 'Rough business,' a style of acting originated by Ichikawa Danjūrō I in 1673. *Aragoto* is muscular, vigorous, and highly stylized.

atoza. The upstage area of the stage. The word is derived from the Nō theatre, in which the orchestra is seated at the rear of the stage.

butai. The stage, to be distinguished from the passageways in both the Nō and Kabuki theatres on which the actor moves to the stage.

chobo. The musical-narrative accompaniment of Kabuki plays taken from the doll theatre.

choboyuka. The second-story area in the stage-left side of the Kabuki 'inner proscenium,' sometimes used by the *chobo* performers.

chū-nori. A device used principally for spectacular appearances of ghosts and other supernatural beings. The actor is lowered from above the stage, or swung in from the side, suspended from a rope.

daijin-bashira. The downstage-left pillar supporting the roof of the Nō stage. In the Kabuki theatre, the upstage edge of the 'inner proscenium' on stage-left.

dammari. Dumb show accompanied by music, used during the Tokugawa period as an introductory piece at the opening of the Kabuki season in November.

debayashi. 'Coming-out-orchestra,' which performs on stage for the accompaniment of Kabuki dance pieces.

degatari. A general name for musicians and singers who appear onstage during the Kabuki performance.

dengakugaeshi. A method of scene change, invented during the 1760's, in which each of the upstage flats is revolved on its vertical axis so that the upstage surface is turned downstage.

283

donchō. Drop curtain, as distinguished from the traditional Kabuki curtain which is drawn across the stage.

doma. 'Earth floor,' the pit of the Kabuki theatre.

furiotoshi. The sudden revelation of a colorful setting by dropping the curtain concealing it to the stage floor.

gakuya. Dressing-room and, by extension, the entire backstage area of the Kabuki theatre.

gandogaeshi. Method of scene change, first used in the doll theatre in 1761, in which a large piece of scenery is turned over to reveal another, and different, surface of the same piece.

gekidan. The hereditary Kabuki troupe.

geza. The Kabuki music and sound effects room on stage-right at stage level.

gidayū. A style of musical narration in the doll theatre, named after its originator Takemoto Gidayū.

hada wo nugu. A partial change of Kabuki costume, in sight of the audience, in which the upper part of the kimono is removed to reveal a kimono of different design or color beneath.

hanamichi. Passageway through the Kabuki auditorium on which important entrances and exits are made.

hanashiten. 'Flower warriors,' who, armed with flowering branches, engage in danced conflict with a Kabuki hero.

hashigakari. The 'bridge' of the Nō theatre, a passageway between stage and dressing-room, on which the actor makes important entrances and exits.

hayagawari. 'Quick change,' a very rapid offstage change of costume and make-up in the Kabuki.

hayashibeya. Alternate term for *geza*, q. v.

hikidōgu. A small wagon stage, used for moving either scenery or actors.

hikimaku. 'Draw curtain,' the traditional front curtain used in the Kabuki theatre.

hikinuki. A rapid onstage change of costume. The parts of the costume are basted together; when the threads are pulled out, the costume falls from the actor's body, revealing another costume.

hyōshigi. Two pieces of resonant wood which, beaten together or on a board, emphasize movement on the Kabuki stage. Also called *ki.*

janome-mawashi. A revolving stage built within the circumference of a larger revolving stage, capable of being operated independently of the outer one.

jidaimono. Kabuki plays based loosely on historical or semi-historical material.

jigazuri. The Kabuki floorcloth.

jikyōgen. Kabuki dances based upon Nō comic interludes.

jōruri. The musical-narrative accompaniment of doll theatre plays.

kabuki jūhachiban. Eighteen short Kabuki plays, the traditional pieces of the Ichikawa troupe. Only seven of these are now performed.

kagami-no-ma. The 'mirror room' in both the Nō and Kabuki theatres, in which the actor studies his reflection before an entrance.

kamishimo. Tokugawa period formal male dress, worn by Kabuki musicians, *kōken,* and actors in certain roles.

kamite. Stage-left.

kanjin-nō. 'Subscription' Nō performances to which commoners were admitted for a fee.

kaomise. 'Face-showing,' the November program which opens the Kabuki season.

kari-hanamichi. 'Temporary' *hanamichi,* on the opposite side of the house from the permanent *hanamichi,* q. v.

kasumimaku. A curtain painted with stylized clouds.

kichirei no kotobuki. Plays of an auspicious or 'congratulatory' nature.

kirido-guchi. The upstage-left low door of the Nō stage and of the adapted Nō setting of the Kabuki.

kizewamono. 'Living' domestic plays, dealing generally with lurid or supernatural matters, which appeared after the beginning of the nineteenth century.

kodōgu. Properties.

kōjō. A Kabuki ceremony, on such occasions as an actor's promotion to a new name, or an anniversary, in which the actors address the audience.

kōken. A stage assistant dressed in formal attire of the Tokugawa period.

koroshiba. Dance-like scenes of murder.

kubijikken. 'Head inspection,' a frequent scene in historical plays. The severed head is examined to determine its identity.

kumadori. Stylized, nonrealistic Kabuki make-up.

kurogo. Alternative term for *kurombō,* q. v.

kuromaku. A black curtain, hung without folds, used to indicate night.

kurombō. 'Black man,' the stage assistant who is dressed in black and wears a black cloth covering his face.

kyōgen kata. He who performs with the wooden clappers which emphasize movement in the Kabuki.

kyōgen. A generic term for play; particularly, the comic interludes of the Nō.

maku soto no hikkomi. 'Exit outside the curtain,' a bravura passage of acting on the *hanamichi* after the curtain has been closed on the stage.

maruhommono. The name given to plays of doll theatre origin performed in the Kabuki.

masu. The 'boxes' into which the pit of the Kabuki theatre was divided toward the end of the eighteenth century.

matatabimono. Plays of 'divided loyalties' in which the chief character owes loyalty to two opposed individuals.

matsubame. The stylized pine tree painted on the rear wall of the Nō stage and of the Kabuki adaptation of the Nō stage.

mawari-butai. Revolving stage. First used in the doll theatre in 1758, in the Kabuki in 1793.

metsuke-bashira. The downstage-right pillar supporting the roof of the Nō stage. Also, the upstage-right edge of the 'inner proscenium' of the Kabuki theatre.

michiyuki. 'Road traveling,' a scene in Nō, doll theatre, and Kabuki involving descriptions of travel. In the Kabuki the travelers are usually lovers.

mie. A self-contained, tense attitude of the male Kabuki character.

miyaji-shibai. Plays performed in temporary theatres on the grounds of temples and shrines during the Tokugawa period.

nami-ita. 'Wave-board,' a low piece of scenery with waves painted upon it, used in front of an ocean backdrop.

nanori-dai. 'Name-announcing-platform,' a small platform attached to the stage-left side of the *hanamichi.* First used in the 1730's, now no longer extant.

naraku. 'Hell,' a name given to the regions below the Kabuki stage and the *hanamichi.*

nezumi-kido. 'Mouse-door,' the spectators' small, sole entrance to the earliest Kabuki theatres.

ningyō-buri. A passage of acting in which the Kabuki actor literally imitates the movement of the dolls of the doll theatre.

nuregoto. 'Moist business': a love scene.

ōbeya. Large room on the third floor of the backstage area of the Kabuki theatre, used both as dressing-room for subordinate actors and as a rehearsal room.

ōdaimono. Plays dealing with ancient or legendary events.

ōdōgu. Settings.

ōiemono. Plays concerning the fall of a 'great House.'

okubyō-guchi. Term used alternately with *kirido-guchi,* q. v.

onnagata. Men who play women's roles in the Kabuki. These men are also sometimes called *oyama,* etymologically a much less complimentary word.

rakandai. A fenced in area on stage-right, used as standing room in the late eighteenth- and early nineteenth-century Kabuki theatres.

sajiki. Boxes in the Kabuki theatre raised above the level of the pit.

sashidashi. A bamboo pole, about six feet long, used by stage assistants to show birds in flight, butterflies, fox-fires, and the like.

seriage. Trap-lift for actors.

seridashi. Trap-lift for scenery.

shibai. Play; also, by extension, playhouse.

shichi-san. The area of greatest acting strength on the *hanamichi.*

shimote. Stage-right.

shimpa. A kind of 'modern' drama, as contrasted with the Kabuki, which flourished approximately from 1888 to 1905. Also, by extension, a contemporary play or film with a modern setting.

shosabutai. The 'dance stage' of the Kabuki, low platforms of Japanese cypress laid on the permanent stage floor.

shosagoto. 'Posture business,' the Kabuki dance pieces.

suppon. The trap-lift in the *hanamichi.*

tachimawari. Ballet-like scenes of Kabuki conflict.

tsukebutai. The forestage of the Kabuki theatre, used from about 1736.

tsukurimono. 'Fictional things,' the stylized set pieces of the Nō theatre.

tsura-akari. 'Face-light,' a lamp at the end of a long pole, used to light the face of an actor.

tsurieda. Hanging floral decorations in the first border position.

waki-za. A stage-left area of the Nō stage on which the chorus is seated.

yagura. 'Drum tower,' an architectural feature of the facade of every Kabuki theatre building until 1878.

Selected Bibliography of Works in Western Languages

Benezet, Alexandre: *Le Théâtre au Japon, ses rapports avec les cultes locaux*, Paris, Leroux, 1901. v, 302 pp.

Blakeney, Ben Bruce: *Rokudaime*, Tōkyō, The Foreign Affairs Association, 1950. 23 pp.

    A memoir of the late Kikugorō VI (1885–1949), reprinted from *Contemporary Japan*, October–December, 1949.

Bowers, Faubion: *The Japanese Theatre*, foreword by Joshua Logan, New York, Hermitage House, 1952. xxi, 294 pp.

    Deals largely with Kabuki; contains translations of three short Kabuki plays.

Clark, Barrett Harper: *World Drama*, Vol. I, New York and London, D. Appleton and Company, 1933. viii, 663 pp.

    Contains translations of a doll theatre-Kabuki play and a Nō-Kabuki *kyōgen*.

Edwards, Osman: *Japanese Plays and Playfellows*, London, W. Heinemann, 1901. viii, 306 pp.

    An early and almost unreadably romanticized account.

Florenz, Karl, tr.: *Japanische Dramen, Terakoya und Asagao*, Leipzig, C. F. Amelang, 1900. 38, 38 pp.

Glaser, Curt: *Japanisches Theater*, mit Beiträgen von Fritz Rump, Friedrich Perzynski, Kazuhiko Sano, Berlin, Würfel, 1930. 192 pp.

Iacovleff, A., and Elisséeff, S.: *Le Théâtre Japonais (Kabuki)*, Paris, Jules Meynial, 1933. 94 pp.

    The most reliable and scholarly work, magnificently illustrated.

Inouye, Jukichi: *Chūshingura, or, The Treasury of Loyal Retainers*, Tōkyō, Nakanishi-ya, 1910. xxxviii, 269 pp.

Kawatake, Shigetoshi: *The Development of Japanese Theatrical Art*, Tōkyō, Kokusai Bunka Shinkokai, 1935. 42 pp.

Keene, Donald: *The Battles of Coxinga, Chikamatsu's puppet play, its background and importance*, London, Taylor's Foreign Press, 1951. x, 205 pp.

    Complete, annotated translation, with an informative introduction.

Kincaid, Zoë: *Kabuki, the popular stage of Japan*, London, Macmillan and Company, 1925. xvi, 385 pp.

Lequeux, André: *Le Théâtre Japonais*, Paris, E. Leroux, 1889. 79 pp.

Lombard, Frank Alanson: *An Outline History of the Japanese Drama*, Boston and New York, Houghton Mifflin Company, 1929. 358 pp.

    Contains translation of *The Death-Love of Kamiya-Jihei*, 'A Kabuki, by an unknown author of the early nineteenth century . . .'

Maybon, Albert: *Le Théâtre Japonais*, Paris, H. Laurens, 1925. 140 pp.

Miyake, Shūtarō: *Kabuki Drama*, Tōkyō, Japan Travel Bureau, 1948. 102 pp.

Miyajima, Tsunao: *Théâtre Japonais de Poupées*, Ōsaka, Société de Rapprochement Intellectuel Franco-Japonais, 1931. (3rd ed.) viii, 109 pp.

    Contains summary translations of portions of five doll theatre-Kabuki plays.

Miyamori, Asatarō, tr.: *Masterpieces of Chikamatsu*, London and New York, E. P. Dutton and Company, 1926. xiv, 359 pp.

    Summary translations of six plays.

——: *Tales from Old Japanese Dramas*, G. P. Putnam's Sons, New York and London, 1915. xii, 401 pp.

    Summary translations of eight doll theatre-Kabuki plays.

Okamoto, Kidō: *The American Envoy (Townsend Harris)*, tr. by Masanao Inouye, Kōbe, J. L. Thompson and Company, 1931. 56 pp.

——: *Drames d'amour*, tr. by Kuni Matsuo and Steinilber-Oberlin, Paris, Stock, 1929. 197 pp.

——: *The Mask-maker*, a play in three acts, adapted and prepared for stage production by Zoë Kincaid from the translation of Hanso Tarao, New York and London, French, 1928. v, 28 pp.

    Examples of the work of a 'neo-Kabuki' playwright.

Pine Tree, The, a drama adapted from the Japanese with an introductory causerie on the Japanese theatre by M. C. Marcus, New York, Duffield, 1916. 126 pp.

    An incomplete and awkward translation of *Terakoya*, 'The Village School.'

Piper, Maria: *Das Japanische Theater, ein Spiegel des Volkes*, Frankfurt-a.-M., Societäts Verlag, 1937. 286 pp.

    A good study, containing synopses of seven Kabuki plays, four doll theatre plays.

Sadler, Arthur Lindsay: *Japanese Plays, Nō, Kyōgen, Kabuki*, Sydney, Angus and Robertson, 1934. xxiv, 283 pp.

    Contains translations of four Kabuki pieces.

Sakanishi, Shio; Addington, Marion H.; Perkins, P. D.: *A List of Translations of Japanese Drama into English, French, and German*. Washington, American Council of Learned Societies, 1935. viii, 89 pp.

    Kabuki and doll theatre plays listed on pp. 60-71.

Scott, A. C.: *Genyadana, A Japanese Kabuki Play*, Tōkyō, The Hokuseido Press, 1953. 52 pp.

    Translation of an act of *Yowa Nasake Ukina no Yokogushi*,

Scott, A. C.: *Kanjinchō, A Japanese Kabuki Play*, Tōkyō, The Hokuseido Press, 1953. 50 pp.

Shioya, Sakae: *Chūshingura, An Exposition*, Tōkyō, The Hokuseido Press, 1940. xii, 236 pp.

Shively, Donald H.: *The Love Suicide at Amijima: A Study of a Domestic Tragedy by Chikamatsu Monzaemon*, Cambridge, Harvard University Press, 1953. 173 pp.
    Complete, annotated translation, with a valuable introduction.

Sugiyama, Makoto, and Fujima, Kanjūrō: *An Outline History of the Japanese Dance*, Tōkyō, Kokusai Bunka Shinkokai, 1937. 28 pp.

Umemoto, Rikuhei, and Ishizawa, Yukata: *Introduction to the Classic Dances of Japan*, Tōkyō, Sanseido Company, 1935. 32 pp.

Index

Actor: 'detachment' of, 192–3, 195–6, 198–9, 202; names, 83; onstage positions, 180–3; regulations concerning, 6–7; relation to audience, 5, 7, 65–6, 81–2, 83–4; relation to setting, 132–5, 146, 187–9; training, 176–7, 194; use of theatrical space, 132–5, 177–8, 180–3; use of theatrical time, 189–92; versatility of, 201–2

Admission prices, 48, 56, 69, 212
Aeschylus, 243
Aesthetics (*bigaku*), 80
Ah, Wilderness, 270
Aibiki, 144
All About Eve, 270
Amaterasu, 15, 164
Amateur performances, 12
Anderson, Judith, 176
Andreyev, 253
'Anniversary Celebration,' 106, 140, 201, 235
Anti-Confucian thought, 15
Antoine, 19, 255
Appia, Adolph, ix, 21
Aragoto (rough-business), 21, 162, 167, 168, 171, 172, 177, 179, 184, 196–7, 211
Aristophanes, 220, 224, 264
Aristotle, 23, 240
Arrow Maker, The, 106, 140, 148, 155, 156, 162, 168, 205, 206
Artist, comparison of Japanese and Western, 75–6
Audience, 69, 76–7, 88–91; relation to performance, 76, 80–4, 103–4, 210–11, 274–5
Aural continuity, 118–9
Ayame-gusa, 195
Azuma Tokuho 'Kabuki', viii

Bach, 17, 267
Barrier at Ataka, The, 206
Bashō, 14, 73, 193
Battle of Ichinotani, The, 95, 133, 135, 224, 234, 238
Battle of the Geisha, 215
Battles of Coxinga, The, 197
Beautiful Story of a Prosperous Country, The, 250

Belasco, viii, 19, 147
Benkei at the Boat, 168, 197
Benshi, 115–6
Benten the Thief, 81, 96, 144, 153, 224, 232
Berg, Alban, 118
Berlioz, 17
Blind Masseur, The, 219, 224
Bloodshed at Ise, 233
Bon festival, 166
Bowers, Faubion, vii, 259
Boxes: *masu*, 48, 59–60; *sajiki*, 25, 36, 37, 41, 44, 45, 49, 59–60, 63; outfittings of, 37, 42, 60
Bridge (*hashigakari*), 32–6, 37–8, 42, 55–6, 103; decline in strength of, 55; expansion of, 43, 49, 57, 65
Brieux, 253, 263
Buddhism, 1, 14, 72, 74–5, 87, 178, 196, 238–9, 247, 272; effect upon artist, 75–6

Camel, 219, 220
Center-passageway (*naka-no-ayumi*), 51, 57
Ceremonial Prelude, 206, 207
Chain of causation (*karma; inga*), 239
Chamberlain, Basil Hall, 251
Chekhov, 65, 253, 254, 256, 273
Chikamatsu Monzaemon, 16, 17, 47, 100, 114, 134, 151, 167, 172, 197, 201, 209, 215, 216, 218, 221, 231, 277
Chikugo-shibai, 53
Chitose-za, 59, 63
Chivalrous Gorozō, 102, 184, 235
Chiyo, 87
Chobo, 28, 113–4, 116–8; and Greek chorus, 117–8
Choboyuka, 28, 52
Chopin, 88
Choreographer (*furitsuke-shi*), 166
Chu Hsi, 13–5, 68, 226
Civil Censorship Detachment, 258, 259, 266, 268
Civil Information and Education Section, 258, 262, 264, 265, 268
Color, use of, 146–7, 185–6
Comedy. *See* Kabuki plays
Comic interludes (*kyōgen*), 213, 221–2
Comic relief, 224–5
Communist theatre, 261–2, 263, 267–9

291

INDEX